D1549955

DEADLINE

Collected Journalism

David Leitch

DEADLINE

Collected Journalism

David Leitch

HARRAP · LONDON

For Luke, Miranda and Daisy

ACKNOWLEDGMENTS

Grateful acknowledgment is made to the Editors of *The Sunday Times, New Statesman, The National Times,* and *The Courier-Journal and Times* for their kind permission to reproduce the articles in this collection.

First published in Great Britain 1984
by HARRAP LIMITED
19-23 Ludgate Hill, London EC4M 7PD

ISBN 0 245-54212-4

Designed by Michael R. Carter
Printed and bound in Great Britain
by R. J. Acford, Chichester.

CONTENTS

DEADLINE

'A bounding line, as within the limits of a military prison, the crossing of which by a prisoner incurs the penalty of being fired upon by the guard.'

New US Dictionary (1946)

In his rightly celebrated New Yorker column called 'The Wayward Press' A. J. Liebling once reviewed a manual with the irresistible title 'Do You Belong in Journalism?' It had been compiled by eighteen editors, no less, and promised to aid potential high-flyers to 'Explore Career Opportunities in Newspaper Work'. The aspirants were warned (all too accurately) that journalism wouldn't make them rich. But, in a spirit of consolation, the editors added that newspapers, in Joe's words, 'offer other compensations, among them a dangerous life'.

This piece appeared in the Spring of 1960, and had I read it then it would have done no more than reinforce a conviction that had already driven me to join the ranks of those who thought they belonged in journalism. Indeed, judged by the youth employment standards prevailing nowadays, I was already a precocious veteran. My first Fleet Street stories had appeared — one at least under the resounding by-line 'From Our Special Correspondent' — in December 1957 and January 1958. *The Times* had not only let me work in the august and indescribably dilapidated news-room in the old Printing House Square over the Christmas vacation during my second university year. They had also offered the princely salary of seven guineas a week, thus relieving me of the need to do my usual job delivering Christmas mail, and they had even used some of the stuff I produced. There was, I recall with pride, a zingy account of the New Year's Chelsea Arts Ball being sabotaged with smoke-bombs, and a yet zingier report on the annual January 'Sales Fever' in Oxford Street and Knightsbridge, where ladies from the well-mannered Home Counties fought like demons for the privilege of buying a coat of Persian Lamb for a tenner. That *The Times* would pay a 19-year-old student, let alone permit him to run loose around Fleet Street under their imprimatur, is perhaps a tribute to the freedom of opportunity afforded to the young in those more genial days. In any case I recall a wild exuberance coming over me as I realized that a fellow-passenger on the London tube was actually reading one of these first published stories. There seemed to be a flicker of amusement hovering around his tight English lips — and suddenly my high spirits changed to fear and embarrassment. It seemed momentarily sure to me that he must divine from my expression, or 'the vibes' I was giving off as people said later, that I was the author of the stuff, and start talking to me about it.

Such intense feelings of rapport between the copy, the reader, if any, and myself did not of course long endure. I do not know how many reporters actually read their own work once it's in print. Not many, I suspect, except maybe for a perfunctory glance to verify how it has been displayed, or whether displayed at all. Certainly even when I was in a London office with access to the paper's first edition I would only read the copy through to check for errors or, in rare cases, against some rival's own first edition equivalent, to see whether 'They' had got anything 'We' had missed. Only in special circumstances, usually disagreeable ones where libel or, much more commonly, the threat of libel obtained, was I in the habit of going through the copy word by word as it had appeared in print. This always seemed a great waste of time that might have been spent writing more stories for oblivion. There was also something innately unnatural about the process, like riding a bike backwards.

This instinctive aversion to the journalistic equivalent of what dealers on the Stock Market call 'jobbing backwards', a disinclination towards lingering over stories once they were in the past historic, was probably very healthy. It indicates at any rate an unneurotic acceptance of the inherent disposability of a reporter's output. By the time I was working the international beat the moment that the words 'well received' came up on the telex to confirm the words' safe arrival, I felt that the bird had well and truly flown.

If you were constantly 'relocating' from one distant place to another for a paper published in London the question seldom came up. By the time the paper itself came into your hands, if it ever did, the story was already ancient history. The most tangible evidence of your labours consisted of so-called 'herograms', cables informing you of the copy's safe arrival and (if you were lucky) prominent display. It follows that most of the international stories assembled here, and a fair number of the others, come into a strange category of material I undeniably wrote but yet did not immediately recognize when my editors, Alison Peacock and Simon Scott, resurrected them from their yellowing files in what American papers so aptly call 'The Morgue'.

There was an almost frightening amount of the stuff and it was hard not to feel a certain sympathy for the often misguided and evidently harassed younger version of myself trapped on a treadmill of events he was trying, with varying success, to get into print against yet another deadline. The variety of the material bothered me as much as its unwieldy volume. There seemed to be so many things I once knew about — but no more. This younger ghost's tastes ranged so wide that they argued a lack of centre, a will o' the wisp commitment to the moment where a search for something more durable might have been in order.

Not, of course, that he chose his own subjects. The tunnel vision of editors, an aspect of the trade that Liebling's manual is unlikely to have stressed, ensures that once a reporter has turned in something satisfactory on a given topic, he is immediately type-cast. For months thereafter, and in the gravest cases for a life-time, the moment any roughly similar story can be discerned on the sky-line he will be packing his bags.

At different times I have found myself labelled as the specialist or even expert, on subjects as various as dock strikes; plane crashes and all kinds of natural disaster from floods to earthquakes; sports of varying kinds; crime, especially where frauds and fakes involving fine arts and antique were involved; elections, both domestic and in different parts of the world; espionage, with particular reference to the 'Cambridge' spies working for Russia; multi-national interviews with the (sometimes fleetingly) famous; France; Italy; North Africa; the Middle East; Australia: and even, during certain times of merciless, incessant 'relocation', 'abroad' in general. It was during one of these spells permanently on the run that while attending a party in Singapore I received a cable containing the terse instruction: 'Go Memphis.' The evening was passed in nervous speculation — did they mean the old city of ancient Egypt, or the more contemporary model in Tennessee? Apart from the name they had nothing in common, unless you counted dire inaccessibility.

The ultimate speciality became wars, particularly the one in Vietnam, and its aftermath. In Saigon, if anywhere, you might reckon to find those undefined yet seductive 'compensations of a dangerous life', hard now as they are to recollect in comparative tranquility. Strangely, the topic attracts increasing controversy and considerable animus. This has sprung from the claim made by conservative historians in the USA that the Press, or media, were responsible, largely thanks to their coverage of the Tet offensive, for losing President Johnson the public support which the war had enjoyed since its inception. It was because those on the spot reported Tet as a defeat, so the theory goes, that LBJ decided to quit, and in due course the war was inexorably lost. Increasingly the Vietnam press corps has been getting a lousy press.

They have been blamed not only for delivering the bad news, as if they had somehow invented what was happening, but also for enjoying themselves unacceptably in the process. The correspondent Nora Ephron probably set this hare running in *New York* magazine by claiming that post-Tet the trade of covering the war, as opposed to to actually fighting the thing, had become 'almost the only classic masculine endeavor left that provides physical danger and personal risk without public disapproval'. She went on to advance the view that the macho correspondents freaking out in the Caravelle Hotel, or on a more fastidious (and ever freakier) scale in the Continental or Royale, had discovered that war was not hell: 'but fun.'

What she wrote approached an aspect of truth, though 'fun' gives comprehensively the wrong idea. There were in my memory times of ecstasy, a kind of soaring relief fuelled by the absence of fear and noise and, above all, the knowledge that you were still alive in a world that seemed beautiful beyond description because, contrary to your expectations, you had not been taken away from it. Commonplace professional satisfactions, the fact that you had somehow got into the right place, and got the story, and got out again, and finally filed the thing, became in those conditions causes for thanksgiving and celebration. Such exaggerated sensations, though they didn't seem exaggerated then, only appropriate, comprised the compensations of a very dangerous life.

By no means all of the Saigon press corps felt obliged to go to the edge, or indeed anywhere near it, even if their routines had allowed unscheduled dashes into the boondocks, which they didn't. Many correspondents were representing agencies or daily papers who needed regular up-dates on the 'Stack 'em like cordwood' body-count arithmetic which was how General Westmoreland chose to present the war's progress. They had to stay close and be on hand to file immediately after the daily press conference, or 'Five o'Clock Follies'.

It was different for TV camera crews and different again for photographers: for them it was far worse. Seeing Don McCullin's picture of the marines by the wall in Hue (on page 11) involved a strange shock of recognition, an only too well-remembered place which I had for years suspected nonetheless of having been born in a bad dream. This was precisely the point where my own coverage of the Hue battle and Don's had diverged — because he had crawled forward beyond the wall, while I had crawled, probably faster, back the way we had come.

Questions of mortality apart, there were no professional reasons why I should have continued. This was quite close enough to report what was happening. For McCullin, who by this time had acquired the skills of a combat infantryman, you could never get too close. This had been evident from the moment he had worked on his first foreign action assignment in Cyprus.

During the research for this book we found John Bulmer's previously unpublished picture of McCullin helping an old woman (on page 53) during this first assignment. John Bulmer was on hand in the battle of Gaziveran, a Turkish village besieged by Greeks, where both he and McCullin shot their first ever combat pictures. Bulmer recalls getting his shirt burned (hot cartridge cases from the Bren-gun a Greek next to him in the ditch was firing), the experience of being mortared, which always concentrates the mind, and Don carrying an old woman who had gone off her head in the main street away from the most intense fire zone.

'The way the journalists behaved during the Gaziveran battle divided into precisely three categories', John remembers.

'Category one was crack-up — one guy spent the whole time being sick in a ditch.

The second category, the largest, consisted of those trying to stay alive and work sensibly between intervals of being mortared or sniped at. Don, on his own, comprised category three.

'He just went straight to the centre of the action, and I took a shot of him running, carrying an old lady on sticks who'd been pinned down in the cross-fire and gone out of her mind....

'When it got dark we all went back to Nicosia but Don stayed in Gaziveran overnight. The next morning just outside the village there were two dead Turks lying as if asleep on the dew in a lovely grove of ripe oranges. Don was there too, waiting. We asked some UN troops for a ride in their jeep and the sergeant said "OK. As long as you help load the stiffs on board." I've never forgotten that.'

Working time and again with these same 'photo-journalists' during their baptism of fire in Cyprus, I evolved a personal scale which seldom failed if occasion arose to see their pictures afterwards. The hallmark of a very good photographer was that working with him alerted you to aspects of the story, not all of them visual, which otherwise you would have missed, and which were never trivial. It was a common bonus that they would have a sense of humour, usually on the black side. In later years McCullin could get to look as grim and unearthly as a corpse he had just photographed in a ditch, but in Nicosia then he specialized in the comedian's mock/solemn deadpan. I spent a lot of time trying to crack this expression, which would give way momentarily to a fine Cheshire cat grin.

These collaborations were rich and rewarding — it was a time of team journalism, with colleagues like the late Nicholas Tomalin, co-author of 'A Day in Search Of Vietnam Peace', or Phillip Knightley, who shared both the research and writing of the article about General de Gaulle's assassins and the piece on the Florence floods.

What all the material has in common is that it was composed under the pressures of editors and deadlines. The editors, notably Sir Denis Hamilton, Harold Evans, and Anthony Howard in Fleet Street, and Max Suich in Australia, deserve my thanks for having made it possible at all.

VIETNAM

The 1968 New Year Offensive in Vietnam was a decisive turning point in the war. It brought 'Charleyland' into the heart of Saigon, and made a mockery of the sanguine 1967 'light at the end of the tunnel' prophecies of General William C. Westmoreland, the US Commander. After Tet 1968 the distant south-east Asian battles became real for people far away. In the USA, internal protest erupted into a fully-fledged Peace Movement with political clout. President Johnson announced his impending retirement. Bobby Kennedy and Eugene McCarthy, front-runners for the Democratic nomination, both mobilised the young anti-War activists, whose heads were busted by Mayor Daley's police at the Chicago convention in August.

But Tet unleashed an international youth protest movement — in Paris the student unrest which caused near-revolution in May 1968, first manifested itself with bomb explosions outside the American Express in February. Everywhere 'the political potential of the very young', as I called it in the December 1968 article about French students (and the revolution that evaporated), became suddenly apparent.

The tumultuous, young people's politics of the Dubcek Spring in Prague, the student revolt in France, and the Kennedy campaign in America, all too soon gave way to an autumn of reaction. Czechoslovakia was occupied by Russian tanks. In America the new team was Nixon and Kissinger. While the war continued unabated, the Peace talks ran on, and on...

1968 was the year when the middle-aged asserted their power over the young. Woodstock notwithstanding, the 1960s youth culture was running out of steam. As far as I was concerned the story was still going a decade later. In Darwin, on the tip of the Australian continent, the first 2,000 Boat People appeared across the Timor Sea, causing a storm of protest. The Australians were notoriously rigorous, and 'White Australia' oriented in their immigration laws. Recent arrivals talked to me in French of the horrors of Ho Chi Minh city, and how wonderful old Saigon had been in comparison, even during the war. Flying the three thousand miles south with a group about to spend Christmas in an outer Sydney suburb, I was aware of having myself grown middle-aged with the story.

Charleyland begins right here: with the American forces in Saigon

In a fetid Saigon side street, bordered by palm-fringed villas now pock-marked by rockets, a stone-faced United States military policeman gathered together three buckled and distorted steel helmets. Nearby there were two military armbands, charred and blood-stained. There was live ammunition in the gutter. A Vietnamese soldier giggled and kicked at a piece of bone. 'VC skull,' he said.

This is where 16 US military policemen were slaughtered as their truck cruised innocently into a Viet Cong ambush. It looked as if it had happened the night before. In fact it was nine days ago, but there has still not been time to clear up properly.

Nine days in which the Viet Cong hit this hitherto complacent capital, but did not run, except, that is, to hit again from somewhere else. Nine days in which for the first time they have demonstrated that the principles of revolutionary war they have practised so accomplishedly in the jungle work equally well in a city.

For these nine days the South Vietnamese army, supported in the air by the Americans and their own air force, have retaliated — devastating heavily populated parts of Saigon in the process. Yet the Viet Cong are still here, at least one thousand of them, confidently squatting only a few minutes' walk from the centre of this harassed and demoralised city.

Who is in control? From the US and South Vietnamese army jeeps patrolling the streets it might look like what the Americans like to call the 'Free World "C" forces'. But seven out of the city's nine precincts — under the French they were called arrondissements — are now officially admitted to be 'under VC influence'.

This does not mean that they are in control of all of them. Their stronghold is 'precinct five' — the predominantly Chinese area of Cholon, a section of which has been cordoned off: no US troops are permitted to enter under any circumstances.

'The VC are really gutty bastards,' said Lt. Colonel Richard E. George, Provost Marshal of the Military Police, who are patrolling the perimeter of Viet Cong controlled Cholon. 'They even hoisted VC flags just behind our PX (the GI's NAAFI).'

'You cross the water there,' he pointed half a kilometre south, 'and you're right in Charleyland.'

So far, the Americans have avoided a house to house confrontation with the invaders — at least 1,000 of them, according to conservative estimates. Instead the task of rooting them out has been left to those who hover on the safe side of the barricades and who have not so far shown any uncontrollable appetite for the task in hand. So nine days after their surprise attack on the morning of the Lunar New Year the Viet Cong are able to lord it over fairly limited but psychologically valuable sections of the city.

'They knocked on my door and said they were the new government,' said Mrs Pen Quy, a Cholon resident who has now moved nearer the centre. 'On the first day (February 1) they told me they had captured all the city and I believed them. They had loudspeakers in the street. I gave them food — there were seven in my apartment. Everyone helped them, with food and looking after the wounded; there was no choice.'

Mrs Quy is wary about political comments, but for a member of the middle classes — she owns a shoe shop — she is not as virulently anti-Communist as one might expect. 'They were being correct,' she says. 'They did not destroy anything, they were quite courteous.'

Cholon is a great coup for the Viet Cong. The Chinese quarter, where in the old days tourists could be sure of the most sophisticated chop suey and brothels in a town noted for both, is now silent and dangerous. It seems that the Viet Cong have set up some rudimentary form of government, street by street, in the areas they still have under control. They have been given time to spread propaganda, to recruit, and even to bring in reinforcements.

The South Vietnamese army launch attacks from time to time but they have only been prepared to conduct house to house cordon and search operations in a handful of streets.

Another resident of Cholon, Dr Lawrence Pratt, aged 60, of Detroit, emerged to safety on Thursday after spending eight scary days in his house behind Viet Cong lines. Dr Pratt told how on February 1 he had heard the broadcast order to Americans 'to stay in your billets'. Shortly afterwards he noticed five Viet Cong barricading his street with oil cans and rubbish. 'Then it became particularly quiet,' said Dr Pratt, adding that for safety's sake he removed his electricity fuses to make sure neither he nor his two servants could switch on lights to alert the Viet Cong to the house.

The servants went shopping and came back to report the Viet Cong were telling everyone that they were in control of the area. So it was to prove for the next four days. On the fifth, South Vietnamese ranger troops came to the end of the street,

(Don McCullin)

but Dr Pratt did not reveal himself: 'How could you tell whether they were real or not?' For the next two days the Vietnamese troops ventured painfully slowly down the street, kept out by heavy firing, but gradually they swept the houses and the roofs, still assuming the Viet Cong were there.

Dr Pratt kept mum, until yesterday when everyone in the area was ordered out with the announcement that air strikes would begin. Dr Pratt, at last in contact with South Vietnamese troops, drove his car out as rocket-firing helicopters began blasting houses 100 yards away.

Local US spokesmen have remained determined, but rather hollowly sanquine about recent events, plaintively echoing the publicly optimistic General William Westmoreland. They claim that in the last week's offensive the Viet Cong have suffered over 26,000 dead, compared with an 'allied' (which means almost entirely US) loss of 741 dead. The South Vietnamese army, not noted for the accuracy of their statistics, claim that they have lost just over 1,600 killed and 5,000 wounded.

Even allowing for certain bias — if the Viet Cong issued figures they would doubtless be very different — it still remains that they have suffered bitterly. But on the other hand they have got a foot in Saigon and at the moment there is nothing to indicate when they can be removed.

The South Vietnamese army have already demonstrated the difficulty. House to house fighting in Cholon is a thankless and desperately dangerous job, fighting from back alley to back alley. Certainly American crack troops are capable of doing the job but it is an operation almost as dangerous in political terms as in military ones. And with the likelihood of a major offensive from North Vietnam at Khe Sanh as soon as the rains come to stifle US airpower, there is the question of whether they can be spared.

Already such successes as there have been against the invaders of February 1 have resulted in truly horrific suffering for the civilians of Saigon.

The estimated 129,000 refugess in the Saigon area, many of whom can be seen sitting on the pavements pathetically guarding wardrobes and cookers they have been able to salvage from their devastated homes while their children play in the gutters, have mainly suffered from air-raids.

They have been blitzed out by South Vietnam Air Force sky-raider strikes using rockets. And they have been burnt out by the US armed helicopters, the so-called 'gun-ships', which can bring terrifying fire-power to bear on a target, but have no magic formula for killing the enemy without slaughtering civilians at the same time. Government sources specify that more than 3,000 civilians have been killed and another 8,000 wounded throughout South Vietnam in the last ten days.

The Viet Cong are not noted for their gentleness with civilians who appear to be against them — this week in Saigon they murdered the wives and children of South Vietnamese soldiers they found in an army compound. But with uncommitted civilians, they usually behave more or less correctly. Certainly as far as the dazed inhabitants are concerned, it was the Americans and their own Government who sent the aircraft and helicopters which have this week appeared out of the sky to devastate houses and overflow Saigon's hospitals with dead and dying civilians.

To the north of the city, where Saigon proper overflows into Gia Dinh province, destroyed streets eerily recall photographs of Hanoi bomb damage. But in two Vietnam wars it has never happened in Saigon. Apart from the dive-bomber strafing, rockets and 105 millimetre recoil rifles fired by ground troops on both sides have started countless fires.

Near the Tan Son Nhut airbase, a vicious attack by armed helicopters flattened every house within fifty yards of the Viet Cong contingent, which was their target. The trail of destruction borders the north of the airport — the Viet Cong have been customarily selective in their own targets but have ruthlessly exploited civilians by using them as cover. The South Vietnamese aircraft have actually done most of the damage but everything that flies is popularly supposed to be American.

Touring the damaged areas with Americans, one feels the bitter resentment. Even the children, who normally shriek greetings at any foreigners, just stared, blank-faced.

Food, unobtainable for days, is now filtering back to the market at prices between three and four times the normal. About 2,000 revolutionary development cadres, whose job was supposed to be to 'pacify' the villagers, are now in the capital distributing rice at controlled prices. On Friday 200 tons were sold this way, and officials say a further 120,000 tons are available in warehouses and ships. Water supplies are adequate and electricity almost back to normal.

But this is for the 'haves'. The swollen multitide of 'have nots' — 130,000 refugees many of whom were already casualties of the way in the countryside and have now been hit again — largely have to trust to luck. Some are accommodated in schools, in tents, in hospital grounds; the latest victims in Cholon are simply huddled on the pavements, some with their pathetic flea-market possessions, more with nothing except, invariably, a horde of small children. A Vietnamese doctor working with them said there was enough rice and a little milk. What he most feared were epidemics of plague and cholera. Mass inoculation has begun but the rotting refuse lining the streets attracts rats. The city stinks with the smarting smoke of rubbish ignited with petrol in thousands of tiny fires.

But perhaps the most unbearable and frightening factor of all is the curfew which makes night last from dusk at seven for thirteen claustrophobic hours. In five visits to Vietnam over three years Fred Emery, South-East Asia correspondent of *The Times*, has never before met a curfew that was enforced. This time it is very different. The night streets are empty except for speeding jeeps and lurking, nervous police guards who shoot curfew-breakers on sight. The whole nightmare scene is illuminated by parachute flares, floating above the roofs.

The police are mostly concentrated around the airbase, the massive tribute to American wealth which bristles with technological wonders. From it one can fly anywhere in the world or communicate by satellite, but passengers — no matter how exalted — arriving after seven are trapped for want of a vehicle to take them through three miles of Government-held city to the centre. Disconsolate crowds sleep on the terminal floor waiting for morning, when along with the citizens of Saigon, they are released. At night here the Viet Cong have succeeded in imposing their will on the city.

The Sunday Times, 11th February 1968

Inside Khe Sanh

Stuck up on the red-mud wall of the trench, just above the grenades, there is an amateurish photo of a girl. She is not a very special girl, except she is naked to the waist and has a rather touching look — an amalgam of shame and determination.

Evidently she is not in the habit of posing for semi-nude pictures but her expression says she is determined to do this, and anything else, if it will help her boyfriend while he is in Khe Sanh. All we can do now is to hope that it did help because it certainly is not helping any more.

My Marine friends found the picture in the wallet of a dead soldier whose charred body they dragged, at great risk, out of the wreck of the Hercules C-130 transport plane which now lies in three spiky heaps fifty yards away. They also found the girl's address and they say they'll send the picture back, with a letter of thanks and condolence — if they ever get out themselves.

Looked at from this trench, the likelihood of girl and photograph ever being reunited seems remote. A Marine captain, keeping his head well down, indicates Hill 950 with its jungle-covered tip half-buried in the low cumulus. From this position the North Vietnamese troops can, if they wish and the weather abets them, lay down a murderous fire on the airstrip only yards from our bleak trench.

It is only one of the half-a-dozen positions from which they dominate this pathetic little rectangle, preventing anyone coming in or running away.

We know that there are two divisions of them — say 20,000 — and possibly two divisions more. There are only 4,800 Marines within the meagre Khe Sanh perimeter, and all of them are waiting for the *coup de grâce*.

There has been a good deal of armchair speculation about whether or not the North Vietnamese army intend to attack Khe Sanh. Some people, even experts in Saigon, believe that General Giap is not primarily concerned with achieving another Dien Bien Phu, but is using Khe Sanh as a decoy.

Giap, according to this theory, simply wants to immobilise the US troops, while he skirts them. This may make sense in Saigon or Washington, but when one is huddled inside a flak-jacket, trying simultaneously to watch for troop movements in the scrub on the other side of the wire and listen for the incoming mortar shells, General Giap's intentions seem only too immediately obvious.

Every day this week, the NVA (North Vietnamese Army) troops have moved closer and there seems to be no way to stop them. Every night you go to sleep in Kne Sanh expecting to be awakened by an ill-intentioned North Vietnamese with his Chinese-manufactured automatic weapon. On St Valentine's Day the Marines received their second 'red alert' — troop movements had indicated that the enemy was massing for attack.

Colonel Davie E. Lownds, the 47-year-old commander of this daily diminishing Marine group, has no doubt in his mind. 'Of course, they're coming,' he says in the command bunker. 'But I don't want to put any time frame on it...I wish I knew.'

So do his men, in their vulnerable fox-holes. (There are perhaps two bunkers in Khe Sanh where men would survive after a direct rocket hit. The rest would crumple under a mortar, and their protection value is as much psychological as anything else.)

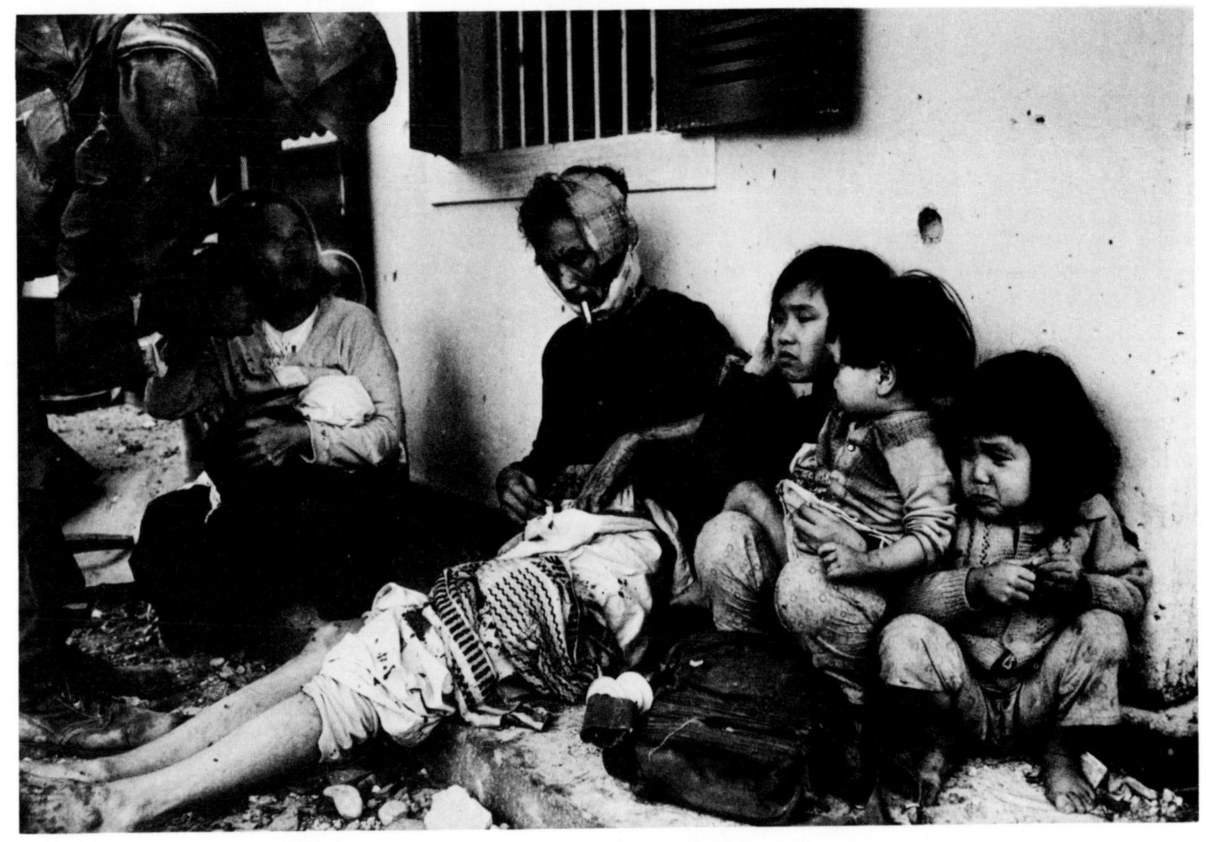

(Don McCullin)

When you see the NVA troops outside the wire, you see brisk, eager little men in jungle kit, going about their jobs with frightening impassivity.

Sergeant W. W. Trottino, a large dead-pan Oklahoman who had kindly offered me the hospitality of his bunker, picked out an advancing section through his binoculars. 'Jee-sus,' he said, 'there's Charley, just like he's going out on an Elks picnic.'

'What does he look like?' asked Private First Class Steve Adrio (an amateur photographer who had been bitterly disappointed that I was what he called a 'writing correspondent' and therefore not carrying any colour film).

'Baby,' said Trottino, declining to relinquish the binoculars, 'he's a small, yellow-looking kind of guy and he speaks with an accent. You'll recognise him by his gun.'

At this point we all heard an agonised, hollow cough from somewhere about 1,000 yards away and lost interest in the cross-talk as we flattened on the red, probably highly fertile, soil which is peculiar to Khe Sanh.

As the mortars come closer, the sound becomes shriller, straighter and faster; you have quite enough time to ponder over your sins of omission and commission between discharge and the arrival. On this particular occasion the nearest explosion was a clear fifty yards away, a dull booming thud, which leaves one with a headache if nothing worse.

Trottino got to his feet with dignity and continued his visual reconnaisance and running commentary. A Negro Marine who had been lying next to me tried to pick mud off his flak-jacket and broke into a huge and deeply frightened grin. 'Kindly get me out of here,' he said. 'I'll go on a chopper, I'll parachute, if you insist, man, I'll walk, but just take me out of this place.'

He was one of the more rational people I spoke to on St Valentine's Day.

Talking, in fact, is rather difficult. This is not because the Marines are taciturn, for everyone in Khe Sanh is so acutely aware of their intermingled destiny that strangers become intimate acquaintances in minutes. It is the noise that inhibits chat — the rippling thud of helicopter blades, the irritable cough of mortars, the fluttering inexorable whine of artillery.

And the sky, on the good days, is black with aircraft — the Skyraider ground-attack planes, jet fighters, and tiny delicate spotter planes, which the Marines talk about like pet dogs as they run through their subtle little arabesques. The spotters are trying to locate gun emplacements beneath the jungle canopy, which comes so near you are aware of it physically, like someone nudging you in the Tube.

These aircraft are delaying the outcome of this battle, taking suicidal risks to help the muddy, frightened men on the ground. But they also have a disturbing message for the Marines in the foxholes because it is clear they are operating each day a little closer to the perimeter.

There is no doubt that the North Vietnamese are moving in, painfully, agonisingly, but still a few yards farther each day. A US Skyraider we watched came swooping in above us, so low we all ducked. But he had not made a mistake.

He dipped down across the perimeter in an arc that seemed inevitably to be leading him to crash, straightened up, and hugging the ground discharged from his belly what looked like a cluster of yellow flame which bounced and swooped, moving perhaps fifty yards parallel to the ground before exploding in a burst of white smoke so close it tickled the throat and made us cough.

'Napalm,' said Trottino. 'Oh, decent, man, isn't that the most beautiful sight you ever saw...' The Marines, disregarding the retaliation that had to come, were jumping up and down, clapping their hands.

The Skyraider wiggled its tail in a half victory roll and gained height for another sweep. We had been looking due east but now there was a deeper rumble dominating the cacophony of lesser sounds coming from the north-west. 'Arclight,' said Trottino, by now an old friend, who had shown me pictures of his children, and asked me to send a message to his wife.

Arclight is the USAF code for the terrifying B-52 bombers which dispense their own kind of justice, God-like, from 55,000 feet, homing in by radar, and destroying an area roughly 1,000 metres long by 400 wide. When their bombs, 500 and 750 pounders (65 tons or thereabouts in all) hit the ground, we were all shaken. The sand started to leak out of the sand-bags. The wooden supports of the bunker teetered. And across the valley, just north of the gap that lead to Laos, the jungle began to ignite.

There is a lot of argument about the B-52 'kill potential'. The efficiency of the raids in military terms may be high or low but psychologically they are crucial. When the Marines see the piles of smoke rising across the valley they feel that someone is remembering them. For the rest of the time they just sit here like so many clay-pigeons, forgotten, they believe, by their leaders, waiting to be sacrificed.

But the air-strikes, the only tactical factor that makes Khe Sanh tenable, tend to be double-edged. If you are dug in even reasonably well — and the Marine trenches and bunkers are now adequate though by no means brilliant — then there is a fair chance of surviving a determined bombardment. As long, that is, as you can hear them coming. An experienced soldier hearing the sound of an approaching rocket, something like the barking of an enormous dog, can get under cover fast enough to be protected from anything other than a direct hit.

But with the aircraft circling overhead one can hear nothing. It is necessary to leave the bunkers to work, to get something to eat, to consult a senior officer. And every time one walks even 25 yards on the mud tracks like 'Buchanan Road' which runs through the base, one is playing a game of Russian roulette. The rockets and mortars come in without warning. They either have your number on them or they don't.

But this is the kind of risk the Marines are happy to live with. Their casualties at the moment are averaging something in the region of 40 a day, which they believe is acceptable.

The real problem is what happens when the weather gets too bad for air support. So far God has been on the side of the United States, and in this situation they badly need supernatural support. The usual torrential monsoon rains have been tardy, and three days in four the weather has been good enough for the support planes to fly from their bases in Da Nang, Saigon and elsewhere. But what is going to happen if the weather changes and a great quiet descends over this valley for two or three days? I asked this question of a section of Marines, who were playing five-card stud poker with military scrip in a trench on the extreme north-east of Khe Sanh position, uncomfortably close to the ammunition dump. 'If the planes can't come any more then the Reds are going to attack,' said a cheery corporal. He had just noisily won forty-five cents by producing three sevens — 'sevens is always been mah lucky numbah' — against a shattered top sergeant who had drawn two aces and a pair of nines. 'What are they going to do? You don't have to ask that question, friend. They just have to start running over that wire when it's dark and we kill a few of them and they keep coming and then we say goodnight. No problem there.'

As long as the planes are there, the North Vietnamese troops are forced to dig in, keep their heads down, and concentrate on avoiding either being roasted by napalm or pulverised by B-52 strikes. But once the weather makes it impossible for these friendly birds to make their complicated passes, fending off the evil day, it all comes down to a question of numbers. There are not physically enough Marines to keep the North Vietnamese out if they are really determined to come, without bothering about the size of their losses, and this has never been something that worried them in the past. At Dien Bien Phu Giap did not try to demonstrate he was a general who kept his losses down.

Khe Sanh is eminently takeable. If Giap decides to take it he can, though it will cost him men. If he waits until weather conditions are better it will be that much easier.

Meanwhile the Marines can do nothing except endure with as much dignity as frightened, potentially defeated men can muster (which, one should say, in their case is a great deal of dignity). As Major Joe Donnelly, the officer who is running one of the hill outposts supporting the area, says: 'The game is now completely in their hands. We wait — it's up to them to move.'

This has been all the more true for the last couple of weeks. Before that the Marines were at least able to send out patrols to spot enemy concentrations and give the command some idea of what they were doing. This is no longer so. Patrols have become too costly. First you send three men, and if they don't come back, you have to support them with a section. If the section too disappears into this unfriendly landscape there is nothing for it but to send a platoon.

The Marines are used to taking heavy losses, indeed they almost glory in them, but this is something else. At the moment Colonel Lownds is trying to preserve as many men in his command as he can. His men sit around and listen to 'Hanoi Hannah' on their expensive transistors — she is the Vietnamese equivalent of Lord Haw-Haw — or play cards, look at their *Playboy* pinups, and pray to God something is going to happen.

Most of them would prefer the NVA to launch a major attack. At least this would be preferable to lying in the red mud and trying to calculate how long you can go before the rocket scores a direct hit. The Marines here are poor boys, ex-truck drivers, labourers and, at the top end of the scale, counter-clerks. They do not have education to help them but their spiritual resources are considerable. They are surviving on companionship and humour.

It makes them the most sympathetic American troops in this country. If you get stuck in Khe Sanh, they automatically accept you as one of them, and talk about newspaper proprietors in the same way they go on about the general staff, forgetting that journalists, unlike soldiers, have a choice about where they go, and do not have to stay to the end of such affairs.

They insist that the people back home do not know what they are suffering. 'I write my parents and my big sister a lot,' said a Negro PFC. 'The first week I was here I wrote eleven letters, would you believe that? Do you think any of them will get there?' Another Marine said: 'I write my wife all the time. Naturally I couldn't get away with telling her what's really going on — nobody Stateside knows that, and if they did know they'd blow their minds.'

My own view is that he is absolutely correct. No Government, one thinks cowering in the trenches of Khe Sanh, has the right to exact this kind of sacrifice from its boys — most of them are boys, literally. The average age of the troops I talked to, perhaps 60 of them, was certainly no more than twenty-two.

They all seemed to be patriots, insofar as they hated the Communists at least. But they combine this hate with a deep and all-abiding cynicism about their leaders, both generals and politicians. The repetitive Marine expletives make it impossible to repeat much of what they say in a newspaper that people will read over their Sunday morning eggs, and they are anyway not very articulate. There is no Wilfred Owen to describe this war.

(It would have to be an Owen. A Rupert Brooke in the age of napalm and revolutionary war would need to keep extremely quiet.)

'Many of us are making plans,
Of what we will do when we hit our homeland
Much as it hurts, it must be said
Some won't hit home for some will be dead.'

This poem was read out in a bunker with the sign above it: 'Friendly place.' Everybody listened, and then went back to their card game, trying at the same time to reserve a measure of concentration for incoming mortars. I asked the dealer whether he liked the poem or not and he grinned: 'Play your cards while you can.'

The one thing that will raise any enthusiasm in this ghost camp is an air strike, not so much, as far as I could make out, because of pleasure at the damage the wheeling planes were doing to the NVA, but rather because it suggested someone was trying to help them, somebody knew they were there.

Most of these people, I feel, have never enjoyed a sense of solidarity with people of their own American generation, except perhaps in gangs. It is sad that it takes a situation like this to turn them into social animals. It is appalling to imagine, after the youthful commitment to violence, how those who survive will react to the world outside.

'You aren't going to believe this, but I volunteered to come here,' said a 21-year-old corporal. 'They told me about the sixty-five dollars a month additional combat allowance. I was in Oakland, California, so bored you know. I thought with that money I could get a tape recorder and so on but of course I didn't know what I was going to buy it with — naturally, in this kind of place all that stuff comes kind of expensive.'

The corporal had made a map pinpointing the mortar and rocket explosions within the camp in the last week. He was hoping to deduce a pattern which would help him to avoid the dangerous sections, though they all looked equally bad. He gave me the map as a souvenir to send to his girl-friend, on the assumption that I would get out (which on St Valentine's Day with the clouds closing in seemed fairly unlikely) and that he wouldn't.

Getting into Khe Sanh has been extremely difficult for two weeks and is now

(Don McCullin)

becoming more so. Despite all the US air strikes, the NVA mortars and rocket fire, zeroed on the runway which at some points is no more than thirty yards within the perimeter, continue unabated.

At the south-east end of the runway, where the incoming planes touch down, there is an NVA .50 calibre machine-gun, or a group of them, which have managed to survive all the rockets and napalm from the air. Now that this gun, which destroyed a C-130 transport last Saturday, is calling the tune the Communists appear to have the potential to dominate the situation.

The C-130s no longer fly because they are reckoned to be too easy targets: instead they have been replaced by smaller C-123s, which have to make more runs to bring in the same amount of supplies. These are slow, awkward planes and their approach run involves them hugging the surface of the innumerable knolls and rises which surround the Marines' camp on all four sides.

This ground-hugging goes on for perhaps five miles on the run-in and the passengers have the impression that this lurching, juddering cow of a plane could be knocked off by someone on the ground with a strong arm and a cricket ball, let alone rockets.

When you finally hit the runway you are encouraged by the wreck of last Saturday's C-130, parked in three pieces on the perimeter. And when you actually come to a stop all hell breaks loose. The apron section of the runway, where the aircraft turn round, is known as 'the Mortar Magnet'. The NVA have now had weeks to zero in on this area and if you survive the machine-gun bursts at one end of the runway you find yourself faced by the mortar fire at the other.

The C-123s keep their engines going all the time, spill cargo and passengers out of the back, taxi and take off within three or four minutes. In this time, under the sound of the engines, the mortars — if you are lucky — and rockets — if you aren't — rain in on the apron. The NVA have been sufficiently harassed from the sky for their fire to be rather erratic.

The plane I came in on attracted one mortar 15 feet from the tail after standstill, which was the best try, and a fusillade of mortars and rockets that came screaming in to land from anything up to seventy-five yards from the turning area. They naturally achieved casualties but the plane itself got away.

The worst job in Khe Sanh is unloading these arriving planes which carry either fuel or ammunition, and loading them with wounded. Twenty-year-old Howard Hunt from Atlanta, Georgia, explained the job to me in a ditch where we spent twenty minutes after the C-123 I had arrived in had made its battered, cumbersome way back up the strip towards Da Nang and safety.

'Every time I go out on the strip my mind goes blank,' Howard said. 'Sometimes the ammo boxes get stuck and I scream — you can't hear it for the noise of the jets and the guns but it seems to make me feel better. I don't do it on purpose, you understand. I just seem to find myself screaming.'

Hunt and his nine friends doing the same job are all in a state of advanced mental exhaustion. 'You know those planes have got to get in here,' said PFC Jim Veron. 'But all the same you get to dread seeing them come because of the fire. It's funny because you know that the plane is the most dangerous thing, the real mortar magnet. But once you get inside it to pick of the cargo you tend to linger, like it's protecting you.'

Once the planes stop flying even for forty-eight hours, Giap will probably launch his attack. If he really has four divisions in the area, say 40,000 men, as some observers believe, and not two divisions only, there can be little doubt about the NVA's ability to over-run the strip. He is rumoured to have a dozen tanks, but it is not certain that tanks are within striking distance of Khe Sanh. The Marines fear they are — the plane I flew in on was carrying anti-tank rockets.

The Marines are bitter when they say: 'You tell them they're using us as bait.' But the anger they feel at their own situation is directed at the Communists as well as the world in general, and there is no doubt they will fight well when the attack comes. Most of them say things like: 'It's time Uncle Sam lost his patience. We ought to drop the big one on Hanoi and put an end to all this.' Most of them think America should withdraw from Vietnam, but initiate a kind of scorched earth policy first. (After seeing the damage to Hue last week one wonders whether, in effect, such a policy is not being carried out already.)

At the 'mortar magnet', the apron where supply planes turn round, a brawny military policeman crouches in a bunker checking that in the general confusion no Marine decides to hop on the plane for Da Nang and leave Khe Sanh to sort out its own problems. So far there has not been a single case of this happening. The only Marines leaving are the dead ones in rubber bags or the wounded on stretchers.

Departure is even more terrifying than arrival because getting the wounded on board up the slippery ramp in the C-123's tail is an awkward and slow performance. The noise of the engines drowns any 'incoming'. Helmets are blown off in the slip-stream and sometimes the plane starts to taxi in its eagerness to take off before everyone is on board.

I went up the ramp hanging on to one end of a stretcher carrying a quiet and patient Negro who looked uncannily like Cassius Clay. There were two other stretcher cases — one a comparatively minor shrapnel case, the other a soldier so covered in bandages that he looked like a white mummy. God knows what wounds the bandages concealed or how the medical orderly managed to attach the saline drip during the flight.

The plane had been strafed by the usual .50-calibre machine-gun on the way in but for some reason got off the ground without attracting a single shot. The stretchers on the floor lurched crazily, the engines screamed and we were above Khe Sanh.

None of the fifteen walking wounded on board showed any emotion, or spoke a word, partly because the noise level was too high, partly because they were just past speaking. At one point the man who looked like Clay indicated he was cold and as there were no extra blankets was given a couple of combat jackets. A Korean Ranger, who had taken a shrapnel burst on his left arm, side and leg removed the cellophane from a cigar with one hand and after long consideration put it in his mouth the wrong way round. He proceeded to smoke it gingerly, the cigar held between swollen black fingers.

With great gentleness a sallow corporal, probably from the Philippines, was fitting a filter cigarette into the small hole in the bandages that must have been the mouth of the Marine in white. I don't know whether he died during the flight but by the time we reached Da Nang he was no longer managing the tiny puffs.

He was carried off, his bloodstained medical card pinned to his bandages, his helmet fastened to the stretcher. On it was written his name, blood group ('A'), a calendar of his service in Vietnam, and a couple of slogans. 'Kill all Gooks' and 'Make war not love.'

The walking wounded followed him still not speaking. They had got out of Khe Sanh, the hard way, but seemed past caring.

The Sunday Times, 18th February 1968

How the Viet Cong could paralyse Saigon

In Cholon, Saigon's Chinese quarter, leaflets, like tuberculosis, undernourishment and unpredicted violence are a part of everyday life. When the Americans drop them exhorting patriotism, the local children are delighted: this is something to play with in the same way kids at home joust with snowflakes.

But the pamphlets distributed on Dong Bang boulevard, north of the Chinese pagoda, on Wednesday, were something different. The hastily produced message on shoddy brown paper announced that the Viet Cong intended to level Saigon to the ground.

They were hot to handle, like a grenade. No children used them as playthings and terrified adults discussed them in the twittering, near hysterical groups which quickly formed in doorways.

For the message was not simply that Saigon was on the verge of destruction. It was that Armageddon, Vietnamese style, was scheduled for this weekend at the latest.

The Chinese in Cholon were not the only people who reacted as if someone had just shown them a delayed action bomb ticking in their hearth. The local police, known because of their uniforms and size as 'white mice', shot at shadows even more haphazardly than usual.

Guards were doubled. Booby-traps, like the shrapnel-spreading Claymore mines that make every trip to the post office a hazard, were set up round potential targets.

A mother stopped me in the street and asked me to use my influence to get her children away to Bangkok. Poor woman, if only she knew.

The South Vietnamese Government, which whatever its defects is certainly no slouch when it comes to protecting its own interests, also reacted to the new threat. Thich Tri Quang, leader of the extreme Buddists, was taken, as the phrase goes, 'into protective custody'. So were two other prestigious anti-Government politicians.

General Loan, the widely-admired police chief, announced that he was flying north — to Hue — to investigate alleged complicity between local policemen and the North Vietnamese troops. There, doubtless, he will be carrying out his usual policies for winning the hearts and minds of the people and encouraging the faint-hearted.

The Americans also took account of the new threat. They added to the already-heavy concentration of US troops protecting the north and north-west perimeter of the town. In the process they denuded their potential farther west between Saigon and the Cambodian border.

In the meantime, the population of Saigon waited, and worried, and tried to calculate what it would mean to them if the local racketeer turned overnight into the local commissar.

From the roof of the biggest hotel, foreigners watched Communist rockets making their elegant fiery arches into Tan Son Nhut airbase, three miles away, and wondered how soon before they started devastating the centre of Saigon.

General Westmoreland and his staff have their headquarters at Tan Son Nhut and those rockets must make it hard for them to get any sleep at night. Like everyone else in Saigon they have been puzzling over the Communists' intentions and this week for the first time it has been possible to piece together a clear and detailed picture of how Westmoreland is thinking.

At least one certain conclusion can be drawn from these reflections of the US General Staff. They fully support Nhan Dan, the Hanoi newspaper, which boasted on February 16 that since the lunar New Year offensive on February 1 'the whole balance of forces, military and political, has changed'. This is so, but it does not follow that the balance has changed conclusively or permanently.

In the meantime, General Giap, to use the local jargon, is 'calling the shots'. The Americans and the South Vietnamese Army are being forced to react to him, rather than initiate themselves. At Hue, Khe Sanh and, probably most crucially, Saigon, US troops are committed. Giap, whether he intended it or not, has achieved almost maximum dispersion of the enemy and maximum concentration of his own.

Do Giap's moves add up to one coherent and subtle strategy? Many leading American military men seem to think they do. There is, however, a good deal of evidence to suggest that the Communist forces have arrived where they are, to some extent at least, by chance. In the long term they may turn out to be less well placed than they think.

But at the moment it looks good for the Communists and very bad for the city of Saigon. Understandably when an ancient taxicab backfires in Tu Do, a main thoroughfare to the water-front, the whole street freezes in fear.

Everybody knows how desperately close Vietcong and North Vietnamese troops are. In the last few days there has been heavy fighting less than four miles from the presidential palace and the US embassy (now protected like a fort). According to the military there are enemy concentrations 'in multi-regimental strength' within two nights' easy march of the centre. Even this dire assessment is probably a shade over-optimistic.

In round figures, there are something like 20,000 troops of the Seventh Viet Cong and the Ninth North Vietnamese divisions positioned in an arc north and north-west of the city. There have been fierce minor engagements this week 11 miles from the centre and other equally determined battles as near as four miles.

If one accepts the US estimates of the number of troops fanned out north of the city limits, one has also to accept that most of them could walk to the presidential palace in a matter of hours if it came to it.

South-east of the city there are heavy mangrove swamps and it is not thought there are many troops about, but most nights this week there has been heavy fighting around the Bien Hoa bridge, to the north-east. Due south there has been little activity but going south-west into the country both My Tho and Can Tho have taken a horrifying battering and they look vulnerable.

But it is perhaps the area westwards that poses the greatest problem of all. The pressure on Saigon has forced General Westmoreland to attempt the solution of a very delicate military equation.

There are three US divisions placed around Saigon now, which means Westmoreland has been forced to reduce the forces whose job it was to prevent infiltration of Communist troops, and, even more important, of material from the other side of the Cambodian border. Intelligence sources are apparently convinced that truckloads of supplies are passing through Cambodia and continuing, probably by boat, until they reach Communist troops in the Saigon area and the delta.

Cambodian soldiers are paid partly in rice, the assumption being that they will sell a proportion of it. Sometimes an officer will dispose of his men's rice for them in a batch: where soldiering and private enterprise go so closely together it is probable that military trucks are also hired out to the highest bidder.

(Don McCullin)

According to normal Communist practice, the troops should have faded away after the hold-up of the Tet (New Year) offensive for a period of retraining, planning and re-supply. But instead they have not only stayed close but built up as far as possible. One explanation of this is their unusually favourable supply position.

How much ammunition has arrived and how many caches survived the confused withdrawal in the first week of February can only be guessed. But the Americans and South Vietnamese have a healthy respect for their opponent's equipment. This week they captured an entirely new weapon, a 107mm rocket which can fire a comparatively light 45lb round ten kilometres.

Don McCullin, a British photographer in the citadel of Hue, has reported that the Marines there were using captured AK-47 combat rifles until orders came to hand them in. This Chinese copy of the standard Soviet infantry weapon is accurate, light (only about 10lb), and can fire a clip of 30 rounds in three seconds. US infantry troops do not think they have anything as effective.

Each night this week there has been only moderate mortar and rocket fire from the Communists on the fringes of Saigon.

Have the Communists kept their fire down because they have supply problems? Or are they waiting for the big night? The fate of Saigon may turn on the answer to this question.

The Communists are so placed that they could cut Saigon's communications and submit the city to economic as well as psychological harassment. But the best military sources do not think this is their object, though they will doubtless try to control communications when they attack.

The American view is that this attack will come soon. The longer they delay, the more their resources will be depleted by daylight encounters which put them at a disadvantage.

For example, last Thursday morning a squadron of the US 25th Infantry Division found a Viet Cong force on the move and, with the help of artillery, helicopters and air strikes, killed 128 men in a four and a half hour battle six miles west of the city.

Fights of this size can be reckoned to occur two or three times a week and there are numerous small engagements invariably advantageous to the Americans. The Viet Cong would find these kind of losses too heavy to bear over more than a short period (though there are reports that by claiming Saigon is aleady virtually theirs the Communists have been able to step up their recruitment since the Tet offensive).

If the Americans once find the enemy in daylight they can fight as they have been taught. But as one learns if one flies by helicopter over the danger areas, even so considerable a body of men can disperse, disappear and yet remain under central control with surprising ease.

The terrain varies from straggle suburbs and woods to dried-out paddy-fields. As usual, the Communists are living in and off the population. As usual, until there is an attack or a daylight movement, it is almost impossible to distinguish the soldiers from the peasants.

American troops do not form a defence perimeter between Saigon and the enemy but move throughout the countryside conducting their search and destroy operations. The South Vietnamese troops, 15 battalions of them, or 7,000 men plus, in the outer suburbs, make up the static defence line.

General Westmoreland is sure that the enemy could only infiltrate in small groups travelling without heavy weapons.

What of those already in the city? Official estimates suggest there are 500 Viet Cong in Cholon, parts of which are still insecure. But this could be an under-estimate judging by some interrogation reports on captured prisoners.

It seems that the Viet Cong set up a much more efficient political and para-governmental structure in certain areas than was previously realised. Most candid US officers admit that they just cannot guess the enemy strength in the city, or the state of their supplies.

The evidence of the Tet offensive suggests overwhelmingly that the population helped the Communists only when they were forced: the myth of the 'popular uprising' is now dead. This war has little ideology left in it as far as the non-combatants are concerned. They are motivated by terror.

Hanoi Radio is not normally noted for its pithy phrase-making but one broadcast last week produced a memorable, but rather sinister image. 'The glorious forces of liberation' said Hanoi, are tightening 'a lasso of steel' round Saigon. Every night the city goes to bed by the light of flares and the flat thump of rockets. Each morning it wakes up feeling that the lasso has closed a little more.

The Sunday Times, 25th February 1968

Hue: Is this one of the war's turning points?

Now that the Viet Cong have departed and the officials have started to count the cost, it is evident that the battle of Hue marks a turning point in the war. Here there has been a truly frightening escalation, but less in military terms than human suffering. In this battle the civilians of South Vietnam have taken their heaviest defeat.

There are now 113,000 refugees in a city with a population of 150,000. A thousand civilians have been killed and 4,000 wounded. 'Ninety per cent of the commercial centre of the city has been wiped out and 90 per cent of the Citadel,' said Dr Ho Dang Le, the public works engineer in charge of the whole province.

Le Thang Minh, a 22-year-old student, or rather former student in the former university, asked me: 'After your blitz-kreig, in your war, had London lost its soul?' I said I thought not. He smiled broadly, as do most Vietnamese when they are about to say something very sad to obviate any possible offence in advance. 'London must be much bigger,' said Minh.

About half of the palaces and pagodas of the ancient Citadel are still standing. In an out-house, the dowager empress's imperial rickshaw, an exotic 19th-century relic with a silken canopy, has been ruined — the Viet Cong used one of the imperial wheels to make their cooking fires.

But, in general, their occupation of more than three weeks was marked by discipline and restraint. They did not loot, or scarcely, unlike the South Vietnamese troops who displaced them. And, according to most people I spoke to, they restricted their killing to men they knew were soldiers of officials.

'I was going to my mother's house and a Viet Cong asked me what I was doing,' a young nurse told me. 'I told him I was taking rice to my sister.'

He asked: 'Are you sure you aren't taking rice or information to the imperialists, little sister?' Then he laughed and let me through.

The Viet Cong let it be understood that if the citizens signed a declaration of faith in the Communist cause and provided a detailed dossier on themselves they would be there-after immune from arrest.

Under the impression that the Viet Cong and North Vietnamese troops were there to stay, a very high percentage of citizens within the citadel and other occupied areas signed the forms. Now they live in fear that the dossiers will be captured by the Americans or the South Vietnamese Army and a purge will follow.

The South Vietnamese police, the Quanh Sat, have now overrun Hue, looking like miniature Tontons Macoute in their dark glasses and black armbands. It is impossible to talk to a student in Hue who will not, providing you speak French, give you the names of colleagues who have been arrested for supposed political sympathy with the VC.

Two of the most important pro-Buddhist student leaders in Hue, both descendants of the royal family, have now been held for questioning.

General Loan's police have used the aftermath of the Viet Cong offensive as a useful occasion to dispose of political opponents who have not already been killed either by the Communists or US airstrikes.

The Buddhists know about martyrdom, but previously the middle-class has been exempt. Now their exquisite villas in the citadel have been razed and their shops looted.

'Suddenly I am poor with my wife and six children,' said Nguyen Quang, a shopkeeper who has lost all his stock through looting, £7,000 in hoarded gold sovereigns, and his two houses.

I drove to the civilian hospital with a seven-year-old boy who had stepped on a grenade. 'He's fine, only flesh wounds,' said the orderly. 'Only he's going to be blind.'

All the way his nine-year-old sister held his hand and talked to him. An hour later she was playing cheerfully and her elder brother explained: 'The children think war is normal life so they are not unhappy. It is the adults who are really scared.'

The Americans are already trying to get the city moving; kindly soldiers are co-operating with civilians, and devoting as much energy to rebuilding parts of Hue as they showed 10 days ago while destroying it.

It is, I suppose, conceivable that given enough work and dollars Hue will be rebuilt. But neither the South Vietnamese nor the Americans will reap any propaganda dividends. This city has been 'pacified' and 'liberated' to such effect that none of its citizens are going to give their hearts and minds to any officials ever again.

The Sunday Times, 3rd March 1968

Khe Sanh — two

St Valentine's Day had started before dawn, waiting for transport from Da Nang base, and my notes read as follows:

05.45. Will there be a flight to relieve 'Operation Scotland' (Khe Sanh) by noon? Met. boys unsure. Only two flights yesterday, one had 329 50-cal. machine gun bullets aft. (Who counted them?) Surroundings grim as normal. Large office split up, vaguely medicinally, into sections with sweating hard-board. A sign says: 'Important — Ignore This Sign'. Institutional humour. One-pipped, bespectacled Lt. Butts is briefing us. He has brought cardboard cartons wrapped in plastic so we can have breakfast out of their gurgling coffee machine. Also some airmail envelopes, again wrapped in plastic, so we can write to our next of kin. A bit premature, lieutenant? Everyone else is writing busily so I shall make a will. Doesn't one need some kind of stamp and witnesses to make it legal?

Lt. Butts briefs us: 'Gentlemen, one thing when the aircraft comes to a halt. Sit tight. The ammunition has priority. Once the ammo crates are cleared get out of the back, turn right at ninety degrees, and run till you hit the support trenches which are located at approximately thirty-five yards off the strip. Charley will be shooting at you.'

'Questions, gennelman?' says the loot. O'Reilly, the mad Irishman from Kansas City who like me had bribed his way on to the flight (what better definition of madness?), raised a languid hand, caricaturing a High School kid.

O'Reilly: You mention in, ah, passing, ammunition, loot.

Butts: Affirmative, sir. Any correspondent who doesn't wish to fly with high explosive just has to say so.

O'Reilly: High, er...

Butts: Right, sir. Ground to ground rockets, plus anti-tank rockets, HE 66 and 72 mm.

O'Reilly (sniffing story): You trying to say Charley's got tanks there too?

Butts (doggedly): You signed your waiver, sir. Still time to get your name off the manifest.

Skip (AP man who previously, like me, has not said a word): Guess there aren't any craft goin' in not carrying HE. Right, Lieutenant?

Butts: Right.

Forty minutes of uninterrupted silence after this. All three of the waiting correspondents go twice to the lavatory during this period. 07.30 we start to talk.

Skip, the AP photographer with a face like a rock someone has been bashing at with a crow-bar, speaks as if to himself.

'I bought this stereo tape recorder in Saigon, four-forty dollars. Really nice sound. All I want to do is sit down in a whorehouse there and play *Kiss Me Kate* and *Madame Butterfly* all afternoon.'

O'Reilly and I pondered this eminently reasonable ambition for a while, nodding sagely. 'Anyone with balls, real balls I mean, would have checked out of this flight the moment he heard that shit about HE,' O'Reilly finally announced.

Skip sighed, and fiddled with the buttons on his flak jacket.

'Maybe Lieutenant Butts was trying to scare us, you know, kind of a joke,' I contributed weakly.

'Give you odds against,' said O'Reilly. 'I mean, does the guy look like a humorist?'

Butts didn't, and wasn't. When, at 0900, the three of us were finally strapped into the C-123 we were separated by a pyramid of wooden crates with steel corners lashed down along the centre of the cargo plane's belly. One, about four feet from my groin, had the following information stencilled in red on the side facing me:

'Warning: Anti-Tank mm72. No naked flames within one hundred yards.'

In case the message left any unresolved ambiguities the stencil concluded with a large skull and cross-bones. The Flight Master was a Virginian called Wild-hack. He wore a cocky ginger moustache, and looked genuinely unfrightened. When I asked him why we were using a C-123, instead of the normal bigger C-130s, he shrugged: 'I guess it's because of the 130 Charley took out Saturday. They make too big a target. You'll see the burned out shell on the runway when we get there.'

After the folding panel at the back of the aircraft had closed, Wild-hack addressed us through a microphone on a wire.

'Gennelmen, when we arrive sit tight. The ammunition goes first, then you follow. In case something not anticipated happens on touch down I ring my bell.' (He rang a bell.) 'That gennelmen is the signal to bale out with no delay, and get the fuck out of it. As far from the aircraft as possible. And you run right, away from the wire. On the perimeter we got Charley.'

With no change of expression he lit a Robert Burns with a match struck on the steel edge of one of the ammo crates. I caught O'Reilly's eyes, and raised my eyebrows in mock despair. He opened both palms to the air, the gesture of a beggar in Jerusalem pleading for alms...

(from *God Stand up for Bastards*.)

Make sure you tell them what's happening, said the US Marine

Waiting to leave Vietnam at Tan Son Nhut Airport, I was stopped by a Marine. 'When you get out of here, make sure to tell them what's happening,' he said, 'because they don't know.'

Now, after 48 hours spent talking to people, and with access to a cross-section of the world's newspapers for the first time in six weeks, I am beginning to think the Marine was right, though not perhaps in the way he intended.

The sufferings of American fighting men are understood, I think, particularly now that casualties are so heavy. (If the post-Tet weekly average of 500-plus continues, the Americans are going to lose nearly as many of their men in Vietnam during 1968 as they did over more than three years in Korea.)

On the other hand, the extent of the military disaster does not seem to have been grasped. Nor does the fact that the pacification programme, the social and political corollary of the military presence, is now in shreds.

In effect, the Americans are back where they were 18 months ago. They are holding on to the towns and their own military bases but, as far as the countryside goes, they are capable of little more than mobile defence.

Constructive social programmes are, given the present circumstances, a thing of the past. They will remain so until Viet Cong control in the countryside has been broken and something has been done for the 600,000 new refugees, the heartbreaking testament of the last seven weeks. This could take America two years; if could also easily take five.

In the light of what one sees in Vietnam, and of what everyone there knows, some recent Pentagon statements, particularly that series about how Tet was being a victory, read as if they had been drafted by Lewis Carroll.

Anyone who wishes America well can only hope that the President, Dean Rusk and the new defence secretary, Clark Clifford, have strong private reservations about their own public statements. (This is, after all, a war, and I see no reason why a head of state should be expected to dwell overly on a major defeat, or a commanding general confide to the Press where he has gone wrong. Contrariwise, it would be tragic if, through a combination of poor intelligence and mutual self-delusion, those running this war were to start believing their own anodyne public remarks.)

One can understand Washington's difficulty at comprehending how their huge, lavish army, a triumph of technology, has been so effectively clobbered by a lot of little men who don't have transport, air support (and sometimes even boots) and yet win major battles.

Why have the American troops suffered this unexpected crushing setback? It does not need a Clausewitz to deduce from ground experience in Vietnam that they are fighting the wrong war in the wrong way.

The French were blasted out of Indo-China because their St Cyr-conditioned officers thought they were fighting World War Two.

If the Americans continue to fail in Vietnam, it will be because their West

(Don McCullin)

Point-conditioned officers, blinded with the orthodoxy of material and technology, are trying to fight World War Three. In Vietnam, officers talk about air strikes like Faustus expounding the alchemist's stone. Their efficacy in jungle terrain has never been established, and a bad case is not helped by phoney statistics.

As for the efficacy of bombing the North (which began in 1965) all one can say for certain is that there are now nearly 25 times as many NVA troops in South Vietnam as there were when it started.

On the ground 'search and destroy' operations, designed to make contact with large enemy concentrations, have been questionably effective. Again the statistics of enemy killed are asininely weighted with either pure optimism or civilian casualties of supporting air-strikes. As they joke in officers' clubs: 'If it's a dead gook (Vietnamese) then it just has to be a VCKIA (killed in action).'

It is a rotten joke.

The famed US Marine Corps in the north is the biggest single failure of the post-Tet war. The troops are brave enough but their training is inadequate, their leadership deplorable. In Hue I saw 18-year-old troops fresh from the States killed because they did not know enough to tell the difference between mortars 'coming in' and those 'going out'.

Their training had been in jungle warfare and they were engaged, and humiliatingly beaten, in house to house warfare.

Correspondents in Khe Sanh were shocked to discover that the Marine Commander there had not read any of the illuminating books published on the French experience in Vietnam, particularly at Dien Bien Phu.

When questioned about the inadequacy of the Marines' Khe Sanh defences their commanding general, Robert Cushman, idiotically remarked that it was against their tradition to dig in. At Camp Caroll, which receives even heavier 'incoming' bombardment than Khe Sanh, more than three-quarters of the battered garrison were spending the night above ground eight days ago because sleeping in bunkers, in the words of a colonel there, 'is bad for morale'.

What can the Americans do? There is no doubt that they should begin by giving their Commanding General, William Westmoreland, a well-earned rest. Last year, in his much-vaunted appearance before the ceremonial Joint Session of Congress, he reassured his worried countrymen that there was light at the end of the tunnel. There was not.

A few months ago he was also suggesting that the first soldiers might be returned home within a couple of years, or even less. We know from Saigon that, following consultations with Westmoreland, joint Chief of Staff Earle Wheeler has reported to President Johnson that 50,000 more troops are required 'as a minimum'. Washington reports suggest that the actual reinforcements now requested are four times more than that.

If a company chairman got his estimates that wrong, the shareholders would soon conclude they would do better without him.

As Westmoreland's successor, the President would need to find someone capable of approaching the war in an entirely different way. There is no military or economic sense in sending more reluctant youths, particularly ill-trained ones, to Vietnam if their only function is to compound confusion and escalate disaster into catastrophe.

The logic of events would seem to dictate a negotiated settlement, and soon.

One hears that the President has recently been patriotically citing the indomitable spirit of the Alamo when engaged in discussions on the Vietnam situation. It is helpful if a country's chief executive is historically sensitive as well as patriotic.

Every schoolboy knows that the Alamo defenders were courageous to the last, and also very dead.

The Sunday Times, 17th March 1968

Only a few centimetres to go in the who-sits-where Vietnam Battle

American diplomats here are hopeful that in the next few days a combination of diplomacy and geometric invention will break the deadlock afflicting the Paris peace talks.

After nearly a month's stalemate over seating arrangements known familiarly as the 'Who sits where? bug', Ambassador Harriman who leads the US delegation seems to have persuaded his tetchy co-negotiator Vice-President Nguyen Cao Ky of South Vietnam to think in terms of compromise.

And at the end of the week, the American delegation was 'within a few centimetres' of reaching agreement on a seating plan which would enable the talks to begin before Christmas.

But so far despite a three-hour meeting with visual aids between Cyrus Vance, the American number two, and Ita Van Lau, the Hanoi negotiator, this is a few centimetres too many.

To date, the long-drawn-out talks have turned on semantic distinctions and delegates in search of inspiration would probably have found it in the pages of Machiavelli or Talleyrand.

This weekend, Euclid and Pythagoras seem more apposite. Square tables are out, by general consent. So, too, for the moment are rectangles, ellipses and probably diamonds, though on Friday they all had their supporters.

The Americans, introducing a much-needed homespun touch into the debate, now favour tables ranged 'like a kind of bisected doughnut with a split in the middle'.

This split, which is really the point at issue, would be filled by stenographers, recording equipment and probably the chap who makes the tea, occupying rectangular tables projecting a few centimetres outside the circumference of the doughnut at each side. This is intended to reinforce the US contention that the talks are 'two-sided.'

Hanoi and the NLF, representing the Viet Cong, want their doughnut round, to symbolise their belief that the talks are four-sided. They have shown no marked enthusiasm for the stenographic diameter between the two camps and when you mention the protruding centimetres to them they say this is another example of the Americans' 'lack of goodwill.'

But at least Mr Ky, who took a very hard line when he arrived from Saigon last week, appears to have mellowed, or at least bent, under American pressure. For him, the table shape is crucial. Any pattern suggesting equality of status between himself and the Viet Cong is hard to swallow.

Sceptics, including of course the North Vietnamese who still refer to President Thieu's Government as 'puppet' or the Saigon administration as if it were a local council, may question the regime's electoral basis. But as Mr Ky is determined to demonstrate, it is indubitably the only Vietnamese Government Saigon enjoys, and must be respected as such.

The triangular pattern had the advantage of confusing the issue even more than

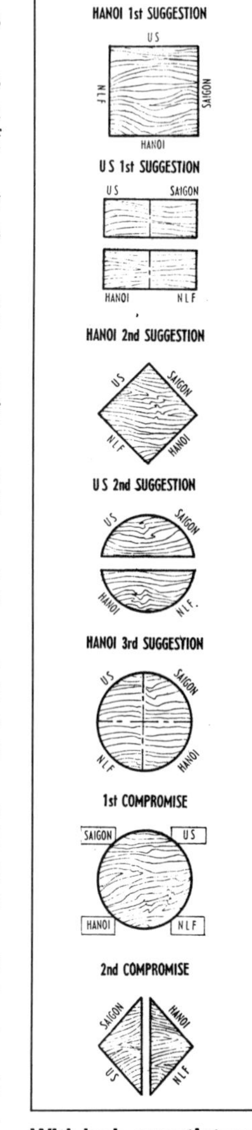

With luck, negotiators at the Paris peace talks will eventually lay their cards on one of these suggested tables.

now, which would have enabled the Americans and Mr Ky to indicate in their propaganda that the talks were really bilateral without inhibiting the other side from letting it be known they were really four-sided all the time.

But for the moment, the issue centres on the broken doughnut, though Hanoi, without much conviction, has also suggested four separate tables grouped in a square or a circle.

Hanoi originally put forward three table plans as against one — two divided rectangles facing each other — from the Americans. This gave Van Lau and his resourceful negotiator Mr Xuan Thuy a slight edge in diplomatic gamesmanship but the Hanoi threesome was really no more than a minor variation on one theme.

The idea was that the delegates should sit normally round a square table, or a round or oval one, as if they were dining together or playing cards. This idea was, however, too simple and came at the beginning of the week when Mr Ky, fresh from Saigon, was carrying intransigence to a point which seemed to irritate his American allies more than his enemies from Hanoi and the NLF.

Since then, apparently thanks to Ambassador Bunker in Saigon, he is taking a much more co-operative line.

The miracle about the talks is that they do accomplish things, albeit painfully slowly. Their progress provides a wealth of interest for connoisseurs as the diplomatic shadow boxing continues. For those fighting in Vietnam, the academic aspects of the exercise probably have less appeal.

The Sunday Times, 15th December 1968

A day in search of Vietnam peace

It is 7 a.m. in Paris, Thursday, March 6, and so cold that the French police outside the American Embassy are stamping their feet. Inside, the round-the-clock communications staff are examining the latest statistics of death direct from Saigon. The news is bad: intelligence reports indicate that the week's death toll of GIs will be the highest since the Vietnam peace talks began here last May.

Later in the day, Ambassador Cabot Lodge is to attend the Seventh Plenary Session of the peace talks, and the news promises to add further acrimony to the debate. In Saigon — seven hours ahead of Paris time — it is the afternoon siesta, but the reports of incidents continue to mount. The ambassador's late news brief is already bulging.

SAIGON, 2 p.m: It is hot, wet and soporific. In a Third Precinct officers' billet an American major sits up abruptly in bed, woken from his siesta by the sudden explosion of a grenade. He runs to the window to see a 50 cc Honda motorcycle roar off, bearing two teenagers in stolen Vietnamese army uniforms.

The sentry box outside his billet has lost a roof, two walls and its sentry. Two lieutenants lie in blood in the courtyard. They were caught coming out of the mess door after lunch. One of them is badly wounded. A seven-year-old Vietnamese child begging on the pavement outside was also caught. He will die.

PHU KUONG, 2.30 p.m: A platoon of the US 25th Infantry Divison, moving through rice paddies near the Michelin rubber plantation, 13 miles north-west of Saigon, drop into the water. Heavy machine-gun fire is coming from a clump of trees shrouding a hamlet beside the paddies. They slither backwards in irrigation ditches and radio for help. In 18 minutes American Supersabres are dropping 500 pound bombs on the trees, and 12 minutes later Huey helicopters are landing the first reinforcements. It is the start of a developing battle that only tapers off after dusk, when the North Vietnamese Army company in the trees pulls back, leaving 51 corpses. One American is dead. One wounded.

CENTRAL VIETNAM, 3.0 p.m: A Phantom jet bomber over the Central Highlands is hit by anti-aircraft fire. The plane falls. Two crew eject. One dies. One survives.

PARIS, 8.30 a.m: There is an early sensation as it is confirmed that Vice-President Ky, 'co-ordinator' of the South Vietnamese mission, has decided to miss the talks and is returning to Saigon on the 11 o'clock Air France flight from Orly. He takes with him messages from Ambassador Phang Dam Lam, who has eight children in Saigon and is worried about the rocket attacks.

Why is Ky going? Are the rumours true about a Saigon Government walk-out? Or has Ky's flattering meeting with Nixon, and the gourmet meal Ambassador Lodge offered him tête-à-tête the previous day, calmed him down?

To observe protocol, so dear to the Vietnamese heart, the US delegation's number two, Judge Lawrence E. Walsh (who replaced Cyrus Vance in January as a Nixon nominee), has been deputed to see him off.

(Don McCullin)

DA NANG, 3.30 p.m: Second platoon, Mike Company, US 7th Marines lose two men and kill 12 in hand-to-hand fighting in a rice paddy. 'That's Van Ryker's mob,' says a brother officer admiringly. 'The wildest goddam Marines in the wildest fightin' force in the world. They could have picked off all them VC from the treeline, neat and tidy. But they'd lost five men from booby traps this week. They were so hepped up with Marine spirit no man could hold 'em. They rushed out to smash in VC skulls with rifle butts. Lost us two good grunts, that spirit. But it sure was worth it.'

The action brings Marine dead in this area to 136 in this post-Tet offensive. Enemy dead are 700. The Marines' job is to protect Da Nang against rocket fire. Rockets have landed on Da Nang every night.

Meanwhile, in Saigon, 500 miles to the South, a worried President Nguyen van Thieu is receiving a visit from the American ambassador, Ellsworth C. Bunker.

PARIS, 9 a.m: Cabot Lodge — who himself has served two terms as ambassador in Saigon — is finishing reading his briefs. Emendations have been made to his speech, and messages are being sent to the capitals of the 'Free World Forces' — Canberra, Manila, Bangkok, Auckland and Seoul. Ambassador Lodge's temporary quarters are in the Hotel Crillon, 45 paces from the Embassy across Rue Boissy-d-Anglas.

The 'Other Side' lives less conveniently and are already getting ready for a long drive in from the suburbs. The NLF are at Verrieres-le-Buisson beyond Orly. The Hanoi delegation moved to the suburbs last summer from the Left-bank Lutetia Hotel after making ungracious remarks about the hotel's standard of rice cuisine. Their villa at Choisy le Roi has its own printing press and a blue steel grill barring visitors. If you ring the bell, a Vietnamese guard tells you placidly that the place is a school.

SAIGON, 4.0 p.m: Correspondents visit the still smoking ruins of Saigon houses in the Kien Hoa district. Twenty-two civilians died here, 25 were wounded in Viet Cong rocket attacks early this morning. Scenes at the hospital were macabre, with bleeding Vietnamese queing for attention, medical orderlies walking the corridors carrying shattered arms for disposal.

But mourning has apparently already ceased. Residents spit at the white men. Kien Hoa is a largely Viet Cong part of town.

Meanwhile at the Gralle Hospital in the rich part of Saigon a French doctor is showing American Embassy officials damage caused by Monday's rocket attack. One landed in the hospital courtyard, smashing an external wall of a children's and maternity ward, breaking one internal window. Three children suffered superficial scratches from the glass. 'We were incredibly lucky,' says the doctor.

SAIGON, 4.15 p.m: A procession of militant anti-Government Buddhists riding three-wheel Lambretta vans adorned with banners is now halfway between one Saigon pagoda and another. Hundreds of police escort them. In a scuffle, they arrest a law student for distributing leaflets calling for peace.

PARIS, 9.30 a.m: Peace here is creating less public concern. When the talks began last May, a grandstand full of 2,000 journalists awaited the delegates outside the Majestic; now there are only 11 reporters, and four of these are Japanese TV men.

But as in Saigon the police are busy. The French Secret Servicemen in their black Citroën are checking that the police with their walkie-talkies are properly in place along the ambassadorial route. Outside the Majestic are 40 uniformed police and a dozen plain clothes men.

SAIGON, 4.30 p.m: Now begin the 'Five O-clock Follies' — the name given by journalists to the daily Saigon press conference at which two Vietnamese and three American spokesmen pop up in turn at a lectern in a dingy hall. First, Mr Huyen for the Vietnamese talks of yesterday's attempted assassination of Prime Minister Tran Van Huong. Huong was saved because a Claymore mine, mounted on a pedicab, failed to explode. Two men were arrested.

We now know, says Huyen, that the attempt was not local Saigon political intrigue — that he was a Communist terrorist. The VC have a list of 2,000 Saigon officials they intend to kill.

Then comes the American political spokesman, Barrett McGurn. He says nothing, in an orotund voice.

PARIS, 10.15 a.m: The delegates as they begin to arrive at the Majestic have their own personal styles of saying nothing. First come the NLF delegates, heralded by a brace of motorcyclists blowing whistles; their leader, Tran Buu Keim, offers only a fleeting skeletal smile. Five minutes later, Ambassador Phang Dam Lam of Saigon fails even to glance at the photographers. Then the Japanese TV men stretch out a microphone on a pole to the American delegation, whose spokesman Harold Kaplan politely says 'hello'.

Finally, the Hanoi men arrive. It is hard to distinguish them from the other Vietnamese delegations. They all wear cheap overcoats; they all look cold; they all arrive in modest black Citroëns and Peugeots lent by the French Government. The Americans, by contrast, in their Ivy League suits and embassy Plymouths look like creatures from another planet, twice as big and a hundred times richer.

VIETNAMESE COAST, 5.15 p.m: The world's only active battleship, the US *New Jersey*, lobs shells on a group of North Vietnamese dugouts just south of the Demilitarised Zone. Each shell costs as much, and weighs as much, as a Peugeot car. The cause of this apocalyptic barrage was a small burst of automatic small-arms fire on an American spotter plane.

QUANG TRI PROVINCE, 5.15 p.m: An American Marine on patrol touches a hidden wire with his boot. He hears the snap of a grenade detonator. He has five seconds to duck and leaps for cover. The explosion blows off his right ankle.

PARIS, 10.25 a.m: Xuan Thuy, leader of the Hanoi delegation, is the last to turn up at the Majestic, and the first to break silence to the press. Waving a pedagogic finger, he makes a long statement through an interpreter — the first dose of jargon in a day devoted to nothing else.

He talks about the indomitable people of Vietnam, their glorious struggle, their imperviousness to threats. There is no mention of the Washington hints about a resumption of bombing, but this of course is what he is obliquely talking about. He takes a long time doing it, as befits the author of an ode to Uncle Ho which ran to ten strophes of four verses each. One verse, in rough translation which nonetheless gives the flavour of Hanoi's style, reads:

The sounds of southern rifles are still echoing,
Bombs are still raining on Vinh Linh and Thanh Hoa
At the international centre of conferences in Paris our voices are also echoing
Demanding that the imperialist Yankee aggressors confess their crimes.

SAIGON, 5.30 p.m: The 'Five O-clock Follies' have ended with a choice selection of statistics from the US military spokesman: 453 American solders have been killed this week, bringing the total killed in the war to 32,326.

2,597 American soldiers have been wounded this week, bringing the total to 204,593.

6,752 enemy troops died this week, bringing the total to 457,132.

208 Vietnamese civilians died last week. But no one has calculated the total.

This morning's rocket attack on Saigon was the worst of the Vietnam war. There were 35 enemy rocket and mortar attacks yesterday, and 31 ground attacks.

Yesterday American Army aircraft flew 11,533 sorties; and B52 bombers dropped 1,500 tons of explosive. Damage assessment by pilots includes 295 enemy fortifications, 357 bunkers, 33 sampans and 49 secondary explosions.

Overwhelmed by blood and percentages, the mind gives up.

CAMBODIAN BORDER, 6 p.m: Machine gun fire brings down an unarmed Medivac helicopter as it takes off with four badly wounded following a firefight in light jungle. Tomorrow they too will be just another statistic.

PARIS, 11.15 a.m: Tran Buu Kiem of the NLF is half-way through a 75-minute speech across the notorious conference table (diameter, one recalls, 8.60 metres). He says 'The US is still unwilling to renounce its aggressive designs and neocolonialist schemes,' a statement delivered with passion and doubtless conviction, though to the Americans it is the tiredest propaganda, He says nothing new: his speech, and those that follow it, are all born of the strange conviction that if repeated often enough one's own vision of the truth will prevail against the opposition.

SOUTH VIETNAM, 6.40 p.m: Dusk falls, and now the time of real danger begins. American and South Vietnamese units have pulled back into the relative safety of base camps and night defensive positions. 105 and 155 mm howitzers begin their random 'H and I' (harrassment and interdiction) barrages which are intended to deter infiltrating Viet Cong, but don't. Flares shoot into the sky every minute or so to illuminate the blackness beyond perimeter defences.

SAIGON, 6.45 p.m: The *Vietnam Guardian* on sale in the streets reports: 'Several deputies in the Lower House are drafting a petition to ask Speaker Nguyen Ba Luong to delay his marriage to a wealthy widow until after his term as Speaker expires next October because the wedding would have a bearing on the credibility of the legislature.'

PARIS, 11.55 a.m: Now it is North Vietnam's turn to speak, with some more serious questioning of the credibility of the Saigon legislature. It is immediately clear that there is no change of line, nor could any be expected.

The North Vietnamese speech lasts for 65 minutes. Then the meeting adjourns for what the opposing sides call coffee break or tea pause.

SOUTH VIETNAM, 7 p.m: American Forces Television is displaying a large blonde. She encourages the troops to keep up their malaria protection. 'Always take the big red pill,' she says. 'I do, and feel secure.' She winks.

But death by malaria is not the only hazard. An hour later, a Marine reconnaissance team codenamed Crazy Bones sights forty VC crossing a river through their 'starlight scope' night binoculars. An artillery strike is called with unknown effect. But a Marine is killed by a falling empty flare canister from an American aircraft.

PARIS, 1.40 p.m: Cabot Lodge makes a brief speech of only 15 minutes in which he calls on the Communists to ponder the words of President Nixon — in itself an idea tantamount to provocation, particularly when we discover what the words are.

The Ambassador has selected a purple passage from the inaugural address in the highest Republican/Evangelical vein. 'The peace we seek to win is not victory over any other people, but the peace which comes with healing in its wings.'

As the wings in the forefront of this week's discussion belong to the B52 bombers, it is easy to see why the Ambassador's words cause resentment.

The South Vietnamese, in a 19-minute speech, add their indignation about rocket attacks on civilians, and by 2.25 p.m. the delegates begin to emerge. The session, less than four hours, has been abnormally short. So short indeed that rumours begin: the impasse is absolute, Saigon intends to quit altogether, it has been the worst meeting yet.

DALAT, 9.30 p.m: A large hole appears in the wall of an elegant villa in this South Vietnamese mountain health resort. One of eight Viet Cong mortar rounds fired on the town. Dalat, a widespread old colonial settlement, 150 miles north of Saigon, is at night almost impossible to defend. This villa is the fifth in the same boulevard to be holed in a month. A sleeping child is killed.

QUANG NGAI, 10.30 p.m: A squad of Viet Cong with flamethrowers and rifles walks through a new refugee village on the sand dunes in this Northern town and set 35 huts ablaze, kill 9 old men and women, wound 25 others, 15 of them children. They keep a military outpost 300 yards away quiet with three mortar bombs. The pacification programme in the area is no more.

PARIS, 4.20 p.m: A hundred reporters attend the delegations' press briefings, in the French Post Office Ministry. Harold Kaplan, the US spokesman, gets up. 'I'll try and keep this short and grim,' he begins.

Kaplan is pressed on US reactions to the rocket attacks on Saigon, and the possibility of resumed bombing of Hanoi. He refuses to commit himself: 'We can only say that the consequences are their responsibility.'

Tran Hoi Nam, the NLF spokesman, wearing rimless glasses, hair sleeked down like a black mouse, gives his version of the morning session. He was contemptuous about US complaints of new attacks. 'This is only a manoeuvre to hide the bloody crimes of the US aggressors and their puppets who are conducting indiscriminate attacks and bombardments.'

A South Korean journalist jumped up and asked vehemently: 'Why have you fired at civilians?' Mr Nam's answer was unusually terse. 'Ask President Nixon.'

SAIGON, 11.40 p.m: The American Defence secretary, Melvin Laird, arrives at Tan Son Nhut airport for his Vietnamese tour and, ringed with guards, declares he is fresh from a breakfast meeting with President Nixon. He says enemy rocket attacks on Vietnamese cities are a violation of the bombing pause agreement. 'I want to reiterate the hopes and prayers for success in Paris. But no one should mistake our patience for weakness.'

SAIGON, 12.0 p.m.: The curfew begins in Saigon. It is strictly enforced and observed. But except for a handful of westerners in girlie bars in Tu Do, the streets have been populated by only police and troops since ten.

HIEP HOA, 1.0 a.m: Fibreglass boats of a river patrol spot ten junks ferrying VC troops, north of Saigon. The junks respond with B40 rocket fire. One American boat, hit and sinking, is towed away by another. A helicopter airlifts naval wounded back to Saigon, but one dies on the way. Other helicopters rocket the junks. They report 12 Viet Cong killed.

LAOTIAN BORDER, 1.30 a.m: Marines of the 3rd Division moving through jungle north of the Ashau Valley discover yet another hidden store of enemy weapons, and an underground vehicle repair station deep enough to withstand even

(Don McCullin)

B52 bombs. This is operation Dewey Canyon, one of the most successful of the war. They have captured 450 tons of Communist weapons and explosives, the biggest haul so far. Their triumph is marred only by the explosion, a week ago, of 370 tons of *American* ammunition in a barge moored in Da Nang.

DA NANG, 3 a.m: The First Marine Division military band (Conductor: Warrant Officer Andrew Olesak) is in Vietnam for musical duties. But the bandsmen also have the military job of guarding the division's camp perimeter at Hill Ten, 500 feet above Da Nang. The Viet Cong choose to hit the band perimeter this night.

A rocket-propelled grenade kills the French horn (his name is Ziegler) and wounds a saxophonist. A bass fiddler, two snare-drummers and an E flat clarinettist race for cover as 40 VC sappers come charging through wire they have been secretly cutting for five days.

Another grenade blasts a Negro trumpeter bodily out of his spider hole. He jumps into the next hole. Both band and Viet Cong, taking him for enemy, blast away from either side.

For half-an-hour Hill Ten is enemy territory. A VC flag is placed on top of the hill overlooking the entire base. Two more bandmen die. An air-control radar centre, worth half a million dollars, is exploded with TNT.

Then a headquarters reaction force, including 4 stenographers, 3 cooks, a barman and pay clerks, — and led by a lawyer — charge Hill Ten and restore it to American control.

'Ah knows army musicians in England is non-combatant,' says conductor Olesak, compiling his Silver Star recommendations after the action. 'But I tell you when the muck hits the fan I'd rather be playing my old M 16 than any clarinet cadenza.'

PARIS, 8.0 p.m: Now it is all over, the Press and TV teams have drifted away. But even after a day when there had been words by the thousand a few reporters had lingered round the Hanoi spokesman, Nguyen Than Le, avid for more. He was asked in French what he thought — and then, for fear of yet another ideological outburst, it was added 'in two words'. He smiled and surprisingly replied in English. 'No progress.'

The Sunday Times, 9th March 1969
(with Nicholas Tomalin)

Waiting for peace

Doctor Henry A. Kissinger slides through Paris as sleek as a grey seal. He keeps mum but the experts claim they can sniff peace in his wake like the aroma of some rare cigar. Are the secret negotiations, the so-called talks behind the talks, reaching their conclusion? Are they, one hardly dares write the words, actually going to stop the war? French officials, reinforced by Maurice Schumann, back from the UN, are optimistic. But what of their judgement? So much French policy has to do with pretending to be in the Big League that a real international event on their doorstep confuses them. They react like schoolboys who discover the Cup Final is happening in their playground. And again they don't really know.

And neither, one suspects, do the Americans attached to the Official Peace Delegation, the old sweats of the Avenue Kléber. Like the national flags in the conference hall, now a bit tatty with age, their function has long been merely decorative. Kissinger's trouble-shooting methods put the career diplomats in a corner. They recall, with bleak distaste, the deplorable habit old Secretary Dulles had of trusting only those who worked in Washington under his nose. 'Now who's clever at Afghanistan?' he would murmur, looking round his assembled staff and, despite the presence of a perfectly sound man on the spot, off would go Kermit Roosevelt, or some other young Turk from Harvard, with results we all know about.

Half the time Washington sent no warning to the man on the spot. So it was this week. Some Paris officials were expecting the presidential adviser to come back again this week to see Le Duc Tho but then up he popped with Gromyko, dining at Fort David and most of the optimistic noises, it is pointed out, tend to be coming from that direction too. President Nixon says something off the cuff intended to repay the faithful for their $1,000 plate of frozen chicken, and the headlines follow. But Nixon has said such things before. Is he the kind of man to buy a second-hand peace from?

But despite such reservations, born of frustration and, in some cases, years of agonising boredom in Paris, a visit to the official negotiations contains some encouragement for those who, following Wall Street, feel bullish about a pre-election negotiated settlement. We start at 10 on the Avenue Kléber outside the old Hotel Majestic, wartime headquarters of the Gestapo. No matter how you tart this place up the air around echoes with bat shrieks of ancient infamies. Coincidentally, the Hotel Lutetia on the Left Bank, where the Hanoi delegates first stayed, has a similar background. It housed Section 3F of the Abwehr under Admiral Canaris, the section that dealt with allied agents. The Vietnamese soon quit the place for very mundane unhistorical reasons; they didn't like the way the hotel prepared rice.

So now they arrive from the outer suburbs in Citroëns and Renaults loaned by the French government. They are totally upstaged by the Americans, who sweep down in monstrous black Plymouths from the embassy car pool only three minutes away along the Champs Elysées. The confrontation of transport and personnel could be from an updated *Gulliver's Travels*. The Americans and their hardware are so huge, the Vietnamese so dinky. Steve Ledegger, until recently the US press spokesman, stood 6 feet 7 inches in glossy black brogues. When he inclined a foot or so to speak to Le Duc Tho, who resembled a prep school swot, the tiny man from Hanoi looked as insecure as a cocktail canapé.

But, contrary to appearances, there seemed to me no doubt who was on top. The Hanoi negotiator contented himself with a shy schoolboy smile but Madame Nguyen Thi Binh, of whom more later, let it be known that as far as the Viet Cong were concerned American bombs were still falling. 'No light in her tunnel,' commented an American journalist, who like so many others came over four years ago and has aged with the talks.

Despite Kissinger the positions apparently have not changed. The Americans insist any new Saigon government must be elected. They claim an enforced coalition would be undemocratic — perish the thought, remembering November '71 — a mere prelude to bloody communistic vengeance. Le Duc Tho thinks there might be blood about too, but on the hands of President Nguyen Van Thieu. Both assumptions are fair ones. Despite all the civics courses the pacification programme threw up there has never been the slightest evidence that any one in Vietnam, North or South, remotely understood democracy as defined by the Americans. Nor is there now. In the afternoon we will be briefed about how long the talks lasted and whether there were any exchanges during the tea breaks.

It seems like tame stuff in this homogenised official building where apparently nothing has changed. The same malevolent old men in dusty work-coats check credentials, their suspicion — like most of the hostility in Paris — a phenomenon exclusive to those venerable enough to bear the psychic scars of our last war. The telephone girls, well permed, still discuss rising prices like a personal affront, still dump their red cigarette ends in the potted rubber plants. It might be four years ago when the point at issue was the shape of the conference table: round? triangular? hexagonal? The US spokesman of the time — one remembers him almost with affection — introduced an imaginative and folksy note. Why not like a doughnut with a kind of slit in the middle, he suggested helpfully.

Certainly there has been progress since those days when Averell Harriman stoically presided. Ar-y-man, the Vietnamese called him. He was an ideal negotiator according to some, being stone deaf. How many, one wonders, have died since then?

The South Vietnamese delegates, the very adjective a fraud, are the most fashion conscious, the most pitiable. Their hysteria cannot be concealed. They give the game away, to the irritation of the American super-pros, by issuing a statement which is tantamount to a plea to Nixon not to sign anything without telling them. 'Le Président Thieu', one says reverently, small palms turned heavenwards, 'would come and take charge personally. But how can he leave Saigon?' How indeed.

The 'puppets' from Saigon, as the Communists call them, are small-time punters who should have taken their profits when the market was on the up. The delegates from Hanoi, and above all those of the Viet Cong, are of a different calibre. Naturally they are just as polite, but one cannot fail to recognise the ghost of the tiger hovering round them. Like the Catholic secret agents who set out from Douai, their obsession with the ultimate makes them regard humanity only in the abstract. Beside them the men from Saigon, with their Protestant concern for human profit or loss, are grocers negotiating with priests.

Madame Binh, Foreign Secretary of the National Liberation Front, is beautiful and implacable. She brings a certain unexpected glamour to the stereotyped exchanges. The first time I came to interview here I fell asleep during the two hours of preliminary statements, during which liberal American representatives of the *Christian Science Monitor* tried to prove through sincere questions that the Communist position is riddled with holes. I was woken by Martha Gelhorn, war reporter extraordinary, formerly married to Hemingway, following the same journalistic trail. Madame Binh attracts a better class of person, and when her press aides call twice in 48 hours to indicate the rumours of a secret peace are simply capitalist manoeuvres, one sees she too is frightened that Washington and Hanoi are by-passing their junior partners. As soon as the White House (still no kudos for the old war-horses of the Avenue Kléber) publicised the arrival of Kissinger's chief aide in Saigon, General Alexander Haig Jr., one understood the alarm. Le Duc Tho insists that the departure of Thieu is a prerequisite of any settlement. In return the Viet Cong's position in the interim government must equally be negotiable. It is scarcely credible that Hanoi is busy electing Nixon for a second term without being absolutely sure he will give them what they want. Kissinger's publicity makes it seem he is running the show but at any time between now and the election Le Duc Tho and his superiors in Hanoi could blow the whistle. It must be very close, this settlement, but it is hard to see what honour the Americans will get along with the peace.

New Statesman, 6th October 1972

A villa in Gîf

The villa's only identification is the number 108 in that dinky French blue-and-white design dear to vogish London and New York house-owners. Here it signifies not sophistication but ordinariness, like its three green shutters and one ragged pine. On the gate stands a security man in dark glasses, whose sunburst capillary complexion is the sole Technicolor touch in the dun November setting. Behind him a six-foot wall: behind the wall, the elusive Vietnam peace, or intimations of it.

For this villa in the forgettable Paris suburb of Gîf-sur-Yvette presently harbours Kissinger, Le Duc Tho and the rest. The place belongs to the French Communist Party, who had it as a gift from the painter Fernand Léger. Here party worthies meet in an inviolable, clandestine setting strikingly reminiscent of a house the AEU once used for similar sessions in a suburb south of London. The well-tended vine trellis at 108, one can safely guess, was cultivated more with an eye to anonymity than love of horticulture.

Yet this week the Communists, who with their Socialist electoral partners lead the Gaullists in the opinion pools for the first time, have for once been flaunting their rustic hide-away. It is a way of making the point that their own Georges (First Secretary Marchais) has usurped his namesake, President Pompidou, as the real host to the peacemakers.

There are indications that the American honeymoon in Paris is nearly over (Maurice Schumann, the Foreign Secretary, is said to be 'Pro-Hanoi', yet another cross for a man who has long suffered politically for his supposed Anglophilia). Kuala Lumpur, of all the world capitals, has been mentioned as a possible venue for future sessions, though probably at a lower level. And generally this week Kissinger's main concern has been to get as many countries in on the peacekeeping part of the truce as possible.

With this in view a whole series of countries, including Britain it seems, are being approached through conventional diplomatic channels with a view to contributing 'police forces'. The nations named mainly have UN peacekeeping experience (India has been excluded) and the only American information forthcoming is to do with 'the nuts and bolts' of selecting and organising such still hypothetical contingents and defining their duties on the ground. All this, of course, is moving some way ahead of the Hanoi view that a cease-fire, the return of prisoners and whatever follows are all contingent on an agreed political settlement. The American strategy ignores such 'legalistic' quibbles, and officials try to forge ahead as if the signatures are already dry on the treaty.

And despite what President Nixon's security adviser misled the world into briefly believing a month ago, the Hanoi officials, as well as Madame Binh for the Provisional Revolutionary Government, make it clear this is by no means the case. Such American guidance as emerges now blithely refers to Inauguration Day as 'a time scale' for the treaty, whereas just over a month ago it was Election Day. There is plenty of action, lots of copy for those prepared to schlep out to Gîf, but business and progress are not necessarily the same animal. The entire visit has been characterised by a synthetic surface zest which owes as much to show business as to conventional diplomacy. It also suggests the protagonists may, once again, be stalled.

It has certainly been very hard, as the more scholarly practitioners have discovered, to produce a detailed analysis of how precisely the current American position has evolved from the base line of the Nixon eight-point peace plan of last February. On the other hand there is lots to write, and above all to show in 20-second television film clips. There are pictures of the security adviser getting off Air Force One in Camp David, getting aboard again in Washington, disembarking at Orly, and as it turned out, later embarking yet again for Brussels. (President Suharto of Indonesia, the object of this particular un-scheduled dash, is perhaps the most extravagantly unsuitable of the numerous 'neutrals' who have been canvassed in the last days.) No problem in understanding why Le Duc Tho said the Vietnamese for 'Are you kidding?' when the Americans came up with Suharto's name. When Kissinger is not in the air and has time to dine one of those impressive blonde companions he invariably selects the kind of restaurant where photographers are as much part of the decor as the wine-waiter. Before leaving Washington, Kissinger, we are told, specifically indicated, via Ziegler at the White House, that the site of the talks was being kept quiet 'to avoid a circus'. He must either be grotesquely inefficient in his quest for discreet encounters or, more likely, smarter than the paint-work on number 108. In either case, the setting could not have been more circus-like if the state department had summoned Barnum and Bailey from the tomb and erected a Big Top.

From the point of view of negotiating, the famous villa at Gîf is highly unsuitable. The Americans have implied the Vietnamese wanted it that way for reasons of 'face' and it seemed simplest to accommodate the quaint little fellows. Yet it is hard to escape the idea that the set-up suits the Americans very nicely. The site may be inconvenient but ideal if you wish to convey an impression of movement and drama. It may be that Kissinger's personal contribution to international diplomacy, its flamboyant and even slightly sexy quality so alien to normal methods, will finally be a matter of style. It is an approach which, with its heavy emphasis on air travel and continual frenzied activity, has something in common with the electioneering technique perfected by Jack Kennedy. It involves an inordinate amount of smiling and waving and is as dependent on TV as a diabetic on insulin.

Each session of the Gîf circus now begins, or so sincere aides tell us, with a joke request from Le Duc Tho for a chair of Marxism at Harvard. There are altogether too many of these heart-warming anecdotes, and when people from Hanoi make jokes the consequences in my experiences have seldom justified mirth.

These impressions — of something stage-managed and inauthentic — crystallised at Gîf when two tubby lady motorists, spotting the arc-lights and sniffing TV stars, promptly parked. The police had a hard time convincing them to move on since the events weren't worth kibbitzing, or as the flic put it: 'It's nothing serious at all, only politics.'

This made the man from the Hanoi news agency chuckle and so did some NLF friends of his when he explained what the cop had said. It is never easy to gauge exactly what Vietnamese laughter signifies. It can mean fear or rage or a defence against something horrible just as easily as amusement. Perhaps they were tickled by the frustrated autograph-hunters. Perhaps they had heard on their transistors it had been one of the heaviest bombing days of the war. Who knows, perhaps they were struck by the incongruity of their country's affairs being discussed at all in a villa in Gîf.

New Statesman 24th November 1972

Unhappy landings for Vietnam's boat people

Darwin, christened so optimistically to honour the father of evolution, has been having a damn rough ride ever since. Its history is indeed positively masochistic, as if God had a grudge against this dauntingly isolated outpost on 'The Top End.'

Afflicted by a climate many find literally insupportable — we are now in the high 'troppo' or suicide season — the community's spasmodic celebrity invariably stems from either man-made or supernatural catastrophe.

Between 1870 and 1938 there were seven major cyclones. In February, 1942, four days after Australia's 'Dunkirk' in Singapore, Darwin became almost by natural right the target of the first-ever attack launched by a foreign power against the Australian mainland.

Cyclone Tracy, choosing Christmas Day to strike as if to rub salt in the wounds, became Australia's worst natural disaster nearly three years ago. Despite the massive and erratic reconstruction programme, some of the subsidies for which were spent on booze, according to Dr Ella Stack, the blunt-speaking mayor, no one who has seen towns — and not just Vietnamese ones — which have been bombed, can fail to recognise a melancholy kinship.

You might think a community which is no stranger to suffering would be sympathetic to the Vietnamese. All the more so since there are 47 different languages spoken in this most cosmopolitan town in Australia.

Yet the violence of the anti-refugee reaction has been palpable; certainly it came through loud and clear to electioneering politicans of all brands.

The wharf workers' response was the most virulent, partly because they believe, as I learnt in the Darwin Workers' Club, that these Vietnamese are rich crooks, and even traitors. And partly because so many Darwin workers have ethnic connections which have caused them sometimes insurmountable difficulties with the Immigration Department themselves.

They don't like the red-tape being cut so comprehensively, and their initial attitude to strangers, a group which includes Federal politicians, is such that you need to move as nimbly as a gecko to avoid trouble.

Not since the Poor Peoples' March passed through Knoxville and Nashville in spring, 1968, have I heard so much about 'coons' and 'niggers'.

Yet there are plenty of people of different races drinking at the bar and there is little genuine racial tension, though plenty of other kinds. It is a kind of semantic racism they practise here, as if a safety valve is built into the vocabulary.

When 1,200 refugees from Timor arrived (300 more than the Vietnamese total so far) no less than 900, after a spell in the south, came back to settle permanently here. There is now even a Timor Children's Choir which produces an uplifting rendition of a song they call *Washing Mathilda*.

To see Darwin from a Navy tracker aircraft combing the Timor Sea for 'boat people' is to be reminded of the Blitz. The plane is searching for the hordes some sources promise will be entering illegally until Christmas.

Three years after Tracy modern blocks stand side by side with dilapidated empty

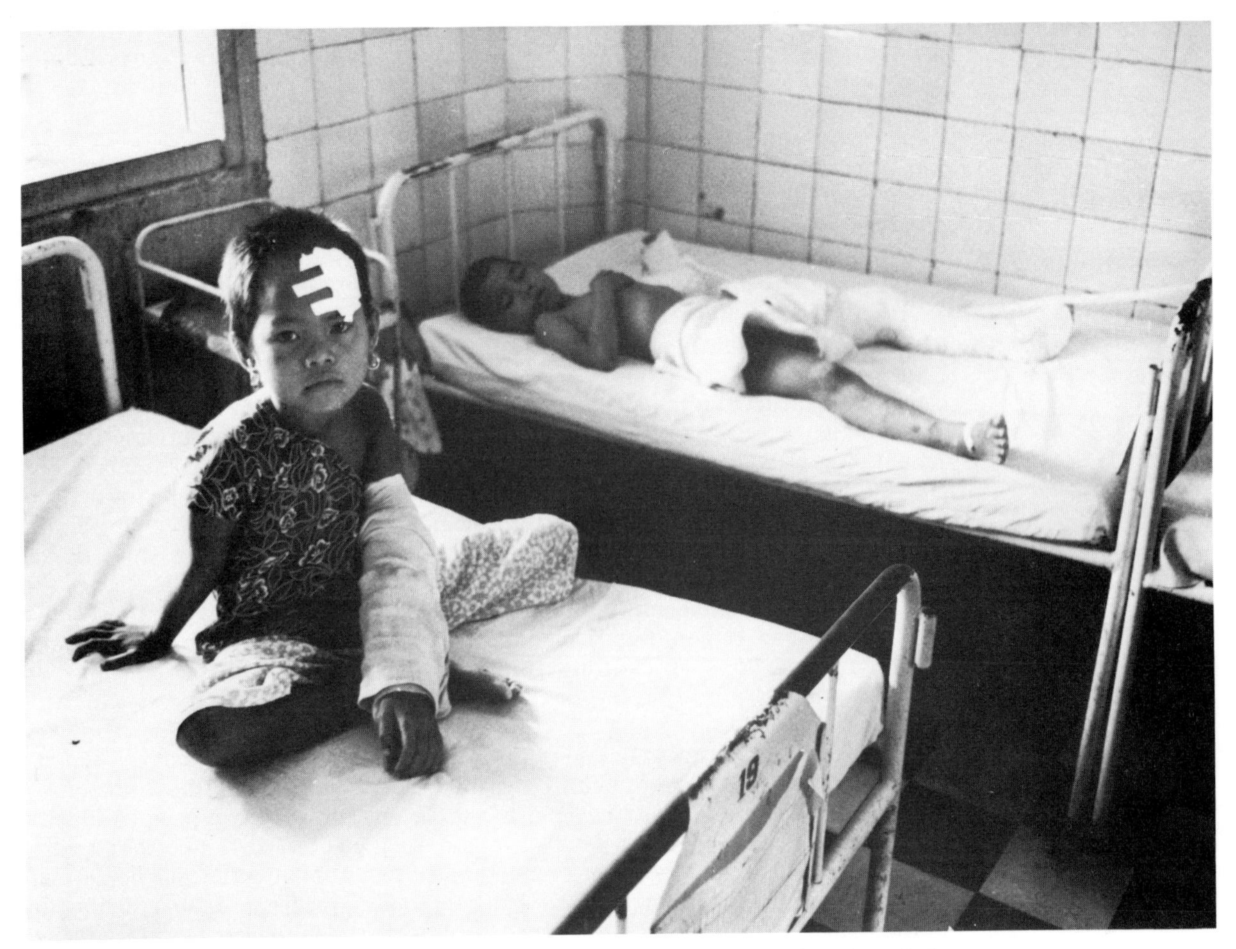

(Don McCullin)

lots and semi-shattered homes, victims of direct hits no one as yet has found the moral resilience — or hard cash — to reconstruct. Local radio punctuates commercials for Christmas gifts of kangaroo skins and buffalo horns with nerve-jangling advice about safety precautions (their intention, presumably, to reassure) issuing from the Tropical Cyclone Warning Centre.

There is also no shortage of human as well as environmental scar tissue. People going out of their minds are advised to call Crisis Line in Darwin. I tried them myself and learnt they had no shortage of clients, particularly after the bars have closed.

Were this an American city strangers would be welcomed with the sign 'Welcome to the Beer Capital of the World,' for Darwin's per capita beer consumption is said to top the universal league. (The Guiness Records book omits to list this distinction under either 'DRINK' or 'HUMAN ENDURANCE,' the two sections that seemed most relevant.) For once, however, here is a Darwin statement a visiting journalist may confidently accept unverified or double-checked.

As in all frontier towns, conning credulous strangers is a minor local art form. (I am less confident, for example, in the claim that Darwin possesses the world live-frog eating record — 'you find the little bastards behind toilet seats and the last challenger was disqualified for chewing,' my frog consumption source insisted with the immobile expression of someone holding the aces.)

It is some consolation that national politicians get at least as rough a ride as 'visiting Pom journos,' the phrase usually employed to describe me when Darwin introductions are made.

Malcolm Fraser, for instance, visited the Schooner bar of the Don Hotel in search of the man in the street, found one eager to proffer a hand shaky from a lifetime devoted to keeping a tight grip of peripheral neuritis and 'handles'.

Expecting an autograph request the Prime Minister did his well-known shark's smile. 'Now you can go back to bloody Canberra and tell them you met Cowboy Jim Garrison the Ringer,' was the highly Territorian greeting he carried away.

Whitlam, to an audience who concealed any enthusiasm they may have felt as unflickeringly as a citizen holding a full house, with aces over, was so overstimulated by the atmosphere that he steamed in with an impressively unstatesmanlike accusation blaming Singapore Premier Lee Kuan Yu for the wretched 'boat people'. Singapore, Whitlam said, supplied the refugees with 'plans and petrol and the maps to get here'.

This sporting effort to link the 'boat people' exodus with ASEAN pique at Canberra's protectionism sounds an inglorious one to anyone whose memory stretches as far back as 1968, when two battalions of hospitable Diggers plus support troops were operating from a climate at least as drear as Darwin's at Nui Dat in Phuoc Tuy Province. It is also a political red herring.

But at least the ALP leader left the (electorally obligatory) anti-'boat people' impression behind him without resorting to the crude off-the-cuff lie which (if the Minister for Immigration is to be believed) marked the happily brief passage of the Federal Transport Minister, Peter Nixon.

(He should not be confused, incidentally, with Darwin's own 'Curly' Nixon, the WWF leader who spasmodically threatens strike action unless the hijacked prawn-trawler *Song Be 12* is returned to Ho Chi Minh City, preferably loaded with 'reffoes'.)

Mr MacKellar on Thursday said that Mr Nixon had assured him that the reports of Mr Nixon's remarks 'were a misrepresentation and distortion of his comments'.

Nixon's performance was so classic an exercise in attempted press manipulation that it repays studying in some detail. It began when he flew in from Perth last week with the Fraser-like intention of pressing some local political flesh to boost Sam Calder MHR, the war-time pilot who has held the NT seat since 1966, and Senator Bernie Kilgariff, the philoprogenitive Alice Springs motel owner (11 kids so far), who won election in 1975.

Supported by a travelling secretariat, including Wentworth Hill, an affable ex-Sydney journalist acting as press aide, Nixon checked into a suite in the grandiloquent Territorian International Hotel, an establishment prominent in this generally stubby landscape both for its height — seven storeys no less — and its extreme ugliness.

The plan was to hold a press conference at 8.15 on Wednesday morning about uranium. The ministerial speech was prepared overnight, though not without difficulty. The down-town power-station blacked-out Darwin in the small hours with a fine bang and a head of steam. Thus, the electric typrewriter, poised to elaborate a scathing attack on Don Dunstan, the South Australian Premier, suddenly became unusable.

Despite this setback, by breakfast time a polemical statement blasting Dunstan for criticising the Government's policy in the NT, while continuing uranium exploration on his native turf, was ready for the waiting world.

Pondering it over their pineapple juice, various locals, including Calder, were not over-impressed. Such grass-roots specialists as Terry Walls, press aide to Paul Everingham who will be the NT's effective Premier after the transitional period in July, 1979, agreed that the hottest local issue still remained not uranium, but refugees.

Come the press conference, the local boys, including an ABC representative, took their hand outs like lambs. However, Neil Dibbs, the AAP Darwin staffman, raised the refugee surveillance issue.

Inspired perhaps by his breakfast briefing, the minister jumped in with both hooves. Now there were immigration authority teams screening refugees in Thailand, Malaysia and Singapore, he said, refugees arriving illegally would not be allowed into Australia. In short, they would be turned round and sent back home, wherever that was supposed to be.

The AAP report of this inflammatory answer went out shortly after nine, local time, and it took a few hours for the other media to graps its import. The ABC, for instance, who had not been interested in interviewing Nixon on Wednesday morning, unleashed the hounds of hell at four in the afternoon to get more on a story which by then was leading their new schedule.

Some time between then and 6.30, when Mr Hill was summoned so urgently he was obliged to leave a campari soda unfinished in the tropical green lounge of the Hotel Darwin and grab a cab, the Immigration Department in Canberra evidently learned what had happened.

From then on the Darwin night was hot with Canberra calls for the Nixon entourage. By noon on Thursday, Mr McKellar, the Immigration Minister, had issued his own statement down south.

'Australia will continue to accept Indo-chinese refugees,' it said, despite the quotes attributed to Nixon in Darwin saying that illegal boats heading for the country would be turned back.

'We will continue to meet our international obligations,' the statement continued. 'Distorted reports to the contrary have no foundation in fact. The Minister for Transport, Mr Nixon, has assured me that reports which would suggest changes in the Government's attitude were a misrepresentation and distortion of his comments.'

Well, I have heard the tape of the controversial exchange, which began when Dibbs inquired what would happen if boat people who saw immigration officials and got no joy decided to sail for Australia anyway.

Nixon: 'They will be sent back if they do.'
Dibbs: (Obviously a bit surprised): 'They will be sent back?'
Nixon: 'That's according to the advice of the Minister for Immigration yesterday.'

Ah, the Nixon tapes. It wouldn't surprise me, once the politicians have finally gone home and the election is forgotten, to hear a Darwin Vietnamese kids' choir belting our *Washing Mathilda* with the best of them.

And by then, with 48 varieties in town, 'The Top End' can challenge Heinz for another place in the record books.

The National Times, 12th-17th December 1977

ACTION REPORTAGE

Cyprus: The army that mustn't shoot

It is now over twenty years since the UN Force described in the following article arrived in post-British Cyprus to keep the Greek and Turkish communities from each other's throats, and July, 1984 marked the tenth anniversary of the Turkish invasion of the island.

The long-suffering Cypriots have continued to be victims of a geo-political destiny that has obtained since antiquity — the intrinsic desirability and even more tempting strategic location of the island has always been more curse than blessing. In 1964, at an earlier stage of woe, it was their fate to be an unusually precise microcosm of post-colonial experience all over the globe.

Nicosia's state of almost permanent emergency attracted as cosmopolitan and raffish a community as can be imagined. Its coastal resort, Kyrenia, was still an elegant English cantonment centred on the jewel-like harbour, and the big retirement or vacation bungalows sited to catch mountain breezes on the exquisite tracts through the olives and vines towards Bellapais, Laurence Durrell's adoptive village, exuded a posthumous whiff of the British Raj.

The Ledra Palace Hotel in Nicosia was a world out of Graham Greene and Eric Ambler — almost everyone was a senior government official or army officer, religious dignitary or international diplomat, journalist, adventurer or spy. Some times the roles overlapped — inevitably, because here was the quintessential Levantine melting-pot, une macédoine *as the Ledra Palace's Frenchified menu proudly christened a special desert composed of variegated mixed fruits.*

Cyprus had seen it all before: close equivalents to the Ledra clientele had very likely been around when the Venetian and Ottoman empires had been obliged to shut up shop. There was, however, a recognizable new breed, as Walter Kent, long-time Sunday Times *Cyprus correspondent, indulgently pointed out over sherry under his celebrated Tree of Idleness. They called themselves by a new name, 'photo-journalists'. Their work was (pretentiously, I thought) christened* 'photo-reportage'. *Very soon it was a burgeoning 1960s cult.*

The photo-journalists I worked with, notably Don McCullin, John Bulmer and Christopher Angeloglou, were leaders of this new wave. (By 1968 it had become a flood-tide and in Vietnam a camera-less reporter was a cause for comment — and disappointment — because he would be carrying no spare film.) McCullin and his fellows were ahead of their time technically and, since many were artists, artistically. Looking at pictures of them taken in 1964, I am astonished how young they look in their jackets and khaki pants. They could be abnormally serious students. After the 1967 Israel-Arab conflict war photographers usually adopted military uniform, and were easily confused with soldiers, sometimes with fatal results. In Cyprus it was all somehow more informal. In those pictures Don and the others could pass for students, only if you look closely, their expressions are too grave to go with youth.

The generation they were rapidly succeeding (and making obsolete) were different animals altogether, invariably big, sweaty Englishmen, often with what were still called 'colonial' antecedents. They sported RAF moustaches with navy-blue blazers, and despite resources of cunning and aggression, were no longer of an age to thrive on man-handling their steel-framed Pathé-Gazette or Movietone cameras in the stunning heat.

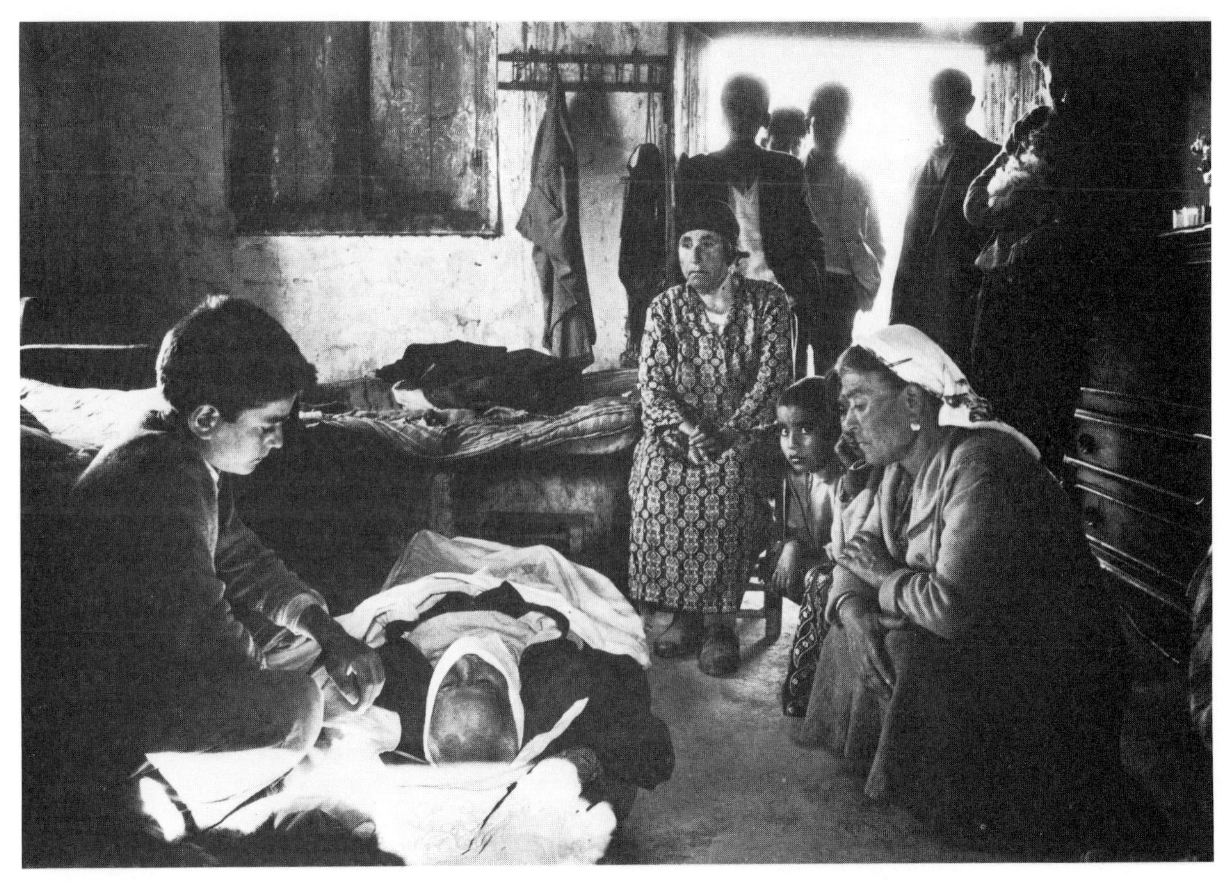

(Don McCullin)

The emphasis was no longer on news-reel footage for cinema audiences but colour photos for the weekly news magazines. The Old School concentrated on ceremonial occasions and events that could be 'set up' in advance. This was how it had been done for over three decades and it accorded both with their equipment and sense of news values. In contrast the new breed of 'photo-reporters', with their Leicas and Nikons, were mobile connoisseurs of 'action', working in nasty conditions at a frantic pitch of physical co-ordination, always engaged in checking light meters or changing film with amazing dexterity.

When I first met Don he was economising by staying in a tiny hotel near Ledra Street, 'Murder Mile' as it had been known under the British, rather than the Ledra Palace. He also made a point of living off his own iron rations, sardines, baked beans and even an HP sauce bottle, claiming that 'foreign food' was alien to his honest, working-class stomach. It was not long before he had cover photos all over Europe and America, a change in financial circumstances which was not at first reflected in what would later be called the McCullin 'lifestyle'. The sauce bottle became a prop in Don's armoury of sardonic humour. He used it to send himself up.

As the photographers were paid hugely better than the reporters they worked with, and the highly romatic cult of photography was soon flourishing, the writers, or 'wordsmiths' as the photographers said, tried hard, though probably with scant success, to keep their uppitty colleagues in line. The ubiquitous Australian veteran, Murray Sayle, propagated the motto: 'The Pen is mightier than the Pentax.'

In fact, when it worked properly, which was more often than you had any right to expect, the two became complementary. Don stalked the picture, as ruthlessly as prey. He didn't know what he wanted in advance but when he saw it the recognition was so instantaneous that he was off like a hare, moving directly towards the centre of whatever action was involved, as nimble as a gymnast when it came to ducking down or getting into the right position to frame his shot. Picture editors, like Angeloglou who, in due course, ran the desk at the Sunday Times for many years, said that the mark of a McCullin picture was not, as you might be expected, the realism, but the sense of composition and light.

It was such a beautiful place that year and so suddenly dangerous. The evening after the killing of four men in Famagusta, Angeloglou and I set off to drive back to Nicosia against the advice of the Irish UN contingent who had escorted us in the Old City. The dusk didn't last long and just after the fork where the road branched north towards the township of Lyssi we had to halt because of a hay-cart drawn across the road.

We kept the interior lights on and out of the darkness I found a gun barrel poking through my window. Horrifyingly, it was an old Sten, least predictable of World War 2 automatic weapons, and, worse, it was in the hands of a boy of around fourteen.

As was (almost always) the way in Cyprus it may have been less dangerous than it felt — we were able to convince the dozen or so Greek irregulars who appeared that we were foreign journalists, or at any rate not Turkish Cypriots, and three hours later we were dining at the Ledra. Yet for years I remember feeling that the incident had been a particularly close call. There were so few occasions when the combination of that weapon and an inexperienced hand didn't lead to an involuntary burst, that it seemed against the odds the boy hadn't got off a few rounds into the car by mistake before anyone said a word.

Everyone seemed to carry arms. Violent death was so commonplace that, as is always the case with protracted bloodshed, the value of any individual life appeared to lose some of its coinage. Death, except perhaps at the moment itself, shed some of its sting through over-familiarity. The risks run by journalists were as nothing to those the locals had been living with through much of the previous decade, and continued to endure in the decade that followed. We always, of course, had the option of a flight out, but I don't think anyone ever lobbied to leave a day sooner than they had to.

The isle was as seductive as Prospero's, and even filled with the wrong kind of noises I remember it as a good time when everyone was at the beginning of things. There were certainly many worse.

It is noon in the Turkish-Cypriot hill village of Louroujina, one of the worst trouble spots in Cyprus. For once, it is very quiet. The UN have moved in.

A young British colonel, Peter Litton, from the 1st Battalion the Sherwood Foresters, is deep in discussion with ten villagers. He is wearing a UN blue beret and the 'ONU' shoulder flash (surplus stock from the Congo, where the UN was the *Organisation des Nations Unies*). After half an hour he seems to be making some progress.

The temperature in the village square is up in the eighties and the sun reflects dazzingly off white walls. Metal parts on the waiting jeep are already uncomfortably hot. The driver, his forearm tattooed with the Foresters' crest, is getting restive. 'Talk, talk, bloody talk.'

'Better than shooting, mate,' says a young corporal with the wireless set. And everyone goes on waiting.

Litton is indicating strong-points on his large-scale map. 'So if I got the Greeks to get out of *here*, you could easily withdraw from here. Of course, you want to end the shooting...'

'Of course — it is we who want peace, but the Greeks are all liars.' The Turkish *muktar* (village spokesman) is a 29-year-old teacher called Erol Huseyn. He had learnt his English at a technical college in Cardiff and, by the sound of them, his

(Don McCullin)

politics from propaganda programmes on Radio Ankara. Another villager who had been in England — 'Chatsworth Road, London, E.5' he told me proudly — translates for the rest. They nod approval of the clichés, half-truths and obvious lies. The café is typical of a thousand in Cyprus, with formal portraits of Kutchuk and Atatürk on the cracked walls, a dominating map of Turkey, and a buzzing circle of persistent flies. There are never any women. Since the troubles the men have acquired the habit of sitting there from dawn to dusk, unless it is their turn to man a gun-point somewhere. I wondered briefly if they would ever start work again.

The colonel interrupts briskly. 'I'm off to tell the Greeks you'll withdraw if they will. It's about time you all stopped shooting and thought about bringing in the corn.' As we leave Huseyn is still describing how Greeks had fired shots into Louroujina the night before.

Less than 15 minutes and we are in the square at Limbia, the neighbouring Greek village (Louroujina, its population artificially swollen by refugees to 3,500, is ringed with Greek-Cypriot communities). An Orthodox Church replaces the Louroujina mosque, with its slender blue minaret, but the other differences are only detailed — the coffee, in the same little cups, is now patriotically called Greek, not Turkish; the cafe portraits are of Makarios and Grivas; the welcome from the Greek *muktar* is equally formal but more muted. There are the same cracked walls, the same flies.

Colonel Litton takes an identical line again. 'If you withdraw your guerillas so will the Turks. Then you can start harvesting the corn.' The muktar wants to talk about Turkish atrocities, and nightly gunfire into Limbia from Louroujina. A group of irregulars, wearing shabby battledress and carrying Stens, sit looking warlike and say nothing.

Thirty minutes later, after a lot more coffee and juggling with maps, there seems to be a hint of concession and, as usual, of a certain Cypriot ambiguity; actions, one feels, might easily not follow words that promise them. But immediately the colonel is off again to report back to the Turks.

'One's got to clutch at any straw, I suppose,' he said as we moved off.

We left him with the Turks and went to the Louroujina school, now flying the UN flag and housing a platoon of Foresters. Jeeps waited beneath the bougainvillea; an automatic weapon stood by the blackboard. In the headmaster's study, a frivolous Dufy reproduction was hung alongside the standard issue bust of Kutchuk. It has now become a signals office.

The Foresters were patrolling from the school, backbreaking, three-hour scrambles across the sheer white ridges overlooking Lourourjina where no vehicles could go. Later they improvised donkey patrols, moving endlessly from one hilltop manned by Turkish guerillas to the next lined with Greeks. We followed the route with a section led by a young corporal, Barry Broadbent.

The Turkish irregulars, all ages between 15 and 70, were welcoming on their fortified hill. They offered cigarettes, plates of boiled rice and meat which were painfully brought up three times a day from the village below. An old man in loose shepherd's trousers crouched with us behind the sandbags and talked about the great day when the Turkish army would invade. Broadbent, carrying a prominent UN flag, climbed across to the Greek position, 1,000 yards away on the next ridge.

The sun reflected off Greek binoculars and gun barrels holding him, and probably us, in their sights.

But we never got to see behind their sandbags. Sweating heavily the corporal finally returned to say his welcome had been far from friendly — 'they're not at all keen on you taking pictures of their armoury. They've got mortars, Brens and God

(Don McCullin)

knows what else up there.' With their old Lee Enfields and shotguns (though they probably had more effective weapons hidden away), the Turks were sorry to see us leave. They welcomed as much UN protection as they could get.

At the school a thickset infantryman, Alan Radford from Mansfield, guessed he had lost 4 lbs. The section went to wash off some of the caked dust under a single tap in the courtyard, eat corned beef and baked beans, and sleep on the classroom floor before going out again. Another patrol had already left to continue the weary process of keeping the two sides apart, even if there seemed little hope of getting them together. We heard Colonel Litton talking to a subaltern. 'For God's sake, make sure they always take a UN flag stuck on a pole when they go out. It may look like Fred Karno's army but I don't want any of the chaps made a nonsense of by mistake.'

It is a necessary precaution. Cyprus has become an island of mistakes, some genuine, some simply convenient. Probably half the sporadic shots which continue throughout most nights in Nicosia and the Kyrenia range are the result of mishandled weapons; teenagers from both sides who wait at roadblocks with their venerable Stens tend to be casual about safety catches. When violence breaks out it always seems like an isolated, inexplicable error — until it happens again. As soon as they have carried away the bodies, that universal Cypriot charm forms a kind of plastic skin over the events. Soon it seems as though nothing really happened at all.

A couple of days after Louroujina we went into the Old City of Famagusta with a UN patrol just after a shooting incident where four men died. A silent Irish platoon already stood by smoking free issue cigarettes; Turkish-Cypriot youths drank Coca-Cola in the pale dusk; Radio Ankara pop songs echoed out of the cafe distorted by a revving prowl car. A juvenile Turkish-Cypriot policeman who had been shooting an hour before was now working on his fingernails with a match.

Murder? The Turkish spokesman, a tradesman in his best suit, was silkily explaining how some Greeks had penetrated the Old City, doubtless to spy...Apart from the empty cartridge cases in the gutter, he might have been saying why the groceries hadn't been delivered on time.

'Mistake?' said a 22-year-old Irish 2nd-lieutenant from County Mayo. 'Funny kind of mistake with four dead.'

UN men all over the island tell similar stories. Sgt. Leroy Macadams of the 22nd Royal Canadian Dragoons talked about a Greek post that had persisted in sending odd shots at a patrol he was leading near the Kyrenia range.

'We had a UN flag flying as well. Finally we went right up, pretty slowly, and they said it was all a mistake. I said we didn't reckon to call being fired on a mistake.'

'It's a curious mentality.' said an English colonel in the bar of the Ledra Palace Hotel, Nicosia. 'As long as a Cypriot says it wasn't done on purpose it didn't happen.'

When, on May 22, Janani Matikainen, aged 22, from Finland, became the first UN fatality, one awaited the predictable official explanation. Sure enough, next day Dr Kutchuk, leader of the Turkish-Cypriot community, expressed his deep grief to General Gyani, the UN Commander, and said there had been a confusion of identity.

Most of the UN troops, of course, went to Cyprus with their eyes open. At full strength the UN Force during the first three-month period consisted of 7,000 men from seven countries. The 2,700 British were Regular soldiers serving overseas, like 50 per cent of the British Army. In Cyprus under the UN because they were posted there, they might equally well have been in Aden or Malaya. By contrast, a good 80 per cent of the other nationalities volunteered for three- or six-month contracts. Almost all had previous UN experience. Canadians, Danes, Finns, Irish and Swedes (plus a small detachment of Austrian civilian police), they came from the traditionally UN-minded 'fire brigade' countries.

What made these volunteer troops become virtually professional peace-keepers?

At 27 Swedish lieutenant Stig Olsson is a veteran of seven UN operations in seven years. One half of the year he spends soldiering, the other as a university teacher of English. When we arrived he was reading an annotated edition of Dorothy Wordsworth's *Journal*.

Why does he do it?

'Partly to preserve a kind of balance — academic world, real world, you know the kind of thing. Perhaps after this I'll stop. I don't want to finish up like some of our men — they find it difficult, you know, to settle in a job at home. Always back to Stockholm for a holiday, and then off again.'

The money is an incentive. Bostrom, who said happily he'd never seen a shot fired (except on the range) either on the Gaza Strip or in Cyprus, had 15,000 Swedish kroner (roughly £1,000) saved for him in a Stockholm bank during his 13 months with UNEF. There is no tax. Many Swedes said they were saving for a house or, more often, a Volvo. (A Swedish private is paid more than £15 a week — about twice as much as his British equivalent.) Special Cyprus allowances are high: Olsson, for example, the Swedish lieutenant with a taste for English romanticism, receives almost £20 a week above his normal pay.

But they don't join just for the money. To the Scandinavians, and particularly the Swedes, internationalism is a middle name, something they've been brought up with. They epitomise neutrality. Unlike the British, they feel completely at home under the UN flag. At the same time we met only one avowed UN idealist — a Finn called Denis Johansson. An Olympic miler turned journalist, he originally visited Cyprus on a writing assignment in 1963. He rushed to volunteer in March 'because I thought the UN is probably the best way of restoring some human values to the place'. Did he think many others had volunteered for the same reason? 'Perhaps. Anyway, 6,000 Finns tried for the 1,000 places.'

A highly militant colonel, just back from Malaya, said in disgust: 'This is one helluva crazy mixed-up army.' Like many British, he objected temperamentally to an operation that was not soldiering as he knew it.

Lieut-Gen. Prem Guani, the anglophile Indian who was first commander of the UN Force, found himself in the same paradoxical position. He graduated at 21 from the Imperial Defence College before going into the Indian Army. And he has remained a spit and polish traditionalist, in some ways more British than the British. 'How many years service have you put in, corporal?' I heard him ask during one of his tours of inspection. 'Seven, sir.'

'Jolly good show,' said the general.

Before his resignation he continually pressed U Thant, the Secretary-General, to remove as many non-military duties as possible for him. He wanted to stick to soldiering and let others get on with the politics. But it was too late. By the time the UN moved in the situation had crystallised; soldiering and politics were inseparable.

Gyani's dilemma is shared by every soldier in the hybrid international force. Their job is a mixture of policeman, mediator, symbol and sometimes even father confessor. Like firemen forbidden to use water, their orders are to prevent violence without themselves fighting. The rules were laid down for them in Oyster Bay, Manhattan — far from the Cyprus world of arbitrary bloodshed and casual deaths.

Realising they were all in it together, the troops we saw co-operated well whenever they had to. The Irish mess at Famagusta H.Q. (christened Wolfe Tone camp) even shared a dinner with their opposite numbers in, of all regiments, the Northern Irish Royal Inniskilling Fusiliers.

'A night with the "Skins" and not a single head broken,' a Republican commandant (major) told us the next morning. 'Co-operation? Indeed it makes you wonder what happened to original sin.'

The British were probably in the most difficult position of all the soldiers in the

Don McCullin under fire in Cyprus.
(John Bulmer)

first peace-keeping force. They had to face the legacy of the Cyprus emergency in the late fifties and the hostility of the Greek-Cypriot Government on top of everything else. Their first loyalties were to country and regiment. Significantly it was a soldier from the Airborne Division (now nicknamed 'Paras' after the French) who is said to have kept his cherry beret on and trampled the blue replacement in the dust.

But all the UN warriors for peace face similar frustrations. Old-fashioned shooting wars were in some ways a lot easier to fight in; the modern UN peace-keeper in Cyprus lacks even the power to disarm those who fire on him. An Irish soldier, Sgt. Hackett, with 24 years' service and two trips to the Congo behind him, summed it up.

During a quiet week in a remote and beautiful section of the island I said it must seem fairly easy-going compared with, say, Elisabethville in December '61.

'Not at all. I'd take the Congo every time,' the sergeant said.

Surprised, I wanted to know why.

'In the Congo we had an enemy.'

The Sunday Times Magazine, 5th July 1964

The Pope mobbed in Jerusalem: Via Dolorosa nuns give him refuge

Pope Paul VI, that rarefied and essentially indoors figure, was nonetheless the first pope to leave Italy for 150 years, the first since St Peter to go to Jerusalem. It is fairly rare that a 'story' instantly establishes itself as a piece of history, as opposed to just another event, in the very process of taking place. This was one.

Its scale was such that it also marked a small watershed in the history of Press coverage of international events. Soon we would be saying 'media', instead of just 'Press', and inhabiting a world where it would be inconceivable that an event comparable in importance to this could ever be allowed to take place without the benefit of colour TV. In the light of what followed those very big stories which took place on the brink of the TV revolution appear curiously spontaneous and uncontrived.

Since the pilgrimage had been announced less than a month in advance it was a distinctly ad hoc and (by Vatican standards) almost impulsive enterprise. The final protocols had only been agreed at Christmas. Until the papal plane actually touched down, there had always seemed a strong possibility that it would either never happen, or suffer some eleventh hour delay.

The Pope had clearly imagined, God knows how, that the visit could be undertaken in a spirit of personal pilgrimage, a surprisingly naive intention which was comprehensively thwarted when Jordan's bureaucracy and the world's Press came into collision. Printed journalism had arrived at a technological moment which made it for a short time as unwieldly as the TV circuses which were in store. While the pictures on the screens were still black and white there was a voracious audience for the American and European magazines which could get on the news-stands fast with spectacular, high quality colour photographs.

There might have been a clue to future things in the coincidence of the Holy Father and Paris-Match, the French weekly photo-magazine, both choosing to employ chartered Caravelles, specially adapted to include the tools of the trade: the Pope's plane had its own portable altar, Paris-Match's *a photo lab. There were about two thousand accredited journalists milling around (about the same number as there were in Saigon after Tet in 1968). The stage was set for chaos.*

Yet there was an honesty about the chaos nevertheless. The Pope's progress through Jerusalem was an authentic event — not an able charade stage-managed from its inception to be acted on camera for transmission via satellite.

All this meant that there was still a valid role for the descriptive reporter, or what in Vietnam was soon to be called a 'writing correspondent' (as opposed to the ever more numerous photographers or TV reporters.)

The participants themselves still took print reporters more seriously than the TV cameras. In Vietnam this faith was particularly poignant since many combat troops genuinely believed that if the reporter managed 'to tell it like it was' then the war would end as the consciences of those far away in 'The World' rose in righteous wrath. The truth was elsewhere. But our young egos fed, or at any rate survived, on the illusion.

All those involved, despite the lure of colour pictures, were much more conscious of words, and susceptible to verbal description, and it didn't last. The pageantry of a later epoch would come to be translated into a set of visual images, or preferably just one overwhelming image, a kind of logo for the occasion.

In the hiatus before these changes in communications technology altered the emphasis a newspaper reporter sometimes took on the literal role of 'correspondent' — it was like writing an (inevitably hurried) letter to share something of importance with people who, unlike the witness crouched over the telex or fighting through the cable-office, lacked the facilities for experiencing what had taken place at first hand.

Pope Paul VI arrived in the Holy Land today to begin his history-making three-day pilgrimage to the places made sacred by the birth, life and death of Jesus Christ. He was greeted in Jerusalem with such wild enthusiasm by the crowds, waving olive branches and palms, that a Jordanian army car had to force a way through to free the Pontiff's limousine.

Crush barriers were overturned. A broadcaster on the spot said: 'The crowd — about 20,000 or more people — is getting hysterical. The Pontiff cannot get out of his car.' A ceremony at the Damascus Gate was cut short and the Pope did not make a speech as intended.

It was nearly 20 minutes before the procession of 45 cars was able to move on.

The Holy Father's spiritual pilgrimage turns into a human traffic-jam on the Via Dolorosa. *(Camera Press)*

Muslims and Christians alike tried to lean into the Pope's car to embrace him. The shouts and cheers almost drowned the church bells.

The Pope was lucky to avoid serious injury. Police with batons lashed out at the crowds but failed to control them or stop them mobbing the Holy Father. His whole itinerary must now be in jeopardy unless the Jordan authorities can improve security arrangements immeasurably.

When he went to the Via Dolorosa to visit the Stations of The Cross he was nearly trampled when crowds crushed him in the narrow street and for a time he was forced to take refuge in a convent. Pushed about, beads of sweat on his brow, the Pope retraced the steps of Christ on his way to Calvary.

It was at the second station by the 'Ecco Homo' Arch, where Christ was given the Cross, that the crowds completely mobbed the Pope. Ahead of him there were 24 men carrying ceremonial staffs which they beat on the ground to clear the way, but they were separated from the Pope and he was engulfed.

An Arab soldier kept trying to reach forward and touch the Pope. The Pope's face was drawn tight with strain.

He sighed repeatedly and several times seemed to be on the verge of collapse, but began to smile as we passed a hospital building where nuns and sisters were sitting on the high wall overlooking the Via Dolorosa. A great cry of 'Il Papa' came from the Italian nuns.

The journey from the Second Station to the Sixth is about 600 yards and several times it seemed that the Pope must fall. An Arab soldier trying to hold back the crowd fell down himself almost in front of the Pope's feet.

At the Fifth Station, where St Simon of Cyrene helped Jesus carry his Cross, a man stumbled in front of the Pope. Security officers picked up the man and pushed him aside.

At the Sixth Station, where the street is very narrow and very steep, it finally became impossible for the Pope to continue. An open door on the left proved to be the entrance to the Convent of a Greek Catholic Order, Les Petites Soèurs de Jésus, and two young nuns dressed white by the doorway found themselves playing hostess to the Holy Father. He was hustled inside.

Outside, the tide of humanity surged on, Christians and Muslims, nuns and priests, schoolchildren, soldiers, tourists and shopkeepers, shouting in a babel of tongues.

Eugene Cardinal Tisserant, Dean of the Sacred College of Cardinals, said: 'This has been a tremendous ordeal for the Holy Father. He has been hustled and pushed all the way through the Via Dolorosa.'

There was a fresh commotion in the Church of the Holy Sepulchre while the Holy Father was celebrating Mass. Fire broke out in the roof when two electric cables for television lamps touched. Flames a foot long shot out. Burning debris rained to the floor. The crowd grew restless as engineers tried in vain to prise the cables apart. Finally, electric power was switched off and the fire put out by an extinguisher.

All this time, the Pope continued the prayers of the Mass by candlelight.

Shortly before, the packed congregation had witnessed a moment of sublime drama when the Holy Father, tired and strained, came to a halt in front of the chapel which stands over the rock-hewn tomb where Christ was buried and rose from the dead.

The Pope knelt. Tears steamed down his cheeks. Bells pealed and the massive organ thundered.

Before the Pope's plane arrived at Amman from Rome cloud and fog suddenly descended on Amman airport and visibility was so bad that, for a time, it seemed likely his plane would have to be diverted, possibly to Beirut.

But at last the big jet broke through the cloud and landed, its engines almost drowning the 21-gun salute. On the tail of the plane was the delicate white and

Pope Paul kneeling in prayer in the Room of the Last Supper (The Cenacle) in Jerusalem. *(Camera Press)*

yellow motif taken up in a thousand triangular flags waving from the airport perimeter.

King Hussein of Jordan and a welcoming party of 30, including 12 priests, waited at the foot of the steps to the plane.

The Holy Father, dressed in a white silk ankle length coat, appeared, then slowly began to descend to meet the King. A fierce easterly wind was blowing and Pope Paul had suddenly to reach up to keep on his hat.

By the time the Pope and the King had reached the saluting base the papal hat had changed to a more manageable white skull-cap. With the King saluting in impeccable Sandhurst style, a military band went through the papal anthem and then the Jordanian one. The Jordanian and Vatican flags were run up ever so slowly. Hussein stepped back and for a moment the Pope was entirely alone, in the land where the Christian religion was born. He raised a hand in blessing. Suddenly an Italian voice cried out from among the crowds: 'Viva il Papa.' Immediately the crowd began to clap.

King Hussein, 'on behalf of the united family of Moslems and Christians alike', offered deep gratitude to the Pope for his visit.

The Pontiff responding by describing his visit as 'a spiritual one, a humble pilgrimage to the sacred places made holy by the birth, the life, the Passion and death of Jesus Christ'. He expressed the hope that God would grant his prayer that all men of good will would live together in harmony.

Then the Pope left for Jerusalem, driving through country rich in Bible history. He crossed the lowest spot on earth — the Dead Sea valley, 1,285 ft below sea level — and drove towards the village of Bethany, home of Mary and Martha, and the place where Jesus raised Lazarus from the dead.

All along the route from Amman to Jerusalem, King Hussein flew his red helicopter overhead to watch over the Pope's safety.

This evening, on the Mount of Olives, Pope Paul met Patriarch of the Orthodox Church Benedictus of Jerusalem. This was the first meeting for 500 years between a Pope of Rome and an Orthodox Patriarch.

The Holy Father completed his devotions tonight with a visit to the Garden of Gethsemane, scene of Christ's agony. A huge crowd awaited him, but there was no repetition of the day's disorders.

In absolute silence the crowd stood as the Pope knelt in prayer and a choir sang *Ave Maria*.

The Sunday Times, 5th January 1964

The Florence disaster

It was the terrified screaming from the old woman in the shanty house next door which shocked Paolo Barracani out of his sleep. To make sure he heard she was banging her fists against the gimcrack plasterboard wall:

'Arno è fuori, Arno è...' Again and again.

What could she mean, the river was out? It was 4.30 a.m. and Paolo, a 52-year-old factory worker, thought is must be a nightmare. Until he went down to the kitchen. He found three feet of brown water lapping round his wife's prized gas cooker. And even while he watched, stunned and incredulous, the level was rising before his eyes.

This was how the flood came to San Donnino, one of Florence's poorest outer suburbs. Just 30 minutes later, 5 a.m. on November 4, the River Arno exploded into the heart of the city. It was still dark, the last hour before dawn, and no Barbarian chieftain in the fifth century could have chosen a more effective moment to strike.

Florence was unprotected, utterly vulnerable. During daylight a flood even of these biblical dimensions — 50 million cubic metres of water released in 15 hours — might have been tamed by using the techniques man has acquired to hold nature off. But at 5 a.m. Florence never had a chance.

The Arno had bluffed everyone for centuries. Not since 1557 had the river turned on the city like this. And in the time between its ever-latent menace had been forgotten.

Thanks to a bureaucratic omission, worthy of a Constantinople official in the last years of the Ottoman Empire, the Arno was not even classified as dangerous. No warning system, no vigilantes, nothing. To the administration, it seems, the Arno was as innocent as Elizabeth Barrett Browning saw it — this 'crystal arrow...in the gentle sunset'.

But not on November 4 when, for example, Signora Ida Leoncini woke up in her flat on the Via San Cristofano — 'feeling damp'.

'I was furious, I thought it must be the new hot water bottle. I lay rehearsing what I was going to tell them when I took it back to the shop. Then I felt the bed rock. I was afloat.'

Signora Leoncini's absurd but terrifying experience was being repeated with minor variations all over the city that dawn. Though the ominous signs had been there for anyone to assess — five weeks' torrential rain, numberless Arno tributaries rich with flood water, a barograph reading tumbling to 990 millibars — everyone slept.

This was partly because Florence has long been a sober slightly withdrawn kind of place, carrying its cultural heritage with a certain gravity. Rome's free-wheeling low life is abhorred. Dawn, as all good Florentines know, is a time to be in bed at home preparing for another responsible, bread-winning day.

Only a handful of professional nightbirds saw the first overflow, and the desperate 100 minutes leading up to it. One was Alberto Maffei, a 40-year-old with a preternatural pallor acquired over two decades of going to bed when everyone else is breakfasting. He works as barman at the Jolly Club in Piazza Santa Maria

Soprarno (or, at least, he did until most of it disappeared down the Arno on November 4).

'Around 2.30 our rock group did an encore of *Yellow Submarine* and then took a break. I went outside for a smoke, and everything was normal except for the rain. And the roaring.'

Roaring?

'The Arno was making a terrible noise that night. You could hear it even behind the music.' It made Maffei feel uneasy and he kept an apprehensive eye on the river during the small hours. Just after 3 o'clock he noticed the brown water swelling. And also something else — a group of shadowy figures in the rain on the 13th-century Ponte Vecchio.

They were goldsmiths who had smelled danger, almost instinctively. One of them, Paris Venturi, proprietor for 20 years of a tiny, glittering shop (now completely destroyed) had received a warning.

'At about 2 a.m. I had a call from Alfredo's Restaurant on the Lungarno A. Diaz [now destroyed, but until November 4 the high temple of Florentine Cuisine]. A civil engineer dining there said he feared a big flood was coming.'

Venturi was on the Ponte Vecchio within minutes, stuffing delicate gold bracelets and jewels in a brown suitcase. He stayed for a while watching the water, listening to it roar. At 3.30 the spray was breaking over the columns at each end of the bridge. 'I decided bed was the best place.'

By the time he was settling down in his silk pyjamas with the jewellery locked in his personal safe, Paolo Barracani, downstream in San Donnino, had evacuated the ground floor.

The frightened family huddled in the bedroom. At 6.15 the water was six feet high. An hour later it was through the ground-floor ceiling. They took to the roof, Paolo's wife Georgina carrying their 30-month-old baby, Mario. Paolo also carried his cheap shot-gun ready to fire distress signals, and there were blankets as it was bitterly cold and still raining. It couldn't last long, they told each other. Anyway they had a packet of biscuits in case Mario got hungry.

He did. The Barracanis stayed marooned on that roof for two days. When Servicemen in a boat finally picked them up, they were suffering from exposure. The biscuits had long gone; so had the shot-gun shells. They had also lost their house; their wedding presents; their furniture — everything. It was not much of a house, but they aren't fussy people, and it had taken them just 20 years to set up a place of their own.

As the Arno rose, the rich began to suffer too. In Piazza de Michelangelo, an elegant middle-class quarter, Signora Armanda Doni got up at dawn. That evening she and her husband were scheduled to fly to Paris and London to attend a series of ready-to-wear dress shows. Signora Doni is frightened of planes so she decided to attend early Mass, to remind the Deity, as it were, to keep an eye on their Comet. When she stepped into the street, a fraction after 6.45 a.m., she was astounded to find her green satin shoes completely soaked.

She rushed home, and shook her sleeping husband to get him down to their boutique in the centre. It was too late, far too late. By now the water was lashing down the Lungarno Acciaoli at 40 m.p.h.; by 7.30 it was at the Ponte San Niccolo; by 8 at the Piazza della Signoria.

The Mayor of Florence, Piero Bargellini, watched in despair from his offices in the 13th century Palazzo Vecchio. Beneath him the water, now filthy with a coat of black crude oil from central heating systems, was washing round the ankles of the enormous reproduction of Michelangelo's David. Ironically, Bargellini had been elected only four months previously after a campaign where he had presented himself as a kind of mini-Malraux...Vote for Bargellini and clean up the buildings of Florence.

Inexorably, the twin catastrophe was moving into its second stage. First, the

Arno had struck at the people of Florence. Now it was threatening 20 museums, 40 churches, and 50 palaces standing in the city centre: the treasure house of the Renaissance, the cultural heart of Europe. The Piazza Santa Croce was the focal point — the worst hit of all. Shortly after 6 o'clock the flood rampaged into the Square, but as it forms a natural basin, the water then remained where it was, building up to form a dam in an area roughly a 100 yards square. In this time it reached 20 feet, rising higher and higher up the façade of the Church of Santa Croce. For once the flood was held. The Franciscans, who had been celebrating Mass at six, barricaded the great mediaeval door and prayed — literally — that it would hold. For three and a half hours it did. Then the battering was too much for it. It burst. Fetid water, a wall 20 feet high, exploded through. The tombs of

Experts examining some of the priceless manuscripts damaged by the floods in Florence.
(Keystone)

Some of Florence's beautiful statues left stranded by the mud and the water.
(Keystone)

Michelangelo, Machiavelli and Galileo were inundated. In the Museo dell' Opera di Santa Croce, the Crucifix of Giovanni Cimabue, Master of Giotto and friend of Dante, became a ruin. Taddeo Gaddi's fresco of The Last Supper was almost covered. By a miracle the Giotto frescoes illustrating the lives of St Francis in the Bardi chapel and SS. John Evangelist and Baptist in the Peruzzi chapel escaped.

Once the water in Santa Croce had filled the cellars, flooded the ground floors, and dealt with Cimabue, it was ready to move on. It formed a second torrent, rushing westwards. The Uffizi Palace, its 42 rooms crammed with the masterpieces which make it the most important Renaissance museum in the world, was vulnerable from both sides.

At 7 a.m. the Chief Conservator, Dottoressa Becherucci, arrived with a dozen museum guides. Until they were altogether cut off two hours later, they worked furiously trying to evacuate the lower rooms, mainly used for restoration and storing the archives. The lady conservator ignored her personal possessions in a ground floor apartment. (It was completely wiped out.) Both wings, used mainly for restoring, suffered equally: one third of the archives; all the prints and ten per cent of the Uffizi's photographic negatives were lost.

At 9.10 the Uffizi's telephones emitted a long whine and then went dead — for six days as it turned out. Dottoressa Becherucci was suddenly afraid, overcome by a sense of isolation. Like thousands of other Florentines she was tortured wondering where the waters had reached. Suddenly there was no electricity, no radio bulletins and, of course, no water supply.

Shouted appeals for information echoed across streets that had become rivers. And all over Florence people were frantically trying to call their friends. There was little time. By noon 30,000 telephones were useless.

Electric clocks had stuck, providing clues for future researchers of the catastrophe. Lifts stopped between floors; television screens went blank; the city was silent — except for the sound of rain still falling.

In the Via dei Bardi, Charles Whittemore, a retired New York doctor, and his wife Amy were watching the Arno creeping up towards their second floor apartment. Their phone failed at the same time as the Uffizi's, their water supply a few minutes later. 'There didn't seem any possibility of the flood reaching the second floor, so we decided to sit it out. We couldn't have gotten out anyway.' On the Lungarno Corsini, Dante Giovannoni, one of the best-known hairdressers in Europe who counts (or counted) Princess Alexandra among his clients, was watching the black water gouging 36 years and 10 million lire (about 5,700 pounds) worth of equipment, including a rare 17th century Venetian table, out of his salon. In the Archaeological Museum the water now filling the cellars, then exploded upwards 'with volcanic force' through the ceilings. The Etruscan collection housed on the ground floor looked as if someone had set off a bomb.

'I've just seen a Citroën DS 15 passing down the river.'

Signora Françoise Neerman of Via Santo Spirito had just rung her friend Signora Nicoletta Livi. They were trying to reassure each other.

Nicoletta: 'Driving?'

Françoise: 'No, floating — upside down.'

It was just before 10 and in the Via delle Casine, near Santa Croce, the flood was claiming its first human victim. A woman, whose name we will keep anonymous, was sitting in her wheel-chair on the ground floor, straining to keep her head above the water line. A team of firemen heard her shouts but they could not get her out — the door was blocked and the windows barred — to protect her from burglars. They rigged a hoist and managed to lift the chair, with her in it, until her head touched the ceiling. Then a wall of water swept round the corner.

It overturned the firemen's boat, almost drowning two of them. Their desperately improvised hoist collapsed and the woman disappeared.

One hundred and twenty-five prisoners in Florence's classically constructed prison, the Murate, shrieked to be let out as they saw the water through their bars. In the end, most of them jumped for it.

'Where are you from?' Signora Giovanna Picchi, who lives 50 yards from the prison, called out of her window at six men clinging precariously to a broken shop shutter.

'No. 2,' they called back (it's the prison's address). She threw them a rope and told them to fasten it to their belts.

'No belts,' came the reply. 'We're prisoners.' Four of them were swept away. The others were hauled to the Signora's comfortable apartment, decorated with her collection of silver icons and 18th-century furniture. Signora Picchi fed them, and gave them dry clothes. She asked what they were in jail for.

'Burglary — of apartments,' the first one said. The other had been sentenced for living off immoral earnings.

'Well,' The Signora said, 'I suppose I'm safe from you at least. I was 70 last week.'

The Florentines, even while the disaster was at its height, were producing their own version of something very like Cockney blitz humour. And some of the more venerable members of the English colony were contributing their personal blend of patrician imperturbability. The oldest British resident of all, Miss Rowena Ashton, who is 97, sagely decided she had passed the stage where she could do anything to help. She settled down by candlelight in her pensione in Via Cavour to re-read one of her favourite books, *Anthony Adverse*. It was the best way she could devise of trying to forget what was happening to the city she has lived in since shortly after Queen Victoria died. Her comparatively youthful compatriot, 91-year-old Miss St. Leger Good, sat in her wheelchair in her apartment in the Costa San Giorgio — complaining: 'If only my legs worked, I'd go down to the centre and help someone. I come from a long line of Navy people...'

The inferno had broken all human barriers. In one of the worst hit areas behind Santa Croce, an American girl painter was feeding a baby belonging to the family in the next apartment while the mother improvised omelettes over a Butane cooker. Previously they had not spoken for three and a half years — since the Italians had discovered their ex-Greenwich Village neighbour occasionally allowed her boyfriends to come for dinner and stay to breakfast.

The reaction of the normally sedate British Consulate officials in the Lungarno Corsini was so remarkable that they are now among the heroes of Florence; in 48 confused hours their efforts were worth decades of diplomacy and official receptions.

At 4 p.m. the American doctor, Charles Whittemore, had his first caller.

At first sight the visitor might have been in a British film made in the forties. He wore a monocle, a tweed jacket, and Wellington boots, with the air of someone on the way to Rotten Row. He was carrying a two-gallon plastic container of fresh water. The British Consul, Mr Christopher Pirie-Gordon, 55, Harrow and Magdalene, was doing his rounds. For once, this urbane figure had not time for diplomatic courtesies; he dumped his water and sloshed off.

With Mr Colin Miler, the vice-consul, Russell Foreman, the Australian novelist, Andrew Crichton, a retired senior executive of B.P., and a group of British colony wives with nursing experience, the consul had an impressive team to call on. Later they were reinforced by Gerrard Lorriman, a Treasury Senior Medical Officer. Miraculously, Whitehall had sent a doctor who spoke fluent Italian, was married to an Italian girl, knew Florence well, and didn't mind walking through four feet of mud to visit an isolated patient — of whom there were many. Headed by Lorriman, the Consulate embarked on a crash vaccination programme in the chaotic first days after the water had receded leaving Florence suffocating in disease-bearing mud. Teams carried candles, matches, water, and tinned food to beleaguered Italians and Britons all over the city.

But this was in the future. Twenty-four hours had still to elapse before travelling, even by boat, to a specific destination, was possible. The waters were still too turbulent and capricious. Dangerous troughs and eddies, cascades and even whirlpools, built up without warning and appeared round corners to ravage people and property.

As late as 4 p.m. in the Piazza della Stazione, near the Medicis' Fortezza da Basso, a vicious whirlpool spun a double-decker bus through the glass window of a bar. It penetrated 30 feet. This was even more powerful than the earlier eddy in the Piazza del Duomo. This had ripped up a ton of paving stones, five centuries old, and skimmed them across the surface like pebbles on a pond.

Five of the gilt bronze panels of Lorenzo Ghiberti's early 15th century Doors of Paradise were torn out of the Baptistery. They were jammed, battered and soiled against a fence surrounding the building, but they survived.

When the long afternoon finally died, just before six, the Florentines descended by candlelight into yet another circle of hell. Isolation was now complete. The only form of communication, as primitive as anything under the Medicis, was the chain of voices eerily exchanging news of the latest disasters — 'Another house has collapsed in Via Condotta' — until they reached Mayor Bargellini and his officials still marooned in their Ponte Vecchio offices.

'What could we do?' said the Mayor, who had a prisoner from the Murate on his chaise-longue, wrapped in a blanket and suffering from shock, 'except tell them to be patient, — and hope'.

Through their windows the waiting Florentines watched for some sign that the flood had reached its peak: it was a long while coming. Then, although the current did not slacken, the roofs of cars, previously totally covered, began to break surface. Along the Via Tornabuoni, where a double line had been parked overnight, a pattern of roofs like a chess-board was emerging infinitesimally. At the same time in the Museum of Santa Croce, the paint on Cimabue's masterpiece was gradually flaking off into the oily water.

'Pazienza'! — the Florentines' patience was tested in the days that followed to endurance point, and way beyond. The waters left dunes of festering mud behind them — with layers of oil and excrement folded in. It filled every cellar in this city abounding with them. Florentine shopkeepers put their money into stock because they don't trust banks. They kept their stock in their basements because they believe that underground storage is safer.

The Arno, no crystal arrow now, but a sullen open-air sewer, was free-freighting God knows what horrors downstream to Pisa. Every morning daylight broke to reveal the same foul-smelling halo of fog hovering above the Ponte Vecchio like a lump of fallen cumulus. Beneath the bronze statue of Duke Cosimo de'Medici Florentines in the Piazza della Signoria stood in line for hand-out bread, spaghetti and drinking water.

They never got enough: it became a mordant slum joke. So did the visiting

Inside the basilica of Santa Croce, a statue of the Virgin Mary stands amid a sea of mud while a soldier tries to clear up.
(Popperfoto)

politicians — Guiseppe Saragat, the President, taken on a conducted tour of the least affected areas like minor Royalty opening a flower show. The proletarian Florentines, at least 10,000 of them now out of work and not many less homeless, greeted him with a bellowed slogan that would have appealed to their ancestors 1700 years before. 'Give us pasta — not words'.

At night the chaos was indescribable. Under improvised searchlights in the Piazza Santa Croce uncomprehending soldiers rushed in to help — but without orders, bulldozers or the greatest need, drain pumps — cast disconsolate shadows on the rippled mud dunes. Military vehicles screamed round the outskirts on improbably urgent errands. The inoculation programme, in a city incubating disease like a laboratory, was a grotesque joke. It was days before any kind of order began to emerge.

Initially the programme of artistic conservation might have had Lewis Carroll as chief executive. Experts and indifferent officials frustrated each other with Ionesco-like inconsequentiality. For three days no one was allowed to enter the Archaeological Museum to aid the decimated Etruscan collection — there was about 6 pounds in the till. Nothing could be done until the appropriate functionary had counted it. Naturally, he was lost. So were some of the many fragments of paint meticulously preserved from the Cimabue Crucifix and reverentially put on a plate. A passing workman used it to eat his dinner off.

For the first long week the Italian Government and press assiduously propagated the idea that the flood was over, and everything was fine in Florence.

The Florentines dug themselves out, as far as they could, with angry energy — spades were more prized than water, blankets, candles or boots. If they didn't start to help themselves, no one else was going to. When the Italian Prime Minister finally got round to inspecting the disaster — ten days after the flood — he was execrated by the mob because of the exquisite Via Condotti lustre on his pointed shoes.

In contrast Sir John Ward, the British Ambassador, ploughed through Santa Croce in gum-boots less than a week after the flood. All along the route Florentines, touched by what they regarded as a compliment, stopped one to explain with pleasure what he had done.

Though they soon created a series of bitter jokes about *'alluvionati'* — those hit by the flood — the city's evident sense of injury was written on every exhausted, strained face. Anyone sharing their situation was welcome to anything they had, with no reservations. As for the outsiders, and particularly the central Government, they had become the object of communal distaste.

The citizens had been shunned like inmates of a mediaeval plague city. No one as much as knew how many Florentines there were any more — how many had been born since the flood, let alone died. The official files had been washed away, though remnants could be found in the mud. If Alfredo B...for example, had passed by the Ponte Vecchio mud dunes on November 10 he could have obliterated with one boot print the record from the State Archives of his conviction on February 18,1944 for 'Dissension in the ranks.'

The Archbishop of Florence, Cardinal Ermenegildo Florit, delivered a sermon suggesting in passing that God had sent the flood to rebuke the city's materialism. A Jesuit suggested it was because the Holy Father had delayed his decision on birth control.

The city took little notice. All they knew was that it would take years to get back to November 3 — and that what had happened, a terrifying demonstration of the fragility of civilised life, had changed them as radically as it had the Piazza Santa Croce.

In his uncle's remote farm in Tuscany, Paolo Barracani's normally extrovert 15-year-old son Massimo was having his nervous condition diagnosed by a sympathetic doctor. After 48 hours on the roof Massimo had fled from Florence:

any suggestion of returning produced a reaction bordering on hysteria. There were many similar cases. Florence's latest contribution to civilisation is a previously undiagnosed neurotic condition — flood shock.

Florence, November 1966.

The Sunday Times Magazine, 11th December 1966
(with Phillip Knightley)

Eye-witness in Gaza

The 'Eye-witness in Gaza' article marked the end of my love affair with Israel, some time ahead perhaps of a rupture that so many of my generation were to experience. It appeared about a month after an article by E. C. Hodgkin, then Foreign Editor of The Times, *which described a new phenomenon. Arabs in the lands conquered by the Israelis after the 1967 Six Day War were, Hodgkin said, 'being persecuted into a new diaspora by the armies and people of Israel'.*

Hodgkin's allegations were less specific (and chilling) than mine. They were strenuously denied by the Israelis but they caused an international furore, just as my own piece did. Its genesis was independent of The Times *story and there was no collusion between* The Times *and their Sunday stable-mate, though it was never possible to convince the Israelis of this.*

Our story was based on meetings with two of the most courageous people I ever met, both Israelis. One approached me in Paris, the other wrote initially to the paper in London. Part of this letter, later reproduced in a sworn statement, read as follows:

'I believe that the duty of a Jew now, not only as a human being but as a Jew, is...to be a witness against the things being committed in the name of Israel, not only because they are wrong but because they threaten the honour of the Jewish people.'

I was reminded of several briefings given me years before by the late Dick Crossman MP, always generous to young people, who had directed my attention to the works of Martin Buber. Bred on the ancient Zionist concept of a holy marriage between a land and a people, Buber often cited the words of Isaiah: 'Israel can only be built with justice.'

There was an additional element which was not mentioned in the article. One of the original informants had spent over three years of his childhood in the Dachau concentration camp, and later I was to meet some of his family, the remnants, who had been there with him.

When it came to torture and persecution these people were peculiarly well qualified to make judgements.

It was all very unhappy. My Israeli sources included people of palpable distinction and probity. The same could be said of some of the Palestinian ones. One night in Haifa, talking with a group of young Palestinian poets (and also terrorists) at a secret address I visited blind-folded, I felt a tug of sympathy for what I had previously always instinctively felt was the Other Side.

While I was sure the allegations were true, I was equally sure that I was being used. Those anxious to assist me, to the point of smuggling me through check-points on to the Gaza strip which was off-limits to the foreign press, usually had a propaganda interest. There were sources whose first allegiance was to the Israeli, or maybe Soviet, Communist Party. There were others who were probably British agents, or their employees, who were passionately anti-Israeli and pro-Arab for reasons not dissimilar to the pro-Turkish Cypriot sentiments of their counterparts in Cyprus, or the pro-Muslim feelings of their predecessors in the (still not so distant) last days of the British Raj in India.

The change in Israel and Israelis since the Six Day War humiliation of their encircling enemies had been frightening to behold. There was a sense of hubris and impending doom which so nearly came about in the 1973 Yom Kippur war. It was clear that the society was drifting towards the hard, and essentially imperialist, Right. Even so, it still astonished me that Menahem Begin, a political pariah in the 1960's, could be elected premier. Begin's penchant for blood-drenched political solutions, whether in the Beirut of the early 1980's or the Palestine of the last days of the British mandate, squandered his society's moral capital.

There was also no longer any chance of reporting Israeli affairs with any kind of objective neutrality. You were either unconditionally pro-Israeli and anti-Arab or the reverse. Over the years, culminating in the September, 1982 massacres in the Beirut camps of Sabra and Chatila, I observed a number of Middle East specialists, including probably the best of them, Tony Clifton of Newsweek, forced out of a kind of closet neutrality into taking sides against Israel, or the Israel of Begin and Ariel Sharon, the Defence Minister.

Retrospectively, I am surprised at how much faith I had in Israel as a morally exemplary society, and surprised at my own naivety.

The story cost me virtually all my Israeli friends as well as putting paid to the opportunity to work again in a country I had loved, certainly to excess. For someone who had always secretly fantasized that his, then unknown, forebears were Jews, it was ironic, and strangely humiliating, to find oneself being described as an anti-Semite by the Tel Aviv radio station, Kol Israel.

All the more so when I discovered five years later that the fantasies of Jewishness were no mere sentimental hang-over from an era when brave, beleaguered Israel had captured the imagination and conscience of a post-war generation. Via my maternal great-grandfather, William Eagles, whose own father had come to England from Odessa early in the nineteenth century, I have a clear line of matriarchal Jewish descent, clear enough to claim Israeli citizenship.

In Gaza this week, the market price for grenade throwers — men not machines — is five Israeli pounds, or 12s. 6d. At this cut-price wage they function more days than not. Also more days than not, the Israeli troops pick them up, their unspent wages still stuffed in their shirt fronts. The grenade boys usually harm more of their compartriots than Israelis. They have established a strong claim to being the most inefficient — as well as the cheapest — hired guns of modern times.

Even so, their maladroit manoeuvres have achieved something, perhaps even their masters' aim. In this they have been abetted by Major-General Moshe Dayan. His policy of 'collective punishment,' or let us call it reprisal, for that is what he means, has driven the uncommitted among the Arabs in Israel — and they did once exist — into the arms of the 100 per cent all-or-nothing haters. Between them they have turned this place, which at best was an unlovely armpit of the Middle East, into a city as menacing and as terrified as Saigon after the Tet offensive.

Here, indifferent Israeli conscripts were shooting at heads moving in the windows in the street of Omar El Mukhtar. Here, when there was a bang, groups of tiny uniformed schoolgirls scurried past the town hall like so many terrorised black rabbits. Private houses were destroyed to encourage the others, and the biggest high school was closed to make an army camp. Effectively, this Arab town of more than 60,000 was under siege.

The terrorists, by means of their 12s. 6d. hired boys, have evidently achieved their aim — to alienate the population and their occupiers. There are consequently Israeli officers there who adduce all Gaza's ills to terrorism. They talk of 'last summer' with a certain lyricism. They say next summer, once the Dayan plan has eliminated the terrorists, could be happy.

But was last summer so good? One observer, and he was there before terrorism was making young soldiers trigger-happy, found conditions unacceptable even then. It is reasonable to ask whether what is happening now is a product of what was done then.

He is an observer worth listening to because, apart from anything else, he is an Israeli, by education and by temperament even a Zionist. This is what he found.

The first thing was hunger. During his period of reserve duty on the Gaza strip, which he described later as 'the most horrific three weeks of my life' he was approached by Arab children who were happy to work all day, he says, for leftovers from soldiers' plates, or even waste food which the Israeli army dumps in plastic bags.

During his service he visited two hospitals where parents, usually mothers, were, according to the staff, in the habit of stealing food from the meals served up to their sick children. This was one of his milder legations, and one of the easiest to confirm. Several neutral health workers in the area said that they had often seen this happen. Indeed, as long as they were assured their names would not be cited they said they had come to find it quite normal.

Moshe Dayan, Israel's famous Defence Minister, said himself last spring in a recorded interview that hunger conditions in some parts of the Gaza Strip were unacceptable, and bad for Israeli prestige in the world. But there is no source, apart from this unofficial one, for the method which occupying forces are reported to have used last summer against the occupied. He saw, and heard from fellow soldiers, how the authorities treated Gaza Arabs, months before Israeli officials began to talk about 'environmental or neighbourhood punishment'.

The first approach involved arbitrary curfews of the kind recently used as a reprisal against terrorism, in the village of Beit Sahor, near Bethlehem, among other places. The inhabitants are forbidden to leave their homes for almost the whole 24 hours; they can go out to get food and water for perhaps two hours a day. As Arab homes in Gaza are usually tiny, have no sanitation or running water, and are sometimes shared with livestock, this is a severe punishment. This witness says that such curfews were imposed against small villages at random, even when there had been no acts of terrorism. When there were terrorist incidents in the area he claims the reaction of his unit was 'much tougher'.

In the tougher cases, the same curfew rules applied, but only the women were kept indoors. The men were driven into the desert in trucks and sometimes beaten up on the way. When they arrived at an isolated spot they were divided according to age into two groups. They were then forced to squat on their haunches in the sun under guard for several hours — he says for as long as eight hours at a time.

There were also harsher measures, which the witness says were common knowledge among soldiers serving on the Strip this summer, but which he never witnessed himself. He says that during a coffee party in his tent (the Israeli army is dry) half a dozen soldiers told him the best way to combat terrorism was to bind suspects tightly with electric wire on arms and legs, and leave them in the sun.

These were not young soldiers telling tall stories, he says, but mature reservists chatting unemotionally, without even much interest (which was the single thing that made the deepest impression on him). He also says they reported beating Arab men on the shins with the butts of automatic weapons, sometimes until their legs were broken.

How accurate are these accounts? And do the events they describe result from official policy? The first question is desperately hard to answer. Many Arabs around Gaza have told me similar stories in the last weeks, but even President Nasser could not call them good witnesses. They were vague on details. They were carried away by their own rhetoric (even filtered through an interpreter) and evidently biased.

On the other hand, an Arab professional man — he is under such pressure that I cannot even say which profession — gave a similar account. And this was also largely confirmed in the course of a series of extremely guarded conversations with international workers in the area, most of whom are concerned, above all, to avoid offending the occupying authorities. Moreover they are frankly terrified that any statement of theirs will be used to prevent them from continuing all kinds of essential services.

All of these witnesses, some of whom have spoken at first hand, and others only through hearsay, must be treated with some reserve. But the Israeli soldier, I believe, is in a different category.

He is not only a Jew; he is a devoted one. He has served in the Israeli army during two wars. He is a highly educated man, and indeed one of some distinction in his profession. He knows people, Israelis like himself, who have told me very similar stories. Finally, this witness, who, it should be said, is unlike the majority of dissident sources in Tel Aviv in that he is anti-Communist, has gone so far as to swear a detailed statement which is in the possession of the *Sunday Times*.

The evidence is by no means conclusive. It does, at the very least, establish a *prima facie* case for some kind of independent inquiry. And it is not the only evidence.

The next set of statements, which deal with Arabs under detention in Israel, fall into much the same category. They have been obtained from both Arab and Israeli lawyers and, via access to defendants' statements and court transcripts, I have selected four examples which are, in various ways, typical.

It would be possible, given time, to add about 40 more. But the following are in themselves sufficient to warrant an inquiry. These examples all involve what amounts to torture.

For historical reasons which do not require emphasis this is a subject which is highly sensitive in Israel. It is hard to believe that a government based on all kinds of humane ideals is prepared to make these methods an instrument of policy. Are the allegations true or not? Again, it seems that only an independent group could decide. But again, the evidence available is enough in itself to cause great concern.

The evidence of Lutfieh El Houari

The first statement comes from a woman and, it should be said, a damned tough one. She is called Lutfieh El Houari, she is 25, and she was arrested in August this year in Ramallah.

The charges against her were numerous: being a member of an unlawful organisation and attempted murder were the most serious.

According to her prosecutors, and their case has not been contradicted with any conviction, on June 5, 1969 — the second anniversary of the outbreak of the Six-Day War — she and four girl-friends despatched a bottle of poisoned whisky to some Palestinian Arabs whom they regarded as collaborators.

She confessed to most of the charges against her, but on November 4 before a military court in Ramllah, her lawyer claimed that her statements had been extracted through torture and fear. This is what she says happened:

She was taken to Beit Shemesh and interrogated for 15 days. During this period she was kept in solitary confinement, with both wrists and feet handcuffed. She says her interrogators threatened her with the same punishment that she had received a year earlier while under administrative arrest.

Then, she says, she was put in the same cell as a group of Jewish prostitutes mostly from the Yemen. They attacked her and were encouraged to do so by the guards. She claims that during her solitary confinement she was prevented from using the lavatory, which was particularly painful for her as she was convalescing from an operation for appendicitis at the time of her arrest.

She also claims that police or soldiers (she is not sure which) threatened that her house would be blown up anyway. Miss Houari has given many more details of alleged ill-treatment to her lawyer, who has made an official protest, so far without response.

The evidence of Ichak Ali El Marari

Ichak Ali El Marari was arrested on March 7, 1969, in Jerusalem. After two months of interrogation, during which he claimed he had no access either to his wife or his lawyer, he was charged with being a member of an illegal organisation. Interestingly, though he is still in prison, the charges against him were dropped on June 6, 1969.

He says, and I have seen his statement, that he had been so maltreated during the interrogation period that the marks would have been visible in court.

His story, which is similar to that of many others, tells of being beaten on the hands with a strap, and of being denied water and medical treatment until he had made a full confession.

In his statement, which his lawyer sent on September 15 this year — so far without reaction — to Israel's Attorney-General, the Minister of Defence, and the Minister responsible for police, he names a police chief inspector (he is called Marcus) who directed the interrogation.

On the same date his lawyer, again to no effect, requested an independent medical examination and access to the prisoner's medical files. These are probably easily available because, after his interrogation, Mr Marari was treated in the prison hospital at Ramleh.

He says his most serious injury was a head wound, and he also complains of defects in vision as a result of his treatment during interrogation, and recurring headaches.

His case is particularly interesting because, unlike most detainees who allege torture, there seems to be no convincing evidence, or indeed evidence of any kind, that he was involved in terrorist activities.

He admits a connection with a nationalist front organisation but says he was only concerned with aiding the families of people who had been arrested. He may, of course, be lying but unless there are statements suggesting the contrary, which I have not had access to, there appears to be no hard evidence against him. This does not mean under the system of administrative imprisonment which is now widely used that there is anything to prevent him remaining in prison for an indefinite period.

The evidence of Abdullah Yusuf Oduan

Similarities can be found in the story of Mr Abdullah Yusuf Oduan. The allegations of torture methods are much the same, though he names three different interrogators.

Mr Oduan is, I understand, a Communist Party member, though this is not an offence in Israel, which has two Communist parties with parliamentary representation. By an international irony, he had already served a long period in a Jordanian prison for being a Communist.

He says the Israelis acquired his Jordanian files when they occupied the West Bank, and picked him up as a result. He also says that Israeli interrogators assured him they would do a much better — which in the context means more brutal job than their counterparts in the Hashemite kingdom. Through his lawyer, on September 11 of this year, he submitted various allegations of ill-treatment to the relevant authorities. By the middle of November there had been no response.

The evidence of Abdel Rahim Gaber

A fully paid-up 100 per cent terrorist, Abdel Rahim Gaber made similar allegations. He is serving a life sentence for terrorist activities, including planting a bomb at a bus station in Tel Aviv in 1968. Presumably he knew the risk, and was prepared to pay the price.

He claims to have served a longer period of solitary confinement than most of the other prisoners whose files I have seen.

But, if one can believe the statements prisoners make, there is little distinction between the treatment of an avowed terrorist and a suspect. A lawyer, an Israeli who handles many of these cases, says that experience suggests 80 per cent of the prisoners are tortured during interrogation if what they say it true.

But is it? Prisoners, Communist Party members, men who have been picked up off the street after a grenade has gone off, are clearly not the best witnesses of their own experiences. Unfortunately, given the present system, what they say cannot be verified, or contradicted. Almost all allegations cover the period immediately after arrest. The suspect has not yet graduated to the comparatively enviable status of prisoner — that is, someone detained inside an official Israel prison with certain rights.

I have heard complaints about prison standards but, compared with those levelled against police and military intelligence during the interrogation period after arrest, they are too trivial to be worth repeating.

The prevailing system makes it particularly hard to check. The legal code which covers Arabs in the occupied areas, and within Israel as it existed before the Six-Day war, is so superlatively illiberal that those on the receiving end have almost nothing on their side. Anyone can be arrested, restricted to a certain area and kept in prison for an indefinite period without any charge. The authorities can give them access to outsiders, or they cannot. It depends on how they feel.

The system is disgraceful. For the British, who feel moral indignation when brought face-to-face with an approach apparently so alien, the only reaction is outrage. It is, however, worth bearing in mind that the British themselves are responsible for the system.

It is based, very largely, on the 14 chapters and 170 articles of the 1945 Emergency Defence Laws which the British introduced under their mandate to deal with Jewish terrorism. Stern though the provisions were, they failed. Passionately though Israeli jurists condemned them at the time as a contradiction of the most fundamental principles of justice, they have, with certain amendments, been carefully preserved.

The best objective witnesses of what is going on inside Israel's detention centres are members of the international committee of the Red Cross. For various reasons, they cannot say what they believe is true, one way or the other. If they deny them, the Israelis will exploit their statements.

As Israel refuses to accept that the provisions of the Fourth Geneva Convention apply to the occupied territories, Red Cross delegates have no access to the police stations or detention centres where prisoners are kept after arrest. Neither can they see prisoners in solitary confinement.

If their representatives decide torture charges are justified — their criteria are physical marks on a prisoner — they make a report. These reports are strictly secret. They are not published because they would prejudice the job which Red Cross delegates, within strictly defined limits, are at present permitted to do.

Many observers believe that the Israelis, if they wish to demonstrate the strength of their case, should either give the Red Cross more facilities or let some other unbiassed group look for themselves.

The Sunday Times, 23rd November 1969

A man and his family

Aid flows into Turkey: but does it reach the dying villages?

The late Claud Cockburn liked to tell how he had once won a prize devised by foreign sub-editors of The Times in the 1920's for the week's dullest headline: 'SMALL EARTHQUAKE IN CHILE — NOT MANY DEAD' was Cockburn's winner.

Earthquakes in Anatolia, unfortunately, are common enought to provoke a similar journalistic detachment. Like so many 'action' stories, planes crashing, boats sinking, hotels burning, they blur and merge in memory. The most specific recollections are invariably connected with problems to do with communications.

I filed several earthquake stories from Istanbul and Ankara to The Times *— 'A MAN AND HIS FAMILY' in the Sunday paper was the final wrap-up feature at the end of the week. One account of latest developments was telephoned from a post office in some Anatolian outpost the name of which I've long forgotten. While I was speaking to a* Times *sub-editor I noticed first the light-bulb swaying, then the desk, and finally a sea-like motion of the whole office.*

My style, if that's the right word, was invariably a bit too 'popular' for The Times *as it then was. Nonetheless, I was manic (and frightened) enough to suggest inserting a paragraph referring to the new tremors as they were occurring, along the lines of 'While I write, new tremors...'*

The sub's reaction was frigid. 'I don't think we'll bother with that, Old Boy,' came down the line from the Gray's Inn Road.

'Why won't we?'

'Because, well, Our Readers probably, well, won't believe it's actually happening, er, at this precise moment...'

I remember watching the swaying light and outside through the window snow-flakes blurring and thickening into as nasty as night as you could hope for. Alexander Macmillan, then of the Telegraph, *now, more simply, of Macmillans, was indicating with some passion that he required the phone.*

'Let it go then', I said, preparing to ring off.

'That's the spirit, Old Boy.'

Those were the days...

Almost exactly two weeks before the Anatolian earthquake disaster, fifteen thousand yards of tenting material was released from bond by the Turkish customs authorities. It had been sent by the British Government for earthquake relief. So at first sight it might seem that Whitehall and the Turks shared a mutual prescience worthy of the Delphic Oracle.

Except, that is, for one small detail.

This invaluable lifesaving cloth had actually been despatched to aid the homeless after the Adjipar quake of July 1967. And despite the impressive thirty-three-

Gediz in Turkey where thousands died in the earthquake.
(G. Sipahioglu/Rex Features)

month timelag British officials in Ankara were still uncertain, on Friday afternoon, whether the stuff had even got as far as the relief air-base of Eskisehir, still five hours by truck from the earthquake town of Gediz.

Meanwhile no one knows how many of the ninety thousand homeless in Western Anatolia are facing the near freezing nights with no protection.

Gediz was a disaster the proportions of which were such that none who saw it will ever be able to erase those stricken faces from the darkest corners of the mind. So too was the Varto quake of 1966, which killed 2,400 people.

On that occasion also, aid poured in from the developed countries. The Scandinavians sent, among other supplies, thousands of tins of meat.

But the people of Varto were not used to this kind of meat. Some indeed may never previously have seen tins and they are pious Moslems. So a city boy spread the story it was pork (this was a lie), and brought in trucks to collect the stuff for nothing from the relief teams.

I am told it is still possible to find some of the battered tins on sale in the Bazaars of Istanbul.

Local observers find nothing strange in these facts. But the real tragedy of Gediz — and one must use debased headline words like tragedy and horror for they are the strongest we have, and in this context they have precise meaning — may well yet be that in a couple of years the seasoned oldtimers will be exchanging similar bland anecdotes about the consequences of Saturday, March 28, 1970.

British diplomats preparing for the five day visit to Turkey by Michael Stewart, the Foreign Secretary, which begins tomorrow, may face a difficult problem. The Foreign Secretary has said that after his official talks in Ankara he wished to visit the stricken areas of Western Anatolia.

The Turkish Foreign Ministry first reacted to this request with a flat refusal. The excuse they offered was that conditions in the Anatolia region are too bad for any

VIP trip. But it was speedily rumoured that the Turks were concerned that the Foreign Secretary might receive an unfavourable impression of the way relief is being distributed.

The Turks are now thinking again. Officials here are hoping that Turkish Foreign Minister, Ihsan Sabri Caglayangil, will reconsider the original decision.

To see what is happening one must start with the logistics of relief. They look impressive at first sight. America and West Germany have led the way, and the RAF, mainly out of Cyprus, have flown in huge quantities of material donated by the British Red Cross, Oxfam, War on Want, and Christian Aid.

Within 18 hours of the worst tremors the Americans had a 19-truck convoy on the road, and it would have been faster yet had there not been protocol delays with the Turkish Ministry of Foreign Affairs.

At Eskisehir air base German pilots in yellow flying suits are literally sprinting across the tarmac. Their operation is being co-ordinated by an ex-Messerschmitt pilot resoundingly named Baron Peter Freiherr Von Malapert-Neufville. As he says, they have established a 'permanent air bridge.' It works like this:

Boeing 707s carrying over forty tons of supplies each fly from near Hanover to the US-leased NATO base at Cigli, outside Izmir. The cargo they unload is lifted on to Eskisehir, where the runway is too small for 707s, by a shuttle-service of eighteen propeller-driven C-16s. Lighter aircraft again continue the bridge to Kutahya, the major town nearest to Gediz.

At this point, the Turkish Red Crescent and the Government Emergency Committee take over, and start moving the supplies to Gediz by truck. And here all hell breaks loose.

Despite the appalling confusion, the Mayor of Gediz, Mustafa Bagdatli, was able to say that his town had all it needed. But it might perhaps be more appropriate to say that Gediz has received more than it needs.

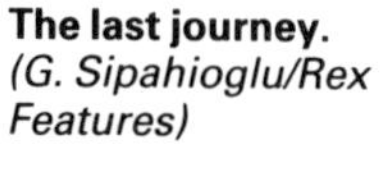

The last journey.
(G. Sipahioglu/Rex Features)

Enormous quantities of supplies poured in by highly-organised Western logistics have reached Gediz. But this little town, although it has become a symbol, is only a tiny part of the disaster-zone — which according to Government estimates, or guesses, may have 'affected' 150,000 people.

And it is scarcely possible for relief supplies to go 'further' than Gediz: the town is very far from being the focus of any sort of transport-system. The scattered villages on the Anatolian plateau are connected by little more than a spider-work of tracks, and to understand the extent of the hidden disaster it is necessary to travel by helicopter.

From the air you can see that only five miles from Gediz, 500 ft higher up the mountainside, there is a satellite village called Akcaalan. When I flew over, four days after the quake, some buildings were still burning there, in this small place that once housed 1,500 people. It is connected with the main town by a rough track certainly negotiable in a jeep. There were no vehicles there, no vehicles have been there, there has been no rescue work.

The lucky ones, or even the lightly injured, could have reached Gediz along the track on foot or by donkey. But around 80 per cent of the buildings there are rubble, and those who were trapped and seriously injured must have found dying a very long-term affair.

Fifteen miles further on in the direction of Emet, which with another village, Simay, was hit by the second round of quakes on Tuesday, there is a fair-sized village. Or anyway there was. A Turkish officer flying with us calculated its original population at around 800.

It has no name on the map we have, but the local cartographers need scarcely bother to worry about the omission. This village — or unvillage — has been reduced to matchwood. The cliché is used precisely; from 100 ft up it looks as if someone had tipped several hundred thousand matchboxes over the side of the hill, and then driven over them with a steam-roller.

There is a track leading to an unnamed, former place; there was no sign of any vehicle within 15 miles. We can, it seems, assume that this is a miniature Anatolian Carthage — total annihilation.

The villagers of Simav Emet have produced a petition claiming that Gediz has got the aid, while they starved. In Emet, population 4,800, the death roll had been fairly light. The headman claims the village needs 2,000 tents, and in 250 tents they had received on Thursday night an average of 5 families or perhaps 25 were sleeping.

One wonders how many villages there are like this. No one knows; no one has been to see. Indeed, there is no way of seeing except by helicopter, truck, or perhaps jeep. I have not been able to discover how many helicopters the Turkish Air Force has, but at Eskisehir, and at a large training base near Ankara last Thursday, there were twenty big Bell helicopters parked in impeccable immobility.

At Emet, the population came to greet us and cheer our big machine from the sky. (The black veiled women were segregated from the men like untouchables.) Why did they cheer? Perhaps they thought we were a sign someone remembered them.

But one wished our chopper-load had contained tents, as well as cameras.

Many foreign rescue-workers have been appalled by the apparent inertia displayed locally amounting almost to indifference. But there are more seasoned ones, some of whom have experienced all of the *fourteen* major quakes which have killed more than 40,000 people along the line of the 'Anatolian Fault' since 1938. They tend to reckon that the Turkish Government's present performance is about the best to date.

There is, in theory, a lot more that could be done: in terms of preventive measures as well as relief work. Japanese technicians who have visited the area have suggested that houses should be rebuilt without the flat roofs which the people

Precious drinking water is dispensed from a lorry in Gediz. *(Bedri Kayabal/Camera Press)*

prefer at present, and that tiles should replace the ponderous layers of clay bricks which are piled on top of the houses for insulation.

But although the local newspapers have been attacking the Government for its inability to control building methods in the danger-area, they admit that it is not easy to think of changing Anatolia.

Some reasons can be discerned for the helpless inertia of the local people, and one, without doubt, is the influence of their religion. There is a clue in the signs which Turkish lorry-drivers tend to have on their cabins: 'Sha' Allah', or 'Masha' Allah.' Precise translation into English is difficult, but a rough effort casts some light. The first means, literally, 'if Allah wills,' but there is a strong undertone of hope that he may in fact be in a good mood. The second simply means 'Allah protects.'

On the dreadful road to Gediz the other day, there was a pile-up which involved three lorries and a car, but it did not cause our driver to slacken his pace from 90 m.p.h. Whatever had happened, Allah was at the wheel.

Apart from Moslem fatalism, there is simple shock. After the earthquake, it was outsiders looking for relatives who used their bare hands to try to shift the debris under which people lay still alive. The local people were not doing this — nor, it should be said, were the soldiers, who just dug graves or slouched around.

And finally, of course, it is just a question of education. A sign outside Gediz says 'Nufus (the Turkish word for population) 7,500.' Before Easter Saturday night the soaring birth rate had made that sign out of date to the tune of about 2,500 people.

Probably after the ultimate body count arithmetical correction will be unnecessary.

Some day, not far off, all this will happen again. The dictator Kemal Atatürk declared that Turkey must be hauled, whatever the cost, into the modern world, and since his time there have been years of more-or-less reform. But an Anatolian earthquake is capable of putting all those ambitions into perspective.

The Sunday Times 5th April 1970

CZECHOSLOVAKIA

Alexander Dubček, whose name I first heard in Vietnam that winter, was only 46 in January 1968 when he succeeded in ousting Antonin Novotný, the Stalinist hard-liner who had run a tight and orthodox ship in Czechoslovakia for 15 granite years.

Dubček's youth gave him rarity value (and appeal) in an age where the post-war 'baby-bulge' generation dominated fashion and street politics, while real power resided immoveably in the hands of a few old men — De Gaulle, Adenauer, Mao, Ho, Giap, Lyndon Johnson and Leonid Brezhnev, the other main protagonist in the Czech tragedy who must have attained late middle-age around the age of 21. Like a seismograph, Dubček instantly began registering the subterreanean impulses and aspirations that were to flare around the world, and largely burn themselves out, by the end of the 1968, that most extraordinary and deluding of all the post-war years.

It was instantly clear that Dubček was special — a figure endowed either with the genius, or tragic political innocence, to mean what he said. His intention was to restore some kind of decency, and even élan, to a country which, like all the Soviet satellites, provided an object lesson in the collective subjugation of the human spirit.

The Czechs thus began 1968 in a society where life for many people, particularly those with minds of their own, was probably not worth living. By March Dubček's first intoxicating acts were to give liberty to the Press and Radio, and freedom of speech, assembly and movement to the exultant Czechs themselves. It was the first taste the country had experienced of these heady, democratic brews for 30 years at the least. No wonder Prague bloomed almost overnight as if the city were suddenly the happy partner in an adolescent love affair.

As if everyone knew it was too naive and beautiful and fragile to stand a chance in hell of making old bones they named it for the shortest, most evanescent season: 'the Dubček Spring'. These were the short months during which Socialism, perhaps for the first time ever, acquired its famous 'human face.'

There was neither Spring nor Socialism in California where my itinerary involved following the Robert Kennedy campaign which was arguably 'peaking' towards the Democratic nomination and the White House precisely at the moment when Sirrhan with his tiny hand-gun and IQ put an end to psephological speculation and the Kennedy presidential dynasty. My own reservations vis-a-vis RFK were considerable. Yet it was hard to see an assassination which gave Richard Nixon the presidency on a plate as anything but a triumph for the forces of darkness.

The way the cards fell in France was similarly comfortless. The freedom of the streets, so unforgettable while it lasted, gave way to the last dog-days of Gaullism, its most reactionary and dispiriting phase. This was all the more so when the General himself resigned in March, 1969.

If his successor, Georges Pompidou, had not had his presidential term amputated by a tragic death, he would have achieved a socio-political vision, one of whose components involved contructing freeways through the heart of Paris and covering the Left Bank, heart of their 'May Revolution', with an eight-lane expressway.

But when it came to the cost of being uppity kids in a world where the old, the cynical, and the implacable called the shots, the Czechs drew the shortest of straws. By the end of July 1968 the Prague leadership was as critically in need of the world's help as it had been just 30 years before when Hitler had moved in. On that occasion the British prime minister, Neville Chamberlain, had sought to justify his policy of appeasement by remarking that it was a small country of which we knew little.

Now once more it was a case of Czechoslovakia versus the Rest. A Soviet invasion seemed inevitable and yet they delayed. Either the Russians were acting with the deviousness of Talleyrand or, more likely, faced with this break in the solidarity of their satellites they genuinely couldn't decide how to respond.

On August 9 at a summit meeting in Bratislava, Leonid Brezhnev, the Soviet party boss, kissed both Dubček and his supporter, Ludvik Svoboda, the Czech President. They had previously held a summit at Čierna with the largest detachment of the Moscow Politburo ever to travel abroad. Could it be the Czechs would squeak through?

Only too soon it was clear that Brezhnev had delivered the Judas kiss. Close to midnight on August 20, while I was having an al fresco dinner in the Place des Vosges in Paris, the Russians, Bulgarians, the East Germans and the Hungarians sent in the planes and tanks.

Retrospectively, it is evident that as occupying forces go the Soviet and other eastern bloc troops behaved well — La Patronne from Fontainebleau would have found them generally 'très correct'. What was particularly frightening about the Soviet presence was the invaders' implacable stupidity. An example that affected me involved communications.

It took the newcomers ten days to discover that uncensored telexes could operate from a number of sources and thus circumvent their entire effort to surround Prague and the whole country with a cordon sanitaire *of propaganda. It reminded you of the Americans in Vietnam — anyone, you felt, who could tolerate so many strikingly dumb men in positions of great responsibility without apparently either noticing their manifest incapacity or letting it remotely bother them must have resources at hand so mighty as to make them invincible.*

As of course they were — wherever you went or looked, Paris in May, Los Angeles in June, Prague in August, Vietnam the whole year long, hopes that there might indeed be light at the end of a tunnel (though not the same one General Westmoreland had in mind when he coined the phrase) ended instantly in tears.

By the end of the year it was a wonder that the international youth movement hadn't lost their capacity to dream. So much utopianism, so it seemed in Paris, had gone up in smoke, leaving little but charred barricades, and maltreated plane trees, and fading slogans the winter would soon obliterate altogether.

The story of Jan Palach, the self-immolator whose Prague funeral so appropriately ushered in the black year 1969, set the tone for what followed. The memorably hedonistic and anti-war pop festival at Woodstock gave way to Altamont, remembered for nothing except violent death and an atmosphere so evil that teenagers solemnly assured each other that Mick Jagger, like Faustus, was in league with the Devil. Manson's family stalked Beverley Hills with blood on their claws like refugees from primitive Greek myth.

The resistance forces are outwitting Russia

Czechoslovak resistance leaders who crossed into Austria at Berg, today, gave the first details of how they have been operating since the invasion.

Their anonymous spokesman, who was carrying a Russian automatic, said that his organisation had enabled the legal Czech Government to function from clandestine headquarters. 'If the Russians issue a false statement after the meeting with Svoboda and Dubček, in Moscow, it will not do them any good,' he said. 'Any agreement in Russia will first have to be ratified by the legal Government of Czechoslovakia.'

He added that Russian troops had continued to flood into Czechoslovakia since midday, yesterday, and it was estimated there were now 500,000 Red Army men in the country. The resistance movement, however, had appealed by radio to railway workers to sabotage the tracks and the Russians were having great difficulty in moving their troops and victualling them.

Ironically, the underground organisation — which includes mobile, clandestine radio stations, printing presses and transport facilities — was set up originally by the Czechs at the instigation of the Russians and with their professional advice. Moscow had warned the Czechs of the possiblity that the Western Germans might invade and insisted that they should make extensive preparations for such a contingency.

The Russian plan for the resistance movement included an extensive, and highly efficient, national grapevine through which they planned to channel propaganda in the event of an invasion from the West. That same grapevine is being used to inform the Czech people of events in Moscow, Washington and elsewhere as well as in their own country.

The spokesman, who crossed the border to organise broadcasting from Austria to Czechoslovakia, in German and Czech, said that the underground had 'at least 40,000 members' and that they were receiving aid from the 100,000-strong national militia. All are armed with Russian or Polish-made automatic weapons. 'We managed to get 1,095 delegates to the 14th extraordinary meeting of the Czech Communist Party within 24 hours, which would have been an extensive operation even in peace-time conditions.

'Not only did we get the delegates to the meeting (in a Prague factory) but we arranged also for them to be taken home. Originally our job was to confuse any West German invaders by changing road signs and to give the Red Army a chance to move. Now the Red Army has its own problems.'

One of the major difficulties for the Russians has been the evident reluctance of Czech political figures, even those notorious for their pro-Stalin views, to take any role in a puppet Government. This, said the spokesman, is because they fear assassination by the underground.

He added that when Cestimir Cisar, the secretary of the Central Committee, was arrested by the Russians, underground agents freed him inside two hours. 'This deeply impressed the Czech people and convinced them that all was not lost. For

A Czech crowd watches as a Soviet tank approaches a flaming barricade at an intersection in Vinohradska Street. *(Jevan Berrangé/ Camera Press)*

the first time, they realised that just because the Russians had a lot of troops it did not necessarily mean that they were able to control everything that happened in our country.

'This was very encouraging for the people and it made the Stalinists think twice before they tried to take advantage of the situation.' Three of the Czechs in Moscow for the talks, he went on, were 'hard-line Stalinists, class of 1944' who have no authority to negotiate on behalf of the people.

'If they come back, we guarantee that they will not draw breath for more than eight hours on Czech soil. They know this because we sent them printed leaflets saying so before they left. I think they will be rather uncertain about coming back.'

The spokesman said that his organisation had been able to warn about half of the writers and intellectuals faced with arrest by the Stalinist elements of the Czech secret police (40 of whom had been sacked since the fall of Novotny but are operating again) to go into hiding before the soldiers and police arrived.

The Czech Resistance claims also that it has escape lines out of the country and that more than 300 prominent people have been moved out one jump ahead of the Russians.

Meanwhile, despite the estimated 500,000 Russian troops in the country, the Resistance is confident that it has the situation well in hand. 'So far, we have avoided violence,' the spokesman said. 'If we have to change our policy, the Russians will find that we learned our lesson in 1939 and 1940. This time we will defend ourselves if every man in the country over the age of 18 dies in the process.'

The Sunday Times, 25th August 1968

Prague endures — politely and with dignity

This morning, I was stopped in a Prague bank by a man who came up and said: 'Can you take me to the border while there is still time?' He was a quiet, dignified man, with glasses and a grey suit. He apologised for bothering me, and when I said no, I could not, he endured the disappointment in a dignified way. That is what Prague is doing this weekend — enduring politely and with dignity.

The Czechs have switched from defiance to deep, unimaginable misery. They seem to suffer better than most people, as if, helped by history, they have acquired a talent for it.

Before their brainwashed leaders returned on Tuesday the towns muted colours sprouted multi-coloured posters screaming defiance and outrage. The statue of King Wenceslas was one enormous collage of insolence. It depicted caricature Russian soldiers, very much as they are in life, sullen crop-haired little men in jackboots. Now instead there are wreaths and candles, memorials to dead patriots and also to a country which is now learning that it too is dying.

Two Czechoslovak tricolours held unsteadily by an acneous youth and a pale girl stand at the summit of the square. They mourn almost professionally, as if they have had a lot of practice and expect the process to continue. Just down the road a little functionary in official cap and moustache diligently erases a wall daub of a blood-red Russian hand and a red Soviet star circumscribed by a swastika. Such gestures of defiance, like the secret radios and the youths who whistled their hate at indifferent tanks, are now 'provocations'.

All the Czechs are now allowed are portraits of Dubček and Svoboda, and a new design which stares bleakly out from many windows with an indescribably bleak message — 'Adapt yourselves', it says.

What a message of hope. As the defiant posters disappear, and the free radios go silent we become, little by little, an island. Our contacts become more sporadic. We are at the mercy of machines, as well as of the Russians in jackboots — who wear rags instead of socks. (Men on the moon, but no socks for soldiers. We have understood the message and the human priorities implied.)

Slowly, a story of how their leaders were treated is seeping through to the people. They believe they know how the fraternal Russians broke Alexander Dubček and the tottering Smrkovsky. How they took Dubček to a mud hut in Poland handcuffed like a felon. How he and his comrades progressed from there to be brainwashed in Mukacevo in the Ukraine, transported like dogs, accused of leading a counter-revolution, prevented from going to the lavatory so they crouched in their own filth. This last point is frequently mentioned as a source of outrage.

Finally Dubček and his friends are said to have been wheeled into a great room in the Kremlin, where they waited an hour. And when the Soviet bosses arrived at last, they looked at the Czechoslovaks 'as if we were strange animals' — that is the versions of the leaders' own words as they are reported in Prague.

Dubček, who was in hospital for a day after his return, came back in such pathetic condition that he could not remember the details of the 'Agreement' with the Russians — none of which was written. Again and again, it is said, the Central Committee asked him: 'What happened? What happened?'

Some details may have accrued to this story with the passage from one outraged Czech to another, but it is what they believe is true, and anyone seeing Prague tonight would understand.

One thing Dubček and Svoboda are said to remember, with great clarity, is that the Russians offered them one thing. They were given permission to liquidate the failed puppet government nominated by the Soviet Ambassador in Prague, Cervonenko.

Did the Russians think that by giving Dubček support to wipe out political opposition, Capone-style, he would be content? Clearly, they never took questions of freedom or anything abstract like that remotely seriously. As one Czech leader said: 'We thought they were politicians and they turned out to be gangsters.'

As far as they were concerned the dispute was entirely pragmatic — one of strategy and of course internal solidarity. Here the Czech leaders, who are beginning to look like boy scouts trying to compete with the Mafia, were confused and they simply found it hard to understand what the Russians were talking about.

But in practical terms, and by this we mean *realpolitik* at its most unadorned, the Russian interpretation of the deal can be seen, only too vividly. It amounts to total control. What are they giving in return? The guarantee that Svoboda and Dubček remain, as long as they do what they are told. The guarantee that there will be no more bloodshed — again, as long as there is no provocation. This is a word which has been stretched a long way in the last 36 hours: as defined by the Russians 'no provocation' means something very near to total subservience.

So the Czechs, having no choice, are behaving with the greatest restraint. Little memorials have sprung up all around Prague's suburbs: they have somehow got candles which stay alight in the drizzle, and boys and girls are keeping vigil over memories in the rain — until the curfew. Even these passive gestures are now circumscribed by the invading armies, and it is now perfectly clear to everyone here that in effect we have a military government and a military theology.

The prudent, which in effect means those over thirty, prepare for the long years ahead. They will have a lot of getting by to do. In practical terms, we saw the first signs of Sovietisation of the ministries in the last two days. We have lost Pavel, the Minister of the Interior, a Dubček man who is loved by the Czechs because he dissolved their police state. It is worth remembering that they had until recently a very fine specimen of a police state, and until 1964 were widely considered the hardest of the hard liners.

Just as the habit of freedom is infectious, so is the habit of obedience. One is wary of making generalisations based on eight days of emergency but the impression is that those who were used to subservience will, to use this bleak new slogan, 'adapt themselves'.

Naturally, the information media must be brought into line, and so the writers' club was smashed up by hairless boys in jackboots. The US Marines read comics before 'pacifying' a Vietnamese village. When the Russians pacify a Czech writers' club they read nothing at all.

The centre of Prague today has a certain spurious vitality, much helped by the microskirted girls who are trying to provoke the Russian troops. But go to the suburbs and it is a stage set for Orwell's 'Nineteen Eighty-four'. To get weak beer you queue fifteen minutes and no one ever pushes or even looks surprised.

If you ask a question in fractured German you are mobbed and hospitably offered bits of salami. They believe any foreigner is German — and therefore a friend. It is a staggering, almost absurd, volte-face. For the Czechs to treat 'Germans' like blood brothers.

The Russian soldiers, in their rag 'socks', are queueing also, for their daily ration

A Soviet tank ablaze in Wenceslas Square.
(Jevan Berrangé/ Camera Press)

of soup and rye bread. They have gone through strange changes this week: last Sunday they were trigger-happy murderers, and you went out at your peril. This went on till about eight on Monday night, when they started to be friendly — presumably someone had fed them some child's guide to the political situation. But on Wednesday we were back at Square One, with tanks trundling absurdly through the streets to demonstrate strength.

However, it is the civilian imports who are now the spearhead of the Czech pacification campaign. These civilians, the absurdly named 'cultural and technical co-operation experts', have frightened the city more than the tanks.

The exodus of intellectuals began in earnest on Friday. Pelikan has been replaced as director of TV and Hejzlar replaced as head of radio. The censors, abolished since last January, are now back in four man committees on the newspapers. The Czechs are back behind the Iron Curtain.

Two interesting signs for the future emerged at the end of the week. The magazine *Literarni Listy* produced a clandestine number calling on the public to reject the Moscow agreement as it had been made in 'abnormal conditions'. Listy said: 'Resist in every way you can, but not on the principle of eye for eye, tooth for tooth. Guns and pistols hardly prove anything.'

The statement was aggressive in the light of what Dubček and the others have been saying, insofar as it advocated passive resistance — the continuation of posters and silent demonstrations, including sitdowns.

But it is no good. The only way they can do anything is to form Vietcong-type organisations, and this they have already shown they are not prepared to do. But one possible future development may be foreshadowed in a declaration from the mammoth CKD factory in eastern Prague, signed by over two thousand workers. It condemns Russian imperialism and rejects the Moscow resolution categorically.

Paradoxically the intellectuals began the liberalisation movement with little worker support and now the workers are showing the strongest determination, while the intellectuals run for the border with their prudently acquired exit visas. Maybe there will be a government in exile, but it will be less relevant than a campaign of resistance launched and conducted by the workers.

The Sunday Times, 1st September 1968

Bus to freedom leaves Czech couple behind

Out of the nineteen Czechs who left Brno, capital of Moravia, on the evening bus for the Austrian border, none looked happy. At least two looked so acutely miserable and frightened that one assumed they were expecting trouble at the Nikolsburg border point.

One was a redheaded woman dressed in the Czech equivalent of the latest St Tropez lounging clothes, a bright red jersey and stretch ski-pants. She had with her a small boy and nine bags, which took her a long time to arrange before our blue bus left gate No. 3 outside the main station.

The second passenger who one suspected might be for the high jump had no luggage at all. He was a man in his middle twenties, dressed in a smart tweed suit worn with plastic sandals and mauve socks. He sat right at the back of the bus chain-smoking a kind of cigarette called 'Sport', glancing from time to time at a magazine about speedway racing, and, when we got near the border, drinking Slivovicz from a half-litre bottle.

Two hundred metres from the border point we were stopped by a Russian patrol, an unusually relaxed one including a soldier playing a guitar. The soldiers came on board briefly and tried to make jokes, but nobody laughed. Eventually they got off and waved us on.

At the border three Czech policemen collected the passports, 19 green Czech ones and one British. They then disappeared into their office and we waited half an hour.

The redheaded woman took her boy and settled herself on a seat right next to the red and white wooden barrier between her and Austria. She flirted energetically with the Czech police and one of them gave the boy a piggy back ride. She was so near the barrier, under a sign saying 'Welcome to the People's Republic of Czechoslovakia' in four languages, that she looked as if she might be going to make a run for it. But it was clearly too far.

At some border points there is only a matter of 50 yards between Czechoslovakia and Austria, and anyone trading on the Czechs' natural reluctance to shoot a fellow countryman in the back might try a quick dash. But at Nikolsburg there is almost a mile of no-man's land and the Austrian arc lights were so far away that one could barely distinguish them across the fields.

The young man with the speedway magazine kept his seat at the back of the bus and after a while threw the empty Slivovicz bottle through the window into the ditch. A party of Russians turned up on a half-track to get water and tried to talk, but everyone, including the Czech police, carefully ignored them. Eventually the man with the passports came out of the office and the trouble started.

Seventeen Czech ones were all right, and so was mine, although the visa had expired four days previously. I was handed it back with a poke in the ribs and knowing laugh. But the redhead and the young man were held back. He, it seemed, had no exit visa, a multi-stamped grey form. She had no passport for her child, and though she kept saying he was too young to need one it was clear she was not getting anywhere.

The two of them stood on the wrong side of the barrier and tried everything. They cajoled, pleaded and at one stage led the policemen off conspiratorially, evidently in an attempt at bribery. At one point they both wept in unison and I realised for the first time that, though they had been sitting apart, they were in fact together.

A bit later on they shouted and pointed imperiously at the barrier. Everyone was very embarrassed, but there was nothing to be done. It went on for 15 minutes and then simultaneously, as if they had agreed in advance, they both gave up.

She painfully extracted her nine shopping bags from the luggage racks, counting them carefully. He left his speedway magazine and the empty yellow packet of 'Sport', and they sat together on a bench next to the barrier. A policeman gave the little boy an orangeade and our bus passed through to Austria, at which point all the other passengers cheered. It seemed a sad way of leaving one's country.

As we crossed the checkpoint we could see the two who had failed, red hair and mauve socks together on the wrong side of the fence. They seemed resigned, serene almost, and one thought for the twentieth time that week how easily the Czechs adapt themselves to subjugation and defeat.

For most of them, particularly outside the towns, life will continue virtually unchanged. The previous day, near the battlefield of Austerlitz, the curator of a museum dedicated to Napoleon asked eagerly whether I had seen any Russians. There had not been any in his area, he said.

In Brno a girl interpreter preparing for the annual trade fair, which had been delayed for a week, regretted that the situation would restrict the number of foreign businessmen coming. 'I have a lot of friends who bring me stockings and things,' she said.

Dubček's so-called temporary measures 'limiting the extent of democracy and freedom of opinion' have deceived no one. They all know that they have been colonised by the Russians and that there is nothing to be done.

In the countryside, anyway, there is almost total compliance on the part of the people. They don't see what they can do except continue getting by. Like the failed emigrants at Nikolsburg they may try their hand at token resistance, but will give in fast.

The Czechs, it seems, have had their morale completely shattered. They see themselves as losers. Why, they ask, keep on trying?

The Sunday Times, 8th September 1968

Prague mourns in fear as Jan Palach is buried

Bells from scores of churches tolled over the suddenly quiet city of Prague today as the mourners moved into line behind the coffin of the 21-year-old student, Jan Palach, who burned himself to death for the ideal of freedom.

First there was his mother, Libuse Palachova, in black, her veiled head bent; she was supported by her elder son, Jiri, and his wife. Then came deans and rectors from universities in the capital and throughout the country, some of them in medieval robes of scarlet and blue. Then such men as Jiri Hajek, the former Foreign Minister, and Josef Kriegel, former member of the Communist party presidium, all removed from office under Soviet pressure.

This was the Czechoslavakia the Russian leaders both fear and wish to crush — a quiet, disciplined people whose slightest gesture nevertheless cries out for freedom and self-respect.

It was a sombre, almost dispiriting, day of driving rain and sleet, and the funeral ceremony, conducted with calculated restraint, had a particular air of tragedy compounded of public and private grief: a nation paying tribute to a martyr beneath the brooding shadow of the Russian occupation, and a mother mourning her dead son.

In the courtyard of Charles University, Mrs Palachova paused momentarily beside the coffin. Sliding her hand along the top, she murmured: 'My son, my beloved son. I never believed a thing like this would happen.' She spoke to herself, but her words were picked up by a bank of microphones accidentally switched on, and transmitted to the silent, waiting crowd outside.

In his tribute to Jan Palach, the University rector, Professor Oldrich Stary, said:

'For love of freedom and truth, Palach made the greatest sacrifice and touched the hearts and minds of men, not only in our land, but in other countries in the world.

'We are not a big country, we are small and we have a tragic history. We cannot use force. Our people must live by the force of their ideals and spiritual values.'

The 45-minutes ceremony ended as pall-bearers slid the coffin into the hearse to the sound of organ music. Mrs Palachova refused to travel in the car provided for her.

'My son, I cannot leave you,' she cried. 'I have to follow you on foot.' For 75 minutes she walked, sometimes ankle-deep in slush, along the cobbled streets, lined by mourners, among them children with lighted candles.

The procession ended at Olsany cemetery on the outskirts of the city. Students had asked for Palach to be buried with the nation's heroes at Vysehrad, but this the authorities refused.

Troops had been brought into the centre of Prague to reinforce massive police cordons stationed round key points since dawn. The Government had been insistent that the funeral ceremony should not develop into civil disobedience and so give the Russians an excuse to bring back the tanks, evacuated since last October's uneasy agreement with the Czechoslovak leaders.

Students drew cards to decide who was to martyr himself as an anti-Russian protest. Though Jan Palach didn't have the lowest card, he nevertheless burnt himself to death when the other man pulled out.
(Camera Press)

The Communist leader, Mr Alexander Dubček, warned the nation last night that disorder might lead to 'unexpected consequences'. As usual he was talking in euphemisms. He was referring to the ever-present threat of a new invasion. Every citizen of Prague has heard sinister rumours that Warsaw Pact forces have been regrouping on the outskirts of the city.

This did not stop them coming to say goodbye to the obscure philosophy student at Charles University. They came first in their thousands, then in their hundreds of thousands by coach from the provinces, in Prague's dreary early morning trams, and above all on foot. The organisers, who included a stricken girl, Helen Zahradnikova, who was Palach's closest friend, expected 50,000 people. They got perhaps 10 times that, perhaps more.

By midnight on Friday, the silent angry queues winding through the city's university district were beginning to overflow into the Mala Strana section across the River Vltava. It might be said that in his life Jan Palach left little mark; but the manner of his death was threatening to provoke a grave political crisis.

Not that the crowds were undisciplined. Far from it. They were controlled, not by police or troops standing by, but by pimply students with home-made armbands. They directed the crowds with informal instructions, always preceded by the ubiquitous Czech *prosim* — please.

They had few difficulties. This country has spent so many years getting used to queueing for cans of sardines, or kilos of potatoes, that it even expresses horror and outrage with the restraint of a well-drilled platoon.

For the first time since the 'normalisation' designed to persuade the Russians to withdraw their troops, Prague has returned to the old August days of wall newspapers, national flags, and photographs of liberal heroes — in this case a line drawing of Palach, looking intense but rather ordinary, as doubtless he was.

From dawn onwards men with trays sold little badges with favours of the Czech red, white and blue tricolour, but with a black mourning stripe mounted across it. This was the badge of August, later banned to avoid 'provocation'.

The nearest thing to disorder was beneath the cloisters of the old Town Hall Square, where people apologetically jostled each other because they did not want to pass the coffin without wearing their badge of mourning.

The coffin itself, of white pine with silver mountings, was placed in the Carolinium, a 14th-century building given to Charles University by a king of Bohemia and used ever since for formal occasions. No occasion could have been more formal or dignified. Palach's funeral was a State occasion with the nation's leaders absent.

Thousands of wreaths smothered the little courtyard where the coffin lay in state. They overflowed into another square outside the building.

When they reached the coffin — at dawn it took nearly three hours to reach it

Jan Palach's mother and older brother, Jiri, at his funeral on 19th January 1969 — a day of National Mourning throughout Czechoslovakia. *(Camera Press)*

from the back of the queue — they removed their ersatz fur hats, stood to attention, bowed or, in many cases, wept. A middle-aged woman, her face scarlet with grief, passed through the courtyard screeching her pain as if she had been shot.

While the people expressed their communal bereavement, and national flags with black sashes suddenly blossomed from the battered houses, the politicians got on with their own affairs. There was Mr Dubček's appeal for calm, there was President Svoboda's appeal to the trades unions (who carried out a token five-minute strike nonetheless) and there were threats from the Ministry of the Interior.

The Government's evident alarm has been increased by the return to the country of the two intellectual fathers of the 1968 post-Novotny Liberalisation, which led to the Russian invasion: Dr Ota Sik, the liberal economist, and Dr Edward Goldstucker, leader of the Writers' Union, have both come under fire from the hard-liners in Slovakia.

Even so, the funeral was conducted with a restraint which made soldiers and police irrelevant.

The Sunday Times, 26th January 1969

How the Czechs always beat the okupanti 4-3

After dusk one night early in January an unlighted train drew into the station of Mlada Boleslav, 35 miles north-east of Prague. A platoon of waiting Russian soldiers herded the porters at gunpoint into the stationmaster's office, with its peagreen walls and crackling stove. Despite these precautions the train's human cargo was noted.

One eye-witness counted 25, and another 28, girls, all wearing what they took to be prison uniform, with forage caps — the Czechs call them 'boat hats'. Some girls were crying. They were loaded into two waiting lorries and disappeared up the hill towards the beige façade of the sprawling 'Barracks of May 9' (formerly Jan Masaryk Barracks) on the road to Jicin, and the Polish border.

Until last September more than 2,000 Czech troops lived here. Since then the grey stone corridors have housed at least twice that number of Russian troops. Locals call them *okupanti* — the occupiers — though it is an offence to use this word.

No Czechs have seen anything of the girls since, except, that is, for two of them. Ten days later these were admitted to the town's modern gynaecological clinic, and treated for what an informant called 'brutalisation'. After 72 hours an armed guard came to take them back. The clinic's staff were reluctant to let them go, even though the girls were Russian, but they stood back. Choice is a word which no longer figures significantly in the Czech vocabulary.

This unelevating but well-authenticated tale indicates how well the *okupanti* have got themselves hated. All armies abroad need camp followers, but rather few are so pushed that they are forced to import their own. Above all, one would have thought, in Czechoslovakia, where decades of privation have made prostitution into a thriving cottage industry.

Some citizens of Mlady Boleslav will tell discreet visitors that last year a handful of local girls were prepared to fraternise with selected Red Army soldiers. But no more. The culprits, they say, received, without the option, Yul Brynner haircuts from outraged compatriots. Other locals deny this. They claim there are no Czech girls with so vestigial a sense of patriotism.

Everyone agrees that one sentence runs like a thread through all conversations here: 'The occupiers are much worse than the Germans.' Old-timers talk of the Wehrmacht almost lyrically: 'They were so correct.'

As one recalls, their colleagues in the Gestapo were not distinguished for 'correctness' in, say, the village of Lidice. There is no evidence that the Russians have behaved badly; it is their very presence which causes such deep offence.

When Russian officers walk the main street, caps well back on their heads, blue breeches set in box pleats, passers-by freeze. They say nothing but simply stare, with the same expression one has seen on the faces of black poor in Tennessee or on Viet Cong prisoners produced in Saigon for the moral delectation of the foreign Press.

Local boys bunch in front of the Roznoi Café opposite the barracks and glare

A Czech youth stands on a Soviet tank waving the national flag.
(Jevan Berrangé/ Camera Press)

fixedly across. Inside, the Russian conscripts, who never go outside except on patrol fatigue duties, peer down from their dormitories like battery hens.

The institutional apartment blocks on either side have national flags and small portraits of Dubček on their notice boards, normally devoted to information about rubbish disposal.

The officers, who look very glossy in their Sam Browne belts, have the freedom of the town, but the privilege is doubtful. In a shoe shop, one captain tried without success to make several purchases, and finally left looking very stiff.

The assistant explained poker-faced that 'We don't have Russian sizes.' Did they perhaps have English or French sizes? She glanced round then shook with laughter: '*Samozrejme*...of course.'

In the Verec Hotel, where on Sunday afternoons local jet-setters come in from the Skoda works for tea and quicksteps, another Russian officer had a hard time. One night last week he waited an hour for dinner, elbows hunched petulantly on the ashy tablecloth. Each waiter who passed his table became afflicted with myopia and deafness.

Eventually, they all grouped beneath an oil-painting depicting five fawns lost on a winter's night and gazed over his shoulder. He then realised what all the other customers had known for half an hour. His cap, the peak chicly reinforced with bent cardboard, had disappeared.

When the officer wanted to know the whereabouts of his cap the room became firmly monolingual though most Czechs study Russian at school. He finally left, hatless in the snow, across the wet cobbles and past a wall decorated with two enormous whitewash numbers: 4/3.

Here in the Bohemian countryside where Smetana composed 'Ma Vlast', the Czech national hymn, these numbers are everywhere. They commemorate the score by which the Czechs enjoyed their ice hockey victory against the Soviet Union last month.

In Prague, the disenchanted grumble about the prohibition of May Day parades. They say that now Alexander Dubček, the national folk hero, has gone, the spirit of the good soldier Schweik has gone with him.

But in Bohemia, in Mlada Boleslav, in Teplice and a dozen other drab towns in a small country of which we know little, he is alive and well. And every night he goes out with a can of whitewash to daub '4/3' on the walls.

The Sunday Times, 27th April 1969

AMERICAN DREAM

My wartime generation dreamed of America, investing the continent with all the romance of enormous frontiers and apparently bottomless resources. Some of these were delivered right to our school, stencilled with the sign 'A Gift from the People and Government of the USA'. And what a gift! Powdered chocolate, when chocolate of any form was unknown to us, arriving in tins we had not yet learnt to call cans, bigger than any tins ever seen in our rationed food shops. Later, according to the process of ineluctable accretion which has marked almost every aspect of European culture in the forty years since, the right expression for those vast tins followed their contents across the Atlantic, entering our vocabularies as another gift from Uncle Sam. 'King-size' was the only word for them.

These generous people, we thought, chewing our GI gum — as in all war things to eat assumed almost primordial importance. These well-trained, rangy soldiers were not only ready, even anxious, to dispense material largesse, but were demonstrating a positively princely munificence by turning up a few thousand miles from home ready to die over German cities or on French beaches, thereby saving us from becoming a North Sea province of the Thousand Year Reich.

So they became our heroes while the older generation's envious complaints about 'Yank' misbehaviour were encapsulated in one over-worked witticism: 'Over-paid, Over-sexed and Over Here.' Their anti-Americanism baffled and enraged me — how could anyone fail to appreciate Glen Miller, or the white Packard Clipper convertible which an airman I knew by sight (for a spell we lived close to an aerodrome used by Super-Forts) drove God-like along the Hertfordshire lanes?

In due course I understood that the roots of enmity derived from a clash of overlapping empires. The British imperial moment was within two decades of becoming a matter for historians, or nostalgia peddlers. The colossal, and by now distinctly ramshackle, organism which had reached its physical peak only ten years before the war was soon hastily dismantled, while its very different American successor took over, much as Kipling had advocated in the notorious and almost universally misunderstood poem, The White Man's Burden. Written in 1899, it was meant to encourage the Americans to annexe, and thus 'civilize', the Philippines. They needed no poetic urging to accomplish the first part of the mission, which was pretty straightforward. As Kipling's British had long known, the second half of the equation was the tricky one.

The wartime Americans, not least their contemporary Roosevelt in the White House, were of course avowedly anti-imperialist. They were nonetheless stuck with their destiny: soon they too would face universal opprobrium for trying to carry the

'Round-eye's' burden on distant shores where the locals were 'Slant-eyes' to a man.

It was the new empire and had many characteristics of our old one, above all a notion of duty to 'lesser breeds without the law' which went deep.

It may be a characteristic of a nation's imperial moment that its citizens insist on eating their national dishes, whether tea or toast or hamburgers, wherever its citizens travel. There is also the tendency to assume that the natives really prefer manufactured breakfast foods, roast beef and Yorkshire, or whatever the dishes prized back home, in preference to their (often more sophisticated) local cuisine.

In the end it all came down to confidence — a confidence we had comprehensively lost, and which the Americans exuded through the pores. You could not imagine a British Norman Mailer, for example, any more than an American Charles Dickens would have been conceivable in the middle of the nineteenth century. Again where but in America could you imagine a Malcolm Forbes? To equal his immense and guiltless expenditure, the sense of innate superiority which obtains from Boston to Bali and permits limitless eccentricity, you need to turn once more to the British nineteenth century, very likely in the land of Forbes's ancestors. He is nothing other than a Scots Highland Duke of around 1830 (a period, incidentally, when dispensing fortunes on ballooning was very much the vogue) masquerading as America's biggest late twentieth-century spender.

This American confidence is fuelled by energy and inventive optimism. The educated Englishman of my generation discovered that such a sanguine (and often impressively arrogant) approach to the world had died with his Edwardian grandfather. Though we accepted the loss of empire with approval and positive relief — we were, after all, passionate anti-imperialists ourselves by then — it was apparent to me as a journalist that, where once international affairs invariably contained a strong 'British angle', increasingly we had no impact on, or even interest in, the Big Story of the day. It was often uncanny, not least in Vietnam where the fortunate absence of British (as opposed to Australian) troops led to periodic insults from crazy officers, usually in the Marine Corps. It was as if our island had disappeared altogether, along with the atlases of childhood where some 12 million square miles were painted imperially red.

But it was the war over London, not the pyrotechnics of Saigon, which had long conditioned my responses to the American Way.

In 1940 the US General Raymond E. Lee came to London as military attache — he was probably as important as anyone in counteracting the anti-British and isolationist position advocated by Joseph P. Kennedy, the ambassador in residence. It was written of Lee's family: 'We regarded ourselves as a modern and improved breed of Englishmen, but equally the heirs of all the creditable achievements of the race, and equal inheritors of English history before our people left the old country to its slower-paced career.'

I think we saw Americans, in many ways erroneously, very like that too, and for me the habit has stuck. Where we retreated into irony, they carried on regardless, exuding enterprise and pursuing a possibly deranged sense of adventure as far as it could be taken, which turned out to be the moon.

In the nation's disinclination to doubt itself, in its probably misguided notions of duty to what it calls the Free World, and in its sublime inability to get the drift of what foreigners could be about, I am pleased to recognize a continuity with my own forbears. But best of all is the optimism, the quality of 'Can-Do', which is the motto of the so-called 'CB's', the US army's bridge-builders and diggers of trenches. They do it better than anyone and if I have one piece of wisdom for my son it is that in the unlikely eventuality of his landing on an American battlefield he should locate the 'CB' bunker as fast as possible. They have never been known to fail.

Norman Mailer's night out

When Norman Mailer flew into London last week he took up residence very discreetly with his fourth wife, Beverley, in Room 776 at the Savoy Hotel. Discreetly, that is, as far as such a word can ever be applied to a man whose private life has attracted headlines for a decade and whose reputation will probably now always travel at least two jumps ahead of him.

Mailer is in London to launch — 'that's what you call it here, in America we just say hustle' — his fourth novel, *'An American Dream'*, which André Deutsch publishes tomorrow. Not that any further publicity, even if constructed on the most massive Hollywood scale, could add to the Mailer myth of anarchic egomania, which is so contagious that one spent the first part of an evening with America's high priest of sensation nervously waiting a cataclysm.

But none came. In the event it was almost a shock to see such a very quiet American in an unmistakably English suit (made in Dover Street, he said) treading his way diffidently across the Savoy carpet and then mildly wondering if he could get a Bourbon and orange juice without disturbing any of the waiters too much. It was an undramatic introduction.

Mailer is short, wide and heavy — he has the humped build of the classic stand-off half — and his physical presence is palpable. Later, over dinner with a group of people, it was noticeable that when conversation passed him by for any length of time the others tended to keep throwing looks at him as if to reassure themselves that he hadn't been up to anything in the last thirty seconds. His face is Celtic rather than Jewish and very kind — he has a faun look, with deep-set eyes, a lot of curly hair getting a bit grizzled about the sideboards he wears long, and a way of looking shrewdly sideways to see if some point has been taken, followed by a big grin. Altogether he has the air of someone who has got used to charming people over the years.

One of the resemblances he shares with Sergius O'Shaughnessy, the hero of his second novel, *The Deer Park,* and Stephen Rojack, who in the new book takes the anti-hero about as far as he will go, is that despite the deliquencies people go on liking him. And his hero's peccadilloes are not the kind that get shrugged off lightly — in the first chapter of *An American Dream*, for example, Rojack manages to get drunk, almost commit suicide, take a lot of pleasure in strangling his wife Deborah; and find the time for acrobatic sex with a German maid before pitching his wife's body ten storeys down in front of a car.

Over his orange juice and Bourbon Mailer was talking mildly and politely, in a voice with more Massachusetts than Brooklyn in it, about how much he likes London. The only note of criticism came when he denied a Sunday newspaper story that he was contemplating settling down here. 'One thing, though, I think your papers are very much worse than ours. In your popular Press most of the stories are so short, and a lot of things just can't be written about shortly. There are also the lies, like this story about me — it's complete invention.'

But he likes it here. 'It's funny, but in a way I grew up in Brooklyn with an English father — he was a South African and came from a Johannesburg Jewish family to Brooklyn in 1920. He's a small, very elegant man who looks like a banker.

Norman Mailer at the Savoy in 1965 — the author is in the right-hand corner.
(Neil Libbert)

He used to play the role of an Englishman, he used to wear spats and talk with an English accent — say 'vanilly' instead of 'vanilla', this kind of affectation. When I come here I feel at home — say, like a Colonial.'

He carried on the family tradition and stood up when his wife, formerly the actress Beverley Bentley, came in. (All through the evening he got to his feet whenever a woman joined the party and was highly punctilious about going through doors last.) On the way out of the Savoy he wondered whether the doorman should have been tipped and demanded a rundown on the local habits. 'That's the kind of thing that gets you nervous in a foreign country.'

Later he elaborated on what he liked about London, mainly in terms of its differences from New York. One wondered how accurate it was, but Mailer at least was deeply convinced. 'Here there must be maybe 5,000 street corners that have been the same for a hundred years. People who grow up there, a clerk or someone, they're like spirits of the place, they see every little change and they do something to the mood. New York is different. We waste everything in America, we waste our substance. I suppose we just get more so we waste more. We don't allow our tree stumps to hang around, we blow them up or bull-doze them. You don't have modern architecture here in the same way — it depends on sensation, which is electric rather then sensuous, and shatters all mood. Most modern architecture induces a sense of shivering and awe, it doesn't give you relaxation or pleasure.'

New York, he thought, was getting like Berlin in the twenties. 'Everyone is looking for something to break that awful bleak tension of the city which comes down on you like a smog and gets into your nerves. Everyone's crazy for abrupt sensation. Say a man thinks in the morning he wants to go to bed with his wife that night — well, he realises that something is sure to go wrong so the best thing to do is to have a row in the early evening and hope it will somehow get patched up later on. That's why 'camp' has run right through New York, so people will break into a conversation say about the Yankees and come up with something completely disrupting just for a laugh — "I like mustard on my Rocquefort", something crazy like that. It came originally from the upper East Side, where you'd find a painter firing bullets at balloons with pigments in them so they'd explode on the canvas — that's the last child of Dada.'

The fragmentation and tension of the city he kept talking about is reflected in the way he wrote his new novel. Towards the end of dinner he started to talk about it. 'I knew I wanted to write a novel about a man who was violent,' he said. 'You know it first came out in eight instalments in *Esquire*. Ten days before the first deadline I still had the idea in my mind of a completely different book, and even when I'd got going there were times in the first two or three instalments when I felt scared I'd dry up — but then it was all right.' The whole method is typical of Mailer (though not one he intends to try again; now he is working on a big novel that 'might take two or might take five years'). It was a kind of literary gamble, the only kind he really takes seriously.

He does a bit of the other kind of gambling. 'Personally, the biggest bet I've ever had was $500 at evens on the Torres-Pastramo Fight. Torres is a friend of mine and I know what a good fighter he is. I was sure he was going to win. I thought of betting a thousand dollars, but then I got scared and didn't want to be too greedy and maybe wreck the whole thing.' (Mailer won his $500; Torres beat Pastrano in nine.)

True to the Hemingway-James Jones tradition Mailer likes to fight and constantly feels a need to prove his physical courage. 'Just before I came here I sparred three rounds with Torres. It was like fighting a puma — a very kind puma who gave me a couple of jabs now and then to make me feel remotely honest.'

And the violence, of course, is reflected in his books.

'I don't think anyone ever condemns murder *really*. Society may be founded on Kant's categorical imperative, but individual murder gives a sense of life to those around the event. Take newspaper readers — doesn't the suburban commuter get a moment of pleasure on the subway reading about murder? Is he perverse or is it really something life-giving? I prefer the second view of Man, the less bleak one.'

By this time they had brought coffee. The conversation got round to Vietnam. Mailer thought that Johnson was using it as a substitute for what he called a 'national myth'. 'I think the politicians have it in their minds that the Civil Rights movement will go on more easily if there's a war somewhere.' Gesturing with his surprisingly small and plump hands he talked about gas and the new Lazy Dog weapon in Vietnam. He agreed that it probably wasn't any worse than napalm. 'Napalm, yes, but napalm's been used up aesthetically — you have to have a new weapon to get a new psychic release. Every time a new weapon is produced every cadet gets a free ride.'

And about the outraged reactions in the States to his hero Rojack's pleasurable sensations after murdering his wife and the social consequences of this kind of writing, Mailer said, 'I don't know about the consequences; all I know is that a man feels good when he commits a murder — immediately after, that is. Have you ever seen soldiers coming back from a killing spree? They're happy. If I wrote any other way about it, it would be meretricious.'

But eventually we finished up at Annie's Room, an after-hours jazz club. There Mailer drank brandy and champagne for an hour and then decided the only way to finish this interview was in his hotel.

It was 2.25 when we got back to the Savoy's grey carpets and white bedspreads, and Mailer celebrated the homecoming by ordering chicken sandwiches and six glasses of Pimm's from room service. Against an un-Maileresque background of tastefully arranged flowers he started to talk about the bad period which comes to almost every novelist who has an infant prodigy success, as he did almost exactly twenty years ago when *The Naked and the Dead* became an overnight best-seller. The next two novels, *Barbary Shore* and *The Deer Park*, were both attacked and in certain cases virtually dismissed by the critics. 'It's hard, there's something in the seed of American culture that throws up writers all the time and then destroys them. Yes, it happened to Fitzgerald, but he had it a lot easier than me all the way up, and I think of myself being about five times tougher than he was.'

With interruptions (mainly for Beverley to ring New York to find out how their thirteen-month-old son Michael was getting on) we moved to the more cheerful subject of what Mailer has made out of his writing. From *An American Dream* alone (for which Warner Bros. have taken up their option) he has so far netted something approaching the equivalent of £170,000.

'Of course, it's a lot of money,' said Mailer, looking suitably modest as he attacked a chicken sandwich, 'but my situation is I have to make $30,000 — say a good £10,000 — a year after tax before I can spend a cent.' (There are four children from his three previous marriages.)

'I'll go on record on one thing in the advice to young writers department — I was too greedy: either get married once or not at all. Though I suppose you learn one thing: by the time you've been through the four stages of women — courtship, marriage, motherhood and divorce — you may be gentlemanly enough *not* to talk about it, but if you do then you certainly know in your heart that you're well qualified to speak.' He seemed to muse on his former marriages. 'After a divorce all I can say is at best there's a dead reserve and at worst an active bitchery back and forth.'

He started on another Pimms (it was 3.15) and talked about the death of Kennedy — 'For a time we felt the country was ours, now it's theirs again, — and then about the Mailer whose personal life once created melodrama for the New York newspapers. 'Yes, maybe in the first instance I used to create situations myself, but then they started to come on at me when I didn't expect them. That's not funny at all. And I'm not at all happy with many of the slogans I coined years ago — there's still a lot to be done with the novel, a lot of reality no one dares to write about, a whole new area of perception on the other side of writing — think of what Lawrence did in 1912. But it's hard, you've got to destroy something in your readers, their unwillingness to open their mood, and if you do it too many times it's at your peril because they either get shocked or don't understand and either way they don't read your books any more. That's the disadvantage of my reputation, it's helped in the sense that I get talked about perhaps, but readers also tighten up in advance.'

3.45. The hotel corridor deserted except for a grey ghost with a vacuum cleaner, and Mailer, finally ready to sleep, having the last word. 'Say, how would you feel being interviewed at this time in the morning?' Grinning disreputably round the door he finally went to bed.

The Sunday Times, 25th April 1965

March of the Poor Brothers has Washington worried

A shambling, untidy line of men, women and children appear through the evening drizzle. A marshal with a megaphone bellows exhortation at them in the thick, scarcely comprehensive accent of the deepest south.

'Poor brother, why are we marching?'

For freedom, they chant back, like a lesson they have learned by rote.

'Brothers, where are we going?'

To Washington.

We were walking through the circus ground in Nashville, Tennessee, but it could equally well have been Alabama, or Mississippi, or Georgia. One contingent of the Poor People's Campaign — they are marching and riding to Washington as a protest against racial discrimination and poverty — is coming from Boston in the North-East. They all look much the same — casual, untidy, and as undisciplined as an army in retreat. But they are advancing.

They have been delayed by bus break-downs, recalcitrant mules, accommodation problems. But each day the different contingents, perhaps 5,000 in all, have been straggling closer towards the capital.

And the prospect fills Washington with disquiet to such an extent that Senator Jacob Javits says the apprehension 'borders in some quarters on hysteria.'

Washington is jumpy for two reasons. The first worry is whether the comparatively small number of marchers, now planning to erect a shanty-town called 'Resurrection City' not far from the Lincoln Memorial, may be swollen by thousands of other demonstrators from cities on the way, or even from Washington itself. The second is whether the Poor People's Campaign will initiate another summer's violence.

Dr Ralph Abernathy, Martin Luther King's successor who leads the campaign, says that this march may be the last attempt to deal peacefully with the problems of race and poverty. But the new leader is far less moderate than King and his statements tend to change from hour to hour.

In Birmingham, Alabama, for example, he told marchers: 'We're going to turn this nation upside down and right side up.' And one of his constant themes this week has been the need 'To go a step further then King.'

Though this demonstration has been publicised as a poverty campaign it does not so far seem to have enthused the poor whites. In Nashville there were not more than a dozen white marchers among 500 blacks. In Knoxville, Tennessee, the next staging point on the road for Washington, the number of whites had risen by perhaps a dozen.

Given the tone of the propaganda which accompanies the march it is not surprising that whites, no matter how poor or wretched, feel out of place. 'You got to get to the stage where you hate all white men,' said one of the guest speakers in Knoxville. 'If you don't fight you're all going to finish up in a concentration camp being exterminated.'

The trail from Memphis to Washington has been fairly well prepared and the

Gerald Scarfe's drawing of an overnight halt in Tennessee on the Poor People's March.
(Gerald Scarfe)

marchers' schedule is the same each day. They travel most of the road in air-conditioned coaches but have set-piece demonstrations when entering and leaving cities. This has given hostile local papers a chance to sneer at the demonstrators, calling them 'mechanised marchers'.

As there are many young children travelling with their parents, and already by Knoxville one marcher in five had been treated for some minor illness, it is hard to see how else they could have made the trip.

Compared with Marks, Mississippi, and other ghetto communities where demonstrators have come from, the march is something of a holiday. They are fed packed meals, mostly provided by Christian organisations, some of them have never before travelled through the country and in the evenings they troop into vast circus rings and boxing halls where there is music and rhetoric to create an atmosphere of excitement, almost of carnival.

The marchers sway, stomp and swing under awnings advertising brands of bourbon and motor cars they can never afford to buy. The choirs, with names like 'The Soul Sisters' and 'The Wings of Music', harmonise protest songs until everyone is shouting and clapping on the off-beat. The high point of the evening is the speech by the Rev. James Bevel, Ralph Abernathy's chief lieutenant.

Mr Bevel gets the audience going by telling them that President Johnson has $40 million, that nobody could make that kind of money honestly, and that in his opinion the President is 'a common thief from Texas'.

He says that the Vietnam War is an invention of the President 'and his white racist cowboys'. He says that anyone who sends his son to fight there is mad. 'They've got most of the black men there already — and the Mexicans and Puerto Ricans, all getting killed for the white pimps.'

Mr Bevel, with his fringe beard and denim work-suit, appals the vaguely evangelical university girls in Bermuda shorts and the local white Catholic priests who have organised beds and food for the marchers.

But for the poor and dispossessed his speeches are inspirational. When he shouts that the wheels of revolution are turning they jump to their feet and give their salute, a kind of double-armed Mussolini with a hand-clap in the middle.

There is only one other speaker as effective. He is a lanky, bearded man who croons to the audience about 'soul-power' from behind dark glasses and calls himself 'Sweet Willy'. As chief director of 'The Invaders', a Black Power movement in Memphis, he travels with several dozen acolytes.

Apart from their uniform dark-glasses they are conspicuous because, unlike the other marchers, they have no Luther King badges inscribed 'I have a dream' on their lapels. 'The Invaders' are acting as marshals and 'security officers'.

But so far there has been no violence. In Nashville and Knoxville local police sealed off the marchers' area in case of trouble from the white racists but there was no other work for them to do. They spent the evening glowering at Sweet Willy's men who glowered back.

Behind the two potentially hostile groups a female choir sang about studying war no more, their shadows weaving across the arena like an animated daguerrotype. Tomorrow, the first marchers arrive in Washington, pursuing Martin Luther King's dream hopefully to the capital.

The Sunday Times, 12th May 1968

Dr Spock — the world's most unlikely conspirator

Benjamin Spock, America's celebrated baby doctor, this weekend faces five years in jail, and a £4,000 fine. A Boston court convicted him, and three other well-known opponents of America's Vietnam involvement, on charges of criminal conspiracy. This verdict opens the way for draconian Government measures against other war dissenters. Spock is a revered American figure: indeed, almost a national institution. The court has done something akin to condemning everyone's favourite uncle. It took the all-male jury more than seven hours to decide and, as if to make amends, they amazed everyone by acquitting the fifth defendant, Marcus Raskin, a former White House defence aide. All four men said they would appeal. Sentence was postponed until July 10. Five years and a £4,000 fine is the maximum sentence they can receive.

The Boston trial was a running battle between the US Government and its intellectual community. America has seen nothing like it since the late Senator Joe McCarthy's Red-hunting sub-committee.

The five defendants were selected with care. Together they constituted what a pollster might call 'a weighted sample' of American liberal thought.

Spock, as chief scapegoat, provided the focus of interest. The lanky, whiskery pediatrician sat throughout without losing his benign smile. Those gigantic brown hands, ideally constructed for baby-hefting, remained placidly folded. He looked like the unlikeliest conspirator in the world.

Dr. Spock's anti-Vietnam activities became most widely known in October when he was one of the leaders of massive anti-war demonstrations in Washington and was quoted as saying that the American Peace Movement was entering a new phase of action against the war.

He was arrested in December in anti-Vietnam war demonstrations outside the main US Army induction centre in New York when he went through a police barricade to sit down in front of the centre.

The next defendant was William Slaone Coffin Jnr, the Yale University chaplain. The 'Rev. Coffin', as the lawyers called him in a slightly macabre way, has an upper crust New England background; even at 43, there is a public school look about him. He is a model white Anglo-Saxon cleric.

Next was Mitchell Goodman, aged 44, teacher and polemicist and everyone's idea of an American Jewish intellectual.

Fourth was Marcus Ferber, only 23, a dishevelled cherub spouting Camus, and there to stand for the students.

And finally Raskin, 34, who resigned as a White House defence and disarmament specialist over Vietnam.

The defendants then were a kind of symbolic cross-section. Very soon, the scene in the white-tiled, vaguely lavatorial court house took on the appearance of microcosm, mirroring American society and its deep divisions. Educated against

Dr Benjamin Spock, chief scapegoat in the criminal conspiracy trial in Boston in 1968. *(Keystone)*

ignorant; young against old; the tolerant against the bigots. The groups were oil and water.

Stone-faced US marshals prowled the room, ready to quell unofficial smiles or any other subversive acts which the mainly collegiate spectators might devise. The lawmen stared at the students, hostile and uncomprehending. Less threateningly, but with equal incomprehension, the students stared back.

They were in mini skirts, or kaftans with beads. To a man the marshals wore grey two pieces of artificial fibre, heavy shoes, white nylon shirts. One group favoured hair at least ear-length; the other went for that corn stubble look.

The respective allegiances could have been no clearer had they been wearing the uniforms of opposed armies. The spectators, queuing to support Spock, were almost exclusively under 30; the marshals, judge and, most significantly, jury were middle aged or over, and evidently unenchanted by the arty young.

Spock, however, related to the young and they to him. After all he had, by proxy, weaned and pot-trained them along with two generations of Americans. Perhaps his methods, almost universally adopted by enlightened middle class mothers, have contributed to the present generation of unaggressive anti-militarist college children.

The idea would appeal to the John Birch Society who believe that the Russians tried to subvert all-American toddlers by circulating cut-price gramophone records playing subtly anti-capitalist nursery rhymes.

John Wall, the Government prosecutor, omitted to advance this theory as part of his criminal conspiracy case, but he did try almost everything else. (At one point a witness was summoned to testify that he had seen two defendants *applauding* an anti-Vietnam war speech.)

The arguments were repetitive. Wall claimed that by attending peace rallies, making speeches, and taking part in anti-draft induction protests, they had conspired to violate the Selective Service law, and encouraged others to do so.

The defence lawyers, 16 in all, replied that all the activities had been public, and publicised — the reverse of conspirational. Spock, and what he called 'the other peace people', had simply exercised fundamental American liberties of free speech and assembly as guaranteed under the First Amendment.

This was their line, and they stuck to it, but given the American conspiracy laws they made little progress. Criminal conspiracy is a charge used fairly sparingly but it has been an effective one for dealing with Mafia luminaries and gangster bosses. The prosecution burden of proof is so wide ranging it is almost open-ended.

As long as the court is satisfied that at least two people have made an agreement to further an unlawful end the prosecutor is virtually home. The agreement does not have to be written, or even spoken: it can be implied or even deduced from a certain kind of conduct.

Criminal conspirators do not even necessarily have to know each other. (Before the Boston episode Spock and Ferber, for instance, had never spoken with each other. Coffin and Goodman had met, briefly, twice.) They do, however, have to be aware that the end product is unlawful.

Conspirators are also vicariously liable: that is, once they have joined the club they can be punished for misdemeanours by any other member. Because of past difficulties involved in convicting members of criminal rings organised along big business lines the rules of evidence are also wide open. Hearsay is perfectly acceptable.

Over four weeks, defence counsel struggled to demonstrate the absurdity of the benign Spock, or 'reverend Coffin', in a conspiratorial role. Right at the end of the trial the prosecuting attorney explained, with unexpected candour, what the case was really about.

'In the affairs of families,' said Wall, glancing sidelong at the hairy spectators, 'and also of nations, a situation can arise where permissiveness goes beyond the bounds of reason. Collaboration magnifies the risk to society and increases the quantum of harm.'

He then added, in effect, that the five defendants were only symbols, heads on the spike, to encourage the others. He told the jury a story about police patrols and speeding motorists on a dangerous road — throughout the trial he leant heavily on homespun image and simple parable, apparently to some effect.

'You don't need to catch every motorist in the trap,' said Wall. 'You just have to have enough so that the others know the law is being enforced.'

The lawyers called each other 'brother', according to the convention, but Wall evidently inspired a strict minimum of fraternal affection. His Perry Mason-style interruptions — 'objection, your honour' — came out as parade ground barks. His Boston twang, wrenched from the sinus, drowned the genteel Ivy league tones of the defendants' defendants.

Wall is a self-made man, a former paratroop officer, the epitome of Right-wing rectitude. He chose to present his case on a sustained level of extreme moral outrage and it was highly effective.

In his final speech to the jury he managed to make such mild words as 'writer' and 'intellectual' sound like a catalogue of abuse. He launched a particularly savage attack on Raskin, and referred to him throughout, with heavy irony, as 'The Great Thinker'.

Raskin had drawn the fire on himself under cross-examination by saying the Vietnam war was illegal, and the use of napalm immoral. Wall argued that Raskin had failed to grasp that the United States was probably in Vietnam 'for the same good reason' as they had been in Korea.

He made some play with the fact that Raskin had been medically unfit for military service and apparently did not understand that napalm and flame throwers, as used in the second world war and Korea, are both in the same family.

'If you napalm a village with children it's horrible but what difference does it make if you burn them from a tank?' Wall asked the jury. Then he concluded that none of the defendants, including Coffin — 'This great man who knows what's legal and illegal' — was capable of thought at all.

They *feel*, it's all belly feel, or gut reaction. Are we going to have our society tied to the strings of Coffin's conscience?...What about the collective conscience as passed by Congress?

It was crude but at least the bemused, patently bored jury were in no danger of misunderstanding the message. Wall had selected the most amenable subjects. When the trial began the Government objected to two women jurors, presumably to counteract any vestigial Spock worship. Wall also refused anyone under 35, or with the faintest trace of unconventionality.

Eventually 12 satisfactory white male Bostonians took the stand, six blinking behind heavy glasses. They were solid citizens from the upper reaches of the working class or just above. Only one had been to college: only three had graduated from high school.

During the trial they were sequestered in a Boston hotel, and were forbidden contact with their families. Newspapers and television were also banned in case the terse flashes on the trial, slipped in occasionally between the avalanche of commercials, might bias their judgment.

So after four weeks and 15 volumes of evidence they wanted their message simple. Wall obliged. Judge Francis W. H. Ford also eschewed ambiguity. He told them the charge was 'very grave'. And he announced, as he had at the beginning, that the original Spock defence had been excluded and was irrelevant. (The defence had sought to claim burning C draft cards was 'symbolic speech', and so constitutionally guaranteed. They had also tried to plead the Vietnam conflict was unconstitutional because Congress had not declared war, because it was contrary to the UN charter, and also in violation of the Geneva Convention.)

District Judge Ford is 85; he attended Harvard Law School with Franklin D. Roosevelt. He is tiny, irascible, and deaf. And when he leans forward in his black robes to croak an order at a witness to speak louder he can be very menacing.

Spock and his fellow defendants did not expect much sympathy from this Dickensian figure. They were right. Ford opened his summing up by telling the comatose jury: 'You must apply the law as that I lay down.' He then warned them against acquitting a defendant 'merely because he is a person of good character'.

From there it should have been all over but to everyone's astonishment after the jury had shuffled out it took them more than seven hours, and two meal breaks, to come back.

Their verdict, in keeping with what had gone before, turned out rather eccentric. As expected they had convicted Spock, plus three of the others. Perversely Raskin was cleared. Perhaps attorney Wall's attack on him as 'The Great Thinker' had been so vicious that it rebounded.

The unlucky four can now do nothing except hope for a successful appeal on a legal technicality. At least 4,000 other teachers, clerics and youth leaders who have been advising draft-age boys to turn in their cards and refuse to fight are wondering how far the Government is prepared to go to limit dissent. Autumn could bring, in the words of dissenting poet Robert Lowell, 'a new reign of piety and iron'.

The Corner-Journal and Times,
Louisville, KY, 16th June 1968

Robert Kennedy

The big Boeing carrying the assassinated body of Robert Kennedy to New York was late (like every other Kennedy aircraft with which I ever had dealings). Accordingly, it was almost dark, but under the ubiquitous TV arclights the coffin was brightly illuminated as it was let down from the plane on an enormous lift platform, normally employed, so I learned, to load cocktail olives, finger lickin' good plastic chicken and other obligatory ingredients of trans-continental airborne cuisine. For the occasion this gastronomic platform had been draped purple, and lined up in front of it the mourning Kennedy women — God help them — wore Greek Chorus black. They looked as always, dignified and somehow highly drilled. In mourning, as in so many other roles, training had bestowed on them the status of professionals. Their back chiffon hair scarves blew in the slight wind in unison.

The reporters who like me had flown in from Los Angeles on an earlier plane had been brought to the right runway on the other side of the airport in a Kennedy campaign coach. We had been herded into a cross between cattle pen and observation platform by the usual vile-tempered police and now the male Kennedy mourners lifted the coffin with the same ventriloquistic precision the women had shown, it struck me that no one was jostling. This was odd as I was right in the front of the pen in the best observation position. The explanation was bizarre. A cluster of TV crews has set up a line of little monitor screens at the back for their own technical purposes, and these were now surrounded by perhaps three-quarters of the reporters present. They had turned their backs on the tarmac, as if making some collective protest, and were simultaneously peering at the little monitor screens and scribbling notes.

There, a few yards away, was the real thing, yet their impulse was to watch it, and in due course report it, predigested by television. It was hard to think of a more appropriate manner to report the return of what a famous commentator a few yards away was calling 'Bobby's simple casket' to what in due course he also called 'Bobby's native soil'.

It was more or less obligatory at this period for people to remark that Sirhan's two bullets were all the more tragic because Bobby had been killed 'just when he had found himself'. What, one always wondered in silence, had there been to find, except the money, and the ambition, and the self-deforming expertise with the media — what my colleagues writing a book about the election had unkindly christened 'The Bullshit Machine'. This 'finding himself' view was usually reinforced by references to Bobby's emotional relationship with Cesar Chavez and his chicanos, the million or so Mexican Americans working in California's giant and corrupt 'argrobusiness'. It was a eulogistic time, after all, a time for compliments, but like every other positive achievement being laid at Bobby's door, right down even to the apparently self-evident 'he was a wonderful family man', one's reaction was always: 'Yes...But.' And the 'But' part of the equation usually had the suggestion of something fraudulent, something that had been distorted by the media, attached to it.

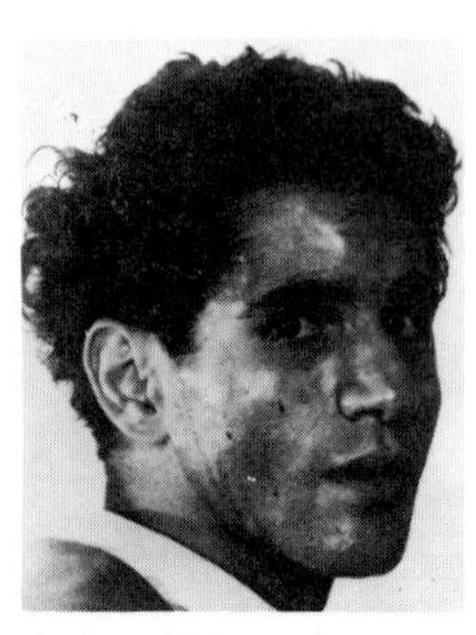

Sirhan Sirhan, the 24-year-old Jordanian who assassinated Robert Kennedy.
(Camera Press)

Yes, out there in California one had seen the 'Stoop' labour force screaming and singing for Bobby. Yes, they had been convinced he was specifically 'their'

candidate, and had accordingly accounted for perhaps half of his slender majority in the last primary, the one that had really mattered, and would equally probably have made him president. But what about the fact that the loser, Eugene McCarthy (whom no one thought was the chicanos' candidate) had actually started public support for this much abused minority some seventeen years previously, precisely at the period in fact when Bobby had been the most dedicated supporter of that other McCarthy, the obscene Joe. What this deranged and criminal witchhunter had thought about the 'Stoop' labour is unrecorded, but it is easy to imagine what would have happened to the idealistic, left-wing Chavez had he and the Bobby of the period still been operating. Still, after the Bullshit Machine had dealt with the question on the little screens...

Kennedy and television were, by this time, as deeply connected in my mind as I think they had been in his. Television had been born for him and he was one of the handful of people I have known who actually look better on it — even on the roughest American colour reproduction — than in real life. The screen made him look younger, though he looked young anyway, and much more handsome. It ironed out the deep-set quality around the eyes that in life spoilt his good looks. It concealed, or usually anyhow, the arrogance, the impatience, the ignorance. It was his right arm, and like certain famous actors, when one met him 'off stage' there was a distinct impression that part of his personality was absent...

Robert Kennedy speaking at a rally during his election campaign in 1968. *(Camera Press)*

How to live like an old-fashioned millionaire

Gaudy as a cockatoo in a custom-tailored red, yellow and blue uniform designed for hot-air ballooning, Malcolm Forbes settles down on the terrace of his immensely grand chateau in Normandy for an authoritative chat about his speciality — money, and the fine art of spending it in very big quantities.

The American publishing tycoon is a spry 60, and as befits one of Nature's hosts, brimming with *bonhomie*. This is more than can be said for some of his guests. After a mere 24 hours of princely Forbesian hospitality (there were 200 for a seven-course dinner the previous night), some of the beautiful faces look ravaged behind dark glasses.

Among them are 20 of Forbes's close chums, who have flown with the millionaire from New York on one of his regular Concorde block-bookings. After a night's rest in Forbes-reserved suites in the Paris Ritz, they have been whisked down to Normandy for 'Balloon Baptisms', maiden flights in the balloons which involve much popping of champagne corks.

Among these insiders is a French artist called Daniel Martin, whose esoteric speciality is creating scale models of the residences of the hyper-rich. He also produces opulent window-displays for the more rarefied stores, Tiffany's, Hermes and so on, and has proved to be a master of social minutiae. 'The lady in the pyjama suit with gold threads talking to Mrs Drew Pearson is Boul de Breteuil,' he informs me. 'She's a French countess domiciled in Marrakesh.'

Just arrived from California, where he has been conferring with Getty trustees about modelling the repro Pompeian villa in Malibu, Martin is a world authority on multi-millionaires and their mores. He does not think any of his clients except Forbes would have added two courses to a gargantuan repast in case the guests finished too soon on a high summer's night for it to be dark enough to enjoy the firework display.

When it comes to the art of enjoying wealth, says Martin with something approaching awe, Malcolm Forbes is alone in the master class. 'Mr Forbes has a way of doing things which gives me a kind of frog in the throat.'

Like Gatsby, the fabulously rich (and mysterious) Scott Fitzgerald hero he somewhat resembles, Malcolm Forbes, though not generally well known outside the USA, generates impassioned interest and wild rumours in every community where he touches down. In Balleroy, site of his Norman castle and ballooning centre, he has single-handedly made the local economy boom. In Tangier, where the restored governor's palace has been modified at frightful cost to contain a museum of Forbes's toy-soldier collection, his spending habits made Barbara Hutton, the Woolworth's heiress, seem a mistress of economy.

The sight of Forbes's personal DC-9 parked like a whale among minnows on Tangier Airport awaiting its master's next travel whim did much to create the common impression in the Arab world during the early 1970s that Forbes was the richest man on the planet.

He never stayed long enough for anyone to verify this thesis. An insatiable traveller with eight major residences from London to the South Pacific, he is capable of flying half-way round the world for a long weekend, and spending millions on a place he will visit — like Balleroy — for only a few days each year.

Forbes pursues his often dangerous hobbies with the same guiltless zest he brings to money-making. In 1971, out of curiosity, he made his first hot-air balloon flight; 15 months later, aged 52, he set six new world balloon records during a 34-day flight across the US from Oregon to Chesapeake.

Exultantly, he spent $1 million or so planning 'the ultimate balloon trip' — a cluster of 13 balloons, 60-storeys high, were set up to carry Forbes and a co-pilot in an Apollo-style capsule across the USA, the Atlantic 'and on round the world if we though we could make it'. They couldn't: seconds before lift-off, Forbes was almost killed when the high technology faltered. Now his insurance assessors, possibly the only restraining influence in his life, have banned record attempts, and his is restricted to taking pleasure rides and acting as the sport's world patron.

Motor-cycling, an unlikely proletarian hobby, gets the same multi-millionaire gloss. He has broken records on his string of Harley Davidsons and, once the Balleroy balloon meet is over, he will don black leathers and ride to Norway's North-West Cape, the first motor-bike expedition to the North Pole.

There is no Forbes residence there, as it happens, but following up the thought that 'it would be funny to have an Empire on which the sun never sets', a team of aides studies the world's plushest real estate brochures looking for houses 'which conform to our requirements'. Those passing the Forbes test include a 40-acre estate in New Jersey; 250-square miles of lush valley set among the Sangre de Cristo mountains of Colorado and a 20,000-acre ranch his wife Roberta runs in Montana.

Farther afield is Laucala, the Forbes copra and game-fishing island in the Pacific; an exotic residential complex in Tahiti, where Zane Grey, the Western writer, once lived; and an estate in Bali, the name of which escapes its owner until an aide fills him in.

In London, Forbes's money has restored Old Battersea House, a mansion attributed to Wren, after years of neglect. But property-hunting in southern Europe has proved disappointing. 'We've been looking in Greece but you'd be surprised how few really, er, adequate buildings you find there nowadays. Italy we were excited about, but once the kidnapping started my insurance people killed that. I lost enthusiasm too. Some places you figure it's best to let the sun set without you.'

If you ask Forbes where all this spending money comes from or, less directly, the secret of his highly demonstrable success, he answers with a grin and a practised one-liner: 'Sheer industry and ability — you spell those words i–n–h–e–r–i–t–a–n–c–e.'

Much of Malcolm Forbes's rarefied quality derives from never having undergone the common-or-garden human experience of being hard-up, let alone poor. His father, Bertie Forbes, did all that for him, in the course of a rags-to-riches biography which started in the finest 19th-century tradition in the village of New Deer, Aberdeenshire, in the 1880s. Bertie was the sixth child in a family of 10. There were, as he used to say, 'more kids than funds'. Accordingly, he emigrated to make his fortune in the New World.

Forbes Senior became first a reporter and then a financial columnist for the Hearst newspaper group and was so successful at it that when, in 1917 at the age of 37, he launched a business magazine, friends advised him to capitalise on his byline by naming if after himself. Hence *Forbes* — a mildly eccentric, staunchly pro-business fortnightly magazine published in New York and still thriving.

Nowadays *Forbes* has a paid circulation of almost 700,000, which puts it a nose ahead of its major rival, *Fortune*, part of the Time Inc stable. The magazine's strength and influence are out of all proportion to its size, since it has been long established as a kind of millionaire's house journal. In fact, according to James J.

Dunn, the magazine's publisher, one in every 13 *Forbes* readers is actually a millionaire. Collectively, the readership owns about $140 billion worth of US corporation stock.

Since Forbes Inc remains a private company what this means in terms of profits is a matter for speculation. Well-informed estimates suggest that the magazine probably made about £5 million last year. However, one fundamental fact about *Forbes* magazine and the unusual commercial empire of which it is the corner-stone is beyond any dispute — Malcolm Forbes, simultaneously President and Editor-in-Chief, owns it all, lock, stock and barrel. As he remarks: 'Our annual meetings tend to be, er, brief.'

This factor of sole and individual proprietorship makes the Forbes wealth special (a quality Malcolm Forbes is determined to perpetuate — his son, Malcolm Jr, will in due course inherit absolute control, though not the same total ownership his father enjoys). In this context the £5 million annual profit, though a handy enough income, is an irrelevance, and certainly far short of the cost of supporting Forbes and his five children in the style to which they have always been accustomed. It also goes some way to explaining why Malcolm Forbes takes such pleasure in denying that he is the richest man in the USA — 'That's silly, I'm not Rockefeller rich,' he says, and manages to make it sound as if he has been accused of something mildly discreditable.

If you explore the matter more deeply, it becomes clear that Forbes is not pursuing the traditional strategy of the super-rich and underplaying his wealth: just the reverse. To own a bank or blocks of stock in mighty corporations in the manner of David Rockefeller, who is a close friend, would be anathema to Forbes. It would be restrictive and mean in all likelihood that he would end up having less disposable money, not more. 'For many years we have been striving, very successfully, to prevent our business getting inordinately big,' he explains.

It takes some delving to comprehend that when he talks in these terms — 'the inordinately rich' is another favourite phrase — Forbes does not mean that a nice middle-sized fortune ought to be enough to suffice any rational man, and the pursuit of more after a certain stage is therefore aberrant. Forbes's philosophy is more simple — beyond a certain point, he believes, you lose absolute control and find yourself answerable to shareholders, or worse the dreaded Internal Revenue Service, every time you sign a cheque for a DC-9, a new yacht, a palace in Morocco, a fleet of hot-air balloons, a Pacific island or whatever it is you need.

'The bigger you are, the more time you spend figuring out ways to structure your business to reduce discriminatory tax laws. Shareholders would never believe that an expense like *Highlander 4* [the new yacht] is an essential part of the business, an indispensable tool if you want to get on intimate terms with the heads of big corporations and their families.'

His usually genial countenance becomes distinctly sombre as he paints in a canvas of hapless Fords, Hugheses or Gettys stalked by the revenue authorities and other modern predators, to the grave and even beyond.

'When you are Henry Ford or David Rockefeller, coming from a family which has undergone several generations of inheritance taxes, you can only keep large hunks of money intact by means of foundations and special funds. The Federal Government controls them rigorously. The foundations can't even hold substantial equity in the stock of the company they were founded with. Henry Ford's probably the best example — he disagrees with the directors of the Ford Foundation and what they do — but do you think he can do anything about it?'

Forbes has given a lifetime's thought to these matters, analysing them in the pages of his magazine and elsewhere. Although he thinks some of the views held by his father — 'a true Aberdonian, a bit of a puritan who *abhorred* spending money' — retain their validity, he is convinced that the late 20th century imposes a different approach.

'He used to say "Waste not, Want not" and that's true. Only a rock star or someone like that gives $100 tips, and that degrades money, shows you have no respect for it. Until the day he died (in 1954), Dad used to remember something Mother said in spring 1929 — just before the crash. Her household bills were exorbitant, and he complained. She said: "But I love to spend money."

'But I love...' Forbes grins, and repeats the credo with zest. 'Ironic, don't you think, that Mother's philosophy is now reckoned essential to society's economic well-being? Anyway she was right. You can say I take after her.'

Forbes's dedicated application of Mother's philosophy has, contrary to what his father believed, pulled in an infinity of jackpots and under the big-spending regimen, Forbes Inc has prospered mightily. Infinitely more so, in fact, than by ways of a programme of financial puritanism. Thus Forbes, smiling on his way to the bank, has been able to rationalise his most Gatsbyesque extravagances. They have all paid off.

The DC-9, for example, with the motto 'Capitalist Tool' emblazoned on its costly nose. Forbes was able to use this aircraft as a family run-around throughout the 1970s, and just about the time he was thinking that Concorde block-bookings provided an even pleasanter (and more luxurious) method of getting himself and friends across the globe, Westinghouse offered to buy 'Capitalist Tool'.

'For $1 million more than I paid, too. It cost $1 million a year to run, and for a Scotsman, a $1 million profit is instant happiness. "Sold," I said,' recalls Forbes.

This Midas touch is the *leitmotiv* of Forbes's biography. It is a constant from his obsession with the Czarist jeweller Fabergé — which led him to acquire the world's largest private collection of these golden eggs at a time when they were (comparatively speaking) dirt cheap — to the scores of Victorian *genre* paintings (again the world's biggest private collection) which line the walls of Old Battersea House in London.

This excursion into capital gains was, for once, not his own idea, but an apparently demented notion of his son Christopher (nick-named Kippie) in 1969. 'Kippie said that my Monet *Water-Lilies* was third-rate,' recalls Forbes, with a glancingly wounded look. 'He persuaded me to sell it, and let him use the cash to build up a collection of stuff I thought, to be frank, was candy-box. Look at the prices now.'

A yet wilder Forbesian fantasy of creating a game reserve in Colorado on the scale of an African safari park led to the inevitable Forbesian windfall profit — this time thanks to the obscurantist intervention of Colorado's Attorney General, a figure to whom Forbes confesses he probably owes a debt, or at least a commission.

Not that the lawyer's intervention was meant in a kindly spirit. 'We bought all this land and were all set to spend $1 million just on the fencing to keep the animals in. There was a legal battle for years. In the end, he ruled we had to drive the existing game off the reserve and re-stock with our own animals from outside.'

Such a project posed too many problems even for Forbes. 'There was nothing to be done, what could you do? We sold 30 per cent of the holding, and we run a real estate business there now, selling the land in sub-division.' How much did Forbes sell his 30 per cent for? 'It was about, well,' the capitalist's capitalist hesitates, as if some spectral Internal Revenue agent is present. 'Well, $50 million, as a matter of fact.'

The only time that Forbes's personal predilection for big spending cost him something which hurt was in the 1950s when he had his eye on a career in politics and was running for Governor in his local fief of New Jersey. As a Republican, naturally.

'In Camden, New Jersey, which is a ship-building community, my opponent announced that I had a yacht (an ancester of the current craft, *Highlander 4*) under construction in Europe, which was true. This made for an, er, highly unstable reception when I campaigned there. When the votes came in I was nosed out — by a landslide.

'It hurt somewhat then. Since I was seven or so I'd been eyeing classmates to see who might beat me for President. Now I see it was a blessing; I'm too selfish to pay the price of public office. You have to kiss everyone's...don't put it like that, I mean you have to go to clambakes and listen attentively to every idiot who grabs you. It's more fun giving advice than taking it, and if I'd stayed in politics how could I have done the things I've done?'

He would not have been able to travel constantly round his world residences, or rebuild the Morocco Palace to accommodate the world's biggest collection (again) of toy soldiers, or ride a Harley Davidson to Moscow and the North-West Cape of Norway. Nor could he have found time to arrange things so an 80ft high hot-air balloon, its panels painted gold and blue with a design of *fleu-de-lys*, suddenly floats surrealistically across the coppery-grey slates of the Chateau de Balleroy, the gem of French classicism (by Mansart, architect of the Place des Vosges).

He waves this wonder on its way with a gesture like a Papal benediction and sets off to change his ballooning uniform for a blue blazer — there is to be a special balloonists' Mass in the private chapel.

By way of farewell he offers a reflection on his idyllic life. 'The hippies had good ideas about pleasure, but they were all wet in thinking the simple life is desirable,' he concludes.

'When you give children balloons at a circus they're in a dilemma. They want them to fly — but to see them do it they have to lose them. So they cry. If you have the cash you just fly away with them.'

The Sunday Times magazine, March 1980

PLACES

In 'When the Going was Good' Evelyn Waugh describes how in the 1920s and 30s he and his (usually well-heeled) friends would take off for foreign parts feeling 'the world wide open before us', an experience 'as remote today as 'Yorrick's' visit to Paris, when he had to be reminded by the landlord that their countries were at war.' Waugh wrote this at the end of World War Two. The frontiers, except to soldiers, had by then long shut.

Between the wars, Waugh and his contemporaries were thus children of an expansive age unfettered by international boundaries. They had roamed 'this wide world' (more than one-third of which, of course, was coloured red on the atlas) with an impunity they had never thought to question. His generation, he writes loftily 'travelled as a matter of course.' Mine, to its claustrophobic chagrin, emphatically did not.

The nearest that British civilians got to 'abroad' between the years 1939 and the early 1950s was watching lads like Humphrey Bogart and Errol Flynn roaring around photogenic foreign fields, often engaged in winning wars, at the local Odeon, Gaumont or Rex. These years coincided with my childhood in an island probably more insular than it had ever been.

Until America entered the war the island's history seemed destined to end as the fiefdom of some psychotic Nazi gauleiter. We expected the Germans to come: signs told us to remove distributor heads from cars, housewives were solemnly told to keep a sharp knife to hand in the kitchen and, should the order be delivered via the BBC, break bottles in the roadways to incommode German transport. People looked up at the skies expecting parachutes. We were alone, cut off from the continent of Europe, and grateful to be so.

The aftermath of victory did not mean a return to Waugh's golden age when, assuming you had the fare, the world was your play-ground. It was a tight little time, with the British physically amputated from the world outside, as large sections of it rapidly became amputated from us. In 1947 there was the worst winter since 1880: blizzards provoking an energy crisis at home, the exodus from India and Palestine, with Foreign Secretary Ernie Bevin having to sign the documents in a Foreign Office lit by candles because of power-cuts, marking the beginning of the end of Empire abroad. For good measure there was also a foreign exchange crisis and devaluation. By 1948 basic subsistence rations had fallen well belfow the wartime average. In 1949 rationing of clothes were abolished — when Princess Elizabeth had married 18 months earlier she had been allotted 100 clothes coupons for her trousseau, and the bridesmaids 23 each. The Lights of Piccadilly Circus now came on again in London

— yet the meat ration was lower than it had been at any time in a decade indifferently hard on carnivores and herbivores alike. Fruit was always in short supply: bananas, pineapples and oranges were rare or unknown. Bread, flour, eggs, sugar and soap could still be obtained via a stamp on a ration book — they were 'on coupons' as people said.

In such a society travel was a luxury beyond imagination, the ultimate extravagance. Until the 1950s the only civilians who ever glimpsed 'abroad' were the very rich. Life across the Channel, yet alone on the far side of the Atlantic, was poignant with distance, inaccessible beyond dreams. A steamer from Harwich to Eskeberg became an adventure as succulent and indulgent as the first foreign fruit, melons and guavas, starting to make an appearance in shops like Harrods.

Hard though it is to convey in a time when twenty million or so British holiday each year in the sun, for us travel was a mistress to be won by privation and cunning. We saved for a year to spend a fortnight hitch-hiking along continental Europe's narrow and comparatively empty roads. We studied languages in the hope that they would qualify us to find a job somewhere 'over there'. Such employment was hard to find. The Empire no longer required educated functionaries as it was shrinking annually, soon to become a topic for historians.

The American 'Beat Generation' writers, Kerouac above all, were seductively appealing to my 1950s undergraduate generation for reasons not strictly speaking to do with their literary merits. We shared their itchy, foot-loose quality and envied their profligate gift for devouring the vast continent, east to west and back again, with no justification except the intoxication of being on the road. Ours was a static world. It was their sense of incessant movement that captured our imagination.

When in 1960 in Rome I had the extraordinary good fortune to spend a few weeks under the tutelage of A. J. Liebling, the great New Yorker foreign correspondent and sports writer, I was hurt to discover that he held these itinerant literary lions in such scant regard. A fastidious man when it came to words (or food and drink, boxers and jockeys, generals and politicians, cities and countries and editors and so much else) he remarked tersely that they did not understand how American prose — or poetry — should be written. Joe himself had travelled more than any of them in order to cobble together those classically limpid — and broadly comic New Yorker *articles, almost none of which I had then read. My own vocation was no longer in doubt.*

Writing and travelling were my obsessions. Journalism, I suspected, offered a probably unique path to explore them both. For once, thank God, a youthful intuition turned out to be absolutely right.

Goodbye, General Oufkir

When Maurice Schumann, the French Foreign Minister, visits Rabat next week his main concern will be to re-stitch the fabric of Franco-Moroccan relations in the light of one man's death. The deceased in question, General Mohammed Oufkir, had effectively put governmental exchanges between the countries into cold storage for nearly five years.

This has been a nuisance because of France's traditional north African interests in the Maghreb — oil and minerals. There are also the 80,000 French citizens still living in Morocco and owning half a million acres under cultivation, not to mention the million or so Moroccans living in metropolitan France and owning next to nothing at all.

In every sense Schumann's visit promises to be a diplomatic collectors item. Moroccan royal hospitality has a unique surreal aspect. When Prince Philip visited Rabat, for example, and intimated he would like to play polo, Moulay Abdullah, King Hassan's brother, detailed a battalion of troops equipped with plastic buckets to quarter the terrain on all fours lest any undisciplined dandelion should impede the royal mallet.

Under the approving eyes of the Rabat jet-set, led in those days by Oufkir wearing gun and dark glasses, the Duke won many plaudits for his unsentimental way with recalcitrant ponies. But these medieval occasions are not always so uplifting. Last year's royal garden party at Skhirat, for example, reached a climax which might have been scripted by Evelyn Waugh: the attendant soldiery started a fire fight among themselves, catching many proud invitation holders in their diplomatic cross-fire. Skhirat thus established an interesting diplomatic precedent, so a Paris protocol expert told me. On no other occasion in living memory have royal invitees been awarded campaign medals just for showing up at a party (though some, it should be added, were conferred posthumously).

Unhappy recollections of this gruesome junket were invoked as a reason to explain the only too notable absence of the US ambassador from the reception line at Rabat airport when Hassan's damaged Boeing came down after yet another coup attempt on 16 August. There are, of course, other less innocent explanations. Over 400 US personnel work in the so-called 'American enclave' at Kenitra, supervising the airbase near Rabat from which the F-5 fighters that so nearly ended the Moroccan monarchy took off.

Certainly Hassan himself was convinced the CIA were in the know, and his gesture in making chief of the airforce the pilot who safely landed his personal 727 was less extravagant that it seemed. Here, anyway, was one pilot he could trust. Of the fewer than 50 others at Kenitra who were graduates of the USAF school in Houston, Colonel Kouera was responsible for orchestrating the coup under Oufkir, and His Majesty had just observed four more Houston alumni firing at him from close range. Hassan, just now, unusually for him, hates Americans more than French.

It was also no secret that Mohammed Oufkir was the kind of man the Americans felt they could talk turkey with (they have been noticeably disenchanted with Hassan since discovering how enthusiastically the royal family had participated in an impressive fraud involving, as victim, the Pan Am airline).

The death of Oufkir has left an enormous hole in the centre of the government which will become even larger as increasing numbers of those who tried so hard to catch the eye of the country's undisputed strong man are carted off to the prisons he himself administered with such zest. The details of his precise role in the abortive coup are now something of an irrelevance, and most of the information furnished to date has evidently come straight out of the top of the royal head.

The French believe Oufkir turned against the king after 15 years' unconditional loyalty because the lessons of Skhirat had so obviously not been learned and no efforts had been made to comb out even the grossest corruption endemic to thc regime. This many be; in any case it would be interesting to learn precisely how this devotee of fire-arms succeeded in committing suicide by shooting himself with at least three bullets, one of which entered his neck and shattered the famous dark glasses on its way out.

On the face of it, Hassan's relations with France were irretrievably ruined by Oufkir's characteristic personal role in the kidnapping, torture and murder of the opposition leader, Mehdi Ben Barka, in Paris. This affair much irritated the French, and not least General de Gaulle, while those of a democratic turn of mind were concerned that a man could be kidnapped in broad daylight on the Boulevard St Germain by French 'parallel police' acting under orders from the head of a foreign security organisation. Theoretically, then, Oufkir's conviction in absentia by a Paris court led to a breach of diplomatic relations: in practice, however, this estrangement was largely a surface one. Oufkir was very much a French colonial product who had learned his tricks in the First Army in Italy and later in Indochina, where he was decorated for extracting his unit from a tricky position after employing a Berber ruse. He showed the white flag to a Vietminh detachment and then machine-gunned them when they came to collect their prisoners. In due course he worked for the French under the Protectorate but after the exile of Hassan's father Mohammed (a downy old bird who protested to the President of the Republic because the French navy refused to deport his harem with him) Oufkir cannily tranferred his loyalties to the Crown Prince. Even then he retained his French 'ties of blood', forged in battle with the paratroops and in murky cells with the inquisitors of the anti-OAS French government button men, the notorious 'Barbouzes'. One of these, an outgoing Corsican named Raymond Sassia, who used to be De Gaulle's head bodyguard and achieved literary distinction by writing the definitive work on snap-shooting from the hip, is now in hospital recovering from a wound acquired when the F-5s or one of them, machine gunned the king's plane.

Although officially, Oufkir's name could not be mentioned in reputable French circles, he had retained his connections with the complex of services which were assiduously built up by Jacques Foccart, De Gaulle's security specialist (who, it may be recalled, was responsible for bugging the Elysée Palace during its brief occupation by interim President Alain Poher after the General's referendum defeat in 1969). Oufkir, it was felt, was a man you could do business with, and it is believed that much of the re-investment in Morocco which began this spring, after the understandable hiatus which followed Skhirat, had been negotiated in Paris by Oufkir himself. He was a very practical man, perhaps the only one in Morocco — which was why the Americans had spotted him as the potential leader of an army take-over that would be ostensibly progressive in the Libyan sense while in practice something very like the Colonels' regime in Greece. Both Americans and French have been working on the assumption that Hassan, despite the 'baraka' or miraculous good luck so much admired in the Mahegreb, is a figure of strictly historical interest.

Schumann, one readily sees, is as reluctant to put his money on a loser as any humbler Frenchman doing his Sunday morning tierce, but the King is all the French have left. Hassan, ably assisted by Oufkir, has long removed any real internal opposition groups and, though he announced last September that he planned talks with the opposition as a prelude to restoring the constitution suspended in 1963, he had been much bothered by the problem of finding an opposition to talk to. Istiglal, the party of Moroccan independence, is hardly a serious runner, being reactionary and monarchist.

However, there is one very clear alternative to the King, a group Oufkir himself made predictions about: 'Today,' as he said after the bloody garden party, 'it is the colonels. But what about the subalterns?' The young officers are the ones who interest the Libyans, so much so that Radio Tripoli greeted Skhirat by beaming in a series of intoxicating programmes congratulating the rebels, prematurely as it turned out, on killing their king, and in the process causing much pain to more sophisticated Arab propagandists.

But Colonel Mohammed Gaddafi, who was appalled at what he saw of royal decadence when he visited Rabat for the Arab summit, has kept his very able radio services pumping out the identical propaganda line. Oufkir's generation were as Frenchified in their ideas as Hussein of Jordan's officers are anglicised. For the young officers, France means nothing, and the puritanism of a new Islam, reborn in blood, inspires them where the extravagances of a French nightclub culture leave them disgusted. (To celebrate the king's return, Moulay Abdullah, his notorious brother, invited a group of regulars from Chez Castel in Paris over for a party. Perhaps they too will get medals.)

According to the Tripoli paper *Al Nahar* Colonel Gaddafi has earmarked the sum of 8m pounds from oil revenues for sparking a Moroccan revolution, mainly among the army cadets. King Hassan, who is certain to ask Schumann for a powerful injection of French 'advisers' to stiffen his much purged but still unreliable armed services, may now be regretting he spurned Oufkir's characteristic plan for quietening the Libyans: this involved acquiring a presidential flight plan from Tripoli and blowing Gaddafi out of the air with the F-5s that were in fact used for a different purpose altogether.

The King's fatalism is famous and much admired in the Magreb, but nowadays he does not exclude planning ahead. He has just purchased a chateau 50 miles north-east of Paris where last week workmen were busy enlarging the women's quarters — and also strengthening the fortifications.

New Statesman, 1st September 1972

Worthing on the veldt

The lawns of Berea Park in Pretoria were as green as fresh mint, smooth as billiard baize. But then they needed to be pretty good to honour 'a milestone in South Africa's history'. Lest any dumb wit had missed the point the same man greeted the games' success by carolling: 'Rejoice, the beloved country.' Heady stuff, particularly as there in the stands, gazing benevolently at all that grass, sat John Vorster no less, accompanied by his wife wearing a hat portentious as a giant mushroom.

At the nearby Pilditch stadium athletes of all colours were straining to cope with Pretoria's high-veldt altitude. No such dramas shattered the canonical calm of Berea Park. Here the name of the games was bowls, and one competitor assured me the place was the Mecca of the sport, finer even than Worthing. Vorster nodded mildly over the woods, a tiger at a tea-party.

Even so it must be admitted the bowls finals were not all that impressive from the multi-racial aspect. During the early rounds the only black face I encountered belonged to the man whose poetic function it was to keep refilling the quivers of lady archers striving on an adjoining lawn. Bowls, the Prime Minister may have noted, has for some reason failed to capture the black imagination. The finals he enjoyed matched an Englishman and a Scot, both as white as their flannels. And the women's singles were between the formidable Mavis Steel, also English, and Mrs Lucy Springett, whose nationality is either Rhodesian or stateless depending on how legalistic you are. Our competitor won to earn a headline accolade 'IT'S MAVIS THE GOLDEN GIRL...'

Pretoria, notorious even within the republic for its white supremacy and provincial obscurantism, has experienced a very strange fortnight. In a normally rigidly segregated community whites have run against blacks, and sometimes been beaten by them. Black athletes have been accepted, if not always precisely welcomed, by security men skulking behind the aspidistras in the Burgers Park Hotel. Usually the only black men admitted there are carrying trays. Efforts were made to remove the 'nie-blanke' and 'non-white' signs. All the accepted Pretorian verities were challenged, and not only racist ones. The track attire of the West German girls was enough to provoke mild cultural shock. As the local *Sunday Times* announced across seven columns on page one: 'PRETORIA BOUNCES INTO BRA-LESS AGE.'

The government's satisfaction at inducing 673 foreign athletes and officials to make the trek to Pretoria was clear enough without post-games headlines like the *Rand Dail Mail*'s 'CASH IN ON GAMES TRIUMPH NOW' or this week's glowing *Times* ad.

Of course the Nationalists were looking for a bargaining position, trying to acquire a nugget of moral capital in the international opinion bank, hoping vainly they would thereby get the Springboks to New Zealand for winter rugby. Alas, Norman Kirk in Wellington concluded it had been no more than a cynical charade.

But in Pretoria, or Main Street, Johannesburg — a thoroughfare, incidentally, as empty as the tomb of Lazarus every day after dusk — the games have caused some excitement. Local commentators, profoundly impressed by the fact that 35,000 racially mixed spectators would watch a white against black soccer game in the sun-excited Johannesburg Rand stadium without even the smallest racial incident ensuring, have written with some lyricism of black palms grasping white in amity. It was hard to meet a white man who did not insist he wanted them to win. An appalling current joke about the unexpected white victory indicates the level of local sentiment, or insensitivity. Every time the white players called 'pass', so the anecdote goes, the athletic black forwards stopped running to search frantically in their shorts for the obligatory book. Off the soccer field spot pass-checks by the police currently run at 1,000 a day, 365,000 a year.

Pretoria is hardly noted for its night-life and some competitors, in search of diversion at any price, joined the holiday crowds who visited the extraordinary Voortrekker memorial. This repository of Afrikaner mythology, squatting on the perimeter of town like a granite jelly-mould, could scarcely be modified for the benefit of tender foreign susceptibilities. The sign explaining that the cenotaph can be visited by non-whites on Tuesday mornings only, for instance, is bolted to the *cathedra* in the entrance, which legend says was used by President Kruger. The symbols are in monumental granite, the superman-size friezes in marble from Forti di Marmi marble which recall the Italian 1930s railway station school of inspirational architecture.

For all the memorial's aesthetic inadequacy its spiritual message is unambiguous. It expresses the pioneers' near-semitic impulse not simply to escape via exodus but also to preserve at any cost the purity of doctrine and blood. Their fearless women, captured for ever in monolithic exaggeration, were — one imagines — the travelling ideologists, preserving the flame of purity as carefully as their white skins, protected beneath lace-trimmed Dutch bonnets against both sun and godless sexuality.

I wonder what Mavis Steel would have made of them. Certainly the weekend of what they are calling 'the glorious games' saw a merging of the historical and the immediate. And in Pretoria, under Vorster's gaze, our golden girl Mavis sinks to one knee in a gesture of invocation, rolling a crafty wood across the bland Berea lawns.

New Statesman, 20th April 1973

Italy: the cost of a miracle

In Paris everyone had said this was a bad time to visit Italy and the headlines in the Turin papers seemed to confirm these Gallic warnings. There was, of course, a crisis — no foreign exchange officially, though apparently on the black market, wherever that was, 'Italian Lira Falls 11 Per Cent'. Neither was there a government, despite efforts by Prime Minister Aldo Moro, understandably called 'the stoop-shouldered one', to cobble together a workable minority. The major obstacle derived from the fact that his chosen Interior Minister, Luigi Gui, had been named in connection with an illegal $1.6m Lockheed payment, and looked like staying out of the cabinet as a means of clearing the honourable Gui name. The papers had found a snappy formula for describing the situation — it was now 'the fifth longest of the 37 government interregnums since the fall of fascism'.

Probably the most attractive story, seized on with great gusto by the local press since it boded ill for their Roman compatriots, was to do with a 100-strong wolf-pack, normally confined within the limits of the Abruzzi national park, and now detected making a communal move towards the Eternal City. A day in the Piedmont capital, trying to change cheques and arrange appointments by telephone, made it clear why the problems of Rome should provide light relief. Turin, one saw, was wrestling with enormous troubles of its own.

There is the absence of coins for a start, which includes telephone tokens. To change a cheque it was necessary to find a small shop in the Piazza Carlo Felice normally catering for numismatists. In the window it was exhibiting government bonds of 1919, face value 250,000 lire, which was no mean sum, for the equivalent of £1.50 each. Put not your faith in Italian governments. As part of my own change there were a series of tiny cheques drawn on the local bank of San Paolo, face value 100 lire or about 7p each. In the course of the day I acquired four single cigarettes, an array of Perugina chocolates, and a card entitling me to a free coffee in a bar opposite the Carignano Palace. Locals have mor or less given up using money for daily transactions — the old tradition of signing *cambiali*, or promissory notes, and settling bills once a month on the magic date of the 27th when salaries are paid, has thus acquired a new popularity. Barter is also back and tipping is now unknown.

Outside the coin shop there was a private policeman wearing pistol and cartridge belt, part of the *lotta alla delinquenza.* According to Giorgio Bocca, a local police reporter, the new police chief, Dr Musomeci, has got even more going against him than the unfortunate accident of being born in Trieste. On paper he has 1,700 men to deal with what 15 years ago was a compact city with a population just topping the half million, and is now a sprawling agglomeration extending some 70 square miles and containing 1.5 million inhabitants. In 1953 there were 4,702 burglaries; in 1974 there were 77,642. According to Bocca, most of the crime increase, like every other ill to which the once elegant capital is heir to, can be attributed to immigrants — 700,000 of them — from the impoverished south.

The Torinesi have an unlovely word for these new residents, whose passion for integration takes many unlikely forms, including fanatical support for Juventus, the Turin football team. They are called *terroni*, which means something like peasants. The lucky ones work at Fiat. Over 50,000 workers drive to and from the Fiat factory daily, producing a traffic wave almost beyond belief.

The film director Pier Paolo Pasolini. *(Press Association)*

Gianni Agnelli, known rather chillingly as *l'avvocato,* flies over this mess in a personal helicopter, roundly cursed by all native-born Torinesi who claim that he should have opened plants in the south earlier, instead of bringing the southerners north. The Agnelli family holding company, IFI, amounts to by far the biggest concentration of industrial power outside government control. It goes far beyond car manufacture, extending to steel and rolling stock; chain-stores; Cinzano vermouth; the daily paper of Turin, *La Stampa;* and such hobbies as the ski resort of Sestrière, and Juventus. Umberto Agnelli, at 42 the younger brother, who is managing director of Fiat, works so closely with the vice-president and strong man of the left-wing junta that controls Piedmont, Luigi Libertini, that there is a local joke about it. The 'Fiat-Lamborghini' sports model is to be renamed the 'Fiat-Libertini'.

Thus the super-capitalist from the now smog-bound 'hill' over the river Po, for 100 years the stronghold of the rich of Turin, forms an alliance with a communist deputy from the *sottoproletariato* of Palermo. A characteristic paradox of modern Italy, embodying the crucial principle of *arrangiarsi* — finding a way either to make the system work, or getting round it.

Very likely Pier Paolo Pasolini, the film-director, would have used his skills to conjure something poetic out of the waste land near Ostia where Pasolini the man was murdered last year. It would have been false though, for art is as alien as life in this lunar rubbish dump a mere 30 minutes from Rome in a fast car. Nothing grows, nothing is cultivated, and the few inhabitants emerge from their shanty-huts to peck out some kind of living by scavenging off the human and industrial detritus which has left the scrubland looking like an elephants' graveyard for machines of various sorts, old cars mainly, which no longer work. There is something irredeemable about the place. Even the breezes from the marsh where the Tiber runs into the sea are polluted with sewage smells and some chemical effluvium which makes the eyes water. It is like a metaphor for the 'ruined Italy' of late industrialism that Pasolini was writing about so hysterically in his last months of life. What a site for a final assignation, even for a connoisseur of the squalid.

And even when the chosen lover was 17-year old Giuseppe Pelosi, called *la rana*, or 'the frog', purchased for a promised £12, a dinner of pasta and boiled chicken, and a ride in a sports car.

The car element is primordial — it is amazing how often the word *macchina* turns up in Pelosi's juvenile court trial for the murder, which he confessed to with an alacrity and indifference which perceptibly disconcerted even the hard-boiled Roman police. It was a car, Pasolini's blue Alfa Romeo, which first intrigued the accused boy on the night of 2 November, when he allowed the film director to drive him away from a pick-up bar for prostitutes of both sexes near the grandiose Stazione Termini. He wanted money to repair his own *macchina,* naturally a more proletarian vehicle, an old Fiat 850. Later, on the waste ground near Ostia, it was Pasolini's own Alfa driven *twice* over his body, which inflicted injuries so terrible — a fractured sternum, a lacerated liver, and much more — that the court had at first been in some doubt whether Pelosi's rather small frame could have been capable of doing so much damage. Again it was for dangerous driving and suspicion of theft — what was a slum boy like *la rana* doing at the wheel of an aristocratic Alfa? — which led the Ostia Polizia Sicurezza to arrest the murderer before even the corpse had been discovered.

Compared with the malignant scene of crime, Pelosi's trial has been conducted in an atmosphere that is always cosy and familial — sometimes it has been positively festive. At different times his father, a shop assistant, his mother, his aunt, and even an aged grannie have turned up in the court which is presided over by Sr Alfredo Moro, the Prime Minister's brother.

It is taking place in a small street with an early mimosa in flower and an unusual name, tucked in behind the 'Ministry of Justice and Grace' — the Via delle Zoccolette, which means 'street of the whores' in the Roman dialect. This same *Romano,* a language both blurred and guttural, is heard all day outside the court, where Pelosi's comrades, including his girl-friend Luana, hang around in the current uniform of (well-pressed) jeans and vaguely alpine overcoats of ersatz green tweed called 'loden', hoping to get in on the action. Reporters are not allowed in court so the street, and the nearby Cafe Garibaldi, are used as a kind of information mart. For a contraband Marlboro cigarette, which she smokes as ferociously as a child sucking liquorice, Luana, aged 16, identifies 'the frog's' various relations. She is trying to sell some of his illiterate letters. In the cafe the reporters from the sensational press, younger brothers of the Via Veneto *paperazzi* of the *Dolce Vita* epoch, are busy extracting nuggets from court officials, a process as painless as pulling nails out of rotten wood.

Nino Marazzita, the lawyer acting for Pasolini's aged mother, insists on the 'injustice' of the situation — as a minor Pelosi risks nothing more serious than a few months in a boys' reformatory, where no doubt he would be a hero, and at the least 'provisional liberty', or probation, when he attains the legal majority of 18.

The boy himself obviously feels he is on a lucky streak — a few months older, and he would have faced a minimum sentence of 22 years. As it is, the trial is a formality, or a farce, and Pelosi drags his high-heels when leaving or entering the court, eager not to miss a scrap of attention. He uses the recesses to work on his quiff and shine his shoes with a special rag he carries. When the cameras flash his expression is a distressing mixture of greed, vanity and a kind of narcissistic bliss.

He is apparently lost in a Roman Dream of celebrity, encouraged by the letters he has had from neo-fascists and others congratulating him on 'the fine job' he did, 'cleaning up' a notorious homosexual and left-winger. On television his father exuded slightly confused pride, called Pasolini 'a dirty brute', and hoped he would have done the same as his son had occasion arisen. He seemed genuinely to believe that the affair reflected credit on his own paternal role.

Why in fact did Pelosi murder his victim, let alone continue to mutilate the body as if trying to reduce it to human garbage? The boy felt no inhibition at describing the assault but faltered (and insisted that his mother leave the court-room) when it came to explaining the sexual exchanges that preceded the murder.

It turned out to be a question of pride as much as anything, a surprising variation on the theme of *machismo*. According to the Pelosi code there was no dispute while he performed the masculine role — but when Pasolini wanted him, as he said, 'to be a woman', then he lost his temper and turned on the film director. To Pelosi it was so perfectly logical that he wondered why they had asked him. There was, after all, the matter of his personal sexual *bella figura* at stake. How else could 'a man' have reacted?

Not by any standards an uplifting Roman tale, indeed one so resolutely unsusceptible to moral lessons that it became necessary to reshuffle the facts in the hope that a more satisfactory version could be made to emerge. There might even be, or so it seemed for a few giddy days, a chance of making Posolini into some kind of leftist martyr, or at the least the victim of a conspiracy.

The journalist Oriana Fallaci caused something of a sensation when she wrote in the magazine *Europeo* that there was more to the affair than met the eye — specifically she wanted to know what the police had done about two other young men who she claimed had been seen on a motorbike near the scene of the crime. Ms Fallaci subsequently found herself summoned to appear before an examining

Mourners file past Pasolini's casket at his funeral in November 1975. The director, Bernardo Bertolucci, stands on the left. *(Keystone)*

magistrate, and under pressure her source was revealed as Kay Withers, a well-established Rome correspondent of several American papers, who had mentioned the case to Ms Fallaci while interviewing her in a totally different context. Thus Ms Withers found herself before the magistrate, explaining that she scarcely remembered the few words that had been exchanged, but adding that the only other person she had mentioned the case to had been Robin Lustig of Reuters. So it came to be Mr Lustig's turn. He had actually broken the story first, simply by phoning the Ostia police on a Sunday morning, when the Italian news agency ANSA does not operate. However, he was in no doubt about the two other boys. He had neither heard nor written anything on the subject.

Hardly then had the Fallaci version been demolished when, lo and behold, the police announced the arrest of two brothers, one 16, the other 14, who had been boasting around the bars of Rome's working-class Trastevere quarter that they had been involved in the crime. The boys were called Borsellino, to add a further filmic touch, and their contribution created such a sensation that the trial of Pelosi was adjourned for a week while their statements were verified. To no avail. It was finally established that the Borsellino brothers, like the envious youngsters waiting in their 'lodens' in the Via delle Zoccolette, were doing no more than making an effort to share in the limelight.

The affair still remains of absorbing interest, its overtones so macroscopic that all kinds of explanations are advanced to explain the crime. It is a consequence of the well-known Italian unemployment phenomenon — not only are a minimum 1.5 million of Italy's work force without jobs, but that work force itself is by far the lowest in the EEC. Thus, even according to official figures, for every two Italians with jobs there is a third 'professionally' unemployed, either drawing a pension or living by some such moonlighting occupation as Pelosi's 'amateur' prostitution. Again, the three-shift school system, which leads to children roaming the streets at odd hours and makes it impossible to tell whether they are playing truant or not, causes 'professional delinquency'. Again, Italy's 'current decadence' is at fault. Or again, it's the fault of the Devil, to cite the opinions of four local analysts applying themselves to the case on one day.

Pasolini himself, interestingly enough, had views on the subject dating from his last year of life. During this period he was not only engaged on his sado-masochistic movie about the Mussolini Salo puppet republic but also produced much polemical journalism about how the economic miracle which trebled the country's GNP between 1950 and 1970 had also 'ruined the soul' of Italy.

He saw this ruin everywhere, and in January 1975 gave an interview to the Agnelli-controlled daily paper, *La Stampa* of Turin, in which he even described the decadence of the *ragazzi di vita*, the expression used for boys like Pelosi and the Borsellino brothers, and also the title of the first novel which established Pasolini on the Italian literary scene when he published it in 1955. His remarks, given the circumstances of his death, are all the more stiking.

'The world of Roman sub-proletariat after the war was degraded and atrocious,' he said. 'But nonetheless it retained both its own standards of morality — a code of living — and its own vitality of language, which is no longer the case, and for which no substitute has been found. Nowadays, the boys from these slums have motor-bikes of their own and watch TV but they scarcely know how to talk, or even sneer.'

There is something pathetic about Pasolini's nostalgia for the hustlers *d'antan*. Devitalised and inarticulate as they may be, the *ragazzi* have certainly had the last word; the trial itself has developed in an odd way where the victim has ended up in the dock, and the self-confessed murderer has turned into a star witness testifying against the corpse.

I wonder whether Pasolini explained his theory of alienation to *la rana*, over the pasta and chicken, or on the fast road to Ostia.

New Statesman, 5th March 1976

The flag comes down

By any reckoning the Solomons experience was one of the strangest in the annals of what was once called the British Empire.

It began in 1893, almost evaporated in 1942 when the Japanese arrived on Guadalcanal, the main island, and most of the British left. What happens next is anybody's guess. Our farewell contribution, apart from the Gloucesters' visit and a leather-bound copy of the constitution, will be £26 million over four years. It may not be a lot, but compared with the budgets Whitehall approved for the Solomons over the years it is an munificent as a goodbye present from the Queen of Sheba.

Fewer than 10 miles from Honiara, the largest and indeed only town in Guadalcanal, the bitumen road shows signs of regressing to dirt. Through the palms you catch glimpses of huts made of bark and bamboo. You get to the village of Kakabona across a tree-trunk bridge fording a stream, the bacterial content of which would probably displease the World Health Organisation. Once there, and *persona grata* with Savino Laugana, the Paramount Chief of some 120 inhabitants, you are in a community more primitive, I would guess, than anything to be found in the heart of Africa.

Like between 6,000 and 8,000 other people on Guadalcanal, Savino is an adherent of a strange cult dreamt up – quite literally — by a man called John Moro in 1957.

The Kakabona men are naked except for a kind of genital jockstrap of bark, and their women wear spinifex grass-skirts which are nothing like those bought by American tourists in Hawaii. Baby pigs run around like puppies — they are holy animals required for sacrificial purposes — and without them, the Moro cultists believe, there is no way of eliciting the *mana*, or power, which dead ancestors transmit to aid the growth of vegetables and to preserve health.

Since these pet pigs attract a wealth of virulent insect life from the bush, a visit to Kakabona has its hazards. The day before we went there the ancestral *mana* had failed to protect the elder sister of one of the betel-chewing Kakabona girls being shipped out to Honiara suffering from one of the three types of malaria which were almost eradicated from the Solomons, but are now making a come-back.

Moro transmits messages to his followers after going into a trance with a Bible on his chest. Most of them are ostensibly Roman Catholics. However, they have grafted a kind of pagan Genesis on to the Biblical version the priests taught them. One of Savino's followers, a 30-year-old clerk in a Government office called Seraphin Pero, explained the secrets of the 'Vale Malenggo Tuali', literally the 'House of Something Before', where the community keeps its treasure.

A 'duty' of warriors guard a box containing money, both of the local shell variety used for buying brides, and the more conventional Australia dollars. There is also a piece of burned wood shaped like a banana. They believe it is a fruit given by their first ancestor, a half-bird, half-human deity called Ironggali, to the woman called Lauili he created, originally in the form of a dog.

The women's movement has not reached the Solomons, but the current British form of matriarchal monarchy has made a deep impression. Seraphin Pero explained that the Queen is 'Paramount Chief' of one of the three earthly Moro hierarchies, which is to do with growing things. The Chief of the second, concerned with religion, is the Pope. The third hierarchy is concerned with the poor, and no-one knows who heads it, perhaps Ironggali, or perhaps Moro himself.

It is a complicated theology to explain, a cult whose essence is preserving 'the custom ways' or primitive simplicity. If it wasn't for anomalies, such as the pipe tucked into a girl's skirt, the world of Kakabona must much resemble what the Spanish explorer Mendana found when he discovered the island group in 1568.

However, there are two major differences for which, despite the lack of material improvements, these most backward of the islanders have cause to feel at least qualified gratitude to that outmoded concept, the *Pax Britannica*. The first is that they are no longer in danger of being attacked by marauders from a nearby village and ending in a cooking pot. The present day Moro cultists dine on such delicacies as *tsaurodo,* a kind of giant flying-fox, but cannibalism is extinct.

The second contribution is one of language, specifically that weird invention called 'pidgin' which is as much the *lingua franca* of the Pacific as kitchen Swahili used to be of East Africa.

While the Solomon Islanders' material welfare has been much neglected, they have had an army of missionaries of every conceivable persuasion catering to their spiritual needs for more than a century. Those missionaries who could not learn local languages, and there are at least 70 in the Solomons group, settled instead for pidgin. The common notion that the locals are 'childlike' is very likely derived from the fact that most communications with them were conducted in this special kind of baby-talk.

The missionaries succeeded, with some exceptions, in getting the women to cover their breasts, but the vulgar word 'arse' despite the most heroic efforts, is an essential part of pidgin. It means not only 'buttocks' but foundation' or 'source' in the general sense. This I discovered while trying to elucidate the Moro version of Genesis from Seraphin Pero. The pidgin for 'God is the source of all things' turns out to be: *God I-ars bilong olgeda sameting.*

The Solomon Islands have been protected by distance. Ordinary maps fail to give an adequate impression of the Coral Sea. It amounts only to a fairly small chunk of the West Pacific, yet these specks, marked red on the maps since 1893, are set in an expanse of exquisite ocean which, if superimposed on a map of Europe, would extend from Paris to Kiev. The Solomons are like a divided yoke in a vast oceanic egg, six times larger than the North Sea, and easily twice as large as the Mediterranean. Indeed, the yet more remote Gilbert Islands and Tuvalu — formerly the Ellice Islands — are still colonies, though not for long.

When Mendana, who optimistically named the islands after the proverbially plutocratic King Solomon, showed up in 1568 from Peru he found not the gold and pearls of the Inca Legends, but islands whose exquisite, coral-lapped beauty were dangerous as minefields to the European. He positively refused to believe that the atolls which looked so opulent could yield so little, and returning with colonial and proselytising intentions, died, like so many Westerners after him, of fever.

Even the Spanish sailors, with their hard-bitten South American experience, were nauseated when the natives of Saint Ysabel, one of the five main islands in the 900-mile-long group, approached the Mendana flagship in a canoe and pitched aboard 'a prime portion of boy's shoulder with hand and arm still attached'.

Partly because Mendana's maps were faulty, no Europeans revisited the place for 160 years. It was only at the start of the 19th century that whalers, sandalwood traders, and, finally, 'blackbirders', slavers, in all but name, all reappeared in turn.

The *Pax Britannica* came much later. In the Solomons and much of the Pacific the British were the most coy and reluctant of colonists. Most of the island groups, and the Solomons more than any, were too remote from the major 19th-century trade routes to constitute either a threat or a promise. Despite urgings from Australia and New Zealand, petitions from half-crazed missionaries exhorting

These Kakabona girls believe they are descended from a half-bird, half-human deity. *(Kenneth Griffiths)*

London to be mindful of their moral obligations to the savages, and not infrequently supplications from island kings, or 'pig men', Whitehall turned a blind eye. They did not want the responsibility of administering these distant, equivocal specks. They were even less enthusiastic at the prospect of spending cash to civilise them. Trade did not follow the flag here, just the reverse.

There had been nearly 100 years of intense, often distinctly piratical, maritime commerce in such Coral Seas delicacies as sandalwood and tortoiseshell, sharks'-fin and *bêche-de-mer,* a sea-cucumber which the Chinese prize for its reputed aphrodisiac effects, before the British grudgingly proclaimed the Solomons a Protectorate in 1893.

Only three years later did they get around to appointing a Resident Commissioner, a 6ft. 6in. botanist, C. M. Woodford, whose journal describes the local orchids with rare passion. He was less enthusiastic about the Islanders and the European missionaries, who waged incessant sectarian wars with each other while trying to save souls in the interest of their Anglican, Roman catholic, Methodist or Evangelical churches at home in Europe.

There was already a tradition of clerical martyrs and this was the golden age of *Punch* humour about missionaries in cooking pots. In the Solomons it was no joke. In 1871, the saintly Bishop Patteson, a descendant of the poet Coleridge, was clubbed to death on an atoll off the island of Santa Cruz. The murder caused a sensation in England for Patteson had been the Missionary Chaplain to Bishop

George Augustus Selwyn, most muscular and celebrated of all Victorian muscular Christians.

In 1874 Selwyn himself became a Solomons martyr, killed at Nukapu in the Reef Islands.

Patteson owed his martyrdom to unhappy coincidence — only a few days before he visited the atoll an Australian brigantine, the *Emma Bell,* had kidnapped five young men for tranportation to the Queensland plantations. The Islanders killed the bishop either in revenge, or because they thought he, too, was in the labour trade. Their error was understandable, since most white sailors in these seas were 'blackbirders', in search of what was called 'Kanaka labour'. Between 1863 and 1904, more than 60,000 Islanders were shipped off to the cotton and sugar plantations of Queensland. They went either forcibly, or in return for a gift of trade goods, the most prized being knife-blades which were much superior to the local stone-edged tools, fabrics, tobacco and poor quality alcohol.

The trade goods were given to either the labourers' relations or whoever arranged the deal, so what at some times was no less than slavery, extending almost into our century, stimulated an ancillary slave industry in the Islands themselves. Local chiefs would kidnap labour from neighbouring tribes, or sometimes hand over those among his own people who had displeased him or who were thought expendable in return for axe-blades or rum.

Thus the Islands were an administrator's nightmare, but a happy hunting ground for anthropologists. Central Melanesia attracted such pioneers as Rivers, Haddon, Seligman, Malinowski, Bateson, Mead and Hogbin. At times there must have been almost as many academics conducting field studies as there were Government officers.

A non-academic observer, J. S. Phillips, visited the Islands just before the Second World War and found the slump had reached there too: 'There are about 95,000 natives and perhaps three dozen Government officers. Nearly all these latter — say 30 — live with their families on Tulagi, a small island with a club, golf links and tennis courts, miles away from the wild, jungle-covered islands, where live the bulk of the native population.'

The soft governmental life was too good to last.

For the first, and possibly last time in its history, the much larger neighbouring island of Guadalcanal soon acquired international fame as the site of the decisive battle in the Pacific War.

After Pearl Harbour, when it became clear that the Islands were — for once — strategically placed on an important if uncomfortable route, the Japanese advance on Fiji, Australia and New Zealand, the British lashed together a Defence Force.

It consisted of three officers, two NCOs, and 112 Other Ranks. In the event most of the Europeans were evacuated in undignified haste, the first occasion when most of the Islanders had seen their white masters panic.

However, they remained astonishingly loyal to the flag and showed no disposition either to work for the Japanese or adopt the sun-worshipping religion the invaders tried to promote. This is perhaps surprising since the cult of the ancestor, venerated at so-called 'Kamisa' shrines containing an ancestral jawbone, sounds to the uninitiated much closer to traditional Solomon practice than, say, Seventh Day Adventism, a Christian import which has flourished, despite a schism between Sabbatarians who do not believe in the Advent, and Adventists who have no objection to having a Sunday Sabbath.

The Japanese also promised the Islanders membership in their Greater South-East Asian Co-Prosperity Sphere, but within months of their arrival the Americans launched one of the war's major campaigns. On August 7, 1942, the Americans landed 10,000 men, mainly from the 5th Marines, on Guadalcanal, and by the end of the campaign the Allied forces totalled more than 50,000.

The Japanese losses were around 25,000 and the Americans lost under 2,000, many of them in the appalling terrain of 'Bloody Ridge', which borders the airport, which the battle was largely about.

The Islands acquired a war hero, Sergeant Major Jacob Vouza, who won the George Medal, the American Silver Star, and the MBE for refusing to give information despite bayonet wounds in the chest and throat as a means to persuade him. A Solomon Islander was credited with saving John F. Kennedy after his celebrated PT 109 was sunk. Guadalcanal and Tulagi acquired great benefits after the war simply from what the Americans left behind — an airstrip, roads, and a local hospital, which is still known as 'Number Nine', the Marines nickname. For years after the war 'scrap metal' figured as an important export item in the Islands' budget. It is still dangerous to walk in the bush on the site of 'Bloody Ridge' where tens of thousands of rounds were exchanged.

Most of the 'cargo-cults', including Moro's, contained references to the return of the Americans bearing gifts. Apart from occasional crew-cutted parties of Marine veterans visiting the battlefields, these mythical saviours, and indeed tourists of any variety, have so far stayed away.

But independence, after more than three years of discussion, has finally arrived. Its advance guard appeared last February in the person of Eric Hefford, a retired Colonel formerly of the Royal Lincolnshire Regiment, whose unusual speciality over the past 18 years has been travelling the globe orchestrating the farewell ceremonies and independence parties of former Imperial possessions.

The Chinese dominate the retail trade in the Solomons, as elsewhere in the Pacific. Almost all of them are staying on. *(Kenneth Griffiths)*

He began with Nigeria in 1960, since when he has seen it all. In Sierra Leone independence took place after a state of emergency had been declared and the opposition locked up. In Mauritius fighting broke out between Creoles and Asians two weeks before the big day and Princess Alexandra, who was supposed to preside, had her visit called off 48 hours before the deadline. In Malta Hefford had riots.

The Colonel discusses his role as Colonial undertaker with a sort of illuminated pride and in the tones of Bertie Wooster on a manic streak. Despite the little local difficulties he has already encountered he told me with conviction that the Solomons, despite an apparent atmosphere of calm, was nonetheless his most difficult *accouchement* so far.

'Do you realise,' he said, 'that you can't buy a pair of men's shoes here? I mean proper shoes of course, not those flip-flop things. As soon as I discovered that I knew we'd have problems.'

Initially, they were mainly to do with Prince Charles. 'Of course, they wanted him. Heir to the throne, out of the Queen's womb, the whole shooting match. I told them straight: 'There's nothing to be done, it's your own fault for changing the dates all the time if it's anyone's.' The Family (he speaks the words with obvious capitals) are booked up nine months ahead, the Queen, Prince Philip and Prince Charles even more. Not that the Queen *ever* comes herself, as I tried to explain. Not that they would listen. The Queen just gets on the blower and says: "Look here, I want you to go and represent me please in the Solomons, or whatever it is." '

However, this tricky matter was sorted out after a visit from Simon Bland, Private Secretary to the Duke of Gloucester. As Hefford says: 'The Secretary always comes in advance so we can go over the route beforehand, decide here's a good spot for a little wee-wee, all the detailed staff work people never think of. Not that they ever think of anything. Diplomatic recognition, letters of credentials, for example. I mean half the chaps you deal with think the Geneva Convention's to do with duty-free booze.'

Gloucester is, strictly speaking, a Royal Duke before he is a prince — 'he was born a Prince, and elevated to Duke,' Hefford explains. To make up for the Charles disappointment the Colonel ensured 'the word "Prince" is on every scrap of printed material. I expect the French or the Japanese will spot it. As you probably know, they're absolute devils for protocol. Anyway, Gloucester's eighth in line.'

The Colonel takes over everything, down to matters like importing ball-pens, balloons for the schoolchildren, and special food for important guests. He regards himself, with justification, 'as a bit of a showman, as well as just a protocol chappie'.

His reputation in this admittedly fairly limited field is such that the Dutch invited him to take over for the independence of Surinam, an occasion he recalls with pleasure. 'We had these 60,000 Indian chaps juggling with lighted flambeaux, quite beautiful. Not that it would do here, of course.

'But I've got fireworks, had to import them from Australia instead of using Brocks, the old English people. There's a reason for fireworks. A lot of people are frightfully volatile. Suddenly there's a whoosh-bang, bang, bang, and they go 'aaahhh'. I warn them in advance, don't run away, it's not going to hurt. But you can rely on fireworks to calm people down at the end of a big day.'

You can also rely on Colonel Hefford to handle every detail. He has 'trained up' a bevy of protocol officers, chosen from 130 sixth-formers, all of whom he interviewed personally.

In some places he makes a special broadcast for the schoolchildren. 'I tell 'em what independence means. I say you have a new flag and a new national anthem; apart from that there's no difference at all. Britain's always there to help if you need it, but now you have your own Government to help you. Mum's got to clean the house, Daddy's got to go to work, and you've got to go to school. I say all that because, you know, some people think the sky's going to fall on them.'

Although he won't be broadcasting in Honiara (apart from any other considerations his pidgin isn't up to it) the Colonel has a shrewd psychological point. In the days before the Big Day it was easy to detect a certain unease in the air, and not only among the last of the 'Expats' as they refer to themselves, those members of Honiara's two clubs who will be remaining.

The Guadalcanal Club, 'G Club' for short, and the Pointe Saint Cruz Yacht Club have much in common, including fairy lights whose trivial illuminations fight a losing battle against the enormous and pulsating tropical night sky. The members often have faces as florid as the ever-present hibiscus, and wear the stunned glowering look serious drinkers acquire in territory close to the Equator. Such tensions as exist come from the Yacht Club, a shade less family-minded than its rival 1,000 yards higher up the coral beach, which boasts tennis courts and a big pool. There are a lot of 'commercial' Australian members, mainly from Queensland, in the Yacht Club, and their wives make bitter jokes: 'Don't tell me fishing's a hobby,' they say. 'It's more a disease.'

The Queensland males drink in bunches, 'shout' their rounds in turn, Australian-style, and their idea of a witty jape is to blow up a condom like a balloon.

The Yacht Club's special Queensland atmosphere was a contributing factor to the only incident which marked the run-up to independence. After a quarrel about serving drinks the leader of the parliamentary opposition, Bartholomew Ulufa'alu, and, such is the kinship system in the Solomons, Francis Saemala, who is Special Secretary to Peter Kenilorea, who will be the Solomons' first Prime Minister, were sentenced to two months' jail for 'disorderly behaviour'.

They have both appealed and the Opposition leader made a sporting — but frustrated — attempt to solve his problem by proposing a general amnesty in the final, pre-independence session of Parliament.

It is characteristic of the Solomons both that political opponents should be drinking chums — in pidgin they are called 'wantoks', people who talk as one — and also that the official Government paper should have run the embarrassing story on page one. Francis Mauli, the Chief of Information, and a former priest, is probably the only man holding such a job in the world who phones visiting journalists to find out whether they have heard the Opposition side of a particular question.

'I tell the Chief Minister (Prime Minister after Independence) that he pays me to make sure proper criticism of the Government appears periodically, Mauli says mildly.

Sir Colin Allen, pre-Independence Governor and thereafter as he says, 'One of the last of the few,' remarked that the missionary influence had led to: 'A rather dull kind of society, but an amazing tradition of probity in public life. There's no Gallic spice, but there's no Gallic corruption either.'

Peter Kenilorea, at 36 the first Prime Minister, told me that whether or not the appeal goes against his secretary, he won't be sacking him. 'He's good at his job and his conduct hasn't outraged public morals,' commented Kenilorea, uncannily like a senior Foreign Office man in the days before Burgess and Maclean.

A non-smoker and non-drinker, the Prime Minister's major concern is to prevent his new country being exploited by the queue of outsiders who are waiting to fill the vacuum. He has seen the effects of indiscriminate tourism on Fiji, and of unbridled industrialism in the Bougainville part of the neighbouring Papua — New Guinea territory. The problem is particularly acute as the 200-mile fishing limit has turned the Solomons into a magnet for the Japanese tuna-fishing industry, who have recently signed a contract with the Solomons which, so Kenilorea claims,

'Blackbirders' once ravaged this village.
(Kenneth Griffiths)

guarantees fair participation for the islanders. In the meantime the most popular brand of canned tuna, Three Sevens, cost more in Honiara than it does in England. Such locals as are employed by Taiyo, the major Japanese company, have jobs as bait-fishermen. The technical work, it is said, has to be done by skilled Japanese, particularly the giant Okinawans with their broad-brimmed hats who periodically descend on the capital.

Opposition sources claim that both the Russians and the Chinese are interested in fishing and mineral rights, but the Government won't say.

The newly-elected Governor-General, Baddeley Devesi, won the plum job so unexpectedly after a tight vote that his wife June had gone off to do the laundry. A former top-class sprinter, who celebrated his election by winning the 'D.S. Corner Handicap Snooker Trophy' at the 'G-Club', he is only 37.

'It's a shame we haven't got a better opposition,' he says. 'The Government isn't 100 per cent united. Religion is more important than politics here and they aren't one political party working together, as you might have in England. They're more a lot of Independents temporarily on the same side.

'The main thing', he says, 'is to start slowly. We've never had any money and our society doesn't permit really wealthy men. We mustn't be too materialistic too soon.'

Prime Minister Kenilorea uses as catch-phrase 'the Pacific way', which has acquired some currency in recent years. 'It's more human than materialism and we like to think being close to nature and the land gives a special gratification, but I don't know how well it will survive against the trend of acquisition.'

The answer will be a matter of the wisdom of the Solomons.

The Sunday Times Magazine, 2nd July 1978

Tasmania

As well as innumerable less printable epithets, convicts transported like caged beasts to Van Diemen's Land called their prison home 'Demon's Island' or, more poetically, 'The Land that God Forgot'. They gave up transporting convicts in 1853, and re-christened the island Tasmania (in search, understandably enough, of a classier image) two years later, but you require no psychic powers to detect echoes of the same forlorn isolation of the island today, transmitted through the generations as stridently as the screams of the giant Pacific gulls wheeling along the coastline.

The penal experience may be history, and indeed, suitably cosmeticised, is even flaunted as a tourist attraction. No past history can be applied to the isolation: it remains Tasmania's endemic disease. For the island itself remains marooned.

Thus, David Cherry, a man of apparently sunny disposition and with an enviable job — he edits the excellent and highly profitable daily *Advocate* published in Burnie on the island's north-west coast — was able to remark with striking bitterness during an interview about his thriving township: 'When it comes to priorities we're at the end of the line and the end of the earth.'

Well, when it comes to geography, certainly. This weird and surprisingly wonderful place, a tiny blob of land left indifferently to its own devices just below latitude 40 south, sits more or less on the floor of the world. The west winds of the 'Roaring Forties' have free play across 200 degrees of longitude without encountering any land-mass between South America's barren toe and Tasmania.

Due north, the awesome continental bulk looming like an elephant over an ant, is Big Brother Australia, its vastness emphasising Tasmanian's Lilliputian proportions, its southernmost shores a mere 150 miles away.

Since Tasmania represents less than 1 per cent of Australia's total land area — you could fit it into New South Wales 12 times — it's not surprising that the island, Australia's sixth state, is prone to feel that 'The Mainlanders' hardly treat Tasmania with due respect, let alone deference.

The apparent geographical propinquity is also in some ways misleading. In the first place the Bass Straits separating mainland and island are notoriously tempestuous, as Edward Heath, like other veterans of the 'exceptionally problematic' Sydney–Hobart yacht race, will testify with conviction. Except for the jet-travelling classes, this closeness does not imply accessibility.

'Those Mainland bastards would watch us bleed to death and never stop whistling *Waltzing Matilda*,' commented Phil Manning, a guitarist, talking in Point Sorell, which is on the north coast and about as close to continental Australia as a Tasmanian can get while remaining on terra firma.

He went on to tell a story that recurred many times in interviews around the island. There have been several occasions when cartographers of mighty Australia with its awesome land mass have actually left Tasmania off their maps. Altogether.

When told about this, I always invited the informant to explain why — or speculate how — such a deed could have been perpetrated. The pithiest reply was from a postman who lives in the idyllic community of Osterley which, sited between the rivers Dee and Ouse in the Victoria Valley, is pretty well in the exact middle of the island, and must surely rank as one of the most beautiful natural environments left on the globe.

'For reasons of bloody symmetry, that's why,' he said, and continued on his outraged way.

Winter (our summer) in Tasmania can be very chilly and, above all, very wet. Even this may be perceived as yet another example of continental Australian discrimination. During a spell of dirty weather while I was there, the radio announcers were saying, with an element of insular long-sufferingness: 'Climatic conditions tomorrow, I'm sorry to tell you, will again be generally dominated by the high pressure area over Canberra...'

In fact, the Tasmanians owe their fresh, changeable and distinctly familiar winter weather to visitations from the Roaring Forties — the prevailing wet westerly winds blowing in off the Indian Ocean. The summer is another more conventionally Australian story, with weeks of temperatures in the high 80s Farenheit that in an unusually dry year — 1967 is still remembered with horror — can cause bush-fire epidemics. But in the winter months the Forties roar faithfully enough, even with their effect somewhat mitigated on the east coast by the mountainous nature of the land, the great escarpments of the largely uninhabited south west and the snow-capped Central Highlands, to produce Tasmania's profoundly un-Australian prevailing greenery.

There are places where, especially seen from the air, it is a vibrant tropical green, the jungle foliage reminiscent of Malaysia or Central Vietnam. But more commonly the lush pastures and densely-wooded hill slopes, the rich pastoral valleys like the Derwent with its astonishing oast houses, looking for all the world as if they've been restored at ruinous cost by some successful City gent proud of his little place in Kent, suggest comparisons much nearer home.

Locals who either started off in 'the old country' or have been to the UK, often in search of family roots since genealogy is a common Tasmanian interest nowadays, offered comparisons with the Yorkshire Dales, various parts of Scotland (including the Orkneys) and even, with reference to the rolling downland of the North-east, Sussex-by-the-Sea. Given the agricultural cornucopia of the fertile lowlands which can produce Golden Delicious, a staple for many years after a trial shipment from Britain in 1884, as well as oats, barley, wheat and vegetable crops in rotation, the patchwork-quilted fields are purely British.

So purely indeed, that there is a suggestion of imposture, just as the exquisite village of Richmond, once the third largest community on the island, and conveniently reachable from Tunbridge with a minor detour at Melton Mowbray, leaves you wondering whether it wasn't constructed at Pinewood some time in the 1940s to portray an idealised Engish country setting for a film adaptation of Dorothy L. Sayers, or maybe Angela Thirkell. There is a Georgian country house, so perfect that the National Trust must surely have its logo somewhere. There is the more modest Fernville, which in the 1950s was a school called 'Harrow-on-the-Hill Academy', and is conveniently placed for evensong at St Luke's Anglican Church. All in all it is scarcely surprising that well over half the 55,000 resident Tasmanians born outside the island originated in the UK.

Among them is David O'Connor, a 38-year-old who saw the light in London's Parsons Green and decided in 1966 that 'the most romantic thing anyone ever thought of was hitch-hiking round the world'. He set out, armed with a teaching diploma and a rucksack, and after some tribulations arrived on the Australian continent. By this time his capital amounted to £2 and his worldly goods consisted of a guitar and a pair of Afghan slippers, which the customs men took apart in search of drugs. Despite this not unusual experience of a 'Pom' being given a hard time, he survived some years' teaching around Australia, and has now come to rest in two rooms costing the 'unusually low' rent of £11 a week in Battery Point, Hobart. This promontory is full of mid-Victorian terraced houses and, despite the belligerent name, was used for spotting welcome merchantmen arriving at the Derwent River entrance, and not for blasting them out of the water.

O'Connor decided that his personal caravan was going to stop in Tasmania nearly four years ago, when he arrived at a supermarket check-out and found he had left his wallet at home. 'There was this great pile of goods, so I said to the girl: 'I'll have to leave it here and go and get my money." She said: "No, that's all right, it's all packed up now, come back and pay me later." In a *huge* supermarket — now that's not supermarket behaviour anywhere else in the world. It's also very nice that you can leave your car unlocked overnight, with the key in it if you like, and be sure it's going to be in the same place next morning.'

He found more signs of a civilised kind of living — 'the obvious fact that Tasmanians are surprisingly open people' — during the three years he led what could be called a modified form of drop-out life in and around Hobart. Two days a week he taught 'Educational Drama' classes to adolescents in a district high school. His pupils, he observed, have none of the punk nihilism endemic in the same age group he had taught in New South Wales on the mainland. 'They don't have Big City hardness and sharpness. They're not automatically suspicious.'

To eke out his meagre part-time wages, O'Connor took up busking, in a funny hat and a charcoal moustache, along The Mall, a central pedestrian arcade. Here, since the police arrested and fined him, he thought he might have discovered the point where tolerance broke. It turned out rather differently. Running on a fairly simplistic platform, even by contemporary political standards — he went round the city with a placard, singing 'Why can't we sing in The Mall?' — this refugee from Parsons Green, and innumerable caravan stops since, was elected to the dignity of Alderman O'Connor for a four-year term.

Now, to his mild bemusement, an aldermanic limousine delivers mail to his (not very much) glorified bed-sit, and he can initiate campaigns which might make this civilised city more civilised yet.

One question exercising the rookie alderman has a resonance transcending the parish pump: it involved the destruction of a myth which, because of the successful film *The Last Tasmanian,* has acquired credence far beyond the confines of the island itself. Thanks to the film, many people know how Truganini, a pipe-smoking aborigine whose name meant 'seaweed', acquired melancholy celebrity by her death in 1976, aged 73.

When she died, so it is widely accepted, her people, well and truly finished by 73 years of abuse from the penal system, died with her. They had been snuffed out like a candle. This cheery, ale-bibbing old lady's lifespace had thus exactly matched the period elapsing since the Tasmanian aborigines, who had inhabited the island for 20,000 years at the least, and possibly much longer, had greeted the first white settlers with manifestations of joy. Some experts maintain the aborigines were ecstatic because the red coats of the soldiers were for them something in the nature of a Messianic second coming — certainly red was a colour of sacred significance for them. They used ochre to paint themselves for religious ceremonials, and also possibly for war, though they appear to have been a notably pacific society. There is evidence to suggest they 'acted out' wars, rather then fought them. In any case their ochre paintings of animals, such as their staples, such as their sacred emu and mutton-bird, as well as rock-carvings of circular symbols resembling mandalas, can be seen at Tiagarra, the site of what obviously was a considerable aboriginal settlement on Mersey Bluff, near Devonport on the north coast.

Truganini's people may have believed that the redcoats were the spirits of their ancestors on first sighting. But nothing in their experience had prepared them to adapt to a government which delivered three million lashes to the backs of their own people in Van Diemen's Land and New South Wales, or under which one man, Alexander Green, a former circus clown transported for life for stealing a piece of cloth from a haberdasher in Shrewsbury, acquired his freedom by becoming official hangman and, with the title of 'Government Finisher', executed 490 during his term of office.

The full story, however, is more complex than *The Last Tasmanian* showed. As Michael Mansell, who runs the Aboriginal Information Centre from premises of appropriate obscurity on the edge of Hobart Docks, puts it: 'The film was an example of white man's propaganda, white *liberals'* propaganda, you can say.'

Mansell himself, in fact, is one of a community of 4,000 aborigines of mixed blood, descendants of Truganini's people and their European persecutors. In what in all likelihood is the most discreditable episode in our entire 19th-century colonial history, the settlers with social aspirations, often inhabiting those gracious country houses and worshipping at those quintessentially English churches, saw no moral objection to hunting blacks on horseback with hounds — since Tasmania, despite its exotic wild-life, unfortunately can boast no foxes. It was also socially acceptable, though evidently more Frenchified, to go out in vast, formal hunting-parties, along the lines of a pheasant shoot on a Normandy estate, and flush out the aborigines like game.

On a lower social level, bushrangers and freed convicts used aborigines for human target practice, and the records abound with accounts of black males being castrated to keep them away from their own women. Visiting seal-fishermen established harems of black women as a matter of course. In the context of a white community which treated the aborigines infinitely worse than their horses or dogs, it could even be argued that sexual slavery was comparatively benign.

In any case, as might be expected, the progeny of innumerable acts of rape and, who knows, even on occasions of love, remain as a testament to history as surely as the mixed races of some Pacific islands are a legacy of the occupying forces of the US and Japan.

'People accept the past quite easily now,' says Alderman O'Connor, 'I think people in Tazzy get satisfaction from breast-beating about what their ancestors did. People are even quite proud nowadays of a convict in the family tree. But I don't think it's right that descendants of aborigines should be discriminated against.'

In practical terms this means being barred from jobs and sometimes — an experience Michael Mansell says is commonplace — being turned away from local restaurants, pubs, and even public places.

Mr Mansell is understandably disappointed by *The Last Tasmanian*. 'They promised they wouldn't use that name, so we co-operated with them when they were filming. They shouldn't have used us as film extras and then gone around the world saying we were extinct,' he told me.

Mr Mansell's catalogue of indignities, including, inevitably, police harassment, were perfectly familiar, commonplace even. There was not time for me to verify them *in situ* but there is no doubt that they should be investigated. David O'Connor, the tyro alderman, is himself no stranger to being arrested for reasons that seemed, at any rate to him, discriminatory. With this veteran busker sitting in the city's council chamber there is living evidence that things can be made better if they are embarked on in the right way.

But what of the general moral principle raised by Mr Mansell and his 4,000 aborigines of mixed descent? They are not simply saying they are being discriminated against on racial grounds and for racist reasons, a case I have been listening to in the mouths of minority leaders for the whole of my working life.

Their case goes further than that and is, in my experience at any rate, unique. They are saying not just that their rights are being denied them, but their very right to rights. Their whole human status is at stake because they are treated as invisible men, as ghosts, who have through some inexplicable inadvertence slipped over the rim of the globe.

Incidentally, the question of those who say they are the remaining Tasmanians and demand others should recognise them for what they are, ought to strike a sympathetic chord in white Tasmanians like Mr Cherry of the Burnie *Advocate* who dislike their island being omitted from the atlas because it looks neater that way.

He, or some fellow editor, should unleash his investigative hounds, and point them in the direction of those mixed-blood descendants of the first Tasmanians. These once and future Tasmanians may otherwise find they have suffered a worse fate — and been blue-pencilled off the human map.

Sunday Times, 15th March 1981

FRANCE

The first time I put my schoolboy French to the test of a conversation with a real French person on French soil must have been about the year 1951. A coach-party from school stopped in Fontainebleau and some of us fell into talking with the woman owner of a central 'café-bar' of some pretension — it boasted a juke box, a rarity in those days, and also an oppressive over-abundance of mirrors. This extravagant decor had its part to play in Madame la Patronne's story, not to mention her vision of foreigners.

Instantly establishing from our blazers, caps and poverty that we were English, she announced (enunciating very slowly) that during the war her fine establishment had been occupied no less than three times — by the Germans, the British, and, finally, the Americans.

Which were the ones she like best, one of my comrades inquired? He was probably trying to show his mastery of irregular adverbs. The topic proved close to La Patronne's heart.

To my virgin astonishment she answered without hesitation that she by far preferred the Germans — they had always been 'very correct', and had never so much as cracked one mirror in the especially posh corner labelled 'Salon de Thé.' Then came the Americans, who were still very much around at the local Shafe HQ, soon to become NATO. They were the richest, of course, but also by far the most 'uncontrolled'. They smashed mirrors by the acre — but always paid.

'And the English?' I inquired foolishly. They were the least desirable occupying troops of them all, Madame explained with indifferent relish. When it came to mirrors, or windows for that matter, they were almost as 'uncontrolled' as the Americans, whom they often engaged in drunken brawls. But unlike their transatlantic cousins, they were poor as mice. In her experience, the English paid late, or never.

Here in Fountainebleau all my wartime assumptions about goodies and baddies were exploded. Madame was clearly telling the truth as she saw it. She was not remotely 'pro-German' or 'anti-British'. Neither was she trying to be offensive. She saw clearly and judged without neurotic hesitation. If the rest of the world disagreed, so much the worse.

When it came to complex considerations of war and international politics she stuck to one essential criterion: the broken glass factor.

Later one of our party asked Madame if she had some item that wasn't in stock that day — stamps for post-cards for England probably.

'No', she replied, that undecorated French negative, without apology or

explanation or offence, that I was to hear so often over the years. The same 'No' which British and other political leaders were equally accustomed to hearing from General de Gaulle.

The better I learned their language, the more vulnerable I became to the reflexive verbal brutality, often impartial and even impersonal in tone, which I learned to relish over the years as peculiar to Paris and nowhere else on the globe. The treatment is dispensed to strangers and lovers with identical Gallic aplomb, leaving the young and tender devastated.

Not many years after the Fontainebleau incident in a moment of passion I asked a French girl of 19 or so if she loved me as much as I did her.

'No', she answered, and proceeded to inform me that her true devotion was reserved for a man some twenty years older than her, a figure I had once met but hardly noticed. Thierry's glasses, his wife, his three children all, so I thought, disqualified him as a rival. Not so. Thierry, I now learnt, owned an apartment block, a small yacht, a Ferrari, and a one-third share in a distinguished provincial French football club.

'Would she ever love me as much as Thierry?'

'No.'

And that was that. Yet I stayed hooked on the French, even if they were as narcissistic as cats and seldom showed any inclination to repay the compliment of my devotion. Because they so epitomised foreignness, while remaining so misleadingly accessible in terms of geography, I could not but be drawn to their country. Inevitably, I ended up living in Paris.

In various disguises I have encountered Madame la Patronne many times in France and its former colonies in the years since then. She has almost never failed to surprise and shock me and oblige me to see the world differently, probably about as differently as it can be seen, because France and England are about as different as two countries can be.

The fact that General de Gaulle's great 'No' was reversed after his death has changed things surprisingly little. The French have not become more like the British or Americans, or vice-versa, though they have acquired more in common, like fast-food restaurants, package holidays or a car-oriented economy. For a foreign correspondent of any nationality the country thus provides an ideal training terrain.

If you can get the hang of how they order things in France, which is sometimes superior to everywhere else (though not as often as the French themselves believe) then the rest of the globe is child's play.

How they tried to kill de Gaulle

Three weeks ago a young Frenchman who teaches English at a school near Geneva was dragged into a police car, driven to a police detention centre at the Ile de Ré, near La Rochelle, worked over and interrogated. He was suspected, his captors told him, of being implicated in the murder in 1965 of a *barbouze*, a member of a special police section formed to crush the OAS — the Secret Army Organisation, once a threat to the Fifth Republic, still a threat to the life of President de Gaulle.

The schoolteacher, who admitted to OAS connections and sympathies, was released six days later because of lack of evidence and returned to his home in Savoie. Others have not been as fortunate. A man found gassed in a flat in Lyons, an unexplained murder in Marseilles; all random casualties of a secret and still unfinished war which France inherited from Algeria.

It is a war which has cooled considerably. The time when the OAS could count on the support of a significant section of the French Army, when generals rallied to its cause, when Paris rattled to its plastic bombs and civilians received their OAS 'call-up papers' through the post ended five years ago. Then the OAS realised that its ultimate aim — to keep Algeria French — was an impossible one: 'We became observers...observers through the wrong end of a telescope.' Denied its main hope, a hard core of the OAS fell back to a secondary, probably useless goal, the intensely human one of revenge. It would assassinate de Gaulle.

Four attempts to do this have failed. One OAS man has been formally executed by firing squad, to the accompaniment of martyr's rumours ('Only one bullet hit him. The others fired to miss.') Several sit out long prison sentences. At least thirty men involved in the attempts are still at liberty in various parts of Europe and South America. The OAS may appear forgotten. While de Gaulle lives it is not finished.

The SDECE (Service de Documentation Extérieur et de Contre-Espionage) is the successor to the old Deuxiéme Bureau so dear to many Anglo-Saxon novelists. It is housed in a group of nondescript buildings near the Porte des Lilas on the eastern outskirts of Paris. At the height of the OAS terror it had a permanent staff of about 1,700 and, like all secret services, an undisclosed number of freelances (known picturesquely as 'honourable correspondents'). Abroad there were nine permanent units — two each in Western Germany and Italy and one each in Spain, Portugal, Austria, Belgium and Britain.

It is a parallel too commonly drawn, but of all the secret police operating in Europe at this time none more closely resembled James Bond than the top 'barbouzes' of the SDECE.

They were small-arms marksmen, proficient at Karate, fluent in several languages, experts at torture and interrogation and at home in any capital of the world. But, like many policemen, they considered that they had the right not only of arrest but of passing sentence and administering punishment. More than one OAS member still missing today is believed by his relatives to have been 'eliminated' by the barbouzes.

General de Gaulle's car after the attempted assassination on 22nd August 1962 by Lieutenant-Colonel Jean-Marie Bastien-Thiry and his OAS agents.
(Popperfoto)

Understandably the barbouzes were detested by the OAS and given no quarter if they were captured. (In the last days of the struggle in Algiers an OAS group captured seven barbouzes from 'Mission C' which had arrested Degueldre. They cut off the policemen's noses and ears and then hanged them naked from balconies and lamp-posts.)

Within the SDECE there was an élite of the élite, a group called Action Service, mostly Corsicans, who were trained in every nicety of underground warfare at a special camp at Satory, near Paris. Promotion to this group was highly prized, not only for reasons of prestige but because it carried a salary of over £100 a week.

The Action Service's top priority from April 1961 had been to eliminate all the OAS leaders. As no one was worried about the methods that might be necessary to achieve this aim, a note which arrived on the desk of the Service's director on the morning of February 22 1963 caused little surprise.

It was a copy of a memorandum which the Director of Internal Security had sent to the Minister of the Interior. In part the memorandum said:

> We have succeeded in ascertaining the whereabouts of one of the main ringleaders of the subversive movement, namely, ex-Colonel of the French Army, Antione Argoud. He has fled to Germany and intends, according to information from our Intelligence Service there (Section d'Outre Rhin), to remain for several days...This being so it should be possible to get at Argoud and perhaps seize him.

As the request made by our official counter-espionage service to the competent German Security Organisations has been refused, and these organisations now expect our agents to be on the heels of Argoud and other OAS leaders, the operation must, in so far as it is directed against the person of Argoud, be carried out with maximum speed and discretion.

The same day the director of Action Service received a copy of the reply from the Ministry of the Interior. Addressed to the head of the German section of SDECE, it authorised Argoud's capture 'with all the discretion possible in an operation of this kind conducted in a foreign country'. The memorandum said that the operation would be undertaken 'in agreement with the Prime Minister's Office'.

Three days later, Argoud, who had been in Rome for talks with other OAS leaders, arrived back in Munich. He took a taxi from the air terminal to the Eden-Wolff Hotel, where he had booked a room, and after a call at the desk was walking to the lift when two men accosted him. Speaking faultless Bavarian-accented German, they asked him for his papers. Argoud concluded that they were German immigration police and reached for his passport. Before he could produce it, the two men seized him and hustled him through the doorway of the hotel and into a waiting car.

Argoud lashed at the driver, who swore viciously in French. Argoud now knew who had him, but before he could call for help the sharp palm edge of a hand cracked his nose, a rigid finger drove into his stomach area and a hand sought for a nerve spot in his neck. He collapsed to the floor of the car. He had a vague impression of being kicked and punched and then he fainted.

He recovered consciousness a little after 3 p.m. the following day. A group of curious gendarmes stood around him. His eyes, recently liberated from the blindfold one of the policemen was holding, refused to focus and he had to be helped to find his balance.

His mouth ached from the gag which had just been removed. His face was swollen, bruised and covered with dried blood. When one of the policemen said to him 'Are you Colonel Antoine Argoud?' he automatically mumbled 'Yes.' Then, before he had realised he was in Paris, he was hustled away to the Brigade Criminal headquarters at 36 Quai des Orfèvres.

Officers of Action Service had kidnapped Argoud in Munich, smuggled him across the border into France and left him, heavily bound and unconscious in the back of a blue van in the square behind Notre Dame. Before abandoning him they had exercised their bizarre sense of humour by telephoning the police commissioner, saying that they were OAS and that they were delivering Argoud, 'a package well tied-up'.

Predictably, there was an angry exchange of notes between the German and French Governments. Argoud was, on the international scale, apparently a man of no great importance. A product of the Ecole Polytechnique, he served as a lieutenant under General de Gaulle, took part in the battles for the liberation of France, and finally was given command of a cavalry regiment in Algeria. A little man, he was a brilliant but ruthless soldier. He was reputed to have had FLN terrorists executed in public. There was even a gory rumour in Algiers that the bodies had later been exhibited outside relatives' houses. After the April 1961 putsch he fled to avoid arrest and had hidden for a while in Paris under the alias of Vichard, his mother's name.

To understand why the French Government was prepared to risk damaging relations with the Federal Republic of Germany over a traitor of apparently minor importance, it is necessary to go back to the precious August when, had Argoud and his OAS followers been a little luckier, they would have killed President de Gaulle and toppled the Fifth Republic.

Assassination was no new risk to the General. He had dodged a sniper's bullet in

Notre Dame after the Liberation of Paris in August 1944. Then, on September 8 1961, when the General's column of cars was driving back to Paris from Colombey-les-deux-Eglises, his estate about 120 miles south-east of the city, an exposion at Pont-sur-Seine (Aube) rocked the President's car. The OAS had planted 80lb. of plastic explosive under some sand at the side of the road with a detonator to be set off by the vibrations of the cars. Fortunately it had failed to work properly.

De Gaulle treated the whole incident as 'a joke in bad taste'. The Assize court at Troyes was not amused. An OAS agent named Henri Manoury, who was found to have organised the plot, received twenty years' gaol, three of his companions fifteen years and a fourth ten years.

The OAS in Algeria, who for reasons of professional pride did not want to be associated with this failure, disclaimed any part of it (and privately condemned the Metropolitan terrorists for clumsy amateurishness).

To show the Patos (their impolite name for Metropolitan Frenchmen) how an Operation Ponctuel against de Gaulle should be carried out, a group of Delta Commandos in Algeria launched their own assassination project in April 1962. Although an independent operation it was fully in line with OAS policy (a top secret memorandum from Godard to OAS High Command, dated September 3 1961, read: 'As for our number one objective, Grand Zohra, it seems to me that the team which Jeanine [Susini] has been keeping up should be reconstituted and reinforced tenfold as soon as possible...The only thing that matters is killing Grand Zohra. We don't give a damn about the rest').

The Delta commandos, six in all, left Algiers for France in the last week of April, travelling separately. One of them transported an enormous trunk which was marked 'Jet Engine — Fragile'. They joined up at 15 rue du Dr Finley, a new flat in the 15th arrondissement, and proceeded to celebrate their arrival in the capital after long months of clandestine life in Algiers.

They equipped themselves with expensive wardrobes, and spent their evenings in night clubs redistributing some of the money that had previously been stored in the vaults of various Algiers banks. They were a cheery group; one night they were in such good spirits that the police picked them up, and discovered that their identity cards were poor-class forgeries. When their flat was searched the police found the trunk marked 'Jet Engine' contained a bazooka, a high-powered rifle with telescopic sights, and a fine assortment of detonators and explosives.

SDECE soon discovered that their plan was to hire a room on the sixth floor of a building in the rue de Faubourg St-Honoré. From there the Bazooka could have dealt with the presidential car turning into the Elysée Palace. As an insurance policy, their sharpshooter had arranged to hire a flat in the same street, the balcony of which gave him an excellent view of the main gate of the Elysée (a tourist trying to find accommodation in either of these places will find it hard going). The first Algerian attempt had flopped.

These two bungling attempts on de Gaulle's life did have one important result. The French Service de la Sécurité Présidentielle finally realised that the OAS were not only serious about trying to kill de Gaulle, but were prepared to risk their own lives to succeed. The easy-going security arrangements which de Gaulle had convinced his guards were quite sufficient would have to be revised radically. This turned out to be much harder than it appeared.

De Gaulle is a bodyguard's nightmare. His 6ft.4in. figure is an ideal target. His 'folk tours' of the provinces, when he doggedly shakes hands with all the local dignitaries, makes tight security difficult. His numerous weekend trips to Colombey put him at serious risk. But worst of all is the President's own attitude to security.

Even after the bomb attempt at Pont-sur-Seine he refused to allow more than one car of bodyguards to escort him, and apart from his chauffeur, a gendarme in plain clothes, he would not tolerate any policemen in his car. Only with great difficulty was he persuaded to give up travelling the whole way from the Elysée to Colombey by road, and instead go by car only as far as the military airfield at Villacoublay, by plane to Saint Dizier, then the last twenty miles by car.

To this new schedule the authorities added a series of feints to fool any assassin. Police cars were disguised as tourist cars with foreign number plates. A double was found for the General and he busied himself setting false trails. Departure times and actual routes were kept secret until the last minute. There was an all-round tightening of security procedure, even to the extent of arranging for a container of blood plasma to accompany de Gaulle wherever he went. (Two British Special Branch men delivered the container to Birch Grove, the Macmillan country home, when de Gaulle visited there in 1961 but were rather put out when the Macmillans' Scots cook refused point-blank to have it in her refrigerator.)

All of this made little difference to the OAS group under Colonel Argoud which was planning an all-out attempt on the President's life. Three OAS look-out men took up stations outside the three exits from the Elysée Palace and signalled de Gaulle's every departure. An OAS sympathiser at Villacoublay told the OAS of the President's arrival and departure from the base. Someone on the staff at Saint Dizier kept the plotters informed on de Gaulle's movements to and from Colombey. If anything, Argoud reasoned, de Gaulle was now an easier target than before.

On August 22, the main plot to kill President de Gaulle went into action. De Gaulle's car, a black Citroën, drove out of the Elysee by a side entrance at about 7.45 p.m. and headed south out of Paris. With the President were Madame de Gaulle, their adjutant, Colonel Alain de Boisieu, who is de Gaulle's son-in-law, and the police driver, Henri Marroux. They started late, so Marroux, worried, drove fast.

In the suburb of Petit Clamart, on the Route Nationale 306, Lieutenant-Colonel Jean-Marie Bastien-Thiry and 14 other OAS agents in three vehicles waited for the presidential cavalcade. They too were worried about General de Gaulle's lateness. It was getting dark, making it that much more difficult to hit a moving target.

Bastien-Thiry, like Argoud, was a graduate of the Ecole Polytechnique and had reached the rank of lieutenant-colonel serving in the Air Ministry in Paris. He was married, had three children and in 1961 de Gaulle himself had conferred on him the Knight's Cross of the Legion of Honour.

But what Bastien-Thiry regarded as de Gaulle's traitorous behaviour over Algeria had turned him bitterly against his former idol. He told himself that as de Gaulle threatened the future of France an 'act of tyrranicide' would not only be expedient but morally justifiable. Even if his assassination attempt failed and he was caught and sentenced to death, he was convinced that no French firing squad would raise its rifles at him. He was wrong.

Bastien-Thiry set up his ambush on classic military lines. Two cars were stationed to pin de Gaulle under cross-fire. The first had a driver and four marksmen — two with 9mm machine pistols and two with automatic rifles.

The plan was for them to bring the President's car to a halt with concentrated fire. Then the second car would cut off the cavalcade from a side street, engage de Gaulle in close combat and finish him off. The plan was detailed — Bastien-Thiry had even considered axial shooting problems, and claimed that his marksmen could achieve a degree of accuracy of five inches at 300 yards — and would have succeeded but for the fading light and the brilliant driving of police chauffeur Marroux.

Bastien-Thiry, standing casually at a bus stop, gave the signal to shoot by waving his newspaper. The first OAS car opened up when de Gaulle was only 50 yards away. But the President's car was travelling at 60 m.p.h. and proved a harder target than had been imagined. Two tyres, one front, one rear, were hit and the car went into a skid.

The adjutant, de Boisieu, sitting alongside the chauffeur, yelled to him 'Accelerate,' and then: 'Mon Général, get down!' Marroux spun the wheel, corrected the skid, and picked up speed again. The second OAS car now shot from the side road, but was just too late to cut off de Gaulle and instead found itself sandwiched between a Security Service car and two police motor-cyclists.

Technically the OAS men were trapped, but they refused to acknowledge it. Leaning wide from his window an OAS agent called Georges Watin, alias 'le boiteux' ('the limp') opened fire with his sub-machine gun at the two cars in front of him. He turned out to be the best marksman of all. Ten bullet holes were later found in the President's car and all of them came from Watin's gun. (In all 150 cartridge cases were found at the scene.)

One of Watin's shots hit the rear window of the Citroën and showered the President and Madame de Gaulle with splintered glass. Another tore into the bodywork inches from de Gaulle's head. But Marroux managed to keep the car moving. A few seconds later they reached a major intersection and pressure of traffic forced the OAS cars to abandon their target and swing away.

Marroux kept the President's car at speed despite the rapidly disintegrating tyres, until they reached Villacoublay. De Gaulle got out, said testily, 'A close shave,' dusted the glass from his clothes and without another word boarded the Air Force plane for Saint Dizier. He arrived only fifteen minutes late.

At Petit Clamart the gendarmerie were beginning to arrive only to find that the OAS men were well away. One vehicle was found abandoned a kilometre away outside a bar called 'The Green Carpet'. In it were two automatic rifles, five magazines, a phospherus grenade, two smoke bombs and a kilogramme of plastic explosive. But no real clues to who the OAS men were. Tracking them down seemed a near-hopeless task until one routine check produced unexpected results.

A roadblock near Valence on Route Nationale 7 stopped a Dauphine with four men to check their identification papers. One of them had no papers at all. At the local police station, this man, a *pied noir* called Pierre Magade, was found to be on the list of Army deserters. He was passed to the Criminal Brigade in Lyon for interrogation.

To fill in a long silence, one of the police officers suddenly said, 'What about Petit Clamart?' Magade said, 'Okay: What do you want to know?', and began to dictate a long confession.

Magade, the only genuine *pied noir* in the assassination group, nursed the common resentment of working class French Algerians against the Metropolitan French and, under pressure, this resentment proved stronger than his OAS loyalties. With the information provided by Magade all the major members of the assassination, except Argoud, were arrested within 48 hours.

They went on trial in January 1963. Normally they would probably have received heavy prison sentences. But while the trial was in process a fourth plot against the President's life was uncovered.

De Gaulle was to be murdered during an official visit to the Paris Military Academy on February 15. As he entered the large lecture hall from the courtyard of the Academy he was to be shot in the back by an OAS man on an upper floor of the building using a gun with telescopic sights. The assassin was the same Georges Watin who had taken part in the Petit Clamart affair: one of the few would-be assassins still at large.

But Madame Paule Rousselot de Liffiac, an English teacher at the Academy and OAS fanatic, tried to recruit an NCO on the staff into the plot. He went straight to the police. (There is evidence that he was, in fact, an undercover agent.) Again all the ringleaders, except Watin, were arrested. De Gaulle drove to the Academy in an armoured car and made his speech as scheduled. He also decided that 'this assassination nonsense' had gone far enough and that an example would have to be made to some of the top OAS conspirators 'to deter the others'.

The pinpointing of Argoud's movements by French intelligence agents in Germany made it clear to the Minister of the Interior, Roger Frey, what the first counter-attack on the OAS should be.

Argoud was the tactician behind the assassination attempts. The military brilliance which had made him the youngest colonel in the French Army meant he was now the most dangerous man in the OAS. SDECE reports on Argoud's activities in Munich made it clear he was setting up headquarters there.

He had two post box addresses, one at Post Office number 22, box number 346, under the name of Gaston André: the second at Post Office 33, box 132, under the name of Michel Laberaudière.

But what really alarmed Frey were reports that Argoud and Georges Bidault, who had turned up at 16 Unertistrasse, were preparing to launch a large-scale political propaganda campaign. Argoud, the reports said, had been in touch with the BBC and had arranged a television interview for Bidault. Then SDECE agents in London reported that Bidault had travelled to London on January 15 using a false passport and had recorded an interview at Lime Grove. This had not yet been released (it was on March 4) but was, the French paranoiacally believed, a move by the British Government to embarrass de Gaulle over the breakdown in the Common Market negotiations.

On his return to Munich Bidault had begun a series of interviews with newspapers and television groups, again arranged by Argoud. Obviously Argoud would have to be stopped. Not only was he a danger to de Gaulle's life, but also a potent political problem.

The Petit Clamart plotters were still on trial and there would be ample opportunity to pass deterrent sentences on them.Frey had no doubt about the court's verdict, because Bastien-Thiry had been more than eager in the witness-box to explain why he considered de Gaulle should die. The only point at issue was whether the Petit Clamart plotters intended to kill de Gaulle, as the prosecution claimed, or only to kidnap him for future 'trial and sentence'.

The chance to kidnap and settle with Argoud came first, but the Bastien-Thiry sequel was not long in following. The Supreme Military Court announced its verdict on March 4. Bastien-Thiry was condemned to death. Two others in the box with him were also sentenced to be shot, as were three still at large, including Watin.

There was no legal appeal against this sentence, so the fate of Bastien-Thiry and his companions rested with General de Gaulle as Head of State. On March 8 the General listened for three hours to appeals for clemency. Then he commuted two of the death sentences. But, he insisted, Bastien-Thiry must die.

So at Fort d'Ivry on March 11 1963, at 6.30 a.m., Bastien-Thiry faced the firing squad he believed could never bring themselves to shoot him. The order to shoot came at 6.40, there was a roll of drums, the firing squad marched past the dead officer as a gesture of respect, and the second counterblow against the OAS and its assassination plans had been struck.

Argoud's trial was more a musical comedy that dispensation of justice. It began in the Cour Sûreté de l'Etat in the Palais de Justice, on December 26,1963. Argoud and his lawyers had decided their tactics in advance. Since Argoud had been brought from Germany illegally, he was, in point of law, still there. And since he was legally in Munich, how could he answer questions at a trial in Paris? Accordingly he sat throughout this three-day trial without saying a word.

The presecution responded equally cynically. Argoud had been known as Charles Cinel in Munich and they were quite happy to have Monsieur Cinel repatriated to Germany — if he could be found. Meanwhile ex-Colonel Argoud must remain and stand trial.

This callousness caused a stir in France, and on the second day of the trial, Henri Thorez, the veteran of the French Left, volunteered to give evidence for the defence. He made a speech warning the prosecution about the effect their case was having on world opinion.

Argoud's lawyers withdrew from the case as a protest, but on December 30, despite a wave of liberal indignation, he was sentenced to life imprisonment. If it had not been for the attitude of the German Government he would almost certainly have received a death sentence.

At their trial the Military Academy plotters all received long sentences. The sharp-shooting Watin, however, perhaps the most determined and expert of de Gaulle's aspiring assassins, has never been caught. At one stage he was in Switzerland, but in the last couple of years he has disappeared altogether. Not even in Alicante, where he would be regarded as a distinguished member of the community, will anyone admit to knowing where he is.

So long as men like Watin are at large there must always be a chance of another assassination attempt: the President's security 'gorillas' are as alert as ever. Each year de Gaulle has allowed a certain number of OAS auxiliaries to be amnestied, but the important leaders, and all those involved in the various assassination attempts, are still in prison.

By the end of de Gaulle's term of office he will have probably released all but the very top men. But, in the interests of preserving his life, he cannot proceed too quickly. He is well aware that the sentiments expressed by Big Jo Ortiz are shared by every *pied noir* — 'De Gaulle might pardon me...I'll never pardon de Gaulle.'

The Sunday Times, 24th September and 1st October 1967
(with Phillip Knightley)

Year of the suppressed students

A recent Latin Quarter exhibition showing photographs of the 'May Revolution' brought all the images back, dreamlike. There was the young girl sprawled in the gutter with twisted legs. There was the riot policeman, snout grotesquely masked against his colleagues' gas, bent sensually over her, baton already scything down. And all around a montage of barricades, flying stones, fleeing teenagers — one could almost smell the panic again, and the gas. Here was Paris, spring 1968.

And now, Paris, winter 1968, is another country. No matter how vivid the images, they have already acquired a historical quality like yellowing photographs of Verdun or the Paris Commune. It all happened six months ago. The Republic tottered. But now the visible scars are so faint that casual visitors miss them altogether. The few tree stumps below the Boulevard St Germain (their trunks went to make barricades). The absence of traditional Latin Quarter cobblestones (the municipality prudently tarmacked them over in case some new revolutionaries started casting round for handy weapons).

The crowds shopping in the Rue Gay Lussac, where capitalist cars flamed like roman candles, are today rude, certainly, and anxious but surprisingly docile considering the stresses of a city rapidly rivalling New York in paranoia. An improbable quirk of winter fashion dictates that young men, probably the same young men who carried the black flag of anarchy in May, must now wear navy blue blazers 'English style'.

The smartest have breast pocket badges with 'E II R' or sometimes 'RAF'. The cavalry twills and chukka boots are missing but, these apart, they are a reasonable imitation of all the young Conservatives of one's adolescence. They would have fitted, sartorially anyway, into the England of Eden, or the long Macmillan sleep.

So, as the stolid crowds indicate, France has decided to exorcise what are euphemistically called 'the events' and carry on much as before. The June elections left no doubt about the wishes of the majority, even if they were largely negative. 'The party of fear' won, rather like, one supposes, Richard Nixon's suburban Republicans. France was frightened and therefore voted against the threat of violence and upheaval, above all against the spectre of Red Revolution which Prime Minister Georges Pompidou, who was finally sacked for his pains, exploited brilliantly and with bottomless cynicism. What the opposition, or such of it as remains, has been saying ever since is that France also voted against productive change and even, in the end, against youth.

What that great majority really voted *for* is harder to define (though it certainly was not the General himself, who is probably more disliked than ever, just as he is more powerful). What it boils down to, again rather like the Nixon supporters, is a reasonable preference for quiet nights, continuity and holidays judiciously booked six months in advance. The General is widely said to have referred to the electors as 'sheep'. There was certainly a deep collective reflex against extremism but it doesn't seem particularly stupid. And, in any case, had the Left been united, or even succeeded in producing a figure of any stature, the General's herd might easily have trooped the other way.

What France will now get, in political terms, allowing for such austerities as arise

A tear-gas grenade signalling a baton charge by riot police in the streets of Paris in May 1968.
(Bryan Wharton)

from de Gaulle's refusal to devalue the franc, is well defined. Foreign policy will continue much as before (the General seemed unmoved by the invasion of Czechoslovakia) and there is no apparent hope for Britain joining the Common Market. Domestically, France will remain conservative, but discreetly reformist. Some of the more glaring inequalities between rich and poor will be tinkered with, if not remedied: the Government will accelerate policies designed to narrow the gap between the great centres of wealth, notably Paris, and the vast forgotten areas of France. Unemployment will remain high, school-leavers will still have problems finding jobs if they are not middle-class, and there will be a lot of talk about 'participation' of workers in their factory decisions, and of students in school and university policies. One guesses it will amount to very little. A notable certainty is that France's radio and television services, surely the worst in Europe, will continue under the strictest Government control and censorship. If something happens in the world the General does not like, we will not be seeing much about it on our living-room telly screens in France next year.

Apart from the new jargon word 'participation' and its still very nebulous practical applications, this is very much the same forecast anyone would have made last April — before 'the events'. But for all that, and despite the Gaullist backlash, it would be wrong to think their effect has been either nil, or even counterproductive. There have been direct social consequences (after the strike some of France's worst paid workers emerged with rises of 40 and 50 per cent), in that the apparently most deeply entrenched regimes, *pace* Spain and Portugal, can suddenly be made to look very fragile given the right conditions. And, above all, what happened here has focused attention on the political potential of the very young — many of the most dedicated figures in May were *lycéens* of 16 or 17. No wonder the authorities thought these bearded kids were playing games and failed to see the threat until it was too late. *'Je suis Marxiste, tendance Groucho'* (I am a Marxist — Groucho-style) was one of the funnier bits of May graffiti, and it was also often true. By conventional political terms most of the leading student figures were a joke, naive sixth-form debaters who had read a paperback of Marx or Kropotkin.

Who could expect an M15 man or Home Office official to guess that a campus brawl about, of all things, a rule forbidding boys and girls to visit each other's bedrooms, could paralyse the entire country in five weeks flat?

It was certainly the question of 'free circulation' in student residences which launched Daniel Cohn-Bendit as leader of the extremists at the University of Paris Nanterre campus. And from there the movement extended to protests against Vietnam, against police arrests, against teaching standards and curricula at Nanterre (which in some subjects, particularly History and English Literature, were in fact infinitely better than those at the Sorbonne). In the end, after the famous March 22 occupation of certain buildings at Nanterre, the students seemed to be making a generalised protest against the whole quality of French life. They were, it seemed, very much like Peter Simple's 'Rentacrowd' adherents in the *Daily Telegraph* column.

Their leaders, and those of extremist groups in the Sorbonne who became so important, were invariably intellectuals, of a sort anyway. They were all bohemian in their habits and of Jewish, often Middle Eastern extraction. (This later gave the Right-wing press, and Gaullists, an antisemitic field day.) Cohn-Bedit himself has as much in common with a French motor-worker as Tariq Ali has with a Durham miner. Nanterre was probably the most fashionable university campus in France and few students there, whether they passed their exams or even bothered to take them, were in any danger of running short of cash. Money did not figure in their protest.

It did, of course, when the workers joined the movement in the weeks of May. Thier manifestos were full of ideas about workers' councils and factory 'democratisation', but the priority was higher pay and a lower working week. Their movement was much more conventional, and though it came to overshadow the students' protest simply because it was so much bigger, what happened in the streets of Paris was much more interesting.

Similarly the graffiti said more than the jargon-ridden manifestos. An underwear company had an advertising campaign in the Madeleine Metro based on endlessly duplicated posters of a dream blonde, twice lifesize, lusting at exhausted commuters in her diaphanous bra and pants. Normally she might have attracted a few schoolboy scrawls over the weeks, or grown a beard, but in June some unknown genius decorated twenty navels with the question 'Am I a girl or a product of the consumer society?'

The students had specific grievances, mainly stemming from the bureaucratic procedures which are France's Napoleonic legacy. But their message was really a scream of defiance against the Government and the system which increasingly controlled their lives, and which they could not influence through conventional politics. They were particularly bitter about television, its bias, and its insulting assumption that people could not be trusted with the truth. This was not a question which exercised the workers. They wanted to earn enough money to buy a television, or keep up the payments.

Arriving at the dog-end of 'the events' they seemed very amateurish after the slickness and underlying ferocity of American politics. The students were really running it themselves. In America, probably without even knowing it, the professionals would have been running them. And there was the comparative lack of violence.

People got their heads split; there were bad cases of police brutality. Yet officially there were no more than half a dozen fatalities over the six weeks. Even if one accepts rumours that the true figures were higher, there is no doubt, absurd though it is, that traffic dislocation over the period saved at least 100 people, and probably many more, who, under normal circumstances, would have died on the roads. It is frightening to guess at the death toll had even the mildest version of the Paris disturbances been acted out in any American city.

One night a handful of Gaullist extremists, much tougher than most students, ran into François Mitterrand, the left-wing leader, and manhandled him briefly. Typically he had been dining at the fashionable Brasserie Lipp in St Germain-des-Pres. In America he would have been despatched on the spot by one of those convenient $25 handguns.

Some army deserters and petty crooks joined the action, throwing odd Molotov cocktails and even firing a few shots, but that was all. I had the impression, again when it was nearly all over, that such real fighting as occurred was done by unemployed slum kids rather than students. (Later, when the Russians came to Prague, it was tough young workers rather than students who led such violence as there was.)

In Paris there were plenty of mini-skirted Left Bank Pasionaries urging the students to stand and fight, but usually they were too sensible. Instead they would provoke, throw stones, and run when the riot squads charged. Cold violence was foreign to them. Their best weapons were words, ideas, and their own numbers.

Cohn-Bendit has a genius for propaganda and impertinence, but one cannot imagine him storming the Elysée. Neither was the French Communist Party disposed to take over by force (its leader, Waldeck Rochet, would not have been much use with a pitchfork on the steps of the Winter Palace, but had he practised his Communism in Russia he would have done a skilful job of surviving the Stalinist purges). Rochet hated the student leaders, delving into the Leninist vocabulary of the Twenties to blast them for 'adventurism' and 'Left-wing Communism'. When Cohn-Bendit was invited to march with Rochet, his response was earthier — 'Bloody Stalinist muck' is a fair bowdlerisation. If anything, the Communist-

The Latin Quarter, Paris, May 1968. *(Camera Press)*

controlled CGT Union was even more hostile than the party itself to the students destroying their rigid structures and tight shop-floor organisation. The last thing they wanted was genuine factory democracy or workers' councils. And they were all united insofar as they had no idea about governing, and, in the case of the Communists anyway, no inclination. The students were acting too far outside the established parties to be able to turn protest into control. And the orthodox non-Communist Leftists lacked the man, and the mass support, to step into the vacuum that existed for a week at the end of May and the beginning of June. Without large-scale violence, for which they were temperamentally ill-fitted, there was no way the students could preserve their momentum. So it had to end.

Normality was, and is, slightly anti-climatic. 'The events' were sometimes nasty, always inconvenient, but often very funny as well. For once it was possible to look at this beautiful city without the tyranny of traffic. Parisians, very wryly, made jokes to each other: 'It must have been like this in the Blitz.' Everyone opened up in a normally very closed society and for once one had the feeling that the streets really belonged to the people. But though the young and wild wanted to go on and on (though not really knowing where) their elders had lost patience. For them crisis was no novelty, and this one had lost its point.

The story may go down as a pointer to the politics of the Seventies, a gift from the politically naive to the man they hated most, or simply an eccentric punctuation mark. Maybe the extremists will get off the ground again. It is equally possible that Cohn-Bendit and his friends will merge imperceptibly into the organisations they despised, write film scripts, or make fortunes on the Stock Exchange they came near to burning down. For the moment, the consumer society we have heard so much about has effortlessly assimilated its enemies.

Anyone interested to see the process in action should visit the mindbending chrome drugstore on the Boulevard St Germain and invest a pound on two beers. Beneath the bar the novelty department has been doing a roaring trade in Paris cobblestones. They tell me that at ten bob each (in safe capitalist indiarubber) they are the best-selling Christmas line. For the moment there is no doubt which side is winning.

The Sunday Times Magazine, December 1968

The old comedian dies the death at the Cafe de la Chaise

The old General, wrapped in a double-breasted jacket so big it looked like a military greatcoat, chose the least oppressive night of the Easter heatwave for his Command performance on the little screen. Promptly at 8pm, a few million French TV sets began flickering with a set of images as familiar, and enervating, as those of the long traffic jams limping back into the Capital along National Route Seven.

There he was, The Old Comedian — as one usually obsequious Gaullist commentator described him the next day — pulling out the ritual time-honoured stops. For 50 minutes we had the trembling lips, that index finger raised like Mr Punch's stick in warning, or pointing towards heaven like a monarch's sceptre.

Here, interlaced with pseudo-abrasive questions from Michel Droit, a kind of latter-day French Dimbleby, was that querulous voice, fluting easily into a long screech at moments of particularly emphatic rhetoric. As so often before, France was watching the General fight for his political life. And though the weapons seem rustier each time, no one can deny they haven't failed yet.

That idiosyncratic voice tempts saloon bar wits from one end of the country to the other, and, as this was an occasion so replete in folk ritual, the best observation platform seemed to be a small cafe between the Place de la Bastille and the Place de la République. The General's reception in the Café de la Chaise would have cheered the public opinion pollsters who have characterised French reaction to the referendum campaign with one word: 'apathy'.

When the programme started, a couple of professional anti-Gaullists, both communists, made nasty remarks about the General's advancing years. Nobody bothered to refute them, or indeed to say anything one way or the other. They watched the screen reflectively for a few minutes — the cafe owes its clientele to free TV — but soon everyone had mentally turned off, and the talk was of horse racing and high taxes. It took the General 35 long minutes to reach his carefully-rehearsed peroration, and the announcement that if the French failed to produce a majority of 'Yeses' on April 27 he would regard his political career as ended.

The point was dramatic enough, even though predictable. However, by then no one was listening. In contrast, a few minutes later the whole room gazed enthralled at a deplorable Hollywood-imported thriller, telling the story of an intrepid team of men from the CIA who made the world safe from communism by using a trained tabby cat to steal a secret formula.

This might seem to be a reflection on the audience rather than the performer, but the clientele is probably as representative of France as anything the French Institute of Public Opinion serves out periodically.

There is a coal merchant who, like the café's patron and the assistant manager of a local grocery shop, went on strike last month with millions of their fellow small businessmen in protest against the increased taxes for 1969 which squeeze their already perilously tight margins. There is the restaurant owner whose prices have been frozen, and who says it was hard going to make a profit six months ago, let alone now.

Charles de Gaulle.
(Leon Herschtritt/ Camera Press)

There are the two communists, factory hands in a local small business producing simple tools — they marched along the boulevard next to us last month because they saw inflation eating away the wage increases so painfully achieved after the events of last May.

Apart from their basic orientation, they are bitter about the regime because its communications stooges announced that 60,000 workers were marching (in torrential rain) on a day when there must have been nearly 10 times that number soaking in the streets. And like everyone else present that day, they are still angry that the General should have called a democratic and meticulously non-violent trade-union demonstration an example of the ruthless subterranean forces trying to destroy the Republic.

These unsophisticated, though vehement, responses have apparently little to do with what the referendum is really about. But, for that matter, neither does the propaganda campaign the General and his acolytes have chosen to launch. Five weeks ago Gaullist Ministers and the regime's licensed pundits were telling one in all apparent sincerity that this ragbag packet of constitutional tinkering and regional reform would be offered to the people on its own intrinsic merits.

Now that the French prefects — the Government's sounding-boards of popular opinion — have reported with ill-concealed alarm that neither Senate reform nor a new regional structure have stimulated anything other than indifference or suspicion from the voters, the plan has changed very rapidly. The General is telling the French, as he has told them periodically since 1958, that he and he alone is capable of leading them to the promised land. And, since the events of last year, this message has acquired added sting. The middle-class, the middle-aged, the established — all those who have anything to lose — are being subjected to the crudest kind of political blackmail. They are being told that the choice lies between the General and anarchy.

On the evidence of the past, and given the paucity of Opposition figures, it looks as though the opinion polls are about right. A majority, albeit a slender one, of France's 28 million voters, seem set to opt for the devil they know. The polls indicate hardly any perceptible change in the last 15 days: 25 per cent say Yes! 23 No: 31 are undecided: and 21 see no reason why they should confide their intentions, assuming they have any, to anyone.

The significant point about these figures is evidently the potential floating vote of 52 per cent. These are the mavericks who have been worrying the prefects: and if it is possible to gain votes through cash, skill and energy — which, precedents indicate, is very likely — then between now and April 27 enough of them will be persuaded to keep the General in the Elysée until the end of his term in 1972.

To this end, fourteen Cabinet Ministers are in Strasbourg this weekend using whatever prestige they may enjoy to counteract the alarming news of electoral vacillation in this normally dedicated Gaullist stronghold. In the next fortnight there will be 21 major public meetings throughout the country. Robert Poujade, who under Georges Pompidou was the architect of last June's National Assembly victory, has organised a series of local action groups, known picturesquely as 'Yes Committees', and a propaganda pamphlet called 'France Regions', 15 million copies of which have been distributed throughout the country, printed at a cost and with funds which the Opposition wish they knew more about.

It is already clear that the campaign is going to have no more than a passing relevance to the questions about which the voters, ostensibly at least, are being asked to give their answers. Despite many reservations on the part of his advisers the General has insisted that the people, not their elected and presumably more qualified representatives in the National Assembly, should be asked to sanction a blueprint of radical constitutional change, under one umbrella affirmative.

It is a curious decision, because, ostensibly, the issues surrounding Senate reform and the changes in the constitution, and those concerning the new regional structure, have little in common. For the voter who, for example, is in favour of a reduction in central bureaucracy — even if details of what it will imply tend to disappear in a Celtic miasma of Gaullist rhetoric — and yet would like the safeguard of a second Parliamentary chamber to continue, the choice is schizophrenic. Even the briefest analysis of the 19 constitutional amendments in the referendum packet indicate the impracticality of submitting them to one Yes or No answer.

On the surface, the referendum raises issues which appear remote from France's most pressing domestic problems — economic stability, social equity, and above all, perhaps, the question of who follows General de Gaulle. This apparent irrelevance is one obvious explanation for the high proportion of 'Don't know' voters the pollsters have found in their preliminary surveys.

Yet, as the Opposition parties have been pointing out, among the articles of the constitution which will be modified if the referendum is approved, and the three which will be suppressed altogether, there is one at least which is central to the question of the succession. And in political terms, to put it mildly, it is highly controversial.

Under the constitution as it now stands (it was originally promulgated in October, 1958, after the General's return, and modified in 1960, 1962 and 1963) the clause which provides for a break in the Presidency is perfectly clear. If for any reason, and in present circumstances, it would presumably be due to the death of the incumbent, the Presidency becomes vacant, then the interim period is filled by the president of the Senate. During the three to four weeks before the Presidential election his role is indentical to that of the President himself.

If the new constitution is approved — this interim function changes — it is the Prime Minister who will step in. This seems reasonable enough — the Prime Minister is, after all, the second most powerful man in France. But there is one vital difference. Unlike the President of the Senate under the present system, the Prime Minister is not elected by universal suffrage, or indeed by suffrage of any kind. He is chosen by the President, as are his Ministers, and they do not have to be elected by anyone. In practice, they are invariably active Parliamentarians who have won representation through normal democratic procedures. But they do not have to be.

Like Georges Pompidou in 1962, for instance, a man can be summoned to be Prime Minister from an apolitical though profitable career in Rothschild's bank. He can come, like the current Prime Minister, Maurice Couve de Murville, from the Foreign Office. There is no need, in theory at least, why the Prime Minister should not be the President's son, an old friend that he knew in the Army, or for that matter, a man he met in a bar and thought might be suitable. The only qualification is that he should be chosen by the President.

This may not be an ideal system, but as it operates at the moment it does have one built-in sanction. No Prime Minister could conceivably continue in power without controlling the Parliamentary majority and through it, theoretically at least, enjoying the confidence of the electors. But, as the Opposition has been nervously saying, there is no such sanction should the President decide to choose a Prime Minister on his own death bed, or on the eve of his departure for whatever reason.

Whoever the choice, no matter how unexpected or, in the eyes of people or politicians, unsuitable, he would for the interim period assume legally uncontested control of the State and the whole paraphernalia of Government. He, and he alone, would be legally entitled to command the armed forces, control the police, direct foreign policy, and, of course, do what he wished with radio and television.

It is a possibility hardly likely to commend itself to the clientele of the Café de la Chaise.

The Sunday Times, 13th April 1969

Finding a face for Georges Pompidou

Three weeks ago, almost indecently soon after General de Gaulle's political obsequies, the whizkids of the Pompidou-for-President team were having a row in their plush headquarters, five minutes' stroll from the Invalides air terminal. The problem was choosing a good campaign photo of their boy, and the task proved franky daunting. One snap gave him the unreassuring guise of a man-eating wolf, a second, showing the General's former Prime Minister on holiday at Saint Tropez, suggested an aged debaucheee tottering off some disreputable Greek yacht. The third, and worst, was positively Mephistophelian.

The candidate himself, well padded to the point of being cuddly, but with a pebbly blue gaze that soon stopped the chat, clinched the matter. 'I have no intention,' said Georges Pompidou, 'of being sold like an enzyme.'

Pompidou's comment implied no moral scruples about detergent selling techniques. He was just being sceptical about their efficacy. 'What we must have', he told his brother-in-law and fellow campaigner, Henri Domerg, 'is a picture which makes me look the way the French people believe I am.'

Well, how do they see him? And how far does their collective impression accord with reality? Piecing together an authentic portrait of this consummate dissembler has more than purely domestic interest here in France. It must be exercising the Wilson Government almost as much as the French electorate — because how Pompidou jumps, and what makes him run, will very likely decide the last major foreign policy theme before the general election. Even if this elusive, clever man loses the presidential fight he will exercise a formidable influence over French policies for years to come. Should Alain Poher, the interim president, beat him to the post on June 15th, Pompidou will still control a weighty parliamentary majority. It is hard to envisage any subsequent horsetrading without Pompidou being right in the middle.

France's most recent bout of electioneering has not much clarified the picture of the man. It was more rewarding, in fact, to observe him during the relatively tranquil period of nearly ten months when he was in the political wilderness. Now, from every spare wall a foxy face (the idiot collaborators naturally got it wrong) peers down. Those luxuriant eyebrows palpitate almost daily on the small screen begging support.

The image is pervasive enough, God knows, but at the same time schizophrenic.

Pompidou's problem likewise is twofold. He needs to reassure the fat 40 per cent of French voters who believed in de Gaulle, or Gaullism, or anyway feel jumpy about the alternatives. At the same time he must seduce a packet from the other half of the electorate — those who found the General's rule unsatisfactory — with evanescent images of change, renovation and reform.

Listening to Pompidou's oddly inept campaigners, who are happy to jettison Gaullist policies, but sadly retain that fulsome vocabulary of adulation, their boy is the reincarnation of Renaissance genius, a man for four, if not five seasons. They have not, in my hearing anyway, got around to claiming he has two heads. But the effect of his tightrope campaign has been to produce twin profiles.

But all the same some interesting discoveries made by the opion pollsters suggest

Georges Pompidou. *(Leon Herschtritt/ Camera Press)*

that the voters have got Pompidou's number pretty clearly. Defining a man through his friends, and enemies, is probably as good a way as any. The polls indicate this sort of division:

Those who love him tend to be old — no bad thing electorally in a country where over half the 19 million voters are forty-five plus. Women like him better than men — not so much sex appeal here, one suspects, but security. The female Pompidou voters are invariably full-time housewives, not women who work. Peasants like him, perhaps because of his roots (of which more later) and so rather surprisingly do small businessmen, despite their recent discontent with the Gaullist squeeze.

Employers are split about fifty-fifty: the very grandest, above all the bankers, love him dearly. If ever there was a big-business nominee it is Pompidou.

The doubters are, in a word, progressive France — or anyway that entity as defined by those who like to think they themselves are progressive. They are the workers (except for some of their wives); middle-salary earners; professional men; technologists; and students. It is an instructive division, although in some ways crude. It appears to indicate what the literary reviewers are always calling a dichotomy — old against young; countrified (and often petrified) against urbanised; those who earn middling (and heavily taxed) salaries against those who make the big money, often through inherited wealth or position.

The obvious deduction, which is supported by a close examination of Pompidou's career and background, is that despite efforts to project him as a computer age dynamist, he is in many ways as old-fashioned a character as his former master. As an acute friend of his from England remarked last week: 'I have always seen George as a bourgeois figure out of the French Third Republic.'

There is no French equivalent of the American Horatio Alger hero. If there were, however, it is a safe bet his sterling qualities would have hoisted him, not from rags to riches, but from illiteracy to the chair of philosophy in some eminent and moth-eaten university faculty.

In the France of the twenties and thirties — Pompidou's formative period — there was an almost Jewish obsession with education as a means to social distinction. The Académie Française, now a palpably absurd institution, was the apex of that system. Portnoy's Jewish mother ran along the beach screaming: 'My son the doctor is drowning.' Leon Pompidou, the candidate's Socialist, anti-clerical father, would have shouted: 'My son the professor...'

The family came from Montboudif in the Auvergne, a name so palpably plebeian to French ears that it lends itself as easily to snobbish jokes as Pompidou itself. (In the patois of Languedoc the name means 'the hobgoblin who flies in the wind', which is, after all, not a bad description.) The grandparents were peasant farmers, the father a minor schoolteacher, who dreamt of being an important academic.

He was also a disciple of Jean Jaurès, the French socialist and pacifist, who was assassinated on the eve of the first world war. On the day Jaurès was killed in Paris Leon Pompidou was called up. The war put paid to his academic aspirations but he shifted them on to his son's back. If Georges did not come top he was whipped: fortunately he was exceptionally brilliant.

Pompidou likes to tell friends an anecdote about his reply when asked at the age of seven, what he was going to do when he grew up. No engine driver he. Instead, he said he was going to the Ecole Normale in Paris, the very rough French equivalent of announcing he would win an All Souls Fellowship. In due course he did, and himself became a teacher.

Those who knew Pompidou at his Paris Lycée, and subsequently the Ecole Normale, agree that he was a swot who went to enormous trouble to conceal the fact. He wore eccentric hats, read Baudelaire ostentatiously during lectures, affected an attitude of exaggerated casualness.

He was very much the provincial in the capital, and when he met his future wife, Claude Cahour, the daughter of a doctor from Brittany, it was in a cafe on the Boulevard St Michel.

Like his eminent contemporary, Enoch Powell, he is a Greek scholar, and his first career was as a teacher of classics, with a period in the infantry from August 1939 until the surrender. Unlike virtually all important Gaullists, he had no Resistance record but just went on teaching Greek in Paris.

He first met de Gaulle in 1944 and made a good impression. He was tremendously clever and fast, completely loyal, and during most of the years the General brooded in Colombey — from 1945 to 1958 — Pompidou ran an informal cabinet for him. Pompidou was also prepared to do the kind of menial jobs for which the great man, writing his memoirs and pondering over history, had neither the time nor the taste.

Pompidou looked after the trust fund set up as a memorial to Anne de Gaulle, the mentally-retarded daughter who died young. He arranged sordid financial details with publishers, and drove hard bargains. He reported to Colombey what was happening in the chaotic political world of the Fourth Republic.

His relationship with the General in these years seems to have been curiously similar to the later one between Prime Minister and President. There are supporters of de Gaulle who insist that Pompidou was the reactionary figure who blocked the great man's brilliant designs for social reform during his years of office. But the evidence suggests that the President was so preoccupied with historical visions that he left vulgar domestic considerations largely to his Prime Minister.

The reward of this stewardship came in May 1968, when Pompidou for the first time achieved national stature by mopping up the mess. But, as his opponents are busy pointing out, he did after all make it himself.

The Pompidous were first able to acquire the taste for smart Paris life when Georges worked briefly for the French tourist commission. Eight years later, by joining Rothschilds Bank, he acquired the cash to cultivate his tastes, particularly for modern pictures.

The man who got him into Rothschilds, René Fillon, owns the enormous apartment in the Boulevard de la Tour Maubourg where the Pompidou-for-President campaign now has its headquarters.

The Rothschild experience provided another opportunity for Pompidou to demonstrate his almost unlimited mental capacity, but it was not an ideal breeding ground for economic reform. When the General sacked Pompidou last July, fervent Gaullists, in an attempt to show it was not simply an act of spite and jealously, pointed out that the glacial Maurice Couve de Murville was much more liberal on the domestic front than Pompidou had ever been.

Except for his decision to announce his candidature formally last January and, despite pressure, his subsequent refusal to renounce it as a last minute device to win the referendum, examples of Pompidou standing out against his master are hard to find.

He was in favour of devaluing the Franc in 1959, and his view prevailed, though the General was not passionately committed. He succeeded in persuading the General not to have Jouhaud, one of the OAS generals, executed, after Salan had got away with a life sentence. That was a harder battle.

And in 1968 he delayed the General's political suicide by ten months or so by persuading him to delay his referendum and substitute parliamentary elections.

His friends outside politics, who include most of the Parisian artistic intelligentsia, tend to insist with pride that he has no principles at all. 'He is just a pragmatist,' they say. This 'pragmatism' (a word which evokes a certain chill in anyone who witnessed Harold Wilson's take-off into the political stratosphere) has long been evident.

It enabled a highly cultivated man to preside over the censorship of radio and television. It allowed him to over-ride a personal affection for the state of Israel (apparently unconnected with his indebtedness to the Rothschilds) in order to execute a pro-Arab policy in the Middle East.

He was out of the Government when the General announced his anti-Israel embargo at the beginning of the year — it would have made no difference if he had still been Prime Minister. This was one of the occasions when the General acted completely on his own; not only did he avoid consulting his ministers, he even failed to inform them. (One learnt the news from a radio broadcast; another via a friend in the customs whose department had received the new orders in a circular sent directly from the Elysée).

At the time, Pompidou told a friend that he was deeply distressed. This was one of the few occasions he has been verbally disloyal to his chief. 'This time,' he said, 'the General and I are finished.'

As it turned out they were, though not of course over the Israel issue. Apart from this small affair when he was already in the political wilderness, there have been few signs of the calm, detached Pompidou allowing himself to get worked up about anything. He always left the Matignon (the Prime Minister's office) promptly at nine with a pile of dossiers. One night in two he would go to a big dinner or the theatre, but he was always in early next morning with all the papers completed. 'He only sleeps five hours a night,' said a friend, 'and he is always happy with life.'

But there is no way of telling how he really felt about the General. Was he counting the minutes to his retirement, and simply avoiding open conflict in the meantime? He may have been thinking one thing as Prime Minister while doing another. Pompidou is a man who keeps his secrets.

The voters know this and many are still uncommitted; they are thoughtfully trying to assess both the man and his potential policies. In terms of experience and ability he is by far the best man for the job (with the exception of Pierre Mendès-France, running on an American-style ticket as prime minister alongside the Mayor of Marseilles, Gaston Defferre). In Human terms he is also the most sympathetic. This is the only French Prime Minister who could conceivably combine dancing bare-chested at St Tropez, reading Aeschylus in the original, and queueing up to see the latest Godard film. Surely such a man cannot be quite so reactionary as he has recently been sounding.

When he came to power in 1962, a poll showed that 78 per cent of Frenchmen had no views on the matter, because they didn't know who he was. But under de Gaulle he became the second political figure in France. His image is astutely defined by the crumpled fag drooping our of his mouth; a thousand journalists and TV commentators have talked about Pompidou and his 'ever-present Gauloise', that cigarette which epitomises Frenchness as much as a bottle of Beaujolais.

The first time I saw Pompidou I noticed him chain-smoking a well-known American brand, which came as a mild surprise, like seeing Churchill chewing spearment. One discovered later that he always smokes American — Gauloises make him cough. Not that it matters. Even if he took to smoking pot, the world will go on believing that this is the French politician with the French cigarette. A man who can carry out such a neat public relations ploy with such aplomb is worth watching. There is time for him to surprise and deceive us all yet.

The Sunday Times, 25th May 1969

A baby falls among bureaucrats

For Gloria Ramos, 20, Portuguese by birth and Parisienne by domicile, last Monday was the day the police stole her baby, Sylvie, aged 18 months and named like thousands of other poor French children in honour of a film star, was removed from the bed she shared with her parents. Gloria had left her to do her morning job at the flat of a British resident of the *quartier*, myself. When she returned the door had been forced and Sylvie had been removed. Gloria knew where to look. She and her husband Miguel were living with some Portuguese friends virtually as squatters in a hotel so ancient it can be made out in contemporary prints of Louis XIII's ornate church of Val de Grace. The place is scheduled for demolition and for some time the police have been harassing the last residents. One had been there, Gloria learnt from an excited neighbour, and left with her child. So the mother went in tears to the local police station and here met for the first of many checks. All services were closed for lunch. They told her to come back at 2.30. Then a period of limbo, during which the mother grew increasingly hysterical and with good reason. For as I later learnt this was the time when the policemen involved, Inspector Cassin, had Sylvie transferred to an emergency centre for homeless babies. Worse. He also started an official report justifying his actions.

By the time I got to see him, Baby Sylvie had become Ramos, S., with a number and a dossier. Once on the bureaucratic roundabout there was no unofficial, unbureaucratic way of getting her off. The baby would not be removed without an official paper stamped by a special judge sitting in a tribunal. This means an audience at the Palais de Justice. Unusually, and thanks to a combination of discreet pressure and general good-will, Inspector Cassin said he would try to fix this for the next day. By this stage Miguel had returned from his building site near Orly, found out what had happened and in his serviceable, proletarian French he was telling a policeman that they would never have dared to treat a French citizen like that. The policemen on the receiving end knew nothing of the affair: Miguel had gone to the *quartier's* police headquarters near the Parthéon. But Inspector Vassin's headquarters is a subsidiary commissariat nearly a mile away in the shadow of the Ecole Normale, the high temple of French intellectualism, whose alumni include George Pompidou. It is arguably a longer journey from the school to the inspector's dingy commissariat across the road than from Oporto, the native town of the Ramos family, to Paris. Few of the Ecole's pupils, one imagines, are aware of the concentrated human hopelessness of those waiting at the bottom of the dirty ochre stairs.

During the afternoon, Inspector Cassin had been built up in the imaginations of the women in the condemned hotel as a baby-stealing monster. In fact, he turned out to be one of the rare French new-style cops, precise and with intellectual leanings; he could be a bank manager in his neutral birdeye suit. He had gone to the hotel to serve an expulsion order, heard the baby crying, forced the door and decided on the spot the baby needed care. It was dirty, he said — pointing to the mess on his coat where he had carried it. There was no cot in the room. There was a formula for such cases, and he had carried it out.

This cot, or its absence, figured largely in all the official discussions of the affair

— to Gloria's evident bewilderment. In Oporto, or at any rate her section of the town, babies sleep with their parents, a concept so self-evident to her she could not discuss it. Sylvie had been sleeping happily so, unusually, Gloria had left her alone. The baby was only crying because a strange man was knocking the door down.

They are a very misleading couple. Their most pressing reason for leaving their country was the prospect of four years' compulsory military service. Gloria is wary of officials, with good reason, but on this matter she smiles confidently as she explains, even to an impressive-looking judge with a Legion of Honour ribbon in his lapel. Anyone in their right mind must see the compulsion behind this decision, she reckons. They also, I think, were pursuing some probably cinematic vision of urban prosperity and glamour, revealed in their choice of name for the first born.

Sylvie Vartan, all peroxide curls and décolletage, is the epitome of dime-store chic. When Gloria and Miguel walk on Sunday mornings in the Luxembourg Gardens they are a strikingly handome couple. They could easily be cast in a promotional TV feature on the latest low-price housing project. No one would guess she can scarcely read, or cannot understand the underground system.

Only one incidental confusion, among so many. At one stage, on the telephone, I was assured the couple had been 'definitively expelled'. Seeing the weight of paper that 'Ramos, S. Bebe' had generated I inquired nervously whether the couple were being thrown out of the country, not merely their rotton hotel. Inspector Cassin was shocked at the idea, just as deeply as he had been at finding Sylvie possessed no cot or any other prescribed accoutrements of French bourgeois babyhood. 'No question. Surely you see they are fine people, thoroughly honest types. Industrious...' Yes, I said hastily, I saw all right.

And so, happily, did the judge next day — largely through intuition. Gloria was hopeless at answering his questions. Finally, the judge himself discovered that 'Ramos, S.' had been shifted from one emergency centre to another. He traced her: mother and baby were reunited, within minutes of a public holiday that would have shoved Sylvie back into impenetrable limbo.

The story then has a happy ending, but no likely moral, though one could probably erect a general theory of urban alienation from it if so inclined. Neither the inspector nor the judge nor Gloria erred, it seems to me, unless she was *a priori*, at fault for being poor, and not clever. The French do not generally share an idea, common I think to most English, of the over-riding claims of motherhood *per se*. This was the key to Lindo Desramault's disastrous encounter with French law when pathetically pursuing her baby, though neither she nor her advisers understood it. They assumed the weight of her maternity was self-evident, imperative. The French courts were concerned to protect the inalienable right of the child, via her father, to be brought up speaking the French language in a French setting.

There was perhaps the faintest hint in Gloria's case that someone realised the separation had been unnecessarily brutal. 'In England,' one official pointed out, 'they have just sent a girl to prison for 21 months for taking an infant for 15 minutes...' Gloria sees or anyway saw, no reason why a working mother should not occasionally leave her child for short periods. It is unlikely she will ever take the risk again.

New Statesman, 10th November 1972

Merde de Taureau

For reasons more to do with money than art *The Last Tango* had to be performed, as the title says, in Paris. The distributors were probably canny when they guessed that an opening run in London would bring some publicity-seeking loonie out of the woodwork, set on having their product either censored or banned. I believe they avoided New York, except for what amounted to one sneak preview, because they did not wish *Tango* to undergo too close a scrutiny before the publicity bandwaggon had started to roll — in Gay Paree.

For sex is of course chic in Paris, and to find a time when it wasn't you have to go back almost as far as the Jansenists. Watching the French audiences in two of my local cinemas (one named in honour of Jean 'Donnez moi un verre de sperme' Cocteau, who knew plenty about exploiting people's refusal to appear shocked) it was hard not to be struck by the twinset and pearls respectability, and also the bored faces. This stems only partly from the film's inherent dullness. The sophisticated middle-class could be seen working within the great Paris tradition of appropriating sex, and particularly sexual aberration, and suggesting it is a French invention, the fine flowering of a native — and superior — culture. Adam, they seemed to say, was a Frenchamn, not to mention the divine *marquis*.

Still, half the spectators must have been American, and most of the advance publicity, the fuss and shock, has resulted from people writing about *Tango* from Paris. But for English-speaking readers, as I shall show, it has been deeply misleading. The French have been less shocked — and enthusiastic — than many critics have implied (in the provinces, as always, the story is slightly different). There are no queues; and as long as you are over 18 with a pound to spare you can find a seat anytime. *Tango* can be seen at eight cinemas, just half those showing the really big hit of the moment, *Un homme est mort*. It is a thriller starring Jean-Louis Trintignant, France's box office idol, and set in Los Angeles. He turned down the role in *Tango* that Brando accepted, just as Dominique Sanda declined to play the part of the girl that went finally to Maria Schneider.

Still, *Time* magazine, whose publicity role has been crucial, would never have had Trintignant on their cover with the headline, Lord help us, 'Sex and Death in Paris'. Nor, I imagine, would the director, Bernardo Bertolucci, have called anyone but Brando 'an angel as a man but a monster as an actor...he has the wisdom of an Indian sage...like one of those figures of Francis Bacon who show on their faces all that is happening in their guts — he has the same devastated plasticity'. Here we sniff Brando's contribution, a quintessentially American one. The vocabulary comes straight out of what some colleagues of mine writing a book about a US election once christened 'the bullshit machine'. 'Devastated plasticity' is a peculiarly fine example. Better even than 'Indian Sage'. There was also the especially memorable statement about Bertolucci requiring the set designer to use red, orange and 'flesh' tones as they were 'all uterine colours'. This is not just another skin flick, but a work of art.

The general drift of the action is, I suppose, well-known enough by now. Brando, inexplicably resident in Paris as patron of a shabby hotel, is cracking up because his wife has killed herself, for reasons he cannot understand, or at any rate express. In

The director, Bernardo Bertolucci, with Marlon Brando and Maria Schneider during the filming of *The Last Tango in Paris*. *(Popperfoto)*

an empty flat in Passy, hovering between the Bir-Hakeim bridge and the ritzy 16th arrondissement, he meets Maria Schneider, who looks what she is: a product of contemporary Montparnasse Bohemia, 20 and already distinctly frayed at the edges. He rips her panties, and mimes intercourse against the wall. They embark on a lost three days, a kind of erotic alcoholiday. Its high point, the rupture (we have been told) of some deep taboo, comes when the ageing man sodomises the baby-faced girl (though he doesn't really) using butter as a lubricant.

Here not only Brando but all the critics I have read seem to crack up. According to *Time* 'for boldness and brutality, the intimate scenes are unprecedented in feature films. Frontal nudity, four-letter words, masturbation, even sodomy — Bertolucci dwells uncompromisingly on them all with a voyeur's eye, a moralist's savagery, an artist's finesse'. Stirring stuff. But it is all either misleading, or flatly untrue. Yet the stress on the film's 'honesty' — the adjective 'uncompromising' has been having a field day — has been the *Leitmotiv* of every critical notice I have seen.

The cue came from Bertolucci, quoted as usual in the *Time* canon: 'I decided that to suggest and allude instead of saying it outright would create an unhealthy climate for the spectator.' This is Bertolucci's fundamental statement about the film, his credo. And like virtually everything written about *Tango* it is the reverse of the truth. Allusion, suggestion, obliquity — a refusal to show the eroticism which is supposed to stem from the situation — this is the core of the film. I do not know whether it is unhealthy or not. But it certainly rings as false as a lead nickel.

Brando's ad-libbing, dredged from that area of Hemingway the novelist was almost always too rigorous to publish, speaks for itself. An amazingly deft amalgam of the worst of *To Have and Have Not* and *Across the River and into the Trees:* 'What the hell, I'm no prize. I picked up a nail in Cuba in 1948, and I got a prostate like an Idaho potato, but I'm still a good studman...' Well: is he? There is certainly no way of telling from the film, though Maria Schneider is on record as saying she found him too unattractive 'to screw on the side'.

I hope the Women's Lib propagandists, including Germaine Greer, one of the many people who flew in expressly to see the film, do not hesitate to analyse its ethics. For once 'sexist' is the right word. The frontal nude shots, cited by *Time* and meant to titillate, are of Maria Schneider, never of Brando. Indeed, in order to disguise the paunch he is sensitive about, there are few shots of him below the neck. Far from letting it all hang out, or intrepidly exploring some cinematic hinterland, sexual contacts are mimed, with grotesque and depressing crudity. I am not suggesting, incidentally, that some acid rule exists obliging actors to make love to each other on celluloid in the pursuit of artistic truth. But I am saying that if you sell a product with this kind of publicity it is fraudulent if it turns out to be an empty paper bag.

But the critics have ignored this aspect. Instead *Paris-Match*, the most widely read magazine here, makes a comparison between *Tango* and *Quai des Brumes* in the following terms: 'Ou Gabin sortait son regard blue, Brando sort son sexe.' Except that he does not. Though Brando, Bertolucci and the bullshit machine have succeeded between them in convincing virtually everyone that he does.

I suppose the colour magazines will soon be crediting Brando and Bertolucci with the invention of sodomy. The *Tango* as *Time* says, may be 'a pantomime coitus for the camera'. Brando's fleeting smile, a cry for help from an eagle who has forgotten how to fly, cannot make up for all the missing elements. To tango, as the banal old song recognised, it takes two. Miss Schneider has to do it all alone.

New Statesman, 2nd February 1973

Keeping them off the grass

A nine-year-old came home from her Latin Quarter primary school aglow with virtue. She had received a good mark in the class called 'Morality'. What had she learnt? 'One must never', she recited with gusto, 'walk on the grass in the Luxembourg Gardens.' Ah, that French institutional morality. At the time we thought it a joke. But as spring came to Paris this year it became reality. A translucent Sunday morning, and there was a posse of cops on the main gate. Forbidding entry, it turned out, to anyone between 12 and 40, though this invidious category was applied only to the natives. Tourists (as long as they had short hair) were exempt. And a group of apparently virile Japanese, some of whom were not a day over 35, were herded through without even showing their passports.

This was three weeks ago, and the segregation had been ordered by the Senate. They control the gardens, and have done since the 19th century. They also have no members under 40. Their decision was a riposte to the first student action of the traditional Latin Quarter season of spring manoeuvres. The previous Saturday afternoon, so I learnt from the Senate's Quaestor Department which deals with matters of discipline and morality, kids from the Beaux Arts had behaved disgustingly. Not only had they ignored the First Commandment, and actually walked on the grass. They had paddled in the ornamental lake, played pop music in the normally strictly decorative 1860 band-stand, and generally behaved as though they owned the place. It had been bad for the grass, not to mention the spring bulbs. There had also, the Senate's lady quaestor primly hinted, been other immorality, which I took to be sexual. But as usual in France she was much more bothered by lawns than loins.

Under normal conditions the Luxembourg has a strong university atmosphere. Students use it as a corridor between the Sorbonne and those faculty buildings west of the garden towards Montparnasse. The police accordingly found themselves rejecting thousands of under-40s (or over-12s) every day. The Lycée Montaigne, placed as it is under the sardonic gaze of the Baudelaire statue and just outside the iron-fenced Luxembourg perimeter, reacted very fast. Posters appeared demanding: 'Why have they stolen our green space?' And the spring merry-go-round had begun.

The Luxembourg issue, a local Latin Quarter one, was soon submerged in a national high school strike. Its theme, or at any rate pretext, being the so-called 'Loi Debré', which changes the rules about military-service deferment. This fairly venerable law (of 9 July 1970) was passed without controversy, or even much discussion. No one voted against it, not even the Communists. It was indeed mildly welcomed since its effect will be to prevent the children of rich parents from delaying their 12-month military stint for years, using an unsuccessful academic course as alibi.

The law's authors must have been amazed to find themselves responsible for the conservative *Figaro*'s main headline a week after the gardens were closed: 'The Student Revolt Grows'. More like May '68 than the sedate summer of 1970, when they were doing their legal tinkering. And revolt it was from, for example, Montpellier, which is traditionally leftist, to the Moselle, which just as traditionally is not. In the first the rector closed all secondary schools after premises were occupied by the pupils. In the second area 10 lycées out of 22 were closed. And right across France what the *Figaro* writer called *la farandole* of kids' agitation effectively gave everyone a week's holiday in the sun.

The commentators disagreed naturally about what had caused it all. Everyone suggested it was somehow cyclical, pointing to the unusually long second term — the Easter vacation begins only on 22 April — as well as the expected seasonal friskiness. Certainly the issue was quickly enlarged to a call for the abolition of military service altogether. A stage further, incidentally, than the common programme of the Left, which would have scrapped the *force de frappe* but retained a reduced six months' call-up. Michel Debré, the Defence Minister whose civil servants cooked up the law with their counterparts at the education ministry, thinks the discipline of short-term conscription a crucial weapon in maintaining order. Those on the Left too have noted how the abolition of military service in other countries often made the kids uppity. Certainly its retention in France has acted as a brake on the youth culture as it has flourished in Scandinavia, or even Britain. Georges Marchais is an impassioned (private) advocate for keeping the young disciplined. The Communist Party worked four years at the shop-floor level to repair the ravages made by young *gauchistes* in 1968.

And that, of course, is why *Le Figaro* and the others have been following the education troubles with such flattering attention to apparently trivial detail. When there was a row at Nanterre just about this time five years ago the press ignored it. A young German in the sociology faculty had insulted the Minister of Education at a swimming-pool inauguration, shouting ruderies about sex education. Then there was some other piddling row on the same campus — about male students being banned from the girls' dormitories after 10 at night. Not the kind of thing to enthuse sub-editors, or alarm sub-prefects. Yet five weeks later the Nanterre unrest had led via some obscure process, still solemnly analysed and nostalgically recalled, to a situation where 10 million were on strike and General de Gaulle was bribing the army to preserve the Republic.

The Communist high-school organisation, called UNCAL, has counselled prudence. Its local men have advised students to avoid clashes with police, and they held to the same line even after it became clear the government had decided not to give anything away. The *gauchiste* groups have meanwhile encouraged occupations of faculties and 'police provocation' — not that in the Latin Quarter much is required. Being young is enough in itself.

The French believe we treat our dogs better than our children; baby-bashing they see as a peculiarly English crime. To the foreign observer it often seems that the teenage-student group in France is the worst treated. Teenage culture is regarded with universal loathing by politicians of all parties. One assumption behind the Senate's proscription of the 12 to 40s — that no adolescent would think of walking with his parents, or vice-verse — seems less than bizarre in a French context. This generation gap is seen as *a priori* unbridgeable.

So the spring skirmishes continue, untidy and spontaneous, hard to predict or explain, a mixture of political conviction, a spirit of mischief, and also a symptom of the bottomless *ennui* the French system provokes in many of its most gifted students. No wonder, periodically, people take a fancy to walking on the grass in the Luxembourg Gardens. Which at the time of writing are still closed — unless you happed to be 12-minus, or 40-plus.

New Statesman, 30th March 1973

Melodrama on the waterfront

If the French have a racial problem in the coming weeks, Radio Monte Carlo, the commercial programme so popular on the Côte d'Azur, can claim much of the credit. When a Marseilles bus-driver, Désiré Emile Gerlache, was stabbed to death by a passenger who had just come out of hospital after treatment for brain damage, they did not regard the matter in these terms. Instead on each hourly news bulletin over two days they talked of a 'North African assassin', and when they added he had been virtually lynched by the rest of the passengers it was in a tone of unfortunate warmth. Almost inevitably the deceased bus-driver turned out to be an impeccable citizen with four children. His funeral brought the town to a halt. And local union leaders exploited the situation, ingloriously it seems, to help them in a local work conditions dispute — their case is that for reasons of safety there should be a conductor to punch tickets and take fares, a job at the moment done by the driver. They omitted to add that Gerlache had a colleague on board when the dispute broke out, though it did him little good.

A banal local incident, then, which should have gone no further. Instead within a matter of days Georges Pompidou was warning the French of the dangers of racism and between Marseilles and Nice the holiday territory of the Mediterranean coast became the scene of a series of racial incidents — small ones which under normal circumstances would have been described in a paragraph and forgotten. In the ship-building port of La Ciotat a bomb threat levelled against a hostel for North Africans, probably by another madman, caused one of the inmates to sprain his ankle leaping from bed when the alarm sounded. This incident also attracted headlines, and to read the papers the next morning one might have thought La Ciotat was a scene of mayhem and racial passion. By coincidence I had passed the same evening there watching a water carnival and there was no hint, to borrow a phrase from the local practitioners, of the racial hate simmering in the cauldron of the Côte d'Azur.

Marseilles has been similarly overwritten. Here the 'casbah', as the locals call it, begins at the waterfront and extends for about a mile north of the Old Port as far as the station of St Charles. In theory this area contains 40,000 North Africans which should not be excessive in a city of around a million. In fact there are perhaps three times that number of unregistered immigrants, many of whom have either just arrived or are preparing to return. They are perhaps unduly prominent, being in the exact centre of the town, and their main sin apart from this is the fact that rather few of them seem to have much on their minds apart from a game of dominoes or another glass of mint tea. The overt idleness irritates local citizens in gainful employment but a study of the crime figures indicates that the North Africans are less likely to be involved with the police than Metropolitan French. Contrary to popular belief they are also a much less heavy charge on the welfare services that racist editorialists try to make out. Since they are predominantly young, single and male they make little call, to take an example, on French family welfare services. They do not have children or vices in France, and given the absence of women the rate of sexual crimes is amazingly low. That is not, however, the impression one gets fromreading the Toulon newspaper, *Le Méridional*.

'We have had enough of it. Enough of the Algerian thieves, of the Algerian hooligans, of Algerian syphilitics, of Algerian rapists, of Algerian pimps, of Algerian madmen, of Algerian killers!' This was how they reacted to the killing of Gerlache, and it is a tone of voice which attracts the attention of the poor, the frustrated and not least of the nearly one million former inhabitants of French North African colonies who settled in the Bouches-du-Rhône department after Algerian independence. The recent expropriations in Morocco have added marginally to their number, and have revived old and invariably disagreeable memories. In 1962 when the Algerian exodus was reaching its peak the Marseilles casbah was truly dangerous for reasons that were even then more ideological than strictly racist. OAS supporters had got into the habit of being beyond the law quite apart from the professional criminals and bank robbers who were the detritus of France's unhappy colonial conclusion.

Nowadays, despite what *Le Méridional* says, one can walk in perfect peace and tranquillity. As a Marseilles friend remarked: '20 years ago no Frenchman would have penetrated this quarter after nightfall. Nowadays no problems.' Except, of course, in special circumstances such as the present ones. The Gerlache funeral provided an enviable opportunity for the hard-core racist to exploit. The Gaullist shock troops, the so-called 'Committees for the Defence of the Republic', immediately called public meetings and sent out their activists to paint slogans on walls announcing that neither mothers nor daughters were safe from North African rapists. The Archbishop of Marseilles, Monseigneur Etchegaray, talked about 'a dramatic situation', which was in fact not dramatic in the least, and of 'the flame of racial violence which has been burning along the coast and has reached its apogee in Marseilles'. Maurice Arreck, the mayor of Toulon, decided it was the right moment to announce that his local social security charges were twice as heavy as those of Bordeaux, a comparable town, because of the presence of the North Africans. He also added various useful comments about the way that immigrants put coal in the baths of their new apartment blocks, or introduced sheep and hens into their houses. He will benefit from these remarks at the next elections, and so probably will Joseph Comiti, a Marseilles MP and minister, who weighed in with some fighting words about clearing ghettoes and creating a society where a respectable woman can walk in the streets without being insulted or violated.

Gaston Defferre, the Marseilles mayor, reacted more calmly. The government, he pointed out, had done everything they could over the last 20 years to encourage immigrant workers without providing services to handle them. Since France's prosperity depended on them, and despite appearances there are very few who are not employed, it is, to put it mildly, ungracious to turn round and announce they are sub-human criminals. He is a man of some experience in this area — having handled the repatriation of a million or so French émigrés, almost all of whom returned to the homeland via Marseilles. If ever there was a situation where racial strife seemed inevitable it was 10 years ago when these families were trying to re-integrate themselves into a Metropolitan French society many of them had forgotten or never known. His methods at the time were not particularly gentle, but they worked well enough for him to be a serious alternative presidential candidate. In the event it was François Mitterrand and not Gaston Defferre who stood for the united Left against de Gaulle in 1965, but had events fallen marginally differently, Defferre might have stood and won. In the event his political career was restricted to a local level. One of his major achievements has been to make of Marseilles a town where French and North Africans live together, without much affection probably, but with a minimum of discord. He will probably ride out this brief bad season, as he has dealt with more demanding situations in the past.

But in the meantime the question of foreign labour has been raised and the French government will have to do something about it. They have a shade over 7 per cent of foreigners, one third of them North Africans, in the work force.

Luxembourg has 20 per cent; Switzerland over 16; Belgium just about the same as France. A timely survey by the *Nouvel Observateur* suggests that the French will accept their foreign labourers, having no choice. They recognise that the Algerians, the Moroccans and the others are almost exclusively employed in jobs which local Frenchmen regard as too disgusting, or ill-paid, or both, to take on themselves. Equally, they see that France's quite striking if inflationary prosperity stems in no small measure from their contribution. President Pompidou's basic assumption about the French is that they will put up with anything so long as they are prosperous, or moderately so. It may seem like an outmoded idea, recalling as it does the smash-and-grab bourgeois society of the Second Empire. As an ethic it is perhaps ignoble. But it is the principle on which the Gaullists have run the country for the last 15 years, and despite the incidents stemming from an unusually hot summer nothing has happened to make them reconsider their basic assumptions. It is not a very beautiful society and every so often one sees its dark side. But for the moment it works.

New Statesman, 7th September 1973

The sick man of France

A bodyguard, supposedly detailed to protect the Prime Minister on his Corsican show-the flag tour, suddenly chucks a grenade at him. The intrepid minister survives to inspect a building. Seconds after he leaves it blows up. The Marx Bros you say? Yes indeed. But compared to the travails suffered by the Gaullist majority in the last week Prime Minister Messmer's picaresque trip to combative Corsica seems almost a tonic, a comedy of human mishappenstance instead of a ghoul saga scripted by Spiro Agnew and Roman Polanski.

Compared with what has afflicted the President, the Prime Minister's travails have been light relief. So much so that for once the caricature aspect of recent days has not escaped local observers. When not publishing learned essays, exploring a spectrum of malady from piles to bone cancer, they have coined the headline 'The President's Psychodrama'.

They are right to seek metaphor from a context outside the normal range of public affairs because the issues are no longer strictly political, but rather politico-medical. Suddenly only a handful of doctors (of medicine, not economics or psephology) are qualified to answer questions about oil bills, industrial relations and the exercise of power which in normal times would be the domain of France's generally highly competent technocrats of government.

Such has been the situation since the macabre Diplomatic Corps gala night last week on the eve of which President Pompidou became too ill to greet his Elysée Palace guests. The ambassadors nonetheless galaed on, since it was too late to stop them, diplomatically speculating where their host might be to the accompaniment of a light orchestra chiselling away at Gounod's Spring Song and operetta extracts. Apparently some less sophisticated or more bibulous diplomats arrived home unaware that their host was stricken in his bed, and had not been presiding as normal somewhere beyond the acres of golden furniture in the Salon Murat.

They knew next morning all right and so did the French en masse. As opposed to the insiders or that section of the electorate which bothers with the minutiae of current affairs. A few days' sickness during Easter holidays in the country might have passed unnoticed. As it was, both the occasion and the timing might have been designed to annul the President's heroic battle with his health earlier in the month at the Black Sea summit with Brezhnev, not to mention the Gaullist majority's whole electoral strategy, which had only been cobbled together in the previous 48 hours.

On the very day of the break-down Finance Minister Giscard d'Estaing had been sanguine as a butterfly about the long-term effects of an emergency budget positively Crippsian in its severity. The calculated gamble was to sacrifice short-term popularity during the dangerous upcoming season of industrial and social unrest. This, or so Giscard and his officials were suggesting, would provide lee-way towards the end of the year, an economic base on which to build an election victory in 1975 should the President's health prevent him from completing his mandate (running to 1976).

The economic package was, and indeed still is, since the Government has little alternative, designed to hold down wages and prices, attack domestic consumption with some brutality, and engage in technical manoeuvres intended to make the franc fall against competitive currencies, thus boosting French exports. The proportion of the Frenchman's annual income tax payable in February had already been raised from one third to 43 per cent. The most immediately unpopular Budget measure was to repeat almost precisely this provision for the second slice of annual tax payable on 15 May. Certainly it's tough, the officials said. What can you expect with a forecasted 1974 trade deficit of 18,000m. francs and a rise of between 12 and 15 per cent in the cost of living for the year? But attention. You will have observed provision has also been made for a reduction of 'simplification' of the VAT mechanism. Not yet, of course. But the implication remained that a handful of tax jujubes around the season of goodwill would help the citizens forget the nasty medicine they had been forced to swallow during less convivial seasons. It may have been optimistic, but given the inherent conservatism of French voters it had some kind of sporting chance. Two days later came the Gala, and a need for a French phrase equivalent to 'all the isms are wasms'.

The French presidency is unusually onerous, carrying with it executive powers as sweeping as any a Washington president enjoys under normal conditions yet without an American-style Congress to impose restraint. It was tailored for (and partly by) a Colossus who believed in imperial isolation as an instrument of awe. There is accordingly no vice-presidential machinery, nor apparently for juristic reasons is it possible to create one in the near future.

In many ways the presidential job has become more demanding since de Gaulle was forced by referendum to resign it. His taste was to closet himself with World Affairs and indeed History, leaving Pompidou the office-boy job of keeping the French modestly affluent and docile. Pompidou has retained this responsibility and inherited the global preoccupations as well. The Gaullists are as aware of the majesty of the office as 15 years' propaganda can make them. They fear, above all, a deterioration or recurrence of crippling illness which could prevent the President either continuing in office, or passing it on tactically to a chosen and legitimate successor from the ranks of the faithfull.

Should this happen the interim presidency would be assumed for 40 days by Alain Poher, the Senate leader who knows something about it since he stopped in after the General's departure. He did the Gaullists little good on that occasion and is thought to have learnt more than is good for the Gaullist. Among other things the fact that long before Watergate was a twinkle in any plumber's eye the Elysée Palace had been comprehensively bugged down to the last Louis XV commode. Poher apart, the prospect of internecine strife between, say, the Prime Minister, the Finance Minister, and former Prime Minister Chaban-Delmas, is also very worrying for many UDR stalwarts, even though the party machine is supposedly sewn up by Chaban already. A smooth and orderly succession would make infinitely more electoral sense.

In theory, if no time is wasted, such a course is still open. The President is known to prefer a five- rather than seven-year term of office, certainly for his successors. This constitutional change could be rushed through the post-Easter Parliament in time for a first electoral round on 16 June, which because of French holiday habits is the last possible date before the autumn. In theory, yet in practice going to the country four weeks after the Budget bite would be highly masochistic. So sit it out, and for how long? This time a medical question.

Much more than the future of a man or a political grouping with a habit of power could be at issue. The one French world record no one can hope to challenge is in the arcane and nervous field of constitution changing. Since 1789 there have been alterations, some minor, others revolutionary, on average every 12 years. As French regimes go the Fifth Republic, 15 years old, is already well ahead of its predecessor, which survived from 1946 until De Gaulle finished it by a wholly original technique not unlike a coup d'etat in May 1958.

Many doubted his creation, the Fifth Republic, would survive him. It proved highly durable, increasingly more presidential in character and less parliamentary. The year 1974 is certainly France's hardest since the Algerian war ended. Can the office be transferred, or even retained, once again? This is the real 'psychodrama', not of one admirable president, but of the presidency itself. In this bad year for presidents France is understandably nervous.

Paris *New Statesman,* 27th March 1974

France without Pompidou

Georges Pompidou's sudden death came as a brutal confirmation of the French nation's most fearful premonitions. The immediate reaction was confusion, later characterised as 'stupefaction' by a grieving cabinet minister. By midnight on Tuesday armed riot police were guarding both the Ile St. Louis, where the President had his private apartment, and the Luxembourg Palace across the Left Bank. A pall of rain was falling democratically on both detachments, the second of which was much larger than the first, reflecting, in theory at least, the reality of a still embryonic situation.

For the 36 hours before he moved to the Elysée Palace Alain Poher, President of the Senate, was commanding the centre of power from his official Luxembourg residence. The Senate post is, except for this instance, distinctly honorific, like a US vice-presidency. Only in a state of constitutional emergency does the urbane palace, its lights glowing till dawn, suddenly reveal a functional heart beneath all the architectural frivolities.

In contrast, President Pompidou's apartment in the Quai de Béthune has already acquired an academic, sequestered air, as if preparing for a long future as an historic monument. The power had seeped out of the stones.

It was a place out of the past, a place where an ex-president had been forced to cede despite amazing endurance, a place which had finally repudiated power altogether, like youthful folly. That had shifted elsewhere, to the Luxembourg, which became a magnet in the small hours, with haggard political figures blustering their way through the increasingly impregnable protective cordon like mosquitoes drawn to a fever patient.

The event emerged as a ghastly surprise which was not really a surprise at all insofar as it had been foreshadowed by innumerable hushed conversations and grim forecasts. But when the blow came it was like a black joke on the part of history, a macabre twist which left France with the most difficult problem of all to overcome.

The President had not only died in office before having time to designate a successor, an eventuality almost as odious to the Opposition as to the leaderless majority the ex-president leaves behind him. The moment of severance had come at a time of deep uncertainty. Domestically the widespread industrial unrest resulting from severe inflation was, if anything, hardening. In the wider European context, officials in Paris were in the process of reacting to the threat to EEC posed by the Callaghan speech at the foreign ministers' conference.

The Left, despite strains and tensions, has retained its by no means easy unity and coasted through what can now be seen as a pre-electoral period without hysteria. This is more than can be said either for the fractious Centre Alliance, which had been making much of the trouble surrounding Pompidou's health, or the now battered looking Gaullist majority, which runs a risk of being fragmented kaleidoscopically.

In private talks recently François Mitterrand had been saying how fervently he hoped the Pompidou mandate would be fulfilled to the end of the term in June 1976. He was not, I think, being disingenuous, and it is hard to see the Socialist leader welcoming a divisive national election campaign at so delicate a point in time, even though it might conceivably make him Socialist President of France before mid-summer.

For the Gaullists find themselves trapped at a transitional stage which only a determined and charismatic figure can resolve. The hierarchy of the majority has been considering the various possibilities open to them for some time. Now what from their point of view was the worst eventuality, the nightmare hypothesis of the king dying sans dauphin which I outlined in the NS last week, has comprehensively come to pass. Stoical, tight-fisted, keeping his own counsel until it was too late,,

Georges Pompidou's funeral in April 1974.
(Hurel/Camera Press)

Croesus has passed away intestate, and without so much as recognising a son.

No one was more aware than President Pompidou of the dangers inherent in this emergency constitutional machinery. His intention had been to modify it as soon as possible in the interest of national stability quite apart from sectarian considerations of keeping the majority in power and de Gaulle's Fifth Republic intact. Poher, who was forced to do the same job when de Gaulle left in 1969, is an avowed and very bitter opponent of the regime. He is no friend of Prime Minister Pierre Messmer, who has his own power base through the machinery stemming from his office at the Hotel Matignon.

It is not hard to imagine the interim President giving orders, particularly once the election campaign starts, which loyalist officials either ignore, block, or simply refuse to obey. The elections must take place within a minimum of 20 days and a maximum of 35, thus leaving the country with no elected leader until May, a month with unhappy connotations for Gaullism. Meanwhile there could be no more classic conditions for a coup than those provided by an interim of this kind at this particularly volatile and problematic moment.

With 15 years of power and know-how behind them it may be that the Gaullists will demonstrate a high level of political maturity in the interests of both party and national unity. It is premature to make predictions one way or the other. But it is evident that France faces a nervous period during which the vacuum left by Georges Pompidou attracts all kinds of aspirants, among them some not very respectable ones.

Again, it is easy to deduce from recent initiatives, the presidential dispositions of days which turned out to be the last of his career, that Pompidou was very conscious of the subterranean threats posed by his illness. One of his last presidential acts was to approve the dismissal of three full colonels with a history of ultra-Gaullist political plotting and employed by the DST, a secret organisation responsible for spying and counter-espionage as well as comparatively mundane domestic security chores, like bugging opposition newspaper offices and infiltrating potentially subversive groups. Despite this action, executed by Interior Minister Jacques Chirac, the DST's newly appointed chief, a career policeman called Jacques Charton, is not a figure likely to work easily under the interim President or inspire him with confidence about the safeguarding of democratic procedures.

During the 1969 interim Poher clashed immediately and bitterly with the Intelligence service on the one hand, the Government-controlled radio and television networks on the other. No one doubts his previous experience has made the interim President all the more determined to exercise his constitutional authority to the full this time. Again, his official opponents are likely to prove even more intransigent since the situation is appreciably tighter. In 1969 the industrial scene was quiet, the post-May 1968 backlash was still the determining factor, and above all in Georges Pompidou the Gaullists had an experienced and 'legitimate' leader and presidential candidate, one who had actually been sanctified as successor by De Gaulle himself. Now the majority has at least four strong and mutually exclusive potential candidates — Chaban-Delmas, Giscard d'Estaing, Messmer and Foreign Minister Michel Jobert — and it must try to make its selection without self-destructive internal feuds.

Of these candidates (and there are others too) Finance Minister Giscard is the only one with a considerable appeal to voters as a personality of stature in his own right. The others will all to some extent or another be attempting to present themselves as the true dauphin, the spiritual legatee. Messmer, renowned for his loyalty, Chaban for his Tammany Hall skills and Jobert, who was Pompidou's discovery in the way Pompidou was De Gaulle's, will in different ways aspire to an idea of legitimacy. For Jobert, who was glacially informing the French nation of the British made EEC crisis at about the time the President was transferred to his private apartment to die, the moment is probably premature.

The country, and by extension the whole European Community, is faced with an agonising hiatus as the first black-rimmed special editions reach the streets.

Paris

New Statesman, 5th April 1974

Mimi and the Cardinal

Madame Mimi Santoni, currently holidaying incognito at a secret address in the South of France, is not the kind of girl you meet at a Legion of Mary Lenten breakfast. Were she, such occasions would be more heavily patronised. Mimi's sartorial taste runs to outmoded yet becoming micro-minis, her shaggy mane is ablaze with blonde highlights, and when Mimi talks (an increasingly rare occurrence just recently) both accent and argot at once identify her as a denizen of Pigalle, the fun section of Paris so often awash with visiting football fans. There she worked (again until very recently) in a cabaret bar. Less specifically she herself describes her occupation as 'the entertainment business'.

Yes indeed. As is usual in these fun-loving circles Mimi has a child whom she adores and a husband who has what English criminal lawyers call 'form'. His last peccadillo cost a medium-length stretch in La Santé prison, convicted of prostitution charges.

The family residence of the Santonis is in the Rue Dulong, a moderately fashionable address in the 17th arrondissement. It enjoys the advantage of being close to both Montmartre, which is sleazy and mercantile, and the Parc Monceau, which should be select and innocent. Though not much hope with the Santonis around. The apartment, where Mimi was visited by numerous friends in the long afternoons, is not, as the French pop papers say, 'totally unknown to the services of police'.

These same services received a bothered call from Mimi shortly after lunch on 20 May. She told them to send a doctor fast. One of her friends had just died. When it comes to sudden, unexplained death, the Paris police are very prompt. Within minutes the neighbours were distressed to find a brace of squad cars in the street. In due course they were joined by an emergency medical squad sent by that excellent but indiscreet body of men, the Sapeurs-Pompiers of Paris.

Through some unhappy cross-cultural omission there are no French anecdotes in which the principal characters are the actress and the bishop. But, ironically, as will become apparent, Gallic commercial travellers are full of chirpy tales involving the fireman and the baker's wife. For 30 minutes the fireman of the 17th arrondissement applied mouth-to-mouth resuscitation techniques on Mimi's guest, but to no avail.

At least one of them, who leaked the story afterwards, must have been aware he had stumbled on a new mythological archetype — let us call it the Lady Entertainer and the Cardinal. The fireman in question was a TV addict and he had no difficulty in recognising the man on Mimi's floor. Here was no itinerant Celtic supporter. The corpse, for the visitor had clearly departed for a better world, belonged to no less than Cardinal Jean Danièlou, by some way the best-known and admired church leader in France.

It seems there are more precedents than one might guess for gentlemen, though not as far as I can discover cardinals, expiring of natural causes in circumstances which, to borrow another piece of French journalese, 'involve the perfume of scandal'. The police know the form. They do not like to upset the nearest and dearest with squalid details. The convention is that a statement is issued noting the deceased was struck down by a heart attack in the street outside the incriminating address. This they did, after a conference with Père André Costes, the provincial of the Jesuit order in France to which the cardinal belonged.

However, at some point things began to go wrong with this humane and well-tried system. Before the Jesuits had time to administer the Last Unction the staircase at 56 Rue Dulong was already full of jostling journalists, largely, it was noted, from the gutter press. According to some reports they were actually there before the Commissaire of the 17th arrondissement who was, to put it mildly overwhelmed that a prince of the Church, a member of the French Academy to boot, had chosen to die in such exotic circumstances in his manor. The police had by then discovered that Jean Danièlou had a shade under 300 pound in his wallet, the basis of later yet inconclusive stories of blackmail.

The Commissaire's reaction was to tell the press to get the hell out, and assure them that not one line of the story had any hope of appearing in their newspapers. He said the proprietors would kill any such accounts out of hand, and he was perfectly right. It was nine days before (a wildly garbled) account of the event saw the light of day in *Le Canard Enchaîné,* the French equivalent of *Private Eye.*

The entry of *Le Canard* into the saga was significant because here was one of the few newspapers in France with an ideological axe to grind — it has behind it a tradition of anti-clerical protest dating back more than half a century. This newspaper's reflex, apart from an innocent desire to spit in the face of the Establishment which they would generously have extended to any member of the French Academy, or probably to any Gaullist, therefore had a specific historical slant. In the good old days their job was to ridicule the Church and all her ways. It was doubtless irresistible for them to have a go at even a dead cardinal, particularly one who had made a name as a conservative theologian and who was particularly well known for his severity on the issue of chastity. Cardinal Danièlou's red hat, awarded in 1969, largely stemmed from his exigent moral line on the vexed question of the celibacy of the priesthood. His thundering television attacks on the concept of married clergy were, in fact, the basis for his post-mortem identification by the fireman.

To make him even fairer game, in the eyes of *Le Canard* at any rate, the dead man had also been an implacable opponent of the ecumenical movement in all its forms. They resented him all the more for being a nice and unpretentious man who was always open to the press.

Despite his conservative views he liked to drink with reporters, and was charitably content to engage them in simplistic theological arguments, late in to the night if need be. This moral capital, acquired over many years, goes some way towards explaining why the story was hushed up for so long.

But no more. In recent years the Church in France has been like the dog that did not bark. There were several election issues which might well have had an ecclesiastical overtone — abortion and contraception reforms figure prominently in the programmes of the three major candidates, yet electoral debates were conducted on a strictly secular level. The only point at which any remotely religious consideration was taken into account concerned the over-60 voters and the three marriages of Jacques Chaban-Delmas. It was thought in some circles that his second divorce, conducted against the lush background of country-club Bordeaux, was a shade more scandalous than appropriate for a future resident of the Elysée Palace. Even so the question was more one of appearance and style than conventional (which in this context means Roman Catholic) morality.

Oddly, what is now known as the 'Danièlou Affaire', apparently a sordid yellow press issue, appears to have provoked a serious debate of a kind which has not been heard of in France for a long time. Although they made some kind of inept effort, the hierarchy of the French church have now ceased to deny the details of Danièlou's death, and are adopting a more viable and interesting defence of their lost leader. Why, after all, surprisingly senior members of the hierarchy have been asking, is it so disgraceful for such a man to have died in the arms of a sinner? There have been many references to the epigram of Cardinal Angelo Dell'Acqua on the subject of sins of the flesh: 'Peccate di carne, peccate di niente'. There are more influential churchmen in France referring to the 'aggiornamento' and the need to re-examine the concept of charity in the light of the modern World since the Danièlou affair, than have ever previously been heard in a country where religious change has been fought tooth and nail ever since the failed worker-priest experiment of a decade ago.

There is a real chance, in short, that the matter of how Cardinal Danièlou died will provoke a genuine reconsideration of the relationship between the Church's leaders and its members. It is a long time since the Church made headlines here.

One imagines that Mimi's aspirations to being a moral influence were fairly slender, yet she seems to have cast herself in the role. Similarly Jean Danièlou's death, despite its absurd Maupassant aspect, may easily turn out to have a more profound significance than anything else he encompassed in the course of 40 years' devotion to the ideals of the Company of Jesus. I think, for once, it is possible to say without contradictions it could only have happened in Paris.

New Statesman, 28th June 1974

Prince of 'flics'

'Le weekend anglais' so permeates the French snobbish imagination that only mugs or masochists attempt driving out of Paris on Friday evenings. The night of Friday 14 last month was nonetheless something quite special: traffic leaving the capital attained a kind of apogee of immobility. Seen from the Porte d'Italie the stationary cars apparently stretched as far as Lyons, if not to the Italian frontier itself. The next morning, it emerged, we owed this historic foul-up to one man: the new Minister of the Interior, Prince Michel Poniatowski no less.

'Ponia' (the nick-name implies scant affection) has spent his life in political intrigue. He is now only one step away from ultimate power in France. He is the President's closest chum — perhaps since Giscard is a phoney aristocrat he admires the genuine article, Poniatowski's princely creation dating from Napoleon. In any case wherever Giscard goes Ponia's overweight shadow and Bosch-like countenance are always within whispering distance. His Interior Ministry job gives the prince enormous power. It does not, however, or in normal circumstances at any rate, stretch far enough to creating a kind of vehicular Armageddon to gratify an aristocratic whim.

Not, of course, when one made innocent inquiries about the affair, that the Ponia PR boys described the 14 June fiasco in precisely these terms. Rather they spoke of radical policies, of liberating innovation, of — and here is the crux — that Fortnum and Mason of authoritarian government, law and order.

For the traffic chaos stemmed from a police exercise initiated by Ponia, whose ministerial post makes him, in the words of his intimate enemy and unlamented predecessor, Raymond Marcellin: 'The first *flic* in France.' Depending on how long the memory of one's informant, it is necessary to go back either to the height of the Algerian war or the activities of the Gestapo during the Occupation to parallel an operation on this scale. But, for once, the most eloquent description is statistical.

The 14 June operation started around dusk and went on into the small hours. Three distinct categories of enforcement officers — motorised police, special riot squads and friendly local gendarmes — achieved an impressive work load during this shift. They performed 'controls' on no fewer than 45,695 citizens, mainly in four areas on the outskirts of the capital. Their basis was random: they did not, that is, select people who generated suspicion for some reason or another. They just happened to be there. Those stopped were required to show the identity papers French citizens are legally obliged to carry at all times, questioned about where they were going and why, and sometimes searched too. In the case of motorists their cars were examined as well. It was noted by the Interior Ministry computer that the controlees included 3,595 citizens under 21, and '4,500 foreigners' — the vast majority North African workers, rather than foreign tourists en route for the Costa Brava, although these were naturally not exempt either. Welcome to *la belle France*.

Ponia himself, plus cameramen (and, I presume, bodyguards) lent a hand on the Pont d'Argenteuil, a traffic black spot even without his help. He explained to the weekend drivers how lucky they were to have so dynamic a government. For those who missed his personal touch there was a printed letter with a facsimile of the ministerial signature. 'I am persuaded you will recognise the necessity and utility of this operation, and accept the minor constraints involved...'

In the interests, of course, of the crusade against crime. Well, since there were around 5,000 cops trawling the net, directed by skipper Ponia on the bridge, one might have expected a rich haul of malefactors on 14 June. The actual results might serve as a propaganda exercise for the law-abiding qualities of Parisians: 35 people in all were held by the police (several of whom were later released: I guess they had left their identity cards at home). Those charged broke down as follows: six drunk drivers; four car thieves; four possessing stolen property; four more carrying illegal drugs, and two cases of illegal weapons (the police are vague about the latter — it may well be the weapons in question were unlicensed sporting guns).

Undeterred by so many mackerels employed in hooking so few sprats, Ponia launched yet another similar drive the next night. This time the police swept through Lille, Lyons and the notoriously criminal city of Marseilles in a 'global operation'. It would be wearisome to spell out the details again. Suffice it to say that 100,000 Frenchmen were 'controlled' by about 10,000 police over the weekend of 14 June. A grand total of 86 were held for further questioning; of these an undisclosed number (an educated guess would be one quarter of the total) were subsequently released without a court appearance.

After so paltry a harvest a lesser minister might have drawn a discreet veil and applied himself to some other aspect of abrasive government. But not Ponia. Instead he delivered a rousing, Agnew-esque harangue about the 173-per-cent crime increase since 1963. He dwelt lovingly on the 55,000 burglaries in Paris last year. He curdled the blood by describing the three hold-ups each day in 1973, the four attacks on solitary women in the streets. Questioned in parliament, Ponia reluctantly conceded that French crime rates are in fact markedly lower than in almost any other comparable society. And within 24 hours, on the night of 21/22 June, set up yet another *rafle* — a near forgotten word used for Gestapo sort-outs during the war. He got 60 minor offenders this time out of 52,000 citizens controlled. Enough to call the whole thing off one might think, particularly as the over-worked police were showing signs of restiveness? By no means. Sheriff Ponia continues to fire from the hip. His latest tactic is random controls on the Metro. Here I predict a more impressive kill rate. With luck many a criminal travelling first class on a second-class ticket will get his deserved comeuppance.

Ponia's policy, stripped of rhetorical grace notes, is familiar, and even respectable: getting the cops back on the beat. He is right to insist that too many police are immobilised by guard duties. The Latin Quarter always seems in a state of siege. First-time visitors are often alarmed by the serried ranks of CRS riot troops. Is there an armed insurrection in the offing, they ask? An imminent invasion?

The answer is that the CRS presence is strictly intimidatory. But as the jurist Gerard Soulier wrote recently in *Le Monde*, Ponia's wild antics are swapping one form of intimidation for another. The scheme is partly designed to placate '*les braves gens*', the silent majority who elected Giscard, and as long as they are not controlled too often themselves it may work. But there is a secondary motive to consider, made all the more sinister since the French penal code, repressive though it is, provides no sanction for police interrogating private citizens when there are no grounds for suspicion. To quote Soulier again: *'The policy is a question of habituation. To get people used to the habit of repression. To make it normal, just necessary and finally legitimate. It is a psychological operation. A new step in the technical and ideological apparatus of repression.'*

New Statesman, 12th July 1974

Giscard's hole in the ground

A few days ago a French property developer called Jean-Claude Aaron picked up his pool-side telephone in the Ritzy resort of Mégève. Minutes before, he had been the proud promoter-in-chief of a truly scandalous project to fill some 280,000 cubic metres of the ancient Les Halles section of Paris in the interests of an 'International Trade Center'. But no longer. President Giscard had just flexed his aesthetic muscles. The only thing now left to promote, the shattered Aaron learned from his equally distracted partner, was the most expensive hole in the world.

Giscard made this far-reaching decision entirely alone, and with casual brutality. When a harassed official from the Paris municipality explained that no fewer than 28,000 ten-ton lorries would be needed almost at once to fill the space on which all those machines, the office towers and boxes, should have been erected, the new President smiled grimly. The lorries will have to move fast. Otherwise the noble Renaissance church of St Eustache, which the property boys had reluctantly made a virtue of 'preserving', would disintegrate and slide into the big hole as ineluctably as Pompidou's idea of France.

France's new President exhibited scant regret. He had decided that there were already too many modern offices and hotels in central Paris. He was going to have a big garden in the centre of Les Halles instead (an idea dismissed by Pompidou, who said a nice green space like that would surely attract '60,000 young hippies'). There was also more, and worse, to come from Giscard. He also intended to cancel a second grandiose scheme scheduled for the neighbouring Plateau Beaubourg site, east of Les Halles. This idea was not only bloody-minded, but virtually blasphemous. For Beaubourg was the late President's personal baby. An art gallery-cum-cultural centre intended to make the Metropolitan Museum in New York look like a stall in the Flea Market.

Cannily recognising the late Roman overtones of this impulse, Parisians labelled this new potential edifice the 'Pompidoleum'. The new President said that this site would make a pretty park too (he is not unaware of the ecology lobby). Robert Galley, Minister for Construction and almost the last extant Gaullist, made little impression even when he pointed out that thousands of specially constructed concrete blocks would shortly be transported to Paris for this Concorde of art galleries. They would come in handy, said Giscard, to fill the hole left by the Trade Centre he had aborted five minutes earlier. It was left to Pompidou's spiritual stepson, Jacques Chirac, to pluck his former master's memorial from the jaws of oblivion, with a shrewd historical appeal. Chirac hinted that when (many years in the future naturally) Giscard retired from the great stage he might himself fancy some suitable tribute...They had to build the thing to preserve Pompidou's name. Otherwise it was in danger of being forgotten altogether. Such arguments carry weight in this bad year for presidents.

So the 'Pompidoleum', the creation of two architects called Rogers and Piano whose model resembles a cut-price atomic reactor, will go ahead. (It will probably also house the world's finest Picasso collection negotiations with the Picasso children to take their 20-per-cent slice of death duties in kind, as it were.) But the museum will be an exception. It is now evident that the era of 'real-estate Gaullism' is well and truly over. Giscard has not only made a radical break with the prevailing urban philosophy of the last decade. He has also invented a new political ploy, the vacation *fait accompli*, which to hear those who speculated in the Trade Centre debacle talk is equivalent to stabbing your opponent in the back between rounds.

It is a moot point, for instance, whether the evil news more distressed Aaron in his pool or Maurice Doublet — as prefect for the Paris conurbation he is theoretically in charge of such matters. Even so he was only informed of the decision when the morning papers arrived on his terrace in the Midi. He should have known better. Giscard had announced he would himself take a brief presidential vacation, but omitted to specify when or where. This meant that ministers and top civil servants either had to sweat it out in Paris or risk being by-passed *in absentia*.

Even as old a hand as Jean Lecanuet, Minister of Justice and presidential aspirant, found himself outsmarted. When to everyone's relief Giscard finally set off for the South of France last Saturday he erroneously deduced that the President would henceforth be harmlessly engaged in scuba-diving and other nautically photogenic pursuits. Instead VGE (the Kennedy-style initials are now obligatory in the presidential entourage) did some fancy footwork involving helicopters and visited two prisons in Lyons, in theory part of Lecanuet's fief, on the trip south.

The Les Halles planning decision is only the most amusing and recent development in the creation of what is being called 'Giscard's Paris'. It is mainly a question of preservation. The new President has now killed no fewer than 15 major development schemes for the capital inherited from his predecessor. They include reversing the lunatic, and apparently irrevocable, express motorway which was to have replaced the most beautiful section of the Left Bank, and the less publicised project known as the 'Radiale Vercingétorix'.

This was an engagingly Strangelovian project: it would have produced an umbilical motorway connection between the ring roads round the city and the belly of the disgraceful Montparnasse high-rise tower. 'Vercingétorix' was the kind of thing Pompidou really appreciated. The process of making southern Montparnasse unfit for anyone not driving a car was the very archetype of post-Gaullist urban thinking.

NS readers who know Paris may be interested to learn the effects of some other condemned projects. The merry idea of building high-rise blocks beside the Eiffel Tower, for instance, has passed into history. There will be no more indistinguishable 'buildings de luxe' at La Defence on the western rim, either. The communist stronghold of Belleville in the 19th arrondissement is no longer due to be transformed into a kind of Parisian Slough. In short, VGE's approach to town planning is perfectly sane. Had he decreed that Messrs Rogers and Piano should be hanged publicly from the top of the Arc de Triomphe to encourage urban architects everywhere, it would even be exemplary.

There are, however, political problems involved, as well as nugatory logistic matters to do with filling holes where Les Halles used to be. Giscard's urban ideas coincide almost precisely with those laid down in the common election programme of the United Left, and so eloquently expressed by François Mitterrand during the campaign (also with an eye on young voters). It marks a major departure from the Tory aspect of late Gaullism, the idea that people, the right people anyway, were never so harmlessly engaged as when making large sums of money out of the wrong people. There is also a fundamental aesthetic change.

Under Pompidou and his brief but disastrous Minister of Culture, Maurice Druon, France was moving towards an idea of State Art (familiar to students of right-wing societies). Druon's cultural views were closer to Goering's than to those of his predecessor André Malraux. His notable firsts included using the adjective 'Pompidolien' in a public speech with no detectable ironic intention, and the memorable statement that it is impossible to lie when speaking the French language with perfect correctness. Pompidou's (no doubt well-founded) fear that if one created a habitable environment young people would take advantage of it to enjoy themselves also has French precedents. Druon was speaking in the same voice as President Gambetta, who remarked (apropros of Renoir) that he preferred the Republic to live with mediocre painting rather than die in the presence of great art. Virtually Giscard's first act on moving into the Elysée Palace was to have Pompidou's pictures thrown out. He continues in the same callous spirit.

New Statesman, 16th August 1974

How the French won the war

Shoulder to shoulder with the French TV networks we have spent much of this summer battling our way from the beaches of Normandy to the gates of Paris. If ever there was an example of television over-kill this daily reconstitution of the events of 1944 — at length if scarcely in depth — must win some sort of prize.

After so much martial fore-play one felt profound release, along with a few million other captive viewers, when last Sunday, 25 August, some kind of televisual consummation was finally achieved on the 30th anniversary of the French capital's Liberation. Suffering by now from vicarious shell-shock, we were on the spot with all the ghosts. There was Leclerc's Free French armoured division; there was Hemingway intrepidly liberating the Ritz Hotel and Sylvia Beach's expatriate bookshop: above all, there was General de Gaulle's lanky and easily offended phantom returning to the Ministry of War he had left four years before — one long stride ahead of les Boches.

That marathon documentary of life in the provinces under the Occupation, *Le Chagrin et la Pitié*, created a stir when shown on TV in Britain but was never, for reasons of censorship, put out on the French ORTF networks. As if to make some back-handed amends we have now seen this orgy of ORTF reminiscence and reconstruction, varying from five-minute film clips inserted into each day's news coverage, to whole feature films on specific incidents, such as the liberation of Toulouse in the south, of which more later. This enterprise, which has occupied the moribund ORTF to the exclusion of almost anything else, adds up to a kind of anti-Chagrin.

The initial documentary struck me as openly tendentious — the camera being employed almost sarcastically, for example, when it concentrated on the nervous hands of a Vichy supporter while his self-justifying voice was heard over. Shiftiness, get it? Le Chagrin's emotional well-springs were the masochistic guilt some post war Frenchmen feel about their country's war record. No one could accuse the ORTF of such negative thinking.

What have the French themselves made of it all? Many I've spoken to of an age to remember have been irritated and uneasy — the relentless (and again tendentious) war focus has set their teeth on edge.

When it comes to the kids the story is entirely different: indifference. A survey of lycée students' attitudes to various matters from compulsory maths to sex education underpinned this impression not long ago. As one 16 year old remarked with adolescent cruelty, 'When my old man starts off about the war I just say "Verdun, connais pas" and bugger off with my mates.'

His references to the 1916 holocaust showed more historical sensitivity than he intended. For grim memories of the gratuitous dead of 1914-18 played no small part in convincing the intelligent, reasonable French — all those who had something to lose — that further resistance in 1940 was useless.

Since as a country we have shown ourselves to be dab hands at self-deception in recent years it has been instructive to watch the ORTF's heavy-handed attempt to cobble together a not dissimilar kind of collective illusion.

One of the most specific examples came during an everlasting documentary

General de Gaulle addressing the citizens of Bayeux in June 1944 after his triumphant return from four years exile.
(Camera Press)

recreation of how Toulouse was liberated and the Gaullists pre-empted a Communist take-over, using the same methods they first successfully employed at Bayeux after the D-Day landings in the north. Professor Bertaux of the university described how he had been named as Commissaire de la République for the region — it was an old Jacobin title resurrected by de Gaulle to make sure his boys and no one else's planted themselves in the ornate fauteuils hurriedly vacated by their Vichy-serving predecessors.

There was a special problem in Toulouse, however, an Englishman called George Starr, DSO MC, who since 1943 had become a kind of baron of resistance in the South West. Starr's underground circuit, code-named Wheelwright had benefited from both local hate of the Germans and a more traditional dislike of central government in any form (which still flourishes). When de Gaulle arrived, according to the Bertaux version he denounced Starr as a mercenary, told him to get to hell out of the prefecture, and ordered his arrest. (Bertaux omitted to add that any such initiative would have had to be made in the teeth of several thousand maquisards who regarded the Englishman as their general and hero).

Bertaux quoted Starr as saying after this fracas: 'J'ai dit merde au Général de Gaulle.' A comment which appears in no official histories but sounds in character. However, there was no hint of the part played by British organised and equipped networks, and scant honour done to the Communist ones, which so mercilessly harassed the Germans retreating up the Rhône valley. Soon after this André Malraux wrote: 'We must not forget that the Allies did help us, that we were armed by them, that without them we would have had nothing...In this respect France can be grateful, but Resistance owes no debt.'

And neither, so we have seen, does the ORTF. One wonders how many Frenchmen seeing this anniversary coverage realise that Leclerc's 2nd Armoured Division, which was allowed to be first into Paris, landed on Utah Beach on 1 August, some seven weeks after the Allied forces. Or that they were greeted not by German shells but an escort of GIs. Or that their armoured vehicles, despite being given such Parisian names as Madeleine-Bastille — a bus route — were American and British. Or the trouble Leclerc had finding two French armoured cars for de Gaulle's entry into Paris, since he had refused to use 'foreign vehicles'.

This problem was so thorny that the General had spent a lot of time discussing whether he should ride into Paris on a white horse, a Bonapartist symbol, or a black, with its overtones of General Boulanger. Both animals were presumably impeccably Gallic.

The most controversial question of all, though, is not what the Germans did to the French, or vice-versa. It is what the French did to each other during the open season for settling accounts that began in the spring of 1944. Summary revenge took many forms; the motivations were sometimes political, often less elevated questions of debt, family feud, a desire to grab someone else's property or even girl friend.

The official figure for summary executions is around 10,000. Colonel Passy, the Resistance leader is quoted (at second hand) with a rather different assessment — 109,000. In the interests of national unity de Gaulle insisted on a 'mild' policy after the war when the time came for official tribunals. In a sense he had little choice.

The trials were conducted almost without exception by magistrates who were themselves collaborators insofar as they had served, and often been appointed, under the Vichy regime. Perhaps the one generalisation that can be made about the Resistance is that the most heroic and by far the most active were the (largely Communist) railway workers, followed by the peasants. Lacking Swiss bank accounts or other assets which could be used to bale them out, the poor had, in a sense, little alternative. Their country was all they possessed.

The true story will not be known before doomsday: certainly the ORTF will make no attempt to dip its delicate finger into this poisoned well, from which springs much of the suspicion the French feel for each other, let alone their reflexes where foreigners are concerned.

It may be that documentary film is simply an inadequate medium for dealing with even recent history. Better perhaps to aim at fiction, rather than achieve it inadvertently. The flash-back in *Hiroshima, Mon Amour* of the young girl and her German soldier-lover, the whole of that masterpiece *Lacombe Lucien*, currently showing in London, the recent trilogy *En passant par la Lorraine* — these portray at least an artistic equivalence of truth. The ORTF's creaking cameras have fallen far short of any such objective. But at least they send us back to the source books to try to find out what really happened.

Paris

New Statesman, 30th September 1974

L'aggro des Anglais

'Dear Mr Ambassador, I knew times had changed in England but never in my wildest dreams...' So begins one letter among the dozens which have inundated our man in Paris in the aftermath of the Leeds rampage and on the eve of the referendum decision. Mostly they came from Frenchmen calling themselves simultaneously 'ordinary' and 'Anglophile'. It would have been gratifying if these Anglo-Saxon lovers, who have long constituted an impassioned if outnumbered French minority group, had been affirming their solidarity at an hour of historic commitment on the other side of the Channel. But not so. Their subject has been damage — to their property, to themselves (like the old man I quote who had his glasses smashed) and, ultimately, to what might be called 'a certain idea of England'. They are sad because Major Thomson, the comic Englishman abroad, affectionately derided by generations of French, has died in squalid circumstances on the playing-fields of the Parc des Princes.

And about time too, it is tempting to add, for the major with his umbrella and awful French embodied a monocle-and-muffins image as dead as the Edwardian era from which it largely derived. (Bertie, Prince of Wales, carries the ultimate responsibility for much of this Thomsonry, setting fashions for tennis and golf, adultery between 5 and 7 p.m. and even the *Prince de Galles* tweeds which 'anglicised' Frenchmen like Couve de Murville, the former Prime Minister, still wear as a badge of class.) But this is not much consolation for Sir Edward Tomkins, our Paris ambassador. His skilled diplomatic reflex, of apologising quickly and sincerely to the right people, particularly the media, who had a martyr in the form of a seriously wounded cameraman, worked initially.

But the *Sorry,' dit l'Ambassadeur* headlines were overtaken when it transpired that a junior member of his own embassy, a clerk in registry, had been arrested for pitching a motorised bike through a chemist's window. This unfortunate stalwart of the embassy's soccer side recalled nothing of the incident, which the police were quite ready to forget. He would have finished his Paris tour next month in any case but the special circumstances meant that he had to be sent home at once.

And thus it became that much harder to explain the rampage in terms of *lumpen* dwarfs from satanic industrial hells in the remote north — a picture which many commentators, who leaned over backwards to stress that the bescarved lunatics dancing on car bonnets were a special sub-culture, had already been painting. Take, for instance, Renaud Vincent, *France-Soir's* expert on the changing face of the English:

This soccer violence is called 'l'Aggro' (diminutive of aggression), the word which groups yell in a frenzy while clapping their hands and moving into 'action'...their behaviour is a kind of new tribalism, and like Indians on the war-path they adorn themselves with symbols of battle — club scarves and English flags on which they write threatening slogans. It is a ritual with more shouts than punches. The danger comes when a goal or penalty is disallowed. Then, crying 'Aggro' repeatedly, they smash everything, showering the stadium with bottles and stones.

Le Journal de Dimanche, the leading Sunday paper, also undertook an inquest designed to explain not only what happened — before and after the match — but

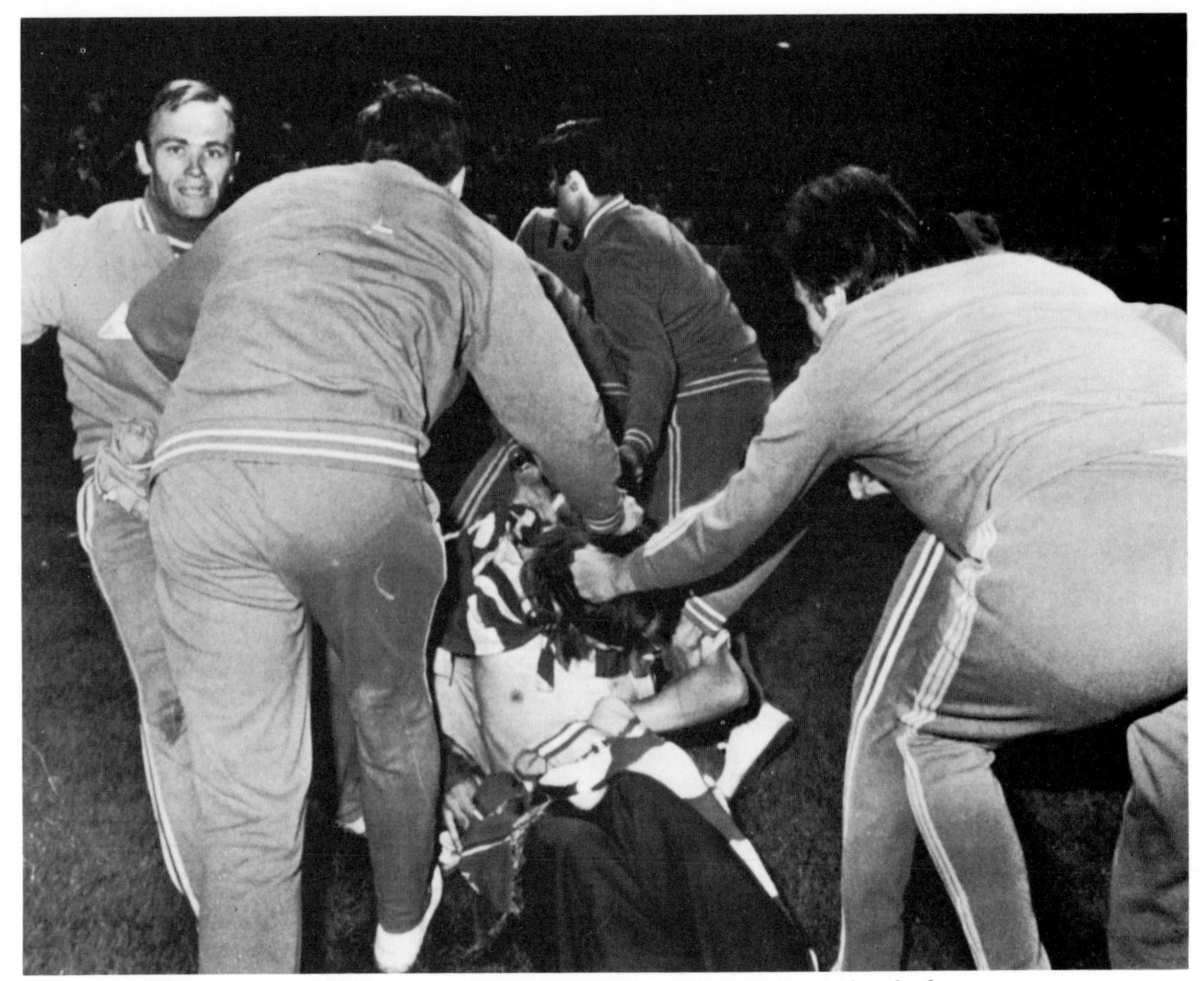

Leeds fans rioting in Paris in May 1975. *(Popperfoto)*

also what this alien cult signifies. 'The Enraged Ones', they found, consisted of 'several hundred fans who were mainly very young and manifestly drunk. On beer, neat *pastis*, and anger in equal measure. They were a pitiful spectacle, according to a policeman who had been called out. Some observers even remarked that these incidents were produced on the eve of the referendum...while we wait for the result it is better to try and smile, all the more since French fans have shown they are not always beyond reproach...'

They devoted their entire back page to war-like photos of the action, captioned in the style of souvenir postcards 'which a Leeds fan might have sent home to his girl while delayed either in a cell or at Calais because of the strike'. One of the most inventive went as follows:

'My God! What a scene! You'll never believe it, darling, but the frog-eating referee refused us a penalty...That's me in the third row with the bare chest cursing the French "bobbies" (flics). We felt fine thanks to a yellow liquor the Frogs call "Pastis". Alleluia — England for ever.'

The tone of both press comments and the embassy letters has been unexpected — no very serious efforts have been made, for instance, to exact compensation from the fans, who were, it was assumed, too poor to have much cash anyway, a judgment founded on the facts of so much theft, largely of liquor, from supermarkets, and the manhandling ticket touts received from supporters whose impoverished state evidently made it impossible for them to get in any other way.

Most letters say that the damage, estimated in total at well over £100,000, will be settled by French insurance companies anyway. The French who have written to the embassy or their newspapers seem less angry than sorry and genuinely confused. Their pain is clearly to do with the loss of a much cherished if wildly inaccurate stereotype which, perforce, they find themselves having to modify.

This factor accounts for the odd critical tone — a kind of benign scholarly attempt to explain what these aliens are about. It is something unprecendented in my experience of French attitudes to us. There is no hostility, no lingering hint of an inferiority complex, no element of rivalry or animus. Instead these chroniclers of the mystery of 'l'Aggro' sound like early anthropologists trying to explain a Masai puberty rite — the English fans do these strange things because they are primitive, not because they are bad. It is not a moral issue; we must try to understand. We must remember that people like this cannot be expected to know that drinks with an anis base are meant to be diluted with water. They drank their Ricard straight from the bottle because they are ignorant; they stole the bottles in the first place because they are poor.

It is not at all what was intended in an important week, prepared for months in advance, since not only the European Cup was on the agenda but the OECD annual meeting; the energy conference; the Le Bourget air show; and even the centennial celebrations for the French Senate had brought no fewer than eight members of the British Government to Paris within a couple of days' span.

The affair has naturally not influenced the French official positions on anything, although it may have reinforced the profound scepticism encountered on so many levels about the 'Europeanness' of present or future British Administrations. We are beginning to sound as European as Mongolia. President Giscard keeps 'explicitly' recalling that economic and monetary union is still the objective of the Community. Officials point out that our inflationary problems are not dissimilar to those of France and other countries a year ago. The difference, between a monthly inflation rate of over 3 per cent in our case, and under 1 per cent in theirs, being attributable to the fact that they took measures, culminating in a return to the 'snake', while we did not.

However, the public is little gripped by all this, while soccer (a game the French usually regard very lightly) has had an odd boost. Some commentators fear the 'bovver' fashion may catch on with their own *voyous*; their fascination with Nazi regalia has faded away in recent years, presumably because the change of stereotypes has now made the Germans gentlemen, not occupiers. It is noted that if the fans of, say, St Etienne copied those of Leeds the police would be less indulgent. The French may be puzzled about how Major Thomson changed into Genghis Khan, or by what process the Germans emerged as arbiters of 'Le Fair-Play', or even how anyone could care whether Leeds wins or not anyway. But one thing has been established. Say 'Aggro' in Paris and, by God, they all understand you.

New Statesman, 6th June 1975

Michel's last demo

The most original and perhaps disquieting of the innumerable student demos that have dislocated French education this spring took place last week in Nevers. Here more than 2,000 high school pupils carrying white banners without inscriptions gathered to express their solidarity with...what exactly? It is hard to explain because the demonstrators themselves were in the grip of powerful and confused emotions.

What set them marching was the death of an 18-year-old called Michel Franchy, not as might be expected the victim of some ill-judged gas grenade or baton blow unleashed by the riot police but, even more disturbingly, of himself. For Franchy committed suicide by hanging himself on the premises of the Lycée Magny-Cours, an 'agricultural high school' which means second-rate establishment for 'non-academic' pupils, set in a grim suburb on the fringe of this notoriously quiet Loire township whose innate melancholy was masterfully captured by Resnais in the flash-back sequences of *Hiroshima, Mon Amour.*

Franchy left a 13-page statement which testified, among other things, to his profound social despair. His suicide note, or *'auto-critique'* as some local activists preferred to call it, painted a monochrome picture of his birthplace. Here was as melancholy a vision as that of Resnais, though sadly lacking the flair that might have provided a more hopeful escape route. The Lycée, seen through Franchy's disabused eyes, was 'a grey-corridored prison': its teachers, like all members of the older generation for that matter, were 'hypocrites who understood nothing and were beyond communicating with'. He found the provincial environs, devoted as they are to the rearing of Charolais herds and other culinary matters, 'mediocre' — a word that with *débile,* the French equivalent of the London comprehensive 'spastic', currently has a prominent place in the student vocabulary. Society, Franchy wrote, was everywhere full of injustice, and religion was simply trickery. 'Et enfin, il ne faut croire en rien' (sic) he concluded.

Although Franchy's death has certain elements about it — of which more below — that have a distinctive ring of 1976, it can of course be seen as part of a longish tradition of French provincial *chagrin.* In another age, most likely, it would have been to do with love, unrequited perhaps, or blocked by the hierarchies of class division. Certainly disillusion with society and its organisation as a whole would very probably have been an insufficient cause for a young man to resort to what Al Alvarez, after Yeats, has characterised as 'the savage God'.

The sense of provincial claustrophobia, so apparent in Franchy's attempt to explain why — one hesitates to use even so tepidly upbeat a phrase as 'farewell note' when discussing his jumbled, despairing jargon — has been implanted in French literature and life at least since Stendhal. Life, to use another word favoured by Franchy, is *'enformé'*: turned in on itself so comprehensively that the sensitive provincial, hero of a thousand forgotten novels, is forced to 'climb up' to Paris.

Paradoxically, in an era of easy journeys, the geographical solution is probably less accessible now than it has ever been. Paris has been depopulated by speculation in office towers and accommodation for the bourgeoisie, which by English standards would mean the rich. The centre of Paris is not designed to accommodate young people without well-paid jobs. It is not only a virtually impossible journey from Nevers, it is equally inaccessible if your point of departure is a proletarian arrondissement like Belleville, or one of the *'alphaville'* suburbs which contain the office-and-service-industry workers in their cement towers.

It is popular, indeed virtually obligatory, to see French society in terms of what is called 'bipolarisation': Left and Right, order and movement, conservatism and anarchy. Those who make their protests manifest and those who brood in morose isolation. Poor Franchy, condemned to the last category, is yet another reminder of the division between parents and children. It is not simply the well-worn question of 'communication'. More, one suspects, the needs, as well as the tastes, of parents and their adolescent children, are seen to be both separate and in conflict. A small residence in some kind of ersatz countryside, at least with a bit of greenery about, so delectable for the *bon père de famille*, and the apogee of a lifetime's industrious ambition, may seem like a desert of emptiness to the children he hopes will share his modest satisfactions. Adolescent suicide, evidently the most extreme expression of malaise, has increased by over 30 per cent in a decade, and the Government, not before time, has just instituted some research on the question.

The experts, we can be sure, will come up with conclusions to do with unemployment and alienation. The unsuitability of rigid structures of education and jobs. But, risking a generalisation, it seems evident enough that France has for some time been in the process of changing both demographically and psychologically in a way that puts young people at a disadvantage. The adolescent no longer finds a society which assumes he is a kind of king simply by virtue of being in the jeans-wearing and record-buying age group. Those in the vanguard of the great 'baby boom', itself a historical memory in a period of zero population growth, are already, in some cases, within spitting distance of early middle age. 'never trust anyone over 30,' wrote Jerry Rubin at the height of the youth culture, offering and awkward hostage to fortune an his own future (which turned out to be obscure).

General considerations of this kind, as opposed to specific questions of how far arts-degree courses should be geared to the needs of the computer industry, may go some way to explaining the unbeautiful desuetude into which French higher education has been drifting this year. There is a collective malaise among students which the Government's late and evidently largely cosmetic 'concessions' hardly affect. In some places strikes and disruptions are now into their fourth month, many lycés and universities, encouraged to accept these 'concessions' which the Communist dominated UNEF claim they have 'torn' from the inept Alice Saunier-Seïte, the Education Minister, are back at work; others are still deciding.

Certainly the student protest has been swamped in the 'polarised' and unionised social conflict which continues, just as their militants were lost among the 150,000 adherents of the CGT and other mammoth unions who turned May Day into the biggest march that has been seen since the eve of the Popular Front victory in 1936, the 40th anniversary of which fell this week. The protest movement, despite its inordinate length and the millions of words it has spawned, has produced neither one memorable phrase nor a single leader, even of Rubinesque, gadfly weight. The nearest, I fear, is Michel Franchy, with his obscure 'militant suicide'.

A banal act committed against himself by a disturbed youth with only banal words to explain it, a local commentator thought. And yet it has stayed with me all week, more powerful than the thousands of words uttered in more sophisticated places like the Dauphine campus, known with Orwellian succinctness as Paris 10, or at *gauchiste* Nanterre, that bleak institution which punctuates the train-ride to the salubrious western suburbs like an unregenerate belch at a gourmet dinner party.

The image of the Nevers *copains* marching with their white banners is haunting. Was it the colour of surrender? A symbol of the emptiness of their present and future? Or were they simply, and understandably, at a loss to encapsulate their feelings in some pert slogan? Franchy has at any rate made some minor historical contribution. I wonder who can find a precendent for 2,000 young people in their prime expressing 'solidarity' with an act of self-destruction?

New Statesman, 7th May 1976

The ghost of Rambouillet

Sometimes, as I take out my trusty notebook and write down a phrase like 'frank and mutual exchanges' or 'climate of reciprocal confidence', I wonder whether TV news has made not only written journalism but the whole language of international discussion redundant. Let us take, as an example, the Callaghan-Giscard summit.

As the first of a regular series of such meetings, usually described nowadays as 'institutionalised bilaterals', it has a certain importance. The urgency Mr Callaghan's government attached to it was evident; the chagrin experienced by British officials when the exigencies of the Commons and Mrs Thatcher delayed Healey, Silkin and Dell in London no less so. The French press immediately started citing figures like 309/310, plunging into the arcana of the parliamentary 'pairing system', and writing pen-portraits of Mrs Thatcher, known here, I'm afraid, as the 'woman of iron'. It was a humiliating beginning, and it soon got worse.

Dinner was an affair on the grandest possible scale and local diplomats were quick to point out the nuances implicit in the French arrangements — the choice of the Chateau of Rambouillet, the unusually lavish food, the fact that there were fires of real logs. The action, such as it was, took place in the enormous dining-room which was once used by Louis XIV and Madame de Maintenon. Then, again as a mark of special consideration since the French President and his wife, like Harold Macmillan and young people, are not much in each other's company, the presence of Madame Giscard was analysed at some length. Other French big guns included Prime Minister Barre, Foreign Minister Louis de Guiringaud, and Jacques de Beaumarchais, the Ambassador in London. A glittering assembly, you might say.

Except for the fact that throughout the length of this banquet Callaghan was obliged to keep in touch with an official humbly established in an ante-chamber (I hope he had sandwiches) with an open line to the House of Commons. Next morning the local press was full of predictions about how long the Labour government could survive. Not surprisingly, they claimed that the Prime Minister had been capable of no more than 'distracted attention' when it came to the preliminary talks on, oh dear, 'wide-ranging topics'. They did, however, put in the bits about 'mutuality' and 'cordiality' (and of course those logs). The man from the nowadays quite influential right-wing daily. *L'Aurore*, also managed to produce one nice phrase. He said that Callaghan, had gone into dinner, wearing 'a circumstantial smile'.

Day two brought more talks, the missing British ministers, and the news that on his desk President Giscard had thought to have placed a small clock which Napoleon was in the habit of using for his councils of ministers. Finally the dogs got to see the rabbits. Giscard and Callaghan appeared for the waiting journalists. They were both wearing their personal variety of circumstantial smiles — the British Prime Minister's broader and cruder than that of the French President's, I think I can say with confidence.

Later, various officials from the two sides were available to comment on, or 'characterise' as they say, the talks. The English said it has all gone much better than anyone had expected. Indeed better than any Anglo-French meetings for years, unless you count Giscard's extremely successful talks with the Queen last

James Callaghan and Giscard d'Estaing at Rambouillet.
(Keystone)

June when these current 'bilaterals' were arranged. I asked what it was that Giscard and the Queen had found to be so friendly about, but no one knew. It is thought they talked about dogs.

All this, of course, raises the point about what Callaghan and Giscard and the others did in fact discuss or agree in Rambouillet. No topics, we learned, were barred. A French spokesman was prepared to go even further. He said that the summit had been 'if not precisely warm, at least impregnated with a spirit of mutual confidence and sympathy'.

The international flags on the town hall of Rambouillet, where all this rubbish was going on, added a wistful, Dufyesque touch. A TV man made some pictures of them which people in England probably saw. It was, in short, an entirely visual occasion. It contained no core, there was no content to speak of, it was a kind of soufflé — all air and elegance and with an entirely empty centre.

Nothing concrete, you ask, nothing at all? Well, the French are going to put in a good word for us with the IMF before 9 December (when we need to borrow the money from Peter to pay last June's debts to Paul). I expect the IMF will be most impressed. Since the French have an overdraft there too, though of only modest proportions compared to our own. I guess their Gallic collateral might be worth a modest meal in a cut-price Paris restaurant designed for coach-parties. At the very least.

So the occasion was a phantom, something which took place indubitably, something that you could take smiling pictures of without doubt, but something that defies retrospective analysis because of sheer lack of nutriment. Its only significance, and one that escaped most of the participants very likely, was historical. In the same place (with different logs) only a month short of 14 years ago General de Gaulle stunned Harold Macmillan by slamming the door on British entry into Europe. It was only weeks after the Cuban missile crisis which Jack Kennedy had weathered (supported, incidentally, by the General). In France the Algerian settlement had just been made, the General had avoided assassination at Petit-Clamart by two centimetres and the French had given him the support he wanted in a referendum establishing the principle (still of course obtaining) of electing a President with enormous powers by universal suffrage. Macmillan went almost directly from Rambouillet to Nassau and in the Bahamas sun agreed with Kennedy the multilateral nuclear force.

When on 14 January 1963 the General gave a press conference explaining his reasons for the British veto, he cited the question of sterling balances among others — the question which only now is about to be definitely and humiliatingly resolved. The great man, less of a phantom I suspect than the current participants, whom I am reliably informed are actually alive, despite appearances, also had something very literate and to the point to say about the Anglo-French alliance:

> Everyone must have allies in the modern world, that goes without saying. But it is also necessary for a great people to have the freedom to dispose of themselves as they wish, and the requisite weapons to fight to retain this freedom. This is a formal necessity. For alliances are not composed of absolute virtues, no matter what the sentiments are on which they are based.

He is dead, Callaghan and the others are said to be living and even smiling; but there is no doubt whose voice remains the loudest. And if the old man had been there, at least I'd have had some beautiful ringing prose to write in my note book.

New Statesman, 19th November 1976

PEOPLE

What in the Soviet Union is called 'kult lichnosti', *the cult of personality, seems always to have characterized the way the Russian ruled have regarded Russian rulers.*

When I did the interviews with Nikita Khrushchev and his entourage I was only 26, which may account for the out-of-the-ordinary impression he made. The little man exuded raw power like a concentrate and I found his human presence uncomfortable, though very funny in retrospect — and from a safe distance.

To do Khrushchev's surreal person credit, to begin to indicate the Dr Strangelove emanations of the Wrong Stuff that hovered around his perky, waddling figure, I would have needed a publication very different from Roy Thomson's Sunday Times *of 1964. It would scarcely have done to compare the Soviet leader to a primed explosive device which not only had the capacity to destroy the world but was also equipped to deliver broad one-line jokes while ushering in Armageddon.*

Within weeks of the interview the man who had succeeded the fearsome Joseph Stalin, and led his country away from the excesses of Stalinism, had himself fallen from power, accused by the Supreme Soviet of trying to run everything (including the disastrous Virgin Lands wheat-growing project we saw) his own way and without consulting anyone. I'm sure that for once they were telling no less than the truth.

Because Nikita Segeievich was only a step away from Stalin you could still smell the old executioner's spoor about the premises and 'Mr K', as we mateyly called him, came across several degrees more frightening by association. The Russians, like the French, have always gone for the Vozhd, *the Big Chief. Khrushchev in the Imperial train was as superlatively* chez lui *as Tsar Nicholas had ever been, just as General de Gaulle fitted into the Salle Murat at the Elysée Palace like a hand-lasted shoe. Indeed the General, by virtue of his height alone, was probably more impressive than the Emperor Napoleon. Khrushchev, contrariwise, relied on his modest and misleadingly comic physical endowments for his impact.*

The 'Kings and Queens of England' kind of history became outmoded in the 1960's, most intellectually self-deceiving of periods, as it became fashionable to study the lives of 'ordinary people', via tax files, church registers, police records and so forth. This was thought to offer superior insights into what life had really been like in the past. It may also have diverted attention for time from the unegalitarian truth that real power, particularly in countries like France, the USSR and the USA who have an imbedded tradition of handing it comparatively unencumbered to one individual and inviting him to run with it like a ball, is something very few statesmen are equipped to do much with, other than hold on to it for as long as possible.

Since I had been brought up at a time when a handful of men — Stalin, Hitler,

Roosevelt and, during the war, Churchill — exercised the most astonishing influence on the world at large, usually promulgating evil and madness, it was hard for me to believe in history as a kind of geological democratic process, the legacy of tiny movements by millions of pebbles or billions of drops of ice-water.

For a journalist, famous people are easier to write about than the others because of the implicit assumption that anyone very celebrated will also be interesting too. You don't need to establish why you are interviewing the person in the first place, even if (as is invariably the case) the moment that you introduce quotation marks involves disclosing that your subject's store of earthly wisdom is as scant as the next fellow's.

It might seem that television has made the whole business of writing about well-known people redundant, but I don't believe it has. Except when focussed on amateurs, that is to say anyone who has not spent the time and effort to become a TV actor, the medium is uniquely unrevealing. An old-style interviewer with pencil and note-book, or maybe just his eyes and a tape-recorder, has every chance of coming up with a sketch that catches at least an aspect of personality in graphic relief.

People may have known their heroes better, I suspect, in the pre-TV days when they would have had difficulty recognising them on the street. At least then there were no accretions of pseudo-familiarity, acquired via countless film clips or set-piece transmissions. People when they appear on television are rarely much like themselves when they are not performing for the benefit of a camera. This might sound obvious enough not to require adumbration. Yet the notion that TV somehow enables you to get the hang of someone you've never met remains a fallacy that many people secretly embrace.

The pure thief

Papillon, or Butterfly, is the nickname of the currently most successful and controversial writer in Europe. This ex-convict's real name in Henri Charrière, and he looks about as literary as a dray-horse. Rocky shoulders, a crushed thumb, and a nose which has known a few fists as well as countless litres of red wine, give Papillon the physiognomy of a professional battler of long standing. This is probably just as well because Papillon now has a classic fight on his hands.

Papillon's literary credentials amount to the 13 years he served — for murder — in France's horrific former penal colonies in South America, including the notorious Devil's Island. Papillon's sentence was life — he was condemned in 1931 at the age of 25 — and he claims he tried to escape eight times, sailing thousands of miles through shark-ridden seas in improvised rafts, surviving two tempests. The ninth time he succeeded and after more picaresque adventures established himself as proprietor of a bar of doubtful repute in Venezuela.

His punishments for the failures included three and a half years spent, in silence, in a black hole. The whole story, told in compelling, racy narrative liberally dosed with the jargon of the Montmartre underworld, is a kind of extended hymn of praise to man's indomitable spirit.

In terms of commercial success 'Papillon' is without precedent. He has earned enough in nine months to make the Sartres and de Beauvoirs of the French literary establishment look like a penny-a-line scribblers. An editor from Robert Laffont, the publishers who had the luck, and flair, to see the book's potential, told me yesterday in tones of awe: 'His only competitor is the Bible.'

But Papillon, riding on the crest of a commercial wave which has enabled him to start drinking his red wine at the Ritz, has run into a little local difficulty. Two other French writers of humbler commercial antecedents have burst into print with the message that the Papillon saga is a load of rubbish.

They claim that the biggest best-seller France has ever known is an extended *Boy's Own* fantasy. There has even been a whispering campaign that he wrote not a word of the book. Next Tuesday he will hold a Press conference to refute these charges which, with film rights and translations in more than 20 foreign languages already signed, involved several million pounds. Yesterday he anticipated the event by giving me a tumultuous two-hour interview.

It began memorably. An enraged Papillon, his battered hand adorned with a Cartier watch and a diamond ring, which if not as big as the Ritz, was at least in respectable range of its annexe, answered my first question by rising to his feet, glass in hand: 'I swear on my mother's heart these bastards are liars,' he growled. 'I was never a pimp — I was always a pure thief.'

He was talking about the main charge in the first book — *Papillon's Four Truths*, by Georges Ménager. The author claims that contrary to Papillon's claim that he was famed in the Montmartre of the late Twenties as an aristocrat among criminals, 'un vrai dur', he was in fact living off the meagre earnings of his mistress, Georgette Fourel, who is now set up in an old people's home with a generous allowance from Papillon's royalties.

It was, in fact, for a shot in the chest which killed a certain Roland Legrand in the

Henri Charrière in London for the publication of *Papillon* in May 1970. *(Popperfoto)*

Place Pigalle on March 26 1930 that Papillon got life — a sentence which meant death as sure as any trip to the guillotine, only slower. Eighty per cent of the deportees, and there were seventy thousand of them between 1852, when the system began, and 1945, when it was abolished, died in the jungle prisons.

Papillon has always denied he killed Legrand. He says his life was signed away through police perjury, and the jealousy of a petit-bourgeois jury — 'the cheeses', he calls them — who took against this handsome, elegantly-tailored young man.

Ménager, who in some mysterious way has seen ancient police files and the documents of lawyers long dead, makes a fairly convincing case for Papillon's guilt. He even suggests he tried to have his mistress convicted for his own crime. Contemporary newspaper reports, however, give a different picture, and it is clear that the conviction was based on the often contradictory evidence of a police informer called Goldstein who paid for his perjury, if perjury it was, when the Nazis occupied France.

Ménager's book ends in 1933 when Papillon arrived in a convict ship in the prison of Cayenne. Gerard de Villiers, who writes paperback thrillers with some affinities to Ian Fleming, takes up the story from there, and casts doubt on much of Papillon's narrative. He claims, for example, that far from being a hero who intrepidly organised the gambling sessions of the real thugs, Papillon was a nurse and a gardener — small fry, indeed, in the world of desperadoes.

Papillon tells how during one escape he was looked after by an English lawyer in Trinidad called Bowen, and describes his charity, and that of his blue-eyed daughter and chestnut-haired wife. De Villiers found Mr Bowen and established he was a life-long bachelor.

One of the most graphic sections in the autobiography describes how Papillon killed an informer in the knife fight, but provoked the other into striking first to claim self-defence. De Villiers has found no record of this. 'Record, my God,' exclaimed Papillon, when I asked him. And he bared a right arm scarred like a relief map with one unmistakable stab mark bisecting his still solid bicep.

He has an answer to most of the accusations. He admits to faults of memory — 'You think I went into the hell with a typewriter?' — and points out that the de Villiers book contains errors of fact about incidents which occurred less than a decade ago.

Papillon and his publishers believe that there has been official backing for a campaign to discredit his book. It is certainly true that both authors have had access to photocopies of documents which, because of the French law of professional secrecy and the habitual suspicion of French authorities towards reporters, indicate friends in high places.

For Papillon has become a pundit as well as a literary celebrity. He has not hesitated to attack the French judiciary — a sacrosanct area. And when a Marseilles school-teacher committed suicide after being sent to prison for having a love affair with a 17-year-old pupil whom she hoped to marry, Papillon attacked the magistrate responsible in a one-hour interview on a French commercial radio programme which probably mobilised public opinion more than anything else. He is now allowed in France only on condition that he eschews radio and TV interviews.

Papillon claims to have rehabilitated himself, and the book, true or false, is infused by an unexpected, almost puritan, ethic and a rigorous if eccentric standard of honour. 'I did not write the book to glorify myself,' he told me. 'But to show people what happens to poor devils who fall into the hands of officialdom gone mad.'

Perhaps his motives were less honourable but the case for or against him, and his book, is still not proven. Papillon comes to England this spring and by then will probably have sold another hundred thousand or so in France. On a more modest level the two anti-Papillons are going pretty well, too.

The Sunday Times, 15th March 1970

Robin Day's zero hour

Spare a thought at 7.30 every weekday morning for a group of rumpled bleary-eyed BBC men and women gathered round a paper-strewn table in Room 330 in Broadcasting House, London W.1.

To be there at this godless hour they have passed through a sombre, distinctly ecclesiastical ante-chamber whose salient feature is an implacable bust of Lord Reith, who would not be impressed with their sartorial standards: some of *The World at One* team show up without ties. But the devotion to duty, the compulsion to communicate what's just happened in the world via the uniquely swift — and unforgiving — medium of broadcasting, retains its Reithian ferocity.

The old man would have applauded the life-style of Carole Lacey, who is one of the programme's producers and the Duty Editor for that day. After 14 years' service, her daily pattern involves an alarm call a few seconds before the first headlines are broadcast on the BBC's 6.30 *Today* programme. Soon she will switch channels to see how LBC — the independent London news station and a rival to the BBC — is getting on. Like the rest of the news acolytes, Lacey consumes broadcast information as a staple, in the way ordinary mortals reach for sliced Hovis.

The World at One news machine, however, begins rolling very slowly fuelled by execrable coffee in styrofoam cups. At 7.30 pre-rush hour Portland Place is so tranquil I identified a blackbird, a thrush and some unknown exotic species, an escapee probably from Snowdon's aviary in nearby Regent's Park Zoo. Inside no birds sing: indeed some of the team, their hang-overs as palpable as their second day drip-drys, find it hard to croak a sentence. Only later will it emerge that the exaggerated languor which marks the conference's start has something in common with the soporific laziness cultivated by combat troops during a battle lull.

Derek Lewis, supremo of both *The World at One* and 5 o'clock *P.M.* programmes, and Julian Holland, the Editor of *The World at One,*, make valiant efforts to initiate discussion about what they will be broadcasting in just five hours and 21 minutes' time. Something (it turns out to be someone) is evidently absent, and I sourly note: 'Room 331 is shabby, inconveniently distant from the studio where, eventually, it will all happen, and as full of creative zest as 20 milligrams of Valium.' Only at 7.42, exercising the star's prerogative for elegant unpunctuality the Presenter — always spoken of with implied capitals — comes through the door with the driving *brio* of a man accustomed to having such fixtures held permanently open for him by someone deferential. Trailing clouds of televisual glory, Robin Day propels his bulk towards the empty chair in the centre of the table.

Without looking at anyone in particular he answers a chorus of 'Good morning, Robins' with a magisterial 'Good morning' to the room at large. Unlike most TV stars, who seem dispossessed and even shrunken off-screen, Day's televisual charisma is surprisingly palpable even in this strikingly unglamorous setting. He is larger, not smaller, than life: the dots on his bow-tie are exotically huge. His first cigar of the morning is big enough to be a stage prop (which in a way it is), and despite these studied details, the overall dishevelment implies someone who doesn't give a damn.

Robin Day, photographed at Broadcasting House on joining the BBC Radio News Programme 'The World at One'.
(Press Association)

Such unashamed self-assurance provokes an egalitarian impulse in a producer called Francis Hailwood.

'Car running OK, Robin,' he inquires sweetly with a glance at the studio clock.

'If you think 10 miles to the gallon's OK,' says Day, brilliantly implying that the deficiencies of his own expensive vehicle are in some way Hailwood's fault.

The news schedule, or 'handover sheet' bequeathed by the night staff, contains the information that China's defence supremo, Yang-Yung, will be visiting the West Wittering RAF base. Stephen Chilcott, the young studio producer, suggests from his seat at the bottom of the table that it's worth covering. Day, an instant conduit through which all discussion flows, delivers a thumbs down.

'He's here for a fortnight. We'll do him when he's in London.'

Hailwood, who sounds Australian but is from New Zealand, and who looks baby-faced, but is actually quite tough, rises once more to Day's bait. Employing an Antipodean whine he decides to stand up for the provinces.

'What's special about London?'

Day: 'Were you aware that 40 per cent of our audience is in London?'

Hailwood: 'That means 60 per cent of them aren't.'

'I never believed those figures anyway,' Day ripostes, so delighted at crushing this smart-alecry from down-under that the whole room, including Hailwood, collapses in laughter. These exchanges, apparently loaded with animus, turn out to be the dominant feature of the conference. It is hard to tell whether Day's unique capacity to generate unease, hovering on the verge of insult and then dousing the impending conflagration with a comic twist, is an actor's routine or simply the product of an ego superlatively at ease with itself. In any case it works. Everyone in Room 331 is now in top gear, speeding up in rhythm with the rush-hour traffic below in Langham Place. The early calm has gone. 'For God's sake close that window,' he says. Three people get up to do his bidding.

Almost at once, without explanation, Day leaves the room. In the interim I remark mildly to Derek Lewis that the TV personality believes in keeping everyone on their toes.

'Robin's a very creative and original personality,' Lewis replies with the deftness of a bureaucrat on the way up.

The main foreign story of the day is a kind of 1979 archetype: an impending oil price rise. No-one knows how to deal with it, though Day, returning with a brief apology about having to make a personal call, squelches, before he has even sat down, the idea of an interview with the syndicated columnist, Jack Anderson.

'For God's sake don't let's have any dreary American pundits.'

'We need a new voice,' says Lewis.

The new voice discussion limps on. Carole Lacey manages to call President Carter 'Nixon' twice in one sentence — 'It would be nice to get that one sorted out,' says Day silkily — and, as a kind of punishment, is deputed by Julian Holland to find out if the Saudi Ambassador speaks English.

At 8.39 a flash from the news-room booms disruptively from a 1940s-looking Tannoy speaker on the north wall: 'Bonn tells us there have been two bomb explosions at BAOR Dortmund, presumed to be IRA. No reports of death or injury so far.' This could evidently develop into the lead story of the morning but the news-team can do no more than wait for it to ramify — or not. So instead they debate how to deal with a statement from Len Murray about the Thatcher Government's impending union legislation.

'Murray said he'd never heard of secondary picketing, had never seen it happen during his years as a trade unionist, and didn't think the problem existed. All on *Today* at 6.30 this morning. Quite extraordinary,' says Holland.

'Let me just say I'm amazed they put it out at that time,' says Lewis.

The next 30 minutes are devoted, with one digression, to establishing whom they should invite to debate the issue. All the names canvassed, among them Alex Wedderburn, John Harvey QC, who helped draft the document, Eric Varley, and a couple of blue-blood-and-thunder Tory backbenchers, are rejected for one reason or another. Day manages to mention that all of them 'are personal friends of mine', which no doubt is the case. Like Derek Lewis, Day is hesitant about the obvious choice Jim Prior, the Employment Secretary, simply because he is so obvious. Also like Lewis, who insists 'it'd better be damn good, that's all I say', the presenter allows himself to be persuaded by the majority.

Now Hailwood tries Prior's home number, plucked from the programme's priceless 14-year-old contact files, and indeed the Minister has left. Worse, he is scheduled to spend the whole morning in a Cabinet meeting. 'Tell his office it's a personal request from me. He'll want to come on,' says Day airily.

Before 9.32, when the conference breaks up, with Derek Lewis withdrawing 'to administer', and the reporters dashing for the phones like starving animals, the rest of the schedule is settled in a more perfunctory manner. An item on a change of Italian Government — 'if you call that *news*,' as Day says — an actors' protest about entertainment tax which sends a reporter called Libby Fawbert scurrying for a tape-recorder and the exit; a Day-inspired suggestion to 'do' Sir Robert Armstrong, new head of the Civil Service, a notoriously rare interviewee, and...surprise, 'a friend of mine': plus a couple of fillers from a choice of five or six personalities.

To an outsider it sounds amazingly *ad hoc,* given there are 30 minutes' air time to fill, and nothing in the bag except Len Murray's mild voice dismissing picketing as a Tory invention. There are now eight phones going at once and snatches of sentences intermingle. Hailwood, using a more English accent, at once soothing and determined: 'The programme goes out at 1 p.m. actually, so if you'd get your skates on...'

Carole Lacey: 'You wouldn't happen to have a number for Willy Brandt in the country to hand...?'

Day: 'Could someone get me that trade union document, the *original*, not some infants' handout...'

From now on the conference room, so claustrophobic during the planning stage, is never still. It has become the axis of movement from the studio and cutting room down the corridor. At 10.30 Hailwood, who has been juggling two phones and has started to sweat, has an audience of a dozen for his triumphant announcement. 'We've got Prior. He's coming in but we'll record him, he's got a lunch.'

Day, by now on his third cigar, is being briefed by the Milan correspondent on Italy's latest political crisis. His facial expression switches from despairing ennui to broad amusement at the incomprehensible alignments of the Italian left. Hailwood, still manic at 'getting Prior', is pleased when Holland returns from the recording studio and inquires gently how he did it.

'By being a genius, that's all. I got hold of his private office first. Then they spoke to the Press office. All you do is talk very quickly.'

Day, who's been writing 'Italian' questions on a pad to be typed up, raises his mane: 'It's because he's a friend of mine, that's all.'

Hailwood picks up a ringing phone, thus foregoing his comeback, and Holland remarks that he'd rather have Prior live. 'We like to record as much as we can, to give us a chance to edit. But some items are better live because the adrenalin gets people going. Some people you wouldn't dare put on live.' In the background Hailwood's voice, heavy with cajolery, stops short. He replaces the phone with a crash and calls across to Day: 'While we're on the subject of your friends, Sir Robert Armstrong says thank you for asking, but he can't.'

'You can tell he's a friend of mine because he refused *politely*,' says Day, without raising his head. 'That's the story of my professional career.' He disappears to the studio to record the Italian story.

Everyone keeps looking at the clock, which astonishingly now indicates there are only 53 minutes left. Virtually everybody is also on the phone trying to find Senator Henry Jackson of the Senate Foreign Relations committee who has made a major statement in Washington — either on energy, SALT, or Teddy Kennedy. No-one knows which.

Holland is asking Day if he's willing 'to do this one on the phone?'

'Jackson?'

'No,' says Holland, 'the bloke from British Caledonian.'

Anyway Lacey's scent sounds more promising. 'What do I say if he comes on? "Hullo?" "Scoop?" ' And then, on a rising crescendo of hope: 'He's not out jogging? He's with CBS, you say? We *can*? Absolutely superb.'

The clock reads 12.30, most ominously it seems to me, and by common consent everyone shifts into a room equipped with a console panel bigger than Concorde's crowned with a long glass through which Day can be seen sitting in front of a microphone wearing headphones. He looks magnificent, as if addressing the nation at some historic crux. His voice comes through ripely saying: 'Go back to the beginning and cut the cobblers about Milan.'

Lacey, now bright pink and distinctly twitchy, is still pursuing Jackson via a phone attached to the wall. The studio clock, more ominous than ever, reads 12.40 and she says, over her shoulder:

'I don't want to worry anyone but we seem to have lost Prior.'

'If the Government fails, does this mean the end of Italian democracy?' Day demands sonorously through the panel. Derek Lewis, as unruffled as a head waiter, chooses this moment to appear and ask Holland, who's jiggling his coins more fiercely now: 'How's it going?'

'We've got one item.'

By common reflex we all look at the clock: 16 minutes left.

'At least we've got no problems cutting,' says Lewis.

'Annie,' says Holland over his shoulder to a hovering researcher, 'Please ask Number 10 if Prior's left.'

Lacey pauses in her Washington phone call to suggest sending a radio car to Whitehall.

'Too late,' remarks Hailwood, who's been writing cues.

'It's broken down, and anyway it couldn't get through the traffic.'

I go in to the cutting room, unable to bear the strain, and find a lady with a pink punk haircut scratching her arm obsessively, and another technician in a floral dress explaining to Hailwood that something's gone wrong. Back in the studio, with eight minutes left, Lewis takes time to sit next to me and with preternatural courtesy, or recklessness, expends another minute explaining: 'We've got almost nothing, but it's quite usual at this time of day. It gets very wobbly sometimes.'

Holland, rubbing his nose, says: 'I shan't be happy till I see Prior come through that door.'

Lacey, still on her Washington call, sounds near tears as she says: 'I think Senator Jackson's gone home. Could you double-check?'

I write a note: '12.54 — disaster?' Lacey's voice suddenly hits an ecstatic pitch: 'Senator Jackson. Thank you, I'll hand you over.'

Day does a little leap in his chair beyond the panel and, precisely as the clock reaches 12.55 and a red light glows, he is saying:

'Hullo, Senator Jackson. Robin Day in London here. We met once in Washington. I'd like to go ahead straight away.' Day's hand is jumping up and down on the desk and he wears a rapt expression as Jackson launches into some high technologese about the energy programme.

'Do you think there'll be rationing?' Day gets in, taking advantage of a pause for breath. Jackson, in Washington, is at least as effective a pro as Day and he ends his piece with a gracious 'Thank you, Robin'. Hailwood, entering the studio in haste, winces involuntarily at yet another example of the Presenter's cosmopolitan acquaintance, and says: 'I gather Prior's bombed out.'

'Not at all,' replies Holland primly. 'The Cabinet's simply not over yet.'

A green light now appears, the clock reaches 13.00, and Chilcott says: 'We're on.' Day's voice comes across announcing the programme, 'And first the news in full from Laurie Macmillan,' — a figure I haven't seen. Her disembodied voice pitches into the news of a 'full alert in Dortmund'. (There are still no developments, no news of casualties.) Lacey is saying something desperate about Prior, which is interrupted by Lewis who enters like a stage manager and says: 'He's here.'

The Cabinet Minister, flanked by two tense young men in suits as dark as his own, floats in with the exaggerated calm of someone about to open an innings. Lacey gives him a beatific smile; Lewis asks him to go straight into the studio.

'Ok,' says Prior, and follows Lewis obediently, which is just as well since there's 60 seconds before Day's first item. 'We'll run Scoop second,' says Chilcott from his console, and almost simultaneously Day's voice is asking Prior whether the Government has mounted 'a major challenge to union rights'.

The Minister's voice is in fruity flow — he makes a reference to 'transport caffs', which produces twin winces in his aides, and he ends up with six minutes 25 seconds. Four minutes 44 seconds of Scoop Jackson follows. An unexpected bonus arrives in the form of 33 seconds of Teddy Kennedy on the fuel crisis, which is clipped in with a cue hastily written by Holland at 1.33. Then, despite a heart-stopping three minutes because it's a little bit short, comes Libby Fawbert's Equity story. 'Can we add two paragraphs instantly?' calls Holland.

At 1.38 Lacey says: 'Oh God, we've lost the headlines'; but Hailwood squeaks: 'I've got them here', and disaster is staved off for the last time.

At 1.39 Day reads the last headline and beams through the panel like a conjuror as an announcer's voice promises: 'Some western areas will still be cloudy.'

Day comes through the door and says to Chilcott: 'That was fine but I knew perfectly well the pay-off had to be brief without being told.' Everyone has now attained a state of advanced euphoria and the canteen lunch in the conference room becomes a celebration.

'Thank you, Robin,' says Lacey. 'Thank you, Carole,' says Day. 'You were wonderful, Jules,' says Libby. 'Libby was spendid, actually,' says Hailwood, at his most English. I ask Day, without irony, how on earth they do it once, let alone regularly. Exuding geniality, he puts it down to confidence and mutual trust. I forgot to ask how much he, or anyone, is paid. Whatever it is, it isn't enough.

The Sunday Times Magazine, October 1979

The fall-girl

Christine Keeler was born in November 1942 — 'the same time as poor Ali, you know, that black boxer.'

She sees it as a time with a cutting zodiacal edge. 'I'm a Fire Horse, that's the name for the year in the Chinese calendar. It only happens once every 60 years, no, really, it's true, apparently. And you know,' she pauses for dramatic emphasis holding bony hands with scarlet nails aloft to witchy effect, 'if ever I marry a man born a Rat — the Rat Year, you know — that man will not live out his full span...'

In her giddy days of high celebrity — 'That Summer of '63' as she calls it — when this refugee waif from the tip-end of Slough nearly perpetrated a successful Guy Fawkes job on possibly the most unflappably Establishment Tory government of the century, the papers tried to conjure her — evidently quasi-mythic — beauty with a phrase of metronomic repetition. 'Madonna-like', was how they described it.

But, then and now, the secret of her compelling visual impact lies not in repose, but in the vital will o'the wisp mobility of a face which can switch from rep company Lady Macbeth to caricature stripper or even a convincing portrait of a Joyce Grenfell boarding-school headmistress, with suitable accompanying dialogue, the one role bewilderingly merging into its successor.

Being 'Chrissie', as her friends call her, she has never managed to exploit her natural gift for acting. She didn't even get to play herself in the catchpenny *Christine Keeler Story* hustled out in Denmark in 1964. It may even have been a blessing, fairly rare visitations in Christine's calendar but ones she awaits almost hourly. Despite the box-office imprimatur of a ban from the Cardinal of Paris himself (by the oddest irony, to expire some years later in the room of a call-girl called Mimi Santoni) the film bombed. Christine, making a token appearance in a kind of celluloid epilogue, remains a collector's item.

She doesn't brood over missed chances. 'I know life will compensate me — but when?' she says.

Christine, striding like a duchess around her distinctly beleaguered home territory, has been making plebeian tea while recollecting distant days of wine, roses (and also handcuffs). Though she has been engrossed reliving the past with obsessional, often highly comic detailed recall, her Micawber-like optimism now briskly takes over from the historian.

She examines her cup as if the tea leaves might disclose what Fate has in store. Will the future bring a career, a man? An unsuspecting Rat possibly, who, as she maintains citing her paperback-acquired Oriental Wisdom, will succumb through force of destiny?

One trigger for her sanguine mood, not everyone's manna from heaven frankly, is an excursion into journalism 'with me writing'. An Agony Column, or 'you know, Personal Counsellor to fellows with emotional problems, in bed I imagine...' as she describes it, more or less straightfaced. Before there's time to inquire whether she plans to combine the Wisdom of the East with that of the East End (where part of her complex tribal roots flourish) her cup-rattling laughter — 'Imagine, a Rat who didn't know, and then read the same book' — has drowned everything else out.

The vitality of Christine's mirth enshrines her youth, the only remaining visual records of which are stark, flash-dominated prints which appeared, invariably on Page One, after cursing, jostling picture-sessions, often conducted through the windows of fleeing limousines.

'I must be getting old,' she says. 'Do you know, my last boyfriend left *me*. I think

Christine Keeler at the height of her fame in the summer of 1963. *(Camera Press)*

he has.' It's a challenging thought for someone whose life, since 16, has been a saga of men who would never let go, pursuing her into flight and hiding.

The Keeler residence, an eleventh-storey council flat in Chelsea, is uncompromisingly bare, stripped to the knuckle of austerity. Christine's two romantic prints, her six tulips, constitute such tiny concessions to decoration that they sit like pebbles beside a sea of deprivation.

There she lives perched in the sky next to a kitchen table empty save for cigarettes and a phone which often rings dire tidings of debts, of eviction even, a few months back; anxious that the lifts won't break down again; terrified that Ziggy the ginger tom, will fall out of the eyrie-like kitchen's window: all this emptiness, the stark pared-down milieu of someone not just hard-up, or even broke but accustomed to being skint as a way of life.

In pursuit of anonymity or warmth she has screened the windows by her door with sack-coloured blankets so at first glance it seems sandbagged as if for imminent blitz.

What a setting for someone whose (constantly changing) addresses during that Keeler summer of '63 were always called 'luxury flats', invariably containing 'wardrobes of model gowns' she was just as invariably leaving behind her.

Throughout that summer her taut face, often frozen in a moment of defiance against unexpected flash-bulbs, retained a charmed invulnerability, while all around her men, sometimes 'of high position' as it was said, tumbled like nine-pins.

They didn't need to be Rats, or even rats, but as Ludovic Kennedy wrote in *The Trial of Stephen Ward*, his contemporaneous account of the trial of Christine's 'father-figure', the society osteopath Ward:

'Was it more than coincidence that so many of the people she had been in contact with had come to ruin? It was because of her, indirectly, that the two West Indians Edgecombe and Gordon had gone to prison; that the Russian naval attaché Ivanov had been banished to some dismal post in Siberia; that the British War Minister Profumo had had to resign and the Government itself been on the point of toppling; that Ward was now in the dock. Without her we would not have heard about (the late) Lord Astor and his friends, Peter Rachman and his slums...Lord Normanbrook and M15. One way and another she was responsible for quite a lot.'

Even more so after Ward took a fatal overdose on the eve of his conviction for living off her immoral earnings, though the verdict, ignoring as it did a wealth of contrary evidence, could not truly be called her fault.

After three days in a coma, unaware of the verdict against him, Ward died in the aptly-named St Stephen's Hospital, Fulham. Most of the other principals, unjustly or not, had ended in disgrace, in prison, and sometimes both.

Yet Christine negotiated the autumn minefield with her custom-made boots from Anello and Davide unscathed, despite the obloquy in Lord Denning's surprisingly tendentious report on vice in high places — he called the late Ward 'this filthy man', and in keeping with the spirit of the time, produced his deliberations in a style which hovered on the brink of a nudge-and-wink, and even employed tabloid-style cross-heads: ' "THE MAN IN THE MASK", CHRISTINE ASKS FOR £5,000', and so on. Even the august judge was not immune to the fever of scandal, rumour and down-right fantasy that had swept through the summer like a freak epidemic.

For once Mandy and Christine, who fought more often about clothes and make-up than over men, and now were scarcely speaking, concurred: they both reckoned the Denning Report was 'a joke'.

But not for Christine, not for very long. The police now knew they had the perjury evidence they had pursued zealously since 'the result' of Ward's conviction. It was back to court, but this time not in the witness-box, but the dock.

'I was terrified', she says, 'of the hate, of the way they'd claw at the car windows.' 'They' were the men and women, mainly women, who queued ten-deep outside the Old Bailey for a glimpse of arriving witnesses and who literally stampeded Christine's car (a chauffeur-driven Rolls, need it be said).

'The women were jealous, they thought I had a better life than them. I did, I expect.' The men? 'They were just, men. What do you expect?'

The Press shots show her still afloat, hanging on as if the normal rules of hubris, so classically played out in the lives of Ward, Profumo and the others, had been miraculously suspended on her behalf.

'If I'd got through 1963,' she says now, 'I might have sat it out. I was very full of my grandeur then.'

She failed. After the legal equivalent of a photo-finish Christine was back in the Old Bailey, this time receiving a nine-month sentence at a court hearing squeezed in before the Christmas holidays.

With the papers pointing up the contasts — 'drab prison garb for the auburn-haired girl who achieved a notoriety to match the great courtesans of history' — she joined 450 other unfortunates inside Holloway.

'That was terrible, that was the turning point, prison. From then on, the most important thing, for me, has been peace of mind. Peace of Mind, Liberty and Love, those are the most important things in life.'

She says this with infinite solemnity, like a creed, and then her face cracks into a huge grin, all cheek-bones and slanted eyes dark as ink.

'A man I knew, a good man, dead now poor old devil, said that ought to be changed. Instead of Peace, Liberty and Love substitute Sex, Social Security and Worrying about the Rent.'

Even 16 years later, Christine Keeler's memories of starting 1964 in Holloway are enough to make her husky, smoker's voice begin to crack. 'I was frightened at first. I thought the other girls would attack me. They left me alone altogether. They could see how bad I was, so they didn't come too near. I'd lost everything, even the milk commercials...'

Her face was too well-known to be commercially associated with anything as wholesome as milk any more. She had even lost her chance of making what the papers called 'a showbiz debut' at L'Hirondelle in Swallow Street. The Keeler 'image', which she remembers her (rapidly changing) business managers, agents, and lawyers discussing interminably, was now so sleazy that the *danseuses* resident at the nightclub had threatened to strike if she as much as started rehearsing.

Ironically, as Christine stepped well and truly out of the spotlight and embarked on her nine-month sentence, her erstwhile junior partner, Mandy Rice-Davies, launched a new career with her name in lights.

Before her opening night at Eve's Bar in Munich in January 1964, Mandy ingenuously told reporters: 'I'm nervous, because of my name, I've got to start at the top.'

Well, Eve's was not quite that — Mandy's predecessor as star attraction had been a monumental 'Parisienne' stripper whose audacious speciality involved appearing suspended over the audience in a cage with three tigers. But to a 20-year-old, innocent of stage or public appearances, apart from her memorable cross-examination in Number One Court, it was a triumph.

An exultant Mandy told reporters that she was angling to star in a film of *Fanny Hill* (in vain, it transpired) and said that her ambition was to be 'a modern Emma Hamilton. I'm looking for another Lord Nelson, only taller,' she added. She compared herself to Nell Gwynn. And there was a glancing affinity between Mandy pouting disdainfully at onlookers mobbing her car, and Nell making a similarly ugly, concupiscent mob give way by calling from her carriage: 'I am the Protestant whore.'

Christine, prim exterior to the fore, was always worried about her Reputation, as Rebecca West observed. Mandy gloried in hers.

She had arrived in London, aged 15, already bearing a True-Brit accolade — a 'Miss Austin' Beauty Contest victory in what she liked to call 'exclusive Solihull'. Already she was a winner.

But when the two girls had first teamed up, the 17-year-old 'Chrissie' had been den-mother — advising Mandy to cut down on the mascara, for instance — as well as the star. Next to Christine's outstanding beauty she had been the sexy soubrette providing comic relief.

Christine's six-month nightmare in Holloway destroyed this dominance, for ever probably. Mandy went her cosmopolitan velvet-lined way, and kept the (right kind of) publicity machine churning. The post-Holloway Keeler was a shell. 'Wherever I went I heard people whispering "pervert", "whore".' A doctor called her 'paranoid' but, to say the least, her feeling of being persecuted, of ending up as fall-girl, was far from devoid of substance, even when seen through an optic less fragmented and narcissistic than Christine's own. 'I wanted to hide, hide, hide.'

Her method of doing so was to return to her roots — and they had never provided much sustenance. Indeed it was her appalling relationship with her stepfather — 'he called my mother a prostitute once and I got a bread-knife and said "I'll stick this in you": he was terrified of me' — which had led her to seek the London lights in the first place.

She stayed for a while in the bungalow near Portsmouth which she had bought her mother with the money, much depleted by agent's and legal fees, she had earned from her idiotic 'Life Story' in the *News of the World*. Soon she married James Levermere, who had been the closest thing to 'the boy next door' in her early teens, except that in those days the Keelers inhabited a converted railway carriage near some gravel pits in a place near Slough called Wraysbury. Next door was a waste-land. In even this insalubrious setting Christine had been an outcast — 'Because my mum wasn't married, the other kids weren't allowed to play with me.'

James Levermere, the new husband by whom she soon had a son, 'Jimmie', had been an exception. They had gone on forbidden swimming expeditions together in the gravel-pits; she remembered happy times with him, and there hadn't been many in her childhood. Even so, nostalgia for an unfallen past was not enough to sustain the marriage.

They divorced, she lost her son, and after licking her wounds married again — this time to Anthony Platt, a wealthy man-about-Belgravia. Again there was a son, Seymour; again within a year the newly-weds had separated.

As Christine reflects: 'It must be something about me. Things begin well, but nine months seems to be my limit.'

Of all the commentators who queued for their Press passes at the Old Bailey, Dame Rebecca West was the most perceptive (and experienced). Struck by the mixture of hatred, lust and envy on the deprived faces of those queueing to enjoy the free spectacle, she noted how the 20-year-old Christine was so bereft 'of the protection we profess to give the young'.

She added, prophetically, 'Admittedly by the time she got into the news, it would have been difficult to protect her save by some such drastic technique as bricking her up in a wall, according to the practice which the cruder kind of Protestant used to believe prevalent in convents.'

What was true in the summer of '63 has held good ever since. It was entirely characteristic of Christine's gift for self-destruction, even when apparently pursuing the main chance, that when Mr Platt, playboy no longer, gave evidence during his bankruptcy proceedings, it emerged that his first wife had received a settlement of some £100,000 and £7,000 a year in maintenance. Christine, contrariwise, had come away with almost nothing. She was already living on the breadline, and in pursuit of £2,500 in unpaid maintenance had spent £1,800 in legal costs.

Her natural intelligence — 'I had the highest IQ of anyone in Holloway, the psychiatrist said' — always lacked a complement of common-sense. And nowadays she is realistic enough to admit that even had she chosen less destructive boyfriends or more scrupulous promoters her material circumstances might easily have turned out much the same.

'I've been skint, destitute, bankrupt,' she says, lighting yet another cigarette. 'But even when I've had money pouring in I've been poor. I just can't handle the damned stuff.'

Mandy could. Her speciality was candour and she made it pay. In the atmosphere of legal hypocrisy which surrounded the Stephen Ward proceedings as impenetrably as a pea-soup fog her off-the-cuff comments were like flashes from a lighthouse.

When Mr Justice Marshall found it incredible that Ward, without cash payment, had let her use a room in his flat for assignations with the late Lord Astor, and had even been at home sometimes on these occasions, she had memorably spoken up for what, like it or not, were the sexual attitudes that had become commonplace. 'Why not?' she fired back, 'it's perfectly normal, isn't it?'

Mandy had made her street-urchin contribution to the cycle of sexual morality prosecutions — Lady Chatterley, Ward/Keeler, *Oz* magazine — which reflected a shake-down and acceptance of 'permissive' mores throughout the society.

Christine, not one of nature's joiners, took no part in the debate and its off-shoots, despite a brief excursion into Release and help programmes for drug-victims in the early Seventies. Much of those other 1970s years were spend hunkering down in pubs and shabby flats.

She was also bringing up Seymour, largely on her own.

'It was as if I was in disguise,' she said one night, buoyant after a dinner where waiters scarcely born in 1963 had jostled to serve her, attracted by her looks as well as those glands which seem to secrete celebrity. They knew she was someone, even though they may not have known her name.

'Now I feel my face coming back, growing into me again, as I was. And,' she adds triumphantly, 'I'm going to have my say.'

By this she means more than her (delicately nebulous) magnum opus: 'One day my book will rest in the British Museum as the best account of What Really Happened.'

A more immediate platform is her new Agony Column in the girlie magazine *Men Only*. It promises to be sensational. Chrissie's advice to the lovelorn, an alchemist's brew of street-insight, surrealist fantasy and her own outrageously complex notions for solving problems could well read like a latterday Anita Loos.

'Had a letter today from a fellow who's always, you know, ripped off by prostitutes.' Answer? 'Well, you're down to finding a Better Class of Person, I suppose.'

More idealistically, she's just counselled a 16-year-old, not for acne, but on how to love his girlfriend. 'No, I didn't go on about sex. It's getting her on the pill that counts, you know?'

Perhaps we have caught Christine growing up at last — making a tardy Chaucerian transition from good-time girl to *grande dame* and guru.

The latter role is so appealing I set a test question. How would she advise a worried husband, whose wife's ardours had grown tepid? The flaring nostrils twitched, the taut bone-structure seemed to tighten as she pondered. Then illumination! An inimitable Christine solution, tailormade to generate mayhem in the *Men Only*-reading suburbs.

'He could get one of his mates to take the wife off for a night, pretending he Knew Nothing About it,' she intones as if tranformed into an oracle. And how was that supposed to make the marriage flourish again?

Eyes flashing, the fine bone-structure recalling Rebecca West's description of her as the Virgin in D. G. Rossetti's *Annunciation,* Christine got quite testy at my obtuseness. 'It would put the wife in a spot, you see. I mean, after that, she couldn't say "No," could she?'

Ms Proops will have to look to her laurels.

The Sunday Times Magazine, December 1979

Khrushchev talks to Lord Thomson

We met Mr Khrushchev on board his private train in the Virgin Lands territory of Russia where no Western reporters have previously been allowed. He came through the door into his private dining room on board the train grinning so broadly that his eyes, always tiny, seemed to have disappeared altogether.

He was wearing a well-cut brown suit. The days of bell-bottomed trousers for Soviet politicians are long gone. He wore a beautifully-ironed white shirt and rather flamboyant mother of pearl cufflinks. He could have passed for a successful executive from somewhere in the American Middle West.

He greeted Lord Thomson with a bear hug, said: 'My friend' in Russian, which his interpreter swiftly translated, and waved expansively: 'Sit down and eat — under Communism there's plenty to go round.'

Mr Khrushchev's 10-coach train (used on normal services when he does not need it) is a lavish affair, full of plush mahogany and Tsarist luxury. The groaning breakfast table added to the impression of a 50-year old time lag between the interior and the view out of the windows — a straggling agricultural settlement, a Red Army soldier, and on the other side of the railway lines a group of workers waiting to see Mr Khrushchev.

Many had wide Asiatic faces, local Kazakhs who were originally nomadic Muslims but now work on the crash programme which has already put just under 9 million acres of the Soviet steppes under intensive cultivation.

The menu ran to caviar (two kinds), omelettes, asparagus, cauliflower, turkey, dumplings and fruit. Mr Khrushchev himself began with yoghurt and curds in a special little cup with a canary painted on the side. One understood the bulge of stomach which must present a challenge to his tailor.

The waiter offered him a piece of black peasant bread — the Russian leader said it was his favourite but his doctors kept him down to one piece — and from then on he took special care to conform to his diet. He drank a bottle of mineral water; he claims it is the secret of his good health and always takes a few crates along with him when he goes abroad. Certainly he was suntanned and looked remarkably fit, even in the middle of an intensive three weeks' tour of agricultural regions in which he has covered several thousand miles of Soviet territory.

Mr Khrushchev began a conversation about the Virgin Lands programme. He has an actor's face, capable of enormous variations from complete and almost frightening impassivity to puckish gleams when he laughs, which is often, revealing one gold tooth.

The conversation was interesting. He mentioned, for example, that latest reports on the harvest indicate the USSR will have a grain surplus this year. Five million tons will go into reserve, a good deal of the rest to Cuba.

Lord Thomson and he got on very well together and the Russian leader suggested we might like to spend the day with him watching him at work. By now the train was under way and as far as one could see out of the windows were flat plains and endless miles of corn.

After a few miles, the train stopped and we embarked on an inspection tour of the 125,000 acre Karakolsk state farm which is in the heart of the Virgin Lands. Mr Khrushchev was greeted by a deputation of farm workers carrying banners who presented him with a huge loaf, which he could hardly pick up, and a bowl of salt. He introduced Lord Thomson and said he was travelling with a friend from the capitalist world.

On the tour we stopped at the boundaries of each two-kilometre section to meet the manager responsible for the next area. Mr Khrushchev was in jubilant mood — he had just received reports of a bumper harvest. Travelling in an open car he and

Nikita Khruschchev.
(Camera Press)

Lord Thomson, who was once a wheat farmer in Canada, discussed technicalities.

At lunch time at one of the farm centres, Mr Khrushchev was presented with a sheep's head which he carved, presenting the ear to the chairman of the local Communist Party, 'so you can hear the complaints of the people,' and the eye to the head of the farm 'so you can see where the crops are good and bad'.

The 40 workers in the room were in no way overawed by his presence. They treated him with respect but also on easy terms. He might have been their uncle. He has a brilliant memory for the names of local functionaries and within minutes he was one of the family, chinking glasses with everybody. At the end he even remembered to call the cook from the kitchen so a special toast could be drunk to her.

We returned to the train and at 4.24 precisely local time — the clock on the wall of Mr Khrushchev's private suite was showing Moscow time, three hours behind — the interview with Lord Thomson began.

The dining table had been cleared for business. The Russian leader was fiddling with a Scottish Television pencil which Lord Thomson had quickly given him and his woman secretary was sternly looking at her writing pad.

Lord Thomson began by asking Mr Khrushchev for his opinion on the future of East-West relations. 'I still like to call a spade a spade and the goals of our society are completely different,' he answered. His line began by sounding tough but after some interjections from Lord Thomson, a firm believer in peaceful coexistence, he became milder.

Except when he was amused and threw back his head in laughter it was impossible to tell how his answer would turn out. His voice, in turn stern, gentle and reflective, varying from a kind of soft growl to harsh well-defined phrases, did not signal what was coming. The translation was often rather a surprise. Mr Khrushchev can be conciliatory rather loudly and aggressive with only two removes from a whisper.

During the interview he drank half a bottle of mineral water. The editor of *Pravda* who was sitting at the bottom end of the table spoke once or twice but Mr Khrushchev's son-in-law Alexei Adjubei, who is normally loquacious, remained silent.

When it was over we had another heavy Russian meal. By the time it was finished we were at Tzelinograd, administrative capital of the Virgin Land area, and Mr Khrushchev completed an 18-hour day with a speech that lasted 145 minutes.

The Sunday Times, 16th August 1964

Nicholas Downie

Nicholas Downie is a war cameraman of unequalled courage and skill. But to his union he is a sinner. Why? Because in an industry of crews, he works solo.

Except for his remarkable eyes, of which more later, Nicholas Downie is a clean-cut Englishman from Central Casting. On first sighting this diffident, bean-pole figure I felt that the year 1956 had been pickled like a gherkin. Pre-punk, pre-Beatles, virtually pre-Suez, the Downie outfit of tweedy coat, cavalry twills and an obscure club tie looking as if it might have put in some time doubling as a belt, adds up to a style which Kingsley Amis (and his readers) found cripplingly comic in the days people wrote Angry Young Man novels.

They don't make them like that anymore (except on TV, where he'd be cast as a lovable, newly qualified vet). And yet the wearer of this mid-century disquise is only 34, with a boyish manner which would allow him to pass for 10 years younger. In the dusk with the light behind him anyway, but only as long as you didn't see his eyes. They don't make expressions like that anymore either, although Downie-style eyes used to be so common in Saigon the expression even had a name — 'the thousand-mile stare'.

Downie is a maker of films, a one-man team that specialises in the extremely hazardous business of producing documentaries about guerrilla warfare. In his own words: 'I do documentaries with an emphasis on clandestine entry. I am my own producer, director, researcher, cameraman, sound-recordist, script writer, typist, narrator and marketing agent. My qualifications for this are diverse. I know Morse, battlefield medicine, astro-navigation, unarmed combat, explosives, sniping, parachuting, and all NATO/Warsaw Pact infantry weapons. I've survived 70 or 80 battles, skirmishes and incidents, from street fighting to the African bush. I've been bombed, strafed, rocketed, mortared, shelled and machine-gunned. I not only have more experience of this sort of work than any other film-maker, I have also seen more actual combat than anyone now in the SAS, the British Army, the NATO alliance, or the Warsaw Pact.'

His films are also astonishingly good. He won the Royal Television news feature award for a film about Polisario in 1977, and again in 1978 for one about Rhodesia. He has a passionate belief in what he is doing. 'The best way to convince a man that war is not an exciting adventure is to kill half his friends, drop a bomb on his family's house, and relieve him of a limb or two. A less drastic but quite effective form of education is to show events like these on colour television.'

Front Line, Rhodesia, his most famous — and best — war film, meant a six-month stint working, unusually for him, with a conventional army, the Rhodesian Defence Force as it was. Even more unusually, Downie had a partner in this venture, Lord Richard Cecil, whose local contacts enabled them to be attached to a Fire Force using helicopters (and old Dakotas from which they did para drops) to initiate close-contact bush combat.

It was so close that a month into filming Downie was only three yards from his partner when Cecil was shot dead by a guerrilla hidden a few yards away. Downie went on filming alone for nearly five months more before Thames were able to produce a *TV Eye* programme running 30 minutes. *The Listener* called the film's treatment of death 'horrifically level-headed'. A *Daily Express* critic wrote: 'With almost obsessive disregard for his own safety he seemed to be determined to confront the raging monster of destruction eyeball to eyeball.'

Unfortunately — or thank Heaven, depending on how you feel about it — Downie's brief career (he started only in 1975) may well be over. He's applied to Thames Television for a full-time job. If he does give up as a freelance, the reasons will be easily identified: money and unions.

A film shot by Downie about the Boat People in February 1979 never saw the light of day because of union objections. Almost exactly a year later one of his most intriguing projects — about Polisario's progress — was still-born when Thames failed to obtain union agreement for him to go ahead. As you might expect, his response has been to raise finance elsewhere.

Downie is by nature a loner, and in a profession where teamwork is thought to be everything, the arrival of an outsider who not only could do everything himself but preferred it that way was bound to cause trouble. The union, the Association of Cinematograph Television and Allied Technicians, saw him as a threat, 'the thin end of the wedge'. The general secretary, Alan Sapper, foresaw the day when management would argue: 'If Downie can make a documentary on his own, why should we send teams of three or four?'

Downie found all this bewildering. 'My income in the past four to five years has averaged out at less than a shorthand typist. It took me all this time to get out of debt and own my equipment. Before that it was one descending spiral of borrowing, interest payments and further borrowing. But even now I can't afford a house for my wife and kids, I can't afford life insurance, I can't replace my car which is falling to pieces, and we haven't had a holiday in five years. How can I be a threat to anyone?'

The other argument from the union is that Downie does nothing a properly constituted staff film crew could not do. He finds this insulting. 'The union's assumption that a life spent in Intercontinental hotels abroad, on location in Europe, or in the studio in London, is suitable training for scrambling around a battlefield in some Godforsaken part of Asia or Africa is, I'm afraid, sadly mistaken. They have no real idea of what it is like.'

He, of course, does. And he has a gift for conveying it in words as well as on film. Take, for instance, the way he describes filming a rebel engagement in Afghanistan. 'The mountain ridge was about 100 yards by 50 and since we were under spasmodic fire — mortar, the odd rocket — from the valley below, well...' he pauses in search of a phrase, 'I could see this was a very, very bad place to be.

'It wasn't just hindsight. That night they started working us over differently. It was suddenly, you know, "Left a bit, chaps, no, too much. Right a bit, now *that's* it, right on the button". I could almost hear the Russian officer in the valley and I thought "Oh God, they're registering targets".

'Just before dawn, 4.15 a.m., I was literally jerked awake straight upright. Boom-a-boom, four times, loud as hell because sound travels like mad there. "Four heavy mortars." I thought, "15 seconds to go".

'I knew from Brigade wireless there were 20 Russians with the Afghani army and they were servicing the mortars themselves because, by God, it was good. Whoomph, right on top, and then they'd work along the ridge one way, and then, you know, you'd hear it coming back. In 15 minutes they put down 300 bombs right on top of us — I got that from Brigade wireless, too, because of course, when it's like that you can't count yourself.

'There was this endless roar, the air was buffeting with shock waves. And the splinters, of course, I was holding my camera, to protect it first, and then to try and stop myself shaking. I felt as if I was alone with my camera in the middle of Wembley Stadium. I thought "I'm never going to live through this. God, what a place to die. What about my family? What's it *for*?" '

Had there been prayers too, I wondered, and promises? The query made him laugh. And even interviewing him in London you hear the echo of the hysteria Downie experienced during that bad dawn in the Afghanistan mountains.

'Pray? It was the most earnest conversation I've ever had with the Almighty. I kept promising "if I ever get out of this alive, if I get out *walking*. I'll never, never, never..." '

'Do anything so ill-advised again?'

'Yes, of course. I expect you've said the same thing yourself. I only hope He's forgiven me.'

Two obvious questions emerge. The first is how Downie has survived; the second, has he become a ghoul with his Aäton 16mm. light-weight camera? What in Vietnam was called 'a war junkie'.

The first answer is, of course, partly luck, but there is another element. While Downie has spent only five years or so filming combat, he graduated to the camera by way of the gun and, more unexpectedly, the corridors of the Middlesex Hospital medical school. Despite an undistinguished spell at Haileybury, he gained ten O levels plus three As and seemed set to follow his father into medicine. Then in his fourth year at the Middlesex, 18 months before his finals, he walked out.

'I'd hated those four years of training because, frankly, I didn't like sick people. I liked the hospital atmosphere, the staff and all that, but the patients got me down. Also midwifery. I'd done 12 deliveries (you had to do 20 to pass then) when there was the final row. Here I was delivering babies and obsessed with guerrilla warfare. Absurd. The Dean couldn't believe it when I said I was joining the army. As for Dad...'

Downie's father is an eminent surgeon, recently retired. Not only did he serve in the war, he ended up a Colonel with a DSO, an OBE, an MC and bar, and a mention in despatches.

'Dad used to make it sound funny — I'd sit on a stool while he was having his bath and he'd tell war stories, not guts and glory stuff, but more "Don't think it's fun, son". He was in a desperate business at Monte Cassino. He had to evacuate 500 men from two battalions. They lost contact for 24 hours. When it was re-established there were 48 men left alive from two battalions, that's out of 800 to 900 men. He got his DSO for that, actually.'

If Downie, the prep school boy, was pretty close to his father, he grew even closer as time went on — 'We can *really* communicate now. I knew he hated war, but not to what extent. He played it down, I think, until I'd been through the same experience myself. He told me, for instance, how he got caught in a British barrage, on his own. He thought: "This is it." He sat behind a rock shaking and weeping. He knew he was going to be killed by his own friends. He only told me about that after Afghanistan.'

The army found their boyish recruit with the Haileybury accent puzzling. But they signed him on as a trooper with the 21st SAS in 1967. Five years later he was serving as Captain in the Sultan of Oman's army.

He admits now that his initial attraction to the army, and guerrilla warfare, his speciality, was far from untinged with 'a boy's romanticism'. It reached a kind of consummation in Oman where for 20 months he led troops in a distinctly (T.E.) Lawrentian desert war.

'I started as leader of an illegal or anyway irregular guerrilla-type operation cross-border. We managed to blow up a fort with a lot of gelignite and, gosh, it was a beautiful sight going. Then I had the most horrendous discussion with a Major-General, who had no idea at all what was going on, just what you'd expect. I was out of the desert and a bit scruffy. They gave me the job of patrolling 1500 square miles of border territory, with never more than about 50 chaps, absolute maximum, and these clapped-out camels. We were called 'Nick's Guides'. Here is the pure voice of Sandy Arbuthnot, the John Buchan character who, like Downie, was 'deceptively boyish', and who (again like Downie) had a weakness for disguises involving nomadic Arab or Pathan costume. Here was the fantasy British hero of an Empire on which the sun, naturally under the aegis of the Almighty who was rather an English sort of chap Himself, would never set.

Sixty years on, transmogrified into a 'media person', with a camera instead of an Enfield .303, and a taste for the underdog substituted for the great moral and ethical myths of Imperial destiny, Downie continues to play 'The Great Game'. Since nowadays he shoots through a lens, not a sniper's V-shaped foresight, there is a certain gratuitousness about his risk-taking. After all Downie, like the UK itself, can have no more than the most peripheral interest in the battles he has bet his life on — either to fight or to capture on camera.

But if that is what Downie wants to do, largely at his own expense, why not let him get on with it? Because, says Alan Sapper, his camera members had to fight long and hard with management before they established the current agreements on war reporting. The agreement calls for a crew of four, and if Downie does not want to work like that then that is his bad luck.

Downie says that if union pressure stops the TV companies from commissioning his work, then he will not be able to carry on. He feels this would be a pity — 'The industry can, and should, be able to afford the occasional eccentric like me.' In his application to Thames, under the section headed 'Comments', he wrote: 'Despite my background, I am a peaceable individual, and though some of my brothers in the ACTT have tried hard to wreck my career, I hereby promise not to do them physical violence.' It is a promise he hopes he can keep.

The Sunday Times Magazine — 7th December 1980

The Di is cast: the making of a princess

When 'poor old Di', as she was so often called at boarding school, is elevated to HRH Princess of Wales before the high altar of St Paul's on July 29, at least 400 million TV viewers will have the chance to see every fumble and mutter, blush or smile, in close-up. And 'live'.

The outside broadcast teams, already fighting savagely over the best pitches, should produce images graphic enough for the viewers to pick up individually each of the 14 diamonds in the $48,000 sapphire engagement ring as easily as snooker balls scattered around the green baize.

But what will the faithful 400 million, plus the additional audiences in the Eastern Bloc or in China, make of their impeccable satellite pictures? Even with a little help from their (probably equally bemused) local commentators trying to translate the High Anglican mumbo-jumbo into Kazakh or Serbo-Croat?

It's likely that what palace officials believe will be the last great State event of the century will come across as an incomprehensible hybrid of religion and grand opera.

We are thus left, in front of our screens or even in the Cathedral itself, in the position of kibbitzer peering over the happy pair's shoulders at a hand already played — and lost — at another time in another place.

In terms of *realpolitik,* of the issues that make the world creak or catch its breath, the venue could as easily be the Grand Duchy of Luxembourg, Ruritania, or Fairyland.

There is one notable exception to this global alienation. And, oddly enough, the place involved, really involved, happens to be Australia.

The Australian people, like it or not, have a connection likely to lead to all kinds of problems and controversy — because the Prince of Poms regards Australia, its land and people, with an undisguised and unmistakably proprietorial admiration.

Charles has been conducting a love affair with the country ever since his exchange visit to Timbertop, Geelong Grammar School's spartan annexe, in February 1966. It sounds pure masochism, but he still likes to remind people how 'they made me chop so much wood I couldn't see my hands for blisters'.

This depth of sentiment — it couldn't have been just the blisters — probably runs parallel to the personal relationship he made, and has retained, with a cheerful, facetious blonde lady, then called Dale Harper. In 1975, when she married Tony Tryon (a chum of the Prince), she became Lady Dale Tryon. It's all the same to Charles, who with that inimitable royal wit, inherited from Dad you can bet, calls her 'Kanga'.

You might expect her to call him 'Chilla', but Kanga just calls him 'Sir'. In 1967 Charles's princely and proprietorial view of Australia emerged in a little known exchange with Lyndon Baines Johnson.

The occasion was Harold Holt's memorial service, all the more painful for the mourners because of the circumstances of his disappearance, swimming off Portsea. LBJ, aboard Air Force One, jetted in ahead of the young Prince's royal flight, and bore down on Charles as if the young man had arrived unexpectedly at the LBJ ranch.

Lady Diana Spencer shortly after her engagement to Prince Charles. *(Keystone)*

'It's good of you to come so far,' he said expansively, shaking the princely hand with Texan bonhomie.

Johnson's gaffe was understandable. Given Harold Holt's alacrity in sending troops to Vietnam, LBJ might easily have been under the delusion that the USA had bought the continent, in the course of some package deal involving Henry Ford, North West Cape and Digger representatives in what were called 'the Free World Forces'.

According to a witness, Charles was shocked and offended. For a moment it seemed he would pass the whole thing off. Then he delivered one of the great royal put-downs of the century, a snub so resonant it might have come from his great-great-grandmother, the old Empress herself.

'Thank you, Mr President,' he said. 'But you know, this is *my* country. And I welcome you to it.'

The Queen was sceptical about her heir's eagerness to visit Australia when anything approaching a pretext could be found. Even after Dale Harper became Lady Tryon, and Charles godfather to the couple's first child, Her Majesty, so it is said, once remarked: 'She isn't some kind of Australian Mrs Simpson, I suppose?'

Since that fateful name is almost as taboo in the household as the word 'abdication', the remark was unlikely to have been casual. But such doubts have since evaporated.

Indeed Lady Tryon, and Charles's other close married woman friend, Camilla Parker-Bowles, formed themselves into an unofficial vetting committee. In the past 18 months, the best sources, including the victims themselves, reckon that these two semi-amateur marriage brokers, or breakers, have frozen out no less than three aspiring Charles followers.

Dale is the senior partner, one of those formidably well-adjusted Australian women, often married to tycoons of one kind or another, who glow with energy and the satisfaction of being universally regarded as 'a good sort'.

Her father, Barry Harper from Melbourne, is said to be rich in his own right. Dale's marriage to a millionaire merchant banker, whose remote retreat in Iceland is a haven for the Prince of Wales on fishing vacations, has done nothing to diminish her capacity for getting things sorted out the way she thinks they should be. Her exclusion of the three unsuitables was as nothing compared with her major coup.

If it hadn't been for Dale, with Camilla as short-stop, then HRH Diana, Princess of Wales, would in all likelihood have never come out on top.

She would still have been 'poor old Di': not very clever; too natural and unassuming for an ambitious marriage; or a life of jet-setting. Despite her impeccable genealogical connections, and no shortage of money, several friends say: 'People always tend to forget about her. She likes to get on with things, cheerfully, but without making a fuss.'

Four years ago, when Charles was too busy conducting his affair with her more poised and noticeable sister Sarah, six years her senior, Lady Diana was only just showing signs of emerging from a classic ugly duckling adolescence.

And with good reasons. Diana still wore the scars of the blitzkrieg divorce her father, Viscount Althorp, had launched against her mother with obsessional bitterness. Overnight, it had amputated mother from daughter.

'Johnny' Spencer, as the bluff Althorp's chums at the bar of Brooks's Club know him, finally won a long, drawn out custody battle, employing evidence of Frances Spencer's adulteries as his weapon to convince the courts she was unfit to exercise care and control.

But the costs, in every sense, had been astronomical. Althorp's health deteriorated. He put in more time at Brooks's and the Turf Club, his other London haunt.

His alcohol intake worried friends. So did an illness initially diagnosed as 'morbid depression', which after remission, cropped up again in the form of a massive brain haemorrhage. This time the diagnosis was deadly: virtually no hope of survival.

Yet Johnny, remembered 'for his bull-like stamina and strength' by a friend who knew him 25 years ago when he was serving as ADC to the Governor of South Australia, somehow survived. He has a slight speech impediment, but so slight it could easily be mistaken for an aristocratic affectation. The Spencer world — one inhabited by a maximum of 500 top families, 'the genuine old nobility' — is probably a cool 100 years out of date. But that was exactly what fitted Diana for the role.

A friend from school, the exclusive West Heath in Kent, describes her as 'withdrawn and somewhat infantile. She liked people younger than her, probably because mentally and emotionally she was more at home with them. Best of all she liked animals.

'She wasn't an outstanding rider, though she had a grey pony with a silly name I can't remember. But there was a guinea pig called Peanuts and a cat called Marmalade she kept a photo of. Frankly she wasn't outstanding at anything, except well-connected. And, of course, dim. I think she got consolation prizes for being 'a good trier', that kind of thing. She was a good diver as well. That's all I can say. Oh no, no boyfriends. But I think she had a photo of Prince Andrew as well as the cat by her bed.'

So she left West Heath at the earliest possible legal age, without passing even one of the indispensable 'O' levels that combine to provide the basic British school-leaving certificate. She was sent to a top finishing school near Montreux in Switzerland. But very soon she hated it beyond bearing and arrived in Daddy's London establishment in Belgravia unannounced after only seven weeks.

For some time there had been an additional cross to bear in the shape of Daddy's new girl-friend, who soon became, in the eyes of all the Spencer children, as *wicked* a step-mother as you could find in the fairy-stories Diana's own life so constantly resembles.

The only good words they had for Raine Dartmouth were that she was 'not so witchy' as the new 'step-granny', Barbara Cartland, the eccentric and prolific writer of romantic novelettes. 'They were all hurt and upset, and Di took it hardest,' a friend says. 'Di was kind of caught in the middle.'

And a very uncomfortable middle it was. Johnny succeeded his father to the Althorp title in 1975. This meant moving to Althorp, an enormous house in Northamptonshire, parts of which are nearly 500 years old. It was in a mess, his finances had taken a hammering, and there were punitive death duties. It's a tough life up there in the top 500.

Raine Dartmouth's unquenchable energy helped the eighth earl, as he now was, to rationalise their expenditure. But this meant dismissing servants, some of whom Diana had known and been close to all her life.

Barbara Cartland's capacity for making money is legendary. Raine lost no time in demonstrating the same huckster hunger. She renovated — and cut down on — the antiquated heating system. She even opened a gift shop, converting a set of stables, an indispensable part of an eighth earl's environment, to make room for souvenir display racks.

When Diana came back from the finishing school her father's health was still uncertain. In the circumstances Raine decreed that the costly 'coming out' debutante season, was not worth undertaking. Particularly the massively expensive ball that would have been *de rigueur*. 'You know all the people you need to know anyway,' Raine reportedly said.

Thus Diana avoided the upper-crust cattle market and began a highly conventional, South Kensington life for non-academic daughters of the upper-classes. It meant leaving the family circle, which took the pressure off.

There is no suggestion that either her father or step-mother treated her badly.

Lady Di fly-fishing with the head ghillie at Balmoral.
(Keystone)

Indeed, Earl Spencer set her up in due course in what is always called 'a suite of rooms' in a rambling apartment block called Coleherne Court, considered part of Earls Court (formerly Kangaroo Valley) until Diana became so celebrated.

Like so many of her contemporaries, Diana's qualifications were so sparse that she hovered on the edge of being unemployable. But she always made friends, often quiet, serious people like herself, and two of these, Victoria Wilson and Kay Seth-Smith, suggested she sign on with them in a new venture that was the nearest to 'a real job' she had ever had.

The girls had taken over a down-at-heel church hall in Pimlico, not far from the Tate Gallery, just north of the Thames. They transformed it into a nursery school, an upperclass one naturally, where the moppets were taught how to shake hands with the teacher and say 'good afternoon' when their mothers came to pick them up on the way home from Harrod's food hall. Diana was popular with children and parents.

She also had boyfriends, contemporary 'Hooray Henrys' on the deb curcuit, but no-one special. At least one friend who questioned her on the topic was told she was 'rather keen' on someone special — a 'Charlie Renfrew'. Had the friend been more historically minded, or a royal expert, she might have guessed. Renfrew, one of the Prince of Wales's numerous subsidiary titles, was employed by his 19th century predecessor, Bertie, Prince of Wales, on low-life ventures in Paris.

The Renfrew-Spencer relationship continued throughout the summer last year without the press, or anyone except a tiny inner circle, getting to hear about it.

Since 1977, with his naval commitments, and his responsibility for organising his mother's jubilee behind him, Charles, so his equerries noticed with professional alarm, appeared to be suffering from a kind of premature menopause. Not to say a tendency to boredom. It was only relieved by indulging in increasingly energetic sports, particularly those involving horses and the pursuit of girlfriends.

Their names would appear in gossip columns for a few days or weeks, sometimes planted by themselves — a guaranteed method of ensuring the end of the affair. But though her two sisters featured from time to time, Diana Spencer was never cited.

Contrary to popular myth, the Royal Family is not sexually prudish. Given the track records of, say, the Prince's great-uncle, the late 'Dickie' Mountbatten, his wife, Edwina, not to mention 'Charlie's Aunt', Prince Margaret, it would be unrealistic. And royals are nothing if not pragmatic.

Generally the gumboots and grouse-shooting gels of his navy days had kissed without telling if they wanted to preserve the relationship.

Lady Jane Wellesley, the journalist descendant of the Duke of Wellington whom he pursued for three years, seems very likely to have been the only candidate who, when asked, actually turned him down. His escorts had no choice but to try to fend off the gossip columnists. But 'the well-brought-up girls', those who knew the rules of the game and played to them, had virtually evaporated by the time he reached his 30th birthday.

Then there were suddenly plenty of ladies around capable of telling as well as kissing, not to mention the Farah Fawcett approach: telling anyway, if possible via a press agent.

Jane Ward, a polo fanatic (good), but also a divorceé (very bad), was pressured out. So was Susan George, the raunchy starlet, and Fiona Watson, whose peccadilloes were less excusable.

George and Farah Fawcett had to make a living after all. Fiona, whose millionaire dad, Lord Norton, relieved her of such sordid exigencies, had posed nude for *Penthouse* — apparently for the sheer hell of it.

It transpired that Fiona had been doubly unfortunate. She had kept mum about her *Penthouse* adventure. The revelations — there had been 11 pages in colour, no less — had not been hers. Instead, a jilted, brooding boyfriend, out-gunned by the most eligible man in the world, had decided on revenge.

It had happened once. All too easily it could happen again.

When it came to a potential Queen, London society did not look promising.

But if London looked unpropitious, Europe was worse. Although the 1701 Act of Settlement barred Roman Catholics, a meeting with Princess Marie-Astrid of Luxembourg and the underground negotiations which led up to it and continued even after Charles had stamped his foot and said 'no', indicated how concerned the palace was.

What about America then? There might be political advantages.

The Prince had loathed his first American experience when Tricia Nixon, according to someone present, had 'thrown herself and her friends at him like baseballs' during the Royal visit in July 1970.

But in 1972 he acquired a troublesome chum called Sabrina Guinness, a disturbing poppet with bitten nails, one of whose minor claims to fame consisted of introducing the term 'laid back' to London. But her pursuit of life in the fast lane appears to have run foul of 'the Australian connection' personified by Dale Tryon.

Her background, in Buck House terms, was dodgy: the family brewery money wasn't good; the family notorious eccentricities, Irish ones at that, were literally beyond the pale — not in social terms, necessarily, but certainly in dynastic ones.

Sabrina's recent foreground was more dubious still. She was fresh from a spell in Hollywood where, she would say with an evil pout, she had acted as 'nanny and spiritual sister' to Tatum O'Neal, whose superstar notoriety derived from supposed sexual precocity.

Sabrina's American rat pack, stretching from Roman Polanski to Jack Nicholson, apparently included other highly undesirable intimates for the realm's heir-apparent.

There was no doubt that Charles and Sabrina were mutually fascinated. But when it came to Guinness versus the Tryon/Parker-Bowles axis there could be only one result. Sabrina was out.

Much more important, Diana was 'in' — barring accidents. From his late teens, Charles had played a game with his successive detectives assessing girls they spotted in the crowd on a scale from one to 10. He had noticed that 'dim Di' had undergone a sea-change via Coleherne Court freedom. Earl Spencer had done his best for his youngest daughter. But the stresses of his own life had nonetheless weighed on her shoulders as heavily as 5,000 acres. Away from it all, above all, away from step-mother Raine, the 'classic late-developer' had at last...developed.

The sympathetic personality was just what Charles himself needed. You could hardly describe him as sexually deprived. But he needed someone sympathetic, stable, decent-looking, and discreet.

And she had to be a virgin.

Di was all these — thanks to being a few years behind her precocious and invariably promiscuous contemporaries. In the 70s and 80s, virgins had attained almost mythical perspective, like unicorns. This sad reality had not escaped the palace. Was Di all right, they wanted to know.

Camilla, who knew her better than Dale, said yes. Dale, who could guarantee her fingernails, but nothing more intimate, said she thought so.

There was a meeting with a gynaecologist. The lady, he said, was 'intacta' — or pure, as her grandfather, Lord Fermoy, later told an impressed and, one had to admit, mildly sceptical press conference. But it made sense, given the biography. Sense enough, anyway.

No sulky old Etonian was going to crop up — in *Private Eye,* the satirical weekly, or worse, the evil German tabloid *Die Aktuelle* — with frontal photos of the future Queen in his briefcase.

The palace likes to think ahead. Charles's extended dalliance had excluded strategy until Di's arrival. It had been reduced to a set of rag-bag tactics, mainly involving saying 'no comment' through tight lips every time some hack wrote a story that he was going to marry Bianca Jagger or one of President Giscard's discarded black mistresses.

But with Di on deck the palace could centre its long-term plans on Australia — in the Royal Family's eyes Coleherne Court would soon be forgotten, like a disused tube station, en route for Government House, Canberra, and, ultimately (in the *very* distant future, since the Queen likes her job and isn't inclined to hand it on) Buckingham Palace and Windsor Castle.

Charles's trip to Australia was part of this strategy to project the Royal line into the 21st century. The Queen is convinced, and all the more since the Sabrina Guinness episode, that Charles must have real experience of rule, albeit in some circumscribed form before he takes over.

First, they have to get the marriage off their hands — Earl Spencer will enjoy it all the more for not having to pick up the bill for once. But the Royal strategists are already busy with their slide-rules.

Suppose the Royal couple were to arrive in Canberra early in 1983 with a baby? Wouldn't that put the *Australian Women's Weekly*, perhaps the whole nation firmly behind them?

Suppose, even more exotically, their heir was actually born there? How about *that* for the Commonwealth connection? And if Australia were to decide to go republic to mark the bi-centenary, Charles would be on hand, with Diana at his elbow, to bow out gracefully on the one hand, and keep the Royal hoof in the Antipodean door on the other.

If Lady Diana hadn't existed, and until 18 months ago no one knew she did, except an assortment of relatives, ponies and cats, it would have been necessary to invent her.

The Australian connection is so important that Charles has recently been trying to reinforce it by making semi-public jokes about his fiancée's family wealth deriving from 'the sheep's back' — a reference to 16th century England, not 19th century Australia, which has left the London hacks even more bemused than usual.

And, interestingly, given her past role, Dale Tryon has received some of the big freeze treatment she meted out to Sabrina Guinness. Now it is all being conducted on Governor-General and Prime Minister level, nothing less. Dale is also suspected by Diana, of having christened her 'The Coleherne Clone', a nickname with enough bite (and truth) in it to hurt.

So Dale's ambition to set up a junior court, equivalent to Bertie's Marlborough House set of 100 years ago, may be stillborn. Day by day almost, Diana is demonstrating that she has a mind of her own.

Diana is aware that she is the lynch-pin in the whole monarchy-preserving exercise. They actually need her more than she needs them.

And if, for instance she said 'no' to Canberra, and claimed health reasons to do with pregnancy, she could very likely get away with it. Her decisions carry almost as much weight as that of the Australian people themselves. Diana has declined to promise 'to obey' her husband ceremonially at St Paul's. She may continue the process unceremonially and in private.

For the first time in his adult life, there won't be a damn thing Charles can do about it. At last HRH is hooked.

The National Times (Australia), 5th July 1981

The infidel who brought his golden hoard to cricket

In the middle 1970s when the 'Packer circus' was still no more than a glint in its inventor's stony eye, a veteran BBC director, Rowan Ayers, was hired by Channel 9 TV in Sydney to boost its prestige.

Arriving for the first time in the headquarters of the Packer organisation the BBC man was taken aback to find the chairman of Consolidated Press Holdings cuddling an elephant gun aimed out of the window towards the busy throng in Castlereagh Street below.

Kerry Packer pulled the trigger as Ayers entered, and said: 'Bang.'

'Got the mug,' he continued. 'That's the 149th today — and every one right between the eyes.'

Although relieved to find the weapon was unloaded — 'Kerry was only *practising* shooting people,' Ayres explained later — the BBC man remained somewhat over-awed throughout the conference which followed. The matter at issue was a 'really big' prestige documentary series to leaven Channel 9's relentlessly down-market output.

Packer, still playing with his gun, evidently found it hard to think about anything much except safaris. Finally he had an idea, *the* idea.

'Africa's big, isn't it?' he said 'Go and do Africa.'

In those days, before playing Big Daddy to more than 50 of the world's leading cricketers took so much of his time, Packer was hard to separate from his elephant gun. He was even toting the weapon when his network chartered a boat to cover the Indonesian invasion of Timor. With some difficulty he was persuaded not to carry it ashore — five Australian reporters had already been killed.

'He was like a boy who'd read all the comics,' one of the Channel 9 journalists said. 'Kerry didn't see it as just a job. He wanted to be blooded. As soon as we got back to Darwin he was on the 'phone telling his wife about the war...'

This was September 1975 and another major project at this time, a kind of dry run for the later cricket adventure, also had a distinctly *Boy's Own* element. The notion was to take over Australia's Open Golf championship.

First, Packer hired Jack Nicklaus to 're-model' 150 acres of his own local golf course, Kensington in Sydney, so that it was up to the highest championship standards. Thousands of tons of soil were shifted and artificial water hazards constructed (a process which made the course, incidentally, almost unplayable for the older members).

By June 1977, Packer was able to bring in the pantheon of US pro golfers — Nicklaus, of course, Weiskopf, Ben Crenshaw, Lee Trevino and the rest, attracted by prize-money totalling £120,000. He also hired Mac Hemion, the top US TV director who had made his name with the Mexico City Olympics, and gave him 37 cameras to play with ('about what the BBC would use for the Coronation,' an Englishman commented).

Channel 9 put out no less than 23 hours of live transmission, all of it for once 'local content' material, not cheap US or UK imports. The ratings soared, there was no shortage of sponsors, and Packer was triumphant. The venture rated his ultimate accolade, the word 'Ripper!' delivered in a throaty growl.

In retrospect the affair of 'Packer's Open Golf' can be seen as a model for his attack on the cricket establishment and his launching of World Series Cricket. The Packer method is founded on an initial audacious idea; the capturing of sole TV rights; almost limitless capital investment; and a final power-play to trample conservative opposition.

But the golf lesson was to press on with exclusive coverage, and control, of sporting events — above all, cricket. For apart from his personal liking for the game (no minor consideration since it soon became clear that he was pursuing very personal sporting ambitions and dreams as well as cash), cricket was ideal for such TV treatment.

When his World Series cricket ambitions were realised during the 1977/78 season in Australia, he acquired 315 hours of top television time for his investment.

Not everyone was pleased by his intrusion into golf. Apart from the older members vainly trying to cope with their 'Packerised' super-champ course, the golf establishment complained bitterly that the major event of the season was now locked into Sydney, instead of rotating to Melbourne and other cities as before. And again they disliked Packer personally. There seems to be a rule that all sporting establishments react to the man in the same way.

Of course, this bothered him not at all. Intimates noted that he was 'happy as a schoolboy', especially with the social success that followed his commercial triumph.

Innocent as he is of the more conventional forms of social snobbery, he was highly gratified to have acquired the *entrée* to the society of millionaire golfers and leading 'personalities'. He was not far off the point of signing autographs himself and of playing in a foursome at Pebble Beach, California, with former President Ford and Bob Hope. Meanwhile, with 'his' championship concluded, Kerry Packer led a party of the top golfers on a hunting expedition to New Zealand, where he could fire his elephant gun with impunity.

Afterwards, the golfing greats presented him with a gold watch as a token of appreciation. 'Ripper!'

It is no accident that Kerry Francis Bullmore Packer's career had to wait for the middle 1970s and his own late thirties to make any impact. His father, the legendary Sir Frank Packer, died in 1974. Until then Kerry was under his father's shadow, and even then it took him two or three years to become known, first in his native Sydney, then abroad, as someone in his own right.

Previously, such limited celebrity as he enjoyed, largely among the Consolidated staff of 2,800 in Sydney, derived somewhat backhandedly from being his father's son. Worse, he was the younger son, and thanks to the cruel family nick-name of 'Boof-head' with which Sir Frank had burdened him, he was widely thought to be 'the dumb one'. Elder brother Clyde, who had made a modest impact on New South Wales politics, was supposed to be the *dauphin* of the Press and TV empire ruthlessly constructed by Sir Frank, an old-fashioned newspaper baron in every sense of the word.

The Packers can trace their family tree back to one John Packer, a (comparatively humble) resident of Donnington Castle in Berkshire in the year 1640. However, the relevant branch of the family emigrated to Tasmania in the 1850s (*not* at Her Majesty's behest), whence sprang a formidable newspaper dynasty, Kerry being the third generation.

Sir Frank's excesses were famous — for instance, he disposed of a Rolls-Royce with 44 miles on the clock because 'it was too small for someone to sit in the back with his hat on'. Such gestures convinced people that he was a barefoot boy who had clawed his way up from the gutter.

This was by no means the case. His own father (and Kerry's grandfather), Robert Clyde Packer, was editor of the now defunct Sydney *Sunday Times*, and Sir Frank's own battered appearance was the legacy of a career as an amateur heavyweight, not early days fighting for boxing booth purses as many assumed. Having married Gretel Bullmore, said to be one of the most beautiful women of his time, Packer *père* built up two tabloids, the *Daily Telegraph* and *Sunday Telegraph,* on a diet of extreme right-wing politics unimaginable anywhere except in Australia during the Menzies epoch.

Sir Frank's temper was famous, as were the occasions when he tried to sack people not on his staff, like a visiting postman who had used the wrong lift in the *Telegraph* building. He dominated the left-wing print unions, sometimes by personal physical intimidation.

Despite protests from his composing room, for instance, he forced through his own inimitable emendation to the bill reading STALIN DEAD OFFICIAL which the *Telegraph* printed to announce the latest news from Moscow in March 1953. The Packer-written version which stunned readers the next day proclaimed: STALIN DEAD OFFICIAL — HOORAY!

Such extravagances, including the famous *Telegraph* leader advocating that black hostages be taken and shot if civil rights riots continued, became part of the folk-lore of Sydney's notoriously 'yellow' journalistic tradition. Sir Frank was quick to extend his range to television in 1956 and used the new technology to add lustre to one of his celebrated open-air parties. He surrounded his garden with TV studio lights, each of which cost a fortune. Outraged at not finding the switch to cut them off once the party was over, he went round kicking them out himself.

By all accounts, including their own, Sir Frank employed a similarly brutal approach when bringing up his two sons. Clyde, who broke with his father in the end, is more reticent, and perhaps has more reservations, than the younger brother.

Kerry's on-the-record comments make the best of what was evidently a difficult childhood.

'I was scared of my father, sure,' he insists. 'But I never knew him to be unfair. I remember him as a strong man who believed in corporal punishment. I mean he used to belt me with, er, a riding whip. He once told me that if ever I believed I was being unfairly whipped, I should call upon him for a stay of execution and tell him why I thought so. He told me this may not stop the whipping, but that if I really thought I did not deserve it, to tell him why not.'

When telling this story he always pauses at this point and adds rather portentiously: 'I can never remember calling on that privilege.'

Kerry Packer is never lacking in filial duty — his intimates say he talks about his father a lot, and even has a special incantatory voice that comes over him when he mentions the old man. There are indications that he was less philosophical at the time, particularly when one considers the full version of a 'Sir Frank' anecdote which is often repeated.

The teenage Kerry transgressed by forgetting to bring his tennis racket home from school for the Easter holidays.

He was commanded to go back to school and get it, a journey of 1,200 miles by train as the boy was attending Geelong Grammar School in Melbourne. Kerry tells the story nowadays to exemplify a lesson well learned; never since that hellish weekend has he forgotten the value of his own property and the need to look after it. Here was Sir Frank being 'hard but fair'.

At the time, it seems, the unfortunate schoolboy saw it differently. With half the punishment journey completed, he sent an angry and sad telegram from Melbourne to his father's grand house in Sidney's élite Bellevue Road, the same street, though not the same house, where he now has his own family of a boy (Jamie) and a girl (Gretel).

'Arrived Melbourne safely.' the telegram read. 'No Love, Kerry.'

If Sir Frank was a difficult act to follow, he was an impossible one to live with.

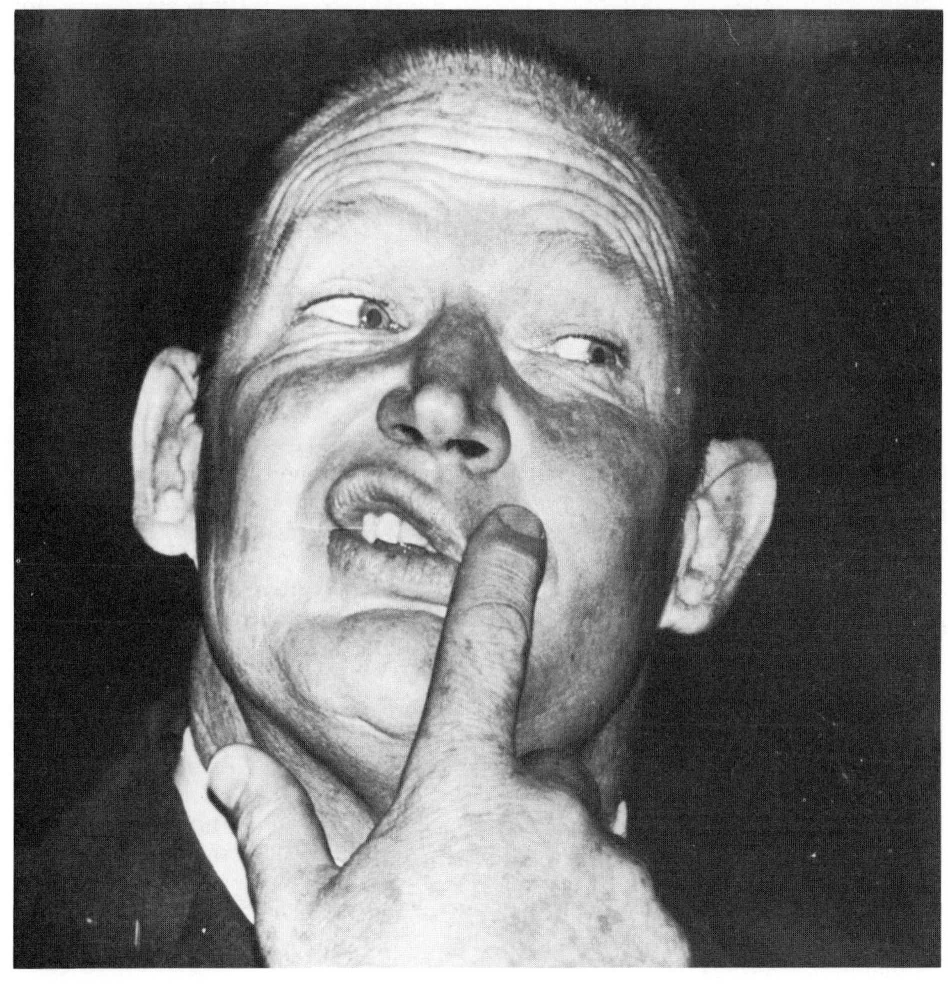

Kerry Packer.
(Keystone)

Although both sons were given important titles during his lifetime, neither was allowed real independence. When the senior Packer took the hardest decision of his life and sold his beloved newspapers to Rupert Murdoch in 1972, one reason advanced was that in the father's eyes neither son was worthy to take over the succession.

Clyde had been made joint managing director of Channel 9 TV, a post that turned out to be more honorific than real when in the same year it became clear that the Labour Party under Gough Whitlam was heading for electoral victory.

A dispute over whether or not the trades union leader, Bob Hawke, should be interviewed on the channel's main talk programme, *A Current Affair*, led to Clyde resigning. As usual the old man had his way. Not only was Channel 9 prevented from giving the Labour leader a hearing, the programme's presenter, Mike Willesee, was himself sacked shortly afterwards.

Since Clyde had walked out in disgust, the obedient Kerry was sent round to the studios with a letter from his father to say that the show was going out for the last time. Again obeying orders to the letter, he stood in the control room while Willesee conducted the live programme, ready to wipe the commentator off the air if he made any reference to Sir Frank's ultimatum.

This was all in the best Sir Frank tradition, for in the 1950s, enraged periodically by Channel 9's (admittedly rare) cultural offerings, the old man would ring the studios and order them to black out what they were showing immediately and screen some footage of one of his horses romping home instead. However, for Clyde this final act of demagoguery was impossible to accept; there was a breach between father and son and Clyde did not speak freely or often to his father thereafter.

But relations with Kerry, who obeyed his father till the end, were not so deeply affected. 'I don't think Kerry and I ever had a real split,' Clyde says. 'We never had a blazing row. We weren't close enough for that.'

Neither mentally, nor — after 1974 — even physically: for, almost as soon as his father died, Clyde wound up his Australian affairs, severed all connections with the family empire, and went to live in Los Angeles.

Until his late 20s Clyde had been favourite son, heir apparent, the bright one whose speed was meant to make up for 'Boof-head's' dullness and lethargy. But, mysteriously, he abdicated before ascending the commercial throne. The matter is now not discussed. When people ask Clyde about Kerry he usually says: 'I'm not my brother's wicket-keeper.'

The details of what occurred immediately before Clyde's departure have never been revealed. But the best information is that the younger brother bought out the elder for some £2½ million — in cash.

The stock market later valued the family holding, which Kerry has dominated ever since, at nearly £12 million; his annual family income from it, probably around the £1 million mark, makes him one of the richest men in Australia. (He is often referred to as 'one of the five most influential men' in the country, though precisely how this judgement is quantified remains mysterious. It is probably true, however.)

On the face of it then, the deal between the brothers seems markedly to have favoured Kerry. Clyde has never expressed any regrets and both men seem content to have gone their very different ways. Apart from the transaction with Clyde, Kerry Packer had already demonstrated that, whatever his father's reservations, 'Boof-head' knew what he was up to when it came to the publishing business. But since Sir Frank regarded the women's magazines he owned with derision, the fact that Kerry had made a success with a 'new product' called *Cleo* won him few laurels.

Kerry's contribution was a watered-down Antipodean version of the US *Cosmopolitan*. (It had male centre-fold pin-ups, a daring innovation, even with the genital area chastely shrouded.) *Cleo's* editor, Ita Buttrose, was a former show business writer on the *Sunday Telegraph*. She became the boss's only close senior colleague who was also a woman. In due course he promoted her to edit a revamped version of *Australian Women's Weekly*, a product she promotes on TV with a genteel lisp. This magazine sells over 800,000 copies weekly (without pin-ups) and was probably Edna Everage's bible before she left home and attained Damehood.

A veteran Packer journalist, King Boyce, commented when he heard the news of Kerry's take-over: 'If this is the slow one, we'd better get the stewards in to take a swab.'

Unlike his father, who is said to have worn a track along the carpet from his suite on the third floor to the composing room on the second, Kerry Packer believes in leaving both his editors and their publications (often known simply as 'the product') in comparative tranquillity. Although his own political views are right-wing, and he is a firm supporter of Prime Minister Malcolm Fraser, his executives insist that the boss is more interested in impact — and commercial success — than ideology.

He is certainly more interested in television than print, despite a hard time as a young man when his father exiled him to a TV station in Cleveland, Ohio, to learn the business from the bottom. It was at this stage in his career that Packer decided to give up drinking 'because it had a worse effect on me than on most people'. His commitment to screen all-night movies on Channel 9, despite the absence of commercials in the small hours, is also a legacy of Cleveland. He learned to appreciate then, he says, that people who worked long hours, particularly those who did not drink, needed late, late TV as a means of winding down.

One of his closest associates, John Cornell, wears a comic life-saver's cap to play 'Strop' in *Laugh In*, a Channel 9 down-market comedy show. 'Strop' is the personification of the 'ocker', the beer-drinking, sports-mad, chauvinistic, moronic Australian male of caricature.

Packer can sound very like 'Strop' — the big-game head collection, the definition of hell as a night at the opera listening to Joan Sutherland, his preferred alternative (watching *Starsky and Hutch* or *Charlie's Angels,* both Channel 9 programmes).

However, since he can be subtle and ironic, there is more to Packer than this stereotype. (There is more to Cornell than 'Strop' for that matter. He acted as link man between discontented Australian cricketers and Packer. Almost blasphemously, some MCC members thought, Cornell used the Melbourne Centenary Test as 'cover' to get the first defecting players signed up provisionally — without, to take one example, a figure as knowledgeable as Richie Benaud hearing so much as a whisper.)

When it suits him Kerry Packer can be at least as devious as Cornell. His much advertised disenchantment with newspapers — 'a second class media nowadays compared with broadcasting,' he says ungrammatically — does not exclude shrewd manipulation of reporters, and particularly women, often it would appear for his own personal amusement.

He plays up to his role as chauvinist pig. One anecdote, much cited by local feminists, has the hall-mark of a Packer invention he has floated into the media for a private laugh. It tells how he decided to extend his honeymoon from one day to three 'because it turned out that the wild pig shooting was so good'.

In the 'ocker' tradition, Packer is most at ease in make company. Since he likes talking, not writing memoranda, there is a ritual drinks session in his Castlereagh Street suite most evenings. Sir Frank believed in the virtues of shabbiness in newspaper offices. His son has had the place polished up and banned the tomato sauce bottles from the dining-room. When he thinks there has been enough chat, Kerry follows his father's tradition by ringing a bell to warn everyone to go home.

He himself only consumes what he call 'softies' — cans of frozen low-calorie drinks. This is pretty heinous in 'ocker' terms, but his friends, most of whom are also employees, forgive him. 'Kerry's a good bloke,' they say.

George Negus, a former left-wing journalist now working for Packer's TV, tried to explain what this ultimate male tribute means in the case of his boss. 'He's not tyrannical, as I expected; he's put up with my politics, so far anyway, and he's quite human, though of course he's tough and aggressive. Nobody called old Sir Frank "a good bloke" in that way, and he probably wasn't. People were physically frightened of him, scared he might land them one. Nobody's scared of Kerry that way.'

Despite his games with guns, there is nothing on the record about Packer shooting anyone (animals are different); and only one account of his being in a fight. Predictably, this was in Sir Frank's day. The Packer and Murdoch interests fell into dispute in 1960 over the take-over of a small Sydney newspaper. There was an impressive punch-up in the streets outside its offices, and Kerry collected two black eyes and a torn shirt.

His great bulk, not far off 18 stone despite the 'no-cals', is usually directed at inanimate not human targets when it comes to physical violence. He has been known to kick his office door open, arriving early and finding it locked, and he once assaulted an Italian chair of David Frost's, which for some reason he disliked. It may be he has created a wrong impression, deliberately even, be telling people so often how much he admires Genghis Khan.

'Not exactly lovable, I suppose, but my favourite historical character because he was so damned efficient.'

The displeased golfers whined and complained about the barbaric changes he had wrought: but the outraged cricketers chose attack as a way of defending themselves against the 'Supertests'. Not very successfully, it emerged. When Packer himself attacked, challenging the right of the cricket authorities to ban players who had signed for him, he attracted so much fear and loathing it might have been a reincarnation of his favourite hero addressing Mr Justice Slade.

One of his own (English) lawyers confessed a certain nervousness about meeting his client on a dark night. As for the cricket establishment, my colleague Philip Norman pleasantly described 'older heroes of the game' watching the invader from down-under 'with spellbound revulsion behind the crooks of their polished walking-sticks'.

Whatever his contribution to cricket, Packer has done a lot to raise the level of invective employed by cricket writers. Robin Marlar compared him to a Tyrannosaurus, Parkinson referred to his 'burglar's licence' and even the amiable Jack Fingleton (a golf partner in the era before Nicklaus and Bob Hope) wrote that Packer was cricket's equivalent of Idi Amin.

In return Packer sweetly points out that 'after over a hundred years running the game' its authorities had managed matters so that players earned £3,000 a year. Certainly young cricketers like David Gower and Ian Botham have seen their income rise 500 per cent (to £15,000) since Packer began to remove their elders making way for them in the England team.

So the cricketers themselves, those who didn't sign for Packer as well as those who did, have profited. In a sense so have the traditional Test series — Cricket As We Know It — since Cornhill Insurance have stepped in with their £1 million sponsorship guaranteeing financial stability for five years.

Packer's own finances looked set for an innings defeat when he began the 'Super-tests' (too early in the season, he later decided) in November 1977. Dennis Amiss, wearing a Packer crash-hat, found himself stitching together an elegant 81 at Adelaide watched by 900 spectators in a stadium designed to accommodate 60,000. Parkinsons's comment — 'I've seen bigger crowds in Barnsley for the quarter-finals of the district shin-kicking contest' — indicated the comfort Packer's opponents derived from these modest beginnings.

But by March 1978, no fewer thatn 354,988 spectators had passed through the turnstiles to see Packer games; 71 per cent of this attendance had been in the second half of the season, with the conventional series between Australia and India ending rather tepidly.

The Packer series still 'lost' about £2 million overall — it cost £3½ million to stage the matches, with a return of £500,000 from the turnstiles, and £1 million from advertising. But, of course, to offset this deficit there was a little matter of 315 hours of TV time on the credit side.

So despite what he calls 'a hatful of mistakes' the TV tycoon had cause to be happy with his experiment. His entourage are confident that this season's results will be spectacularly better, particularly if the depleted Australian side takes a hammering from England. 'I kid you not,' says Packer, 'crowds like to watch their teams *winning.*'

He doesn't think his influence on cricket will cause the game to lose its subtlety — 'It will make it sharper and harder,' he says. Already, he points out, his example has improved the TV coverage of other conventional games: the use of 'two-end' cameras, for instance, in tennis.

Scant consolation, of course, for those 'older heroes' who experienced something akin to physical pain when confronted by the amiable giant in his specially awful clothes — a shirt with a striking cobra on it, a sun-hat proclaiming his golfing apogee at Pebble Beach. To them, a man who calls the game of Grace 'the product' is Genghis Khan indeed.

Many believe he has besmirched the game; it will never be lily-white again. Instead Packer's product will become increasingly plastic, a pseudo-dramatic charade conducted under floodlights on an artificially manufactured surface with a coloured ball by performers in crash helmets representing Mickey Mouse entities dreamed up by commercial barbarians. As an 'older hero' told me bitterly in a Sydney pub: 'Anything Packer invents will turn out to be a lot of yellow balls.'

Like someone's sparring partner on his day off, Packer accepts the opposition with indifferent equanimity. He may not be in *Wisden* but in not much over a couple of years he has manufactured an honorary sporting hero out of himself, one who calls Mike Procter 'Procky' and signs as many autographs as Richie Benaud.

Despite an expensive education at schools modelled on English originals he will never be loved by the kind of people who wear club ties; in Melbourne this is as true as in Marylebone. 'You can't polish Kerry,' commented Elizabeth Fell, a friend of his wife's since school. 'It's like putting nail varnish on a Wellington boot.'

His father, who paid all those school fees, would be neither surprised nor disappointed, very likely. When the brothers were in their early 20s he enrolled them in various clubs, including the Athenaeum (the *Melbourne* Athenaeum, that is). 'By your thirties you'll have trodden on so many bloody corns no good club will have you,' he explained.

He was right about Kerry.

The Sunday Times Magazine, November 1979

Monsieur Cardin's maxim

The exotic, monogrammed universe of Pierre Cardin has its own imperial protocol. Even a simple call to fix an interview or photo session acquires a reverberating international dimension — something between arranging a papal audience, and answering a royal summons.

Like the emperor of fashion himself, the process is intricate and filled with comic surprises. It is also far from immune to sudden hitches: emergency messages arrive from Rio or Peking, even a registered Parisian *lettre recommandée,* addressed in what looks like Cardin's own hand, turns up mysteriously in London one day as if the couturier has an international mail service run exclusively on own behalf.

As you progress, the protocol stakes escalate, culminating in a royal vision of Parisian chic called Gislaine, Princesse de Polignac. The princesse, who copes with Cardin's social calendar, wafts you on to Edouard St Bris, a jet-lagged aristocrat from the Loire, who for six years has dealt with Cardin's licensing operations in no fewer than 93 countries outside France.

It is Edouard's voice that phones at odd hours subsequently from Tokyo or Hawaii to indicate that Monsieur Cardin would like one to be 30 minutes early for an interview in Paris 15 days later.

It is always 'Monsieur Cardin', never Pierre. This universal reverence helps remind me that here is no common-or-garden mortal interviewee, but rather a modern god, whose capacity for mercantile miracle-making defies rational analysis. After all, he has sold so many neckties with his initials on that, knotted end to end, they would encradle the globe.

In the meantime he has come down to earth in the form of a Frenchman, aged 62, whose domain is the Rue du Faubourg St Honoré in the eighth arrondissement of Paris.

Cardin's court relish grandiose metaphors about ties stretching into eternity: press them for more conventional statistics and they come over distinctly sniffy. This is partly a natural reluctance to divulge mercantile secrets, partly a refusal to 'demystify', as they would say, the Cardin phenomenon.

For we are not dealing with normal merchandising where you employ marketing skills to discover what people want, and then sell it to them. Instead Cardin 'creates' a design, for a suit or a butter-dish; his licensees manufacture it: and very shortly people in Dallas or Düsseldorf are trampling over each other to buy.

They are not so much acquiring the thing for itself, but for the name (or initials) on it. Here is the authentic papal touch. The man's monogram is a near-universal imprimatur.

St Bris is prepared to divulge, a shade wearily, that the American operation alone now tops 200 million dollars annually. Menswear, he says, accounts for 40 per cent of turnover, women's 30 per cent, and accessories the same. World sales figures? St Bris sighs that they are so prodigious as to be devoid of definition or meaning. He stretches his Cardin-tailored arms as wide apart as they will go, a gesture indicating infinity.

'We know there are between ninety and a hundred thousand people employed manufacturing Cardin items under licence. But of course we don't use slide rules.

Monsieur Cardin says if he designed babies' teats (which so far he doesn't) it would be easier. We could calculate sales by extrapolating from population figures.'

Although Cardin has two couture shows a year, what goes with, or stems from, the fantastic and often unwearable dresses, far overshadows the opulent confections on the cat-walk.

'For a show he will produce models with, say, enormous very exaggerated shoulders,' St Bris explains. 'What he is doing is preparing the world's eyes for suits with shoulders a little wider four years later.'

Is this, then, the secret of his Gallic alchemy?

'His secret is that he's a genius. And, of course, the publicity.'

Despite all the byzantine, logistical preliminaries, Cardin turns out to be 'delayed' at the preordained time for any audience. There is some waiting on a mauve, triangular stool, next to a sunken table of imitation tortoise-shell and 1920s inspiration.

Then through a door, at a desk containing a bottle of mineral water, a drawing-pad, and a pair of his own glasses, there is Cardin himself, frantically miming being deluged by work.

There are greetings, apologies, and the interview is changed into a lunch at Maxim's. However, he cannot resist a quick detour to demonstrate the view, a superior version of the site chosen in *The Day of the Jackal* for sniping the French president.

From Cardin's window no jackal could miss. You look down on the tricolor flying over the Elysée Palace as if painted by Dufy.

He is not displeased that he 'overlooks' the President of France. Not least since Cardin is no socialist. President Mitterrand, the incumbent, does not wear Cardin suits, though his predecessor, Valéry Giscard d'Estaing, is claimed to have done. 'Presidents move on,' remarks Cardin philosophically, 'but they don't bother me. I am always the same.'

He does look remarkably unchanged since the last time I saw him on successive gala nights in Paris in the 1960s. Two balls, one 'White', the other 'Black', were held to launch the Paris social season. Cardin attended the first with a model from Finland, the second with a Japanese. He seemed to spend about 36 hours dancing, talking, entertaining friends, and ever more friends...Nowadays, he says, social occasions are kept to a strict minimum. 'I cannot allow anything to interfere with creation. I am a monk.'

He somehow manages an instant mime of ascetic life (his first youthful ambition was to be an actor) and emphasises a gaunt quality usually lost in the flow of his talk and gestures. Though his face looks much the same he can look tight and brittle, as if decades pursuing his vocation to chic have consumed inner juices and left him mummified.

What he call 'my first nest' was established here in the Faubourg St Honoré 35 years ago. Since then, whenever property has been for sale in the quartier ('at the right price', he adds) he has snapped it up. Now his writ runs over more cubic metres of the Elysée section of Paris than the President can call on.

Cardin actually owns no less than 12 shops clustering round the Palace, and nowadays Maxim's nearby in the Rue Royale as well. He has his own empire within the concentric Establishment areas of the Palace and the Interior ministry, which runs the French police, across the road in the Place Beauvau.

The concentration of navy-blue vans marked 'Cardin' in familiar lower case easily outnumbers the grey police transport emanating from the Ministry of the Interior. Cardin's vehicles park aristocratically wherever they come to rest — you can't imagine them getting a ticket. The boss himself drives a three-year old Peugeot 504, which causes his entourage great amusement. He has designed aircraft and racing-car cockpits but at the wheel, so they say, 'he's like Charlie Chaplin'.

Pierre Cardin pictured at a reception at Maxim's in Paris. *(Keystone)*

Since Cardin travels constantly — 'my physical presence gives all my licensees a publicity source which is gigantic', he puts it more portentously — when in Paris he likes to walk within his imperial square mile. Thus, he will stroll along the St Honoré pavements, past a score of windows filled entirely with his creations from office suits to milk-jugs, much as a landowner might patrol his woods.

He has the same proprietorial air later when we sit down at the table of Maxim's indicating the newly renovated Belle Epoque decorations which make the place look like a de luxe indoor jungle. One of the entourage has reminded me of the scandal when Brigitte Bardot turned up barefoot in the 1960s. Cardin smiles indulgently, but one is left with an impression it wouldn't happen nowadays.

He declines Maxim's brand-name champagne, choosing Maxim's mineral water instead, and pursues the train of thought: 'In the Sixties the newspapers, not I, you understand, said I was one of the three most famous French in' — he pauses and lowers lids, momentarily demure — 'the world.' He smiles boyishly, waiting. There is no way on earth to dodge an obligation to ask who were the other two.

'General de Gaulle and Brigitte Bardot,' Cardin replies. 'Brigitte is tranquil now in St Tropez. While the General', another resonant pause, 'is dead.'

There is no arguing about this. 'Now time has passed, these people have no dimension besides me. And', he finds this fascinating, 'I had less education than any of the band I knew when I came to Paris. They all had their diplomas, licenses, and thesis even.'

He recounts his early biography with the practised relish of someone on his favourite subject. Born in 1922 of a small farming family from the Veneto in northern Italy — not in Venice, as is often said, but 12 miles out of town; not in a palazzo, but on a tiny farm. The family had gentlemanly pretensions.

Nonetheless, they were ruined by the Great War fought in their backyard and emigrated to France when Pierre was only two. His father, an eldest son, felt he could not dirty his hands with manual work in Grenoble, where they settled. The inherited notion of gentility meant that they were all not too far from the starvation line.

'My father did nothing in France,' says Cardin, who has done virtually everything. 'He vegetated.'

Pierre survived this, and the German Occupation too, where he worked in a minor role in the Vichy administration. He learned the rudiments of accounting — 'book-keeping, more properly' — and acquired a love for reading balance sheets, particularly his own. Once the war ended, like all French heroes he set out for Paris to make a name. His ambition was to be an actor. Instead he was recommended by someone to try for a place in the fashion house of Paquin.

There are several versions of the next story extant. On this occasion Cardin tells me the simplest — he asks a stranger in the street for directions, is asked in turn whom he wishes to see at the address, gives the name of his contact, and, behold, the very man he seeks to impress is there on the pavement before him. The Princesse de Polignac later spells out a more intricate narrative, involving a gypsy fortune-teller. However it really came about, Cardin indisputably found a way of clambering aboard Paquin's stately and prestigious establishment and once he had entered the rarefied world of haute couture the rest was history in an amazingly short time.

At Paguin, and soon afterwards at Dior where 'I learned everything from sewing a button-hole to selling a model dress for $20,000', his route led directly upwards.

In 1947 Dior launched the 'New Look', which took a world accustomed to wartime austerity by storm. Cardin learnt the psychological lessons of change and reaction. Within three years he had his own house employing more than 100 people.

This was the time he first came to England — on a walking tour devoted largely to cathedrals. During it he visited Norwich, where nowadays a factory called Worth Valley Menswear turns our Cardin clothes in the heart of the country's traditional native industry.

But there was little time for vacations as Cardin was obsessed by the need to expand — and also prevent people copying his already extravagant range of production. 'Nowadays I produce seven or eight hundred new haute couture designs annually and work 15 hours a day. Then I probably never stopped.'

In 1959 he dealt with the problem of quantity by 'creating a terrible scandal — off-the-peg clothes from a great Paris house. Unheard of. All the other boys in the business wanted to knife me.'

And now? 'They have probably come to accept it. Everyone has copied me.'

In any case he claims to see few of his contemporaries — he won't admit to having any rivals at all. Is he on bad terms with the 'competition'?

'I see people so rarely because I work when they go out, it's hard to say.'

'In everything I am abnormal. For instance, I don't do market research, never, as a preliminary to creating what experts tell me the customers would like. I create it first, and therefore they like it, and want to have it for themselves, whatever it is. I think not of one country but the whole world.

'Nor do I begin with a girl and find a dress to put on her. I create the dress and put any girl inside. The model I create is the vase; the water you put inside can be Japanese, Danish, it doesn't matter.'

Although this vision of a world where girls resemble water has not always endeared him to fashion writers of feminist inclination, Cardin says how good the British and American press have been to him. To prove it we leave 'the canteen', as the staff call Maxim's and return along the pavement past the British Embassy to explore the Cardin scrapbooks.

Cardin keeps everything. He has every model dress he ever really liked — around 2000, he thinks — and the cuttings books, all identically bound in leather with the year hand-written by Cardin, amount to a small library.

Among the minor eccentricities he shares with General de Gaulle there is a tendency to assume that France and himself are interchangeable and a lack of inhibition when it comes to referring to himself in the third person. The press cuttings delight him like a child.

'Cardin Sensation', he reads happily, from the 1958 volume — the English text describes how 'Maitre Cardin from Paris' has decreed that no English debs should appear at the annual Berkeley Dress show unless their hips were 34 inches or below.

'Cardin on page one, Cardin double spread, imagine what this would have cost; Cardin and the Princesse de Broglie; Cardin Sales-girl Marries Yul Brynner; Cardin Employs Mexican Heiress...Cardin, Cardin, wonderful!'

1963 takes a particularly long time because The Name is linked with another — that of Jeanne Moreau, whose film *Jules et Jim* had made her an international star. We read solemnly over his shoulder accounts of whether or not the two would marry, and if so what kind of dress the bride would wear.

Cardin's lips are moving silently, whether reading the impassioned prose or counting the column inches. Might he have married? Cardin looks solemn and says that the well-springs of creativity imply solitude. The only person he wished to live with now is his sister, Janine, because they know each other's ways.

We have moved to the crunch year 1968, which Cardin surmounted with his customary aplomb. Just before the 'events' of May he claimed a new customer in Mia Farrow, who visited him on her way home from a sojourn with the Maharishi. Later Olivier Guichard, the Gaullist minister, appointed him head of the French equivalent of the Council of Industrial Design.

Had he thoughts of continuing the government link after the fall of de Gaulle?

'It wasn't necessary.' he replies without hesitation. 'For years French fashion abroad has been me.'

He goes on to explain that this was his defence in 1977 during the former President Giscard's onslaught on inflation whereby all shopkeepers were obliged to mark prices on their goods. Cardin refused — and was fined just under 3000 pounds. He makes a gesture of chucking away a fag end, but is distracted from this unhappy story by one more to his taste.

It's a headline from his old friend *Paris Match*, dated January, 1980.

'Cardin Replace Mao in China', he intones. The story tells how his dress show in Shanghai is part of the government campaign to eradicate the blue Mao uniforms for a look which reminds no one of the cultural Revolution. It is a subject he is keen to amplify but a nervous secretary — Cardin is a cat who sometimes scratches — interrupts to plead with him to answer a phone call.

Later, back again at 'the canteen', Cardin talks happily of the inspired idea of buying Maxim's from the Vaudable family, which only came up during a 'dinner I never wanted to attend' in 1979.

'When Vaudable tried to sell me the restaurant I said it's the name I want, that and the chance to develop the trade-mark. He'd never even considered it. Two years later we won a gold medal for Maxim's cigars in London.'

I learn later that within 12 months of the Maxim's brand-name being acquired by Cardin there were 500 French points of sale for a range including everything from Cardin-designed candles to jam pots created by the same hand.

The story is so astonishing that it moves Cardin to modesty. 'Do you know something? Maxim's is one of the few names in the world that does everything. By the end of 1983 we'll have a Maxim's in London, near your Piccadilly somewhere, and another in Peking. You wouldn't think the places had much in common, would you? But they are certain to succeed — just like Maxim's in Tokyo, where I am treated like the Head of State, the Emperor.'

Not unusually, the couturier puts on a solemn expression as if about to disclose some intellectual breakthrough that will change us all. 'You won't believe what we discovered last week. In five years, maybe less, the name Maxim's, my discovery at dinner chez les Vaudables, will have grown until it is bigger than, yes, Cardin.'

We ponder this development over sips of water while I search for a question commensurate with the scale of the subject. It comes out pretty banal. Would he count 'inventing' the name Maxim's for world consumption as his greatest achievement?

The master himself has no hesitations.

'No, that was probably walking in the same space suit Armstrong used on the moon. No other human has done that. At first NASA at Houston said "it's forbidden". Then they let me. The suit has six thicknesses, it's most bizarre, like wearing another body.'

How did he feel, experiencing this apotheosis?

Cardin grins. 'Light', he says ecstatically. 'Very light indeed.'

The Sunday Times Magazine, September 1983